THE COMPLETE POETICAL WORKS OF THOMAS HARDY

THE COMPLETE POETICAL WORKS OF THOMAS HARDY

EDITED BY
SAMUEL HYNES

VOLUME II

Satires of Circumstance
Moments of Vision
Late Lyrics and Earlier

CLARENDON PRESS · OXFORD
1984

Oxford University Press, Walton Street, Oxford OX2 6DP

London New York Toronto
Delhi Bombay Calcutta Madras Karachi
Kuala Lumpur Singapore Hong Kong Tokyo
Nairobi Dar es Salaam Cape Town
Melbourne Auckland

and associated companies in
Beirut Berlin Ibadan Mexico City Nicosia

Oxford is a trade mark of Oxford University Press

Published in the United States
by Oxford University Press, New York

The preparation of this edition was made possible (in part) by a grant from the Program for Editions of the National Endowment for the Humanities, an independent federal agency of the United States government.

British Library Cataloguing in Publication Data
Hardy, Thomas, 1840–1928
The complete poetical works of Thomas Hardy
Vol 2
I. Title II. Hynes, Samuel
821'.8 PR4741
ISBN 0–19–812783–9

Set by Eta Services (Typesetters) Ltd.
and printed in Great Britain by
Thomson Litho Ltd.,
East Kilbride

CONTENTS

VOLUME TWO

ABBREVIATIONS USED IN THIS VOLUME

CP	*Collected Poems* (all reported editions)
CP19	*Collected Poems* (London: 1919)
CP20	*Collected Poems*, 2nd impression (London: 1920)
CP23	*Collected Poems*, 2nd edition (London: 1923)
LL	*Late Lyrics and Earlier* (all reported impressions)
LL22a	*Late Lyrics and Earlier*, 1st impression (London: May 1922)
LL22b	*Late Lyrics and Earlier*, 2nd impression (London: August, 1922)
LL22c	*Late Lyrics and Earlier*, 3rd impression (London: December, 1922)
ME	Mellstock Edition (London: 1919–20): Volume XXXVI, *Satires of Circumstance* (1920); Volume XXXVII, *Moments of Vision* (1920)
MV	*Moments of Vision* (all reported impressions)
MV17	*Moments of Vision* (London: 1917)
MV19	*Moments of Vision*, Uniform Edition (London: 1919)
PE	Pocket Edition (London: 1906–30): *Satires of Circumstance* and *Moments of Vision* (1919); *Late Lyrics and Earlier* (1923)
SC	*Satires of Circumstance* (all reported impressions)
SC14	*Satires of Circumstance* (London: 1914)
SC15	*Satires of Circumstance*, 2nd impression (London: 1915)
SP	*Selected Poems* (London: 1916)
WE	Wessex Edition (London: 1912–31): Verse Volume IV, *Satires of Circumstance/Moments of Vision* (1919); Verse Volume V, *Late Lyrics and Earlier* (with *The Famous Tragedy of the Queen of Cornwall*) (1926)

Adams	the collection of Frederick B. Adams
Bailey	J. O. Bailey, *The Poetry of Thomas Hardy* (Chapel Hill: 1970)
Bancroft	the Bancroft Library, University of California, Berkeley
Berg	the Henry W. and Albert A. Berg Collection, New York Public Library
BL	the British Library
Buffalo	the Poetry/Rare Books Collection of the University Libraries, State University of New York at Buffalo
Clark	correspondence and corrected proofs in papers of R. & R. Clark Ltd., in National Library of Scotland
Colby	the Hardy collection at Colby College, Waterville, Maine
Collins	Vere H. Collins, *Talks with Thomas Hardy at Max Gate 1920–1922* (London: 1928)

DCM	the Hardy collection in the Dorset County Museum; particular documents in this collection are identified as follows: *DCM1* revisions in Hardy's copies of Verse Volumes of the Wessex Edition *DCM2* revisions in Hardy's copy of *Selected Poems* (1916) *DCM3* revisions in Hardy's copy of *Collected Poems* (1923) *DCM4* revisions in Hardy's copy of *Selected Poems* (1917)
EL	Florence Emily Hardy, *The Early Life of Thomas Hardy* (London: 1928)
Eton	the Hardy collection at Eton College
Fales	the Fales Collection, New York University Library
FEH	pamphlets of Hardy's poems privately printed for Florence Emily Hardy
Holmes	the collection of David Holmes
HRC	the Humanities Research Center, University of Texas
LC	Library of Congress, Washington, DC
Letters I	Richard Little Purdy and Michael Millgate, eds., *The Collected Letters of Thomas Hardy*, Volume I (Oxford: 1978)
Letters II	*Collected Letters*, Volume II (Oxford: 1980)
LY	Florence Emily Hardy, *The Later Years of Thomas Hardy* (London: 1930)
Orel	Harold Orel, ed., *Thomas Hardy's Personal Writings* (London: 1967)
ORFW	Evelyn Hardy and F. B. Pinion, eds., *One Rare Fair Woman: Thomas Hardy's Letters to Florence Henniker* (London: 1972)
Pinion	F. B. Pinion, *A Commentary on the Poems of Thomas Hardy* (London: 1976)
PML	the Pierpont Morgan Library, New York
Purdy	Richard Little Purdy, *Thomas Hardy: A Bibliographical Study* (Oxford: 1954, reissued 1978)
RLP	the Hardy collection of Richard Little Purdy
SCC	Viola Meynell, ed., *Friends of a Lifetime: Letters to Sydney Carlyle Cockerell* (London: 1940)
SR	Evelyn Hardy and Robert Gittings, eds., *Some Recollections by Emma Hardy*, revised edition (London: 1979)
Taylor	the Robert H. Taylor Collection, Princeton University Library
Yale	the Beinecke Library, Yale University

cap.	capitalized
del.	deleted
Hol.	the bound holograph printer's copies of the individual volumes of Hardy's verse. Locations are given in explanatory notes at the end of this volume.
ital.	italic type, or underlined (in manuscript texts)
l.c.	lower-case
MS1, etc.	other single manuscripts, as identified in textual notes

om.	omitted
Pl etc.	proofs and revises, as identified in textual notes
rom.	roman type
TS	typescript

SATIRES OF CIRCUMSTANCE

LYRICS AND REVERIES
WITH MISCELLANEOUS PIECES

CONTENTS

LYRICS AND REVERIES

IN FRONT OF THE LANDSCAPE

Plunging and labouring on in a tide of visions,
Dolorous and dear,
Forward I pushed my way as amid waste waters
Stretching around,
Through whose eddies there glimmered the customed land-
scape
Yonder and near

Blotted to feeble mist. And the coomb and the upland
Coppice-crowned,
Ancient chalk-pit, milestone, rills in the grass-flat
Stroked by the light,
Seemed but a ghost-like gauze, and no substantial
Meadow or mound.

What were the infinite spectacles featuring foremost
Under my sight,
Hindering me to discern my paced advancement
Lengthening to miles;
What were the re-creations killing the daytime
As by the night?

O they were speechful faces, gazing insistent,
Some as with smiles,
Some as with slow-born tears that brinily trundled
Over the wrecked
Cheeks that were fair in their flush-time, ash now with
anguish,
Harrowed by wiles.

IN FRONT OF THE LANDSCAPE. 2 Dolorous and] ⟨Corpselike, yet⟩ Bitterly *Hol.* 7 mist. And] mist; and *Hol.* 8 Coppice-crowned,] Foliage-crowned, *SC* 13 featuring] bulking *SC* 19 insistent,] ~— *Hol.*

Yes, I could see them, feel them, hear them, address them—
Halo-bedecked—
And, alas, onwards, shaken by fierce unreason,
Rigid in hate,
Smitten by years-long wryness born of misprision,
Dreaded, suspect.

Then there would breast me shining sights, sweet seasons
Further in date;
Instruments of strings with the tenderest passion
Vibrant, beside
Lamps long extinguished, robes, cheeks, eyes with the earth's crust
Now corporate.

Also there rose a headland of hoary aspect
Gnawed by the tide,
Frilled by the nimb of the morning as two friends stood there
Guilelessly glad—
Wherefore they knew not—touched by the fringe of an ecstasy
Scantly descried.

Later images too did the day unfurl me,
Shadowed and sad,
Clay cadavers of those who had shared in the dramas,
Laid now at ease,
Passions all spent, chiefest the one of the broad brow
Sepulture-clad.

So did beset me scenes miscalled of the bygone,
Over the leaze,
Past the clump, and down to where lay the beheld ones;
—Yea, as the rhyme
Sung by the sea-swell, so in their pleading dumbness
Captured me these.

36 corporate.] ~! *Hol.* 51 ⟨Past the treed hill, down to where lay ⟨⟨those seen⟩⟩ the beheld ones;⟩ ⟨Past the treed hill, and the graves of the beheld ones;⟩ *Hol.* 53 dumbness] ⟨showance⟩ *Hol.*

For, their lost revisiting manifestations
In their live time
Much had I slighted, caring not for their purport,
Seeing behind
Things more coveted, reckoned the better worth calling
Sweet, sad, sublime.

Thus do they now show hourly before the intenser
Stare of the mind
As they were ghosts avenging their slights by my by-past
Body-borne eyes,
Show, too, with fuller translation than rested upon them
As living kind.

Hence wag the tongues of the passing people, saying
In their surmise,
'Ah—whose is this dull form that perambulates, seeing nought
Round him that looms
Whithersoever his footsteps turn in his farings,
Save a few tombs?'

CHANNEL FIRING*

That night your great guns, unawares,
Shook all our coffins as we lay,
And broke the chancel window-squares,
We thought it was the Judgment-day

And sat upright. While drearisome
Arose the howl of wakened hounds:
The mouse let fall the altar-crumb,
The worms drew back into the mounds,

56 live] own *SC* 57 purport,] ⟨message,⟩ *Hol.*

CHANNEL FIRING. *Fortnightly Review*, 1 May 1914
8 worms] worm *FR*

The glebe cow drooled. Till God called, 'No;
It's gunnery practice out at sea
Just as before you went below;
The world is as it used to be:

'All nations striving strong to make
Red war yet redder. Mad as hatters
They do no more for Christés sake
Than you who are helpless in such matters.

'That this is not the judgment-hour
For some of them's a blessed thing,
For if it were they'd have to scour
Hell's floor for so much threatening. . . .

'Ha, ha. It will be warmer when
I blow the trumpet (if indeed
I ever do; for you are men,
And rest eternal sorely need).'

So down we lay again. 'I wonder,
Will the world ever saner be',
Said one, 'than when He sent us under
In our indifferent century!'

And many a skeleton shook his head.
'Instead of preaching forty year,'
My neighbour Parson Thirdly said,
'I wish I had stuck to pipes and beer.'

Again the guns disturbed the hour,
Roaring their readiness to avenge,
As far inland as Stourton Tower,
And Camelot, and starlit Stonehenge.

April 1914.

13 "All nations trying how to make *FR*, *Hol.* 15 Christés] Christ his *FR*, *Hol.*
21 'Ha, ha.] "Ha, no. *FR*
Date om. FR

THE CONVERGENCE OF THE TWAIN*

(Lines on the loss of the *Titanic*)

I

In a solitude of the sea
Deep from human vanity,
And the Pride of Life that planned her, stilly couches
she.

II

Steel chambers, late the pyres
Of her salamandrine fires,
Cold currents thrid, and turn to rhythmic tidal lyres.

III

Over the mirrors meant
To glass the opulent
The sea-worm crawls—grotesque, slimed, dumb, in-
different.

IV

Jewels in joy designed
To ravish the sensuous mind
Lie lightless, all their sparkles bleared and black and
blind.

THE CONVERGENCE OF THE TWAIN. Souvenir Programme for 'Dramatic and Operatic matinée in Aid of the "Titanic" disaster Fund', Covent Garden, 14 May 1912; *Fortnightly Review*, 1 June 1912; Limited Edition, Aug. 1912. *P1* (*LE*) Yale; *P2* (*LE*) Berg; *MS1* 'Replica of Original MS' (Bancroft)

Headnote [*Improvised on the loss of* "*The Titanic.*"] *S.Prog.*

1 a solitude] the solitudes *S.Prog.* sea] ~, *S.Prog., FR, LE, MS1* 4 Steel chambers, late] In retorts that were *S.Prog.* chambers,] ⟨chamber⟩ *P1* 5 fires,] ~ *S.Prog., FR, LE, MS1, Hol.* 6 The cold, calm currents strike their rhythmic tidal lyres. *S.Prog.* turn to rhythmic] turn to rhymic *P1*; tune to rhythmic *P2, LE, MS1* 7 mirrors] ~, *MS1* 8 To flash forms opulent *S.Prog.* opulent] ~, *MS1* 9 The sea-worm creeps—grotesque, unweeting, mean, content. *S.Prog.* 12 sparkles] flashes *MS1*

V

Dim moon-eyed fishes near
Gaze at the gilded gear
And query: 'What does this vaingloriousness down here?' . . .

VI

Well: while was fashioning
This creature of cleaving wing,
The Immanent Will that stirs and urges everything

VII

Prepared a sinister mate
For her—so gaily great—
A Shape of Ice, for the time far and dissociate.

VIII

And as the smart ship grew
In stature, grace, and hue,
In shadowy silent distance grew the Iceberg too.

IX

Alien they seemed to be:
No mortal eye could see
The intimate welding of their later history,

X

Or sign that they were bent
By paths coincident
On being anon twin halves of one august event,

13–15 *om. S.Prog.* 13 moon-eyed] moon-eyen *P1* 14 The daintily gilded gear, *FR*, *P1* gear] ~, *S.Prog.* 15 Gaze querying: "What does all this sumptuousness down here?" *FR*, *P1*; And query: "What does all this sumptuousness down here?" *P2*, *LE* 16 Well:] For, *S.Prog.* 17 This ship of swiftest wing, *S.Prog.*, *FR*, *LE*, *MS1* creature of cleaving] ⟨ship of swiftest⟩ *Hol.* 19 mate] *cap. S.Prog.*, *FR*, *LE*, *MS1* 20 her—so] her so *S.Prog.* 27 How closely welded was their later history, *S.Prog.* 28 And so coincident *S.Prog.* 29 In course as to be meant *S.Prog.* 30 On being] To form *S.Prog.* event,] ~: *MS1*

XI

Till the Spinner of the Years
Said 'Now!' And each one hears,
And consummation comes, and jars two hemispheres.

THE GHOST OF THE PAST

We two kept house, the Past and I,
The Past and I;
Through all my tasks it hovered nigh,
Leaving me never alone.
It was a spectral housekeeping
Where fell no jarring tone,
As strange, as still a housekeeping
As ever has been known.

As daily I went up the stair,
And down the stair,
I did not mind the Bygone there—
The Present once to me;
Its moving meek companionship
I wished might ever be,
There was in that companionship
Something of ecstasy.

It dwelt with me just as it was,
Just as it was
When first its prospects gave me pause
In wayward wanderings,
Before the years had torn old troths
As they tear all sweet things,
Before gaunt griefs had torn old troths
And dulled old rapturings.

31 Spinner] Mover *S.Prog.* 32 And each one] The which each *S.Prog.*, *FR*, *P1* hears,] ~*MS1* 33 jars] clouds *S.Prog.*
Date April, 1912 *S.Prog.*; April 24, 1912 *P2*, *LE*, *MS1*

THE GHOST OF THE PAST. 2 I;] ~, *Hol.* 3 Through all my tasks] I tended while *SC* 19 its prospects] ⟨a figure⟩ its visions *Hol.* 20 wayward] ⟨western⟩ *Hol.* 23 torn] wrecked *SP*

And then its form began to fade,
Began to fade,
Its gentle echoes faintlier played
At eves upon my ear
Than when the autumn's look embrowned
The lonely chambers here,
When autumn's settling shades embrowned
Nooks that it haunted near.

And so with time my vision less,
Yea, less and less
Makes of that Past my housemistress,
It dwindles in my eye;
It looms a far-off skeleton
And not a comrade nigh,
A fitful far-off skeleton
Dimming as days draw by.

AFTER THE VISIT*

(To F. E. D.)

Come again to the place
Where your presence was as a leaf that skims
Down a drouthy way whose ascent bedims
The bloom on the farer's face.

Come again, with the feet
That were light on the green as a thistledown ball,
And those mute ministrations to one and to all
Beyond a man's saying sweet.

29 autumn's look] ⟨autumn shades⟩ autumn's eye *Hol.* 30 chambers] ⟨chambers⟩ parlours *Hol.* 31 When] The *SC* autumn's] ⟨slowly⟩ *Hol.* shades] ⟨shades⟩ ⟨shade⟩ *Hol.* 32 Nooks] ⟨Spots⟩ *Hol.* 33 my vision] ⟨the moments⟩ the chambers *Hol.* 35 Makes of] ⟨Make of⟩ Retain *Hol.* 36 Its mien smalls in my eye; *Hol.* 39 A flitting fitful skeleton *SP*

AFTER THE VISIT. *Spectator*, 13 Aug. 1910. *MS1* (*S*) RLP
Dedication om. MS1, *S*, *Hol.*
2 leaf] waft *S* 6 green] lawn *S* 8 a man's] the tongue's *S*

Until then the faint scent
Of the bordering flowers swam unheeded away,
And I marked not the charm in the changes of day
As the cloud-colours came and went.

Through the dark corridors
Your walk was so soundless I did not know
Your form from a phantom's of long ago
Said to pass on the ancient floors,

Till you drew from the shade,
And I saw the large luminous living eyes
Regard me in fixed inquiring-wise
As those of a soul that weighed,

Scarce consciously,
The eternal question of what Life was,
And why we were there, and by whose strange laws
That which mattered most could not be.

TO MEET, OR OTHERWISE

Whether to sally and see thee, girl of my dreams,
Or whether to stay
And see thee not! How vast the difference seems
Of Yea from Nay
Just now. Yet this same sun will slant its beams
At no far day
On our two mounds, and then what will the difference weigh!

12 cloud-colours] cloud-shadows *S* 13 dark corridors] night-filmed doors *MS1*; dusk corridors *S* 16 pass] glide *MS1*; ⟨flit⟩ *Hol.* 18 large] great *S* 19 inquiring-wise] ~, *MS1*, *S* 20 As] Even as *S* weighed,] ~ *MS1*, *S* 21 consciously,] ~ *MS1*, *S* 22 Life] *l.c.* *MS1* 23 by whose] what sad *S* 24 Made us crave that which could not be! *S*

TO MEET, OR OTHERWISE. *Sphere*, 20 Dec. 1913. *MS1* DCM; *MS2* Yale
Title ⟨To Meet, or Not⟩ *Hol.*
1 sally] ⟨sail⟩ *S* girl of my] ⟨child of⟩ *Hol.* 5 will] shall *S* slant] ⟨shed⟩ *Hol.* 6 At] ⟨On⟩ *Hol.* 7 On our two mounds,] ⟨Upon our turves,⟩ *Hol.*

Yet I will see thee, maiden dear, and make
The most I can
Of what remains to us amid this brake
Cimmerian
Through which we grope, and from whose thorns we ache,
While still we scan
Round our frail faltering progress for some path or plan.

By briefest meeting something sure is won;
It will have been:
Nor God nor Daemon can undo the done,
Unsight the seen,
Make muted music be as unbegun,
Though things terrene
Groan in their bondage till oblivion supervene.

So, to the one long-sweeping symphony
From times remote
Till now, of human tenderness, shall we
Supply one note,
Small and untraced, yet that will ever be
Somewhere afloat
Amid the spheres, as part of sick Life's antidote.

THE DIFFERENCE

I

Sinking down by the gate I discern the thin moon,
And a blackbird tries over old airs in the pine,
But the moon is a sorry one, sad the bird's tune,
For this spot is unknown to that Heartmate of mine.

II

Did my Heartmate but haunt here at times such as now,
The song would be joyous and cheerful the moon;
But she will see never this gate, path, or bough,
Nor I find a joy in the scene or the tune.

8 maiden] ⟨phantom⟩ *Hol.* 16 been:] ~ *MS1*; ~; *MS2*
17 Daemon] ⟨Demon⟩ *Hol.* 21 ⟨Remain as now they are ⟨⟨till⟩⟩ until⟩ *Hol.*

THE SUN ON THE BOOKCASE

(Student's Love-song: 1870)

Once more the cauldron of the sun
Smears the bookcase with winy red,
And here my page is, and there my bed,
And the apple-tree shadows travel along.
Soon their intangible track will be run,
And dusk grow strong
And they have fled.

Yes: now the boiling ball is gone,
And I have wasted another day. . . .
But wasted—*wasted*, do I say?
Is it a waste to have imaged one
Beyond the hills there, who, anon,
My great deeds done
Will be mine alway?

'WHEN I SET OUT FOR LYONNESSE'*

(1870)

When I set out for Lyonnesse,
A hundred miles away,
The rime was on the spray,
And starlight lit my lonesomeness
When I set out for Lyonnesse
A hundred miles away.

What would bechance at Lyonnesse
While I should sojourn there
No prophet durst declare,

THE SUN ON THE BOOKCASE. *Subtitle date om. SC*; ⟨1872⟩ *Hol.* 7 have] be *SC* fled.] ~⟨!⟩. *Hol.* 10 *wasted*,] *rom. Hol.* 12 who,] ⟨whom,⟩ who, *Hol.*; whom, *SC14* 13 deeds] deed *Hol.*

'WHEN I SET OUT'. *MS1* Adams
Date om. MS1, SC

Nor did the wisest wizard guess
What would bechance at Lyonnesse
While I should sojourn there.

When I came back from Lyonnesse
With magic in my eyes,
All marked with mute surmise
My radiance rare and fathomless,
When I came back from Lyonnesse
With magic in my eyes!

A THUNDERSTORM IN TOWN*

(A Reminiscence: 1893)

She wore a new 'terra-cotta' dress,
And we stayed, because of the pelting storm,
Within the hansom's dry recess,
Though the horse had stopped; yea, motionless
We sat on, snug and warm.

Then the downpour ceased, to my sharp sad pain,
And the glass that had screened our forms before
Flew up, and out she sprang to her door:
I should have kissed her if the rain
Had lasted a minute more.

14 eyes,] ~ *MS1* 15 None managed to surmise *SC*; *variant line del. MS1* 16 What meant my godlike gloriousness, *SC*; *variant line del. MS1* fathomless,] ~ *MS1* 18 eyes! *SP*, *CP23*] ~. *SC*, *CP19*, *WE*

A THUNDERSTORM IN TOWN. *Headnote date om. SC*
2 stayed,] ~⟨,⟩ *Hol.* storm,] ~ *Hol.* 6 sharp sad] lasting *Hol.*

THE TORN LETTER

I

I tore your letter into strips
No bigger than the airy feathers
That ducks preen out in changing weathers
Upon the shifting ripple-tips.

II

In darkness on my bed alone
I seemed to see you in a vision,
And hear you say: 'Why this derision
Of one drawn to you, though unknown?'

III

Yes, eve's quick mood had run its course,
The night had cooled my hasty madness;
I suffered a regretful sadness
Which deepened into real remorse.

IV

I thought what pensive patient days
A soul must know of grain so tender,
How much of good must grace the sender
Of such sweet words in such bright phrase.

V

Uprising then, as things unpriced
I sought each fragment, patched and mended;
The midnight whitened ere I had ended
And gathered words I had sacrificed.

VI

But some, alas, of those I threw
Were past my search, destroyed for ever:
They were your name and place; and never
Did I regain those clues to you.

THE TORN LETTER. *English Review*, Dec. 1910
2 airy] tiny *ER* 5 In darkness] Thereafter *ER* 9 Yes,] Yea, *ER*, *Hol.*
19 whitened] faded *ER*; ⟨faded⟩ *Hol.*

VII

I learnt I had missed, by rash unheed,
My track; that, so the Will decided,
In life, death, we should be divided,
And at the sense I ached indeed.

VIII

That ache for you, born long ago,
Throbs on; I never could outgrow it.
What a revenge, did you but know it!
But that, thank God, you do not know.

BEYOND THE LAST LAMP*

(Near Tooting Common)

I

While rain, with eve in partnership,
Descended darkly, drip, drip, drip,
Beyond the last lone lamp I passed
Walking slowly, whispering sadly,
Two linked loiterers, wan, downcast:
Some heavy thought constrained each face,
And blinded them to time and place.

II

The pair seemed lovers, yet absorbed
In mental scenes no longer orbed
By love's young rays. Each countenance
As it slowly, as it sadly
Caught the lamplight's yellow glance

25–7 And having missed, by rash unheed,
My first, last, only means to know you,
It dawned on me I must forgo you, *ER*
29 born] got *ER* 30 Throbs on;] Comes back; *ER* 32 But that you will not, cannot know. *ER*

BEYOND THE LAST LAMP. *Harper's Monthly*, Dec. 1911. *MS1* HRC
Title Night in a Suburb *MS1*, *HM*; ⟨Night in a Suburb⟩ *Hol.*
5 downcast:] ~; *MS1*, *HM* 7 And blinded them] And made them blank *MS1*, *HM* 10 rays.] light. *MS1*, *HM* 12 glance] ~, *MS1*, *HM*

Held in suspense a misery
At things which had been or might be.

III

When I retrod that watery way
Some hours beyond the droop of day,
Still I found pacing there the twain
    Just as slowly, just as sadly,
    Heedless of the night and rain.
One could but wonder who they were
And what wild woe detained them there.

IV

Though thirty years of blur and blot
Have slid since I beheld that spot,
And saw in curious converse there
    Moving slowly, moving sadly
    That mysterious tragic pair,
Its olden look may linger on—
All but the couple; they have gone.

V

Whither? Who knows, indeed. . . . And yet
To me, when nights are weird and wet,
Without those comrades there at tryst
    Creeping slowly, creeping sadly,
    That lone lane does not exist.
There they seem brooding on their pain,
And will, while such a lane remain.

14 At things which might, or might not, be. *MS1*, *HM*; *variant line del. Hol.* 16 droop] death *MS1*, *H* 20 were] ~, *MS1*, *HM* 23 slid] flown *MS1*, *HM* 25 sadly] ~, *MS1*, *HM* 29 indeed. . . .] ~! . . . *MS1*, *HM* 34 There] Still *MS1*, *HM*
Date Sept: 1911. *MS1*

THE FACE AT THE CASEMENT*

If ever joy leave
An abiding sting of sorrow,
So befell it on the morrow
Of that May eve. . . .

The travelled sun dropped
To the north-west, low and lower,
The pony's trot grew slower,
Until we stopped.

'This cosy house just by
I must call at for a minute,
A sick man lies within it
Who soon will die.

'He wished to—marry me,
So I am bound, when I drive near him,
To inquire, if but to cheer him,
How he may be.'

A message was sent in,
And wordlessly we waited,
Till some one came and stated
The bulletin.

And that the sufferer said,
For her call no words could thank her;
As his angel he must rank her
Till life's spark fled.

Slowly we drove away,
When I turned my head, although not
Called to; why I turned I know not
Even to this day.

THE FACE AT THE CASEMENT. 2 ⟨Sting of wry remorseful sorrow,⟩ *Hol.* 4 May] June *Hol.* 8 Until] And then *SC14* 13 to—marry] to marry *SC* 21 said,] ~ *Hol.* 25 drove] moved *Hol.* 27 ⟨Called from backward—why, I know not⟩ Called; and why I did I know not *Hol.* Called . . . I] Called; why I so *SC14*; Called; why so I *SC15*

And lo, there in my view
Pressed against an upper lattice
Was a white face, gazing at us
As we withdrew.

And well did I divine
It to be the man's there dying,
Who but lately had been sighing
For her pledged mine.

Then I deigned a deed of hell;
It was done before I knew it;
What devil made me do it
I cannot tell!

Yes, while he gazed above,
I put my arm about her
That he might see, nor doubt her
My plighted Love.

The pale face vanished quick,
As if blasted, from the casement,
And my shame and self-abasement
Began their prick.

And they prick on, ceaselessly,
For that stab in Love's fierce fashion
Which, unfired by lover's passion,
Was foreign to me.

She smiled at my caress,
But why came the soft embowment
Of her shoulder at that moment
She did not guess.

30 an upper] a bedroom *Hol.* 34 It] ⟨Such⟩ That *Hol.* 41 Yes,] ⟨Yea,⟩ *Hol.* 49 ceaselessly,] ~ *Hol.* 51 lover's] ⟨Love's mad⟩ *Hol.* 54 the] ⟨my⟩ *Hol.*

Long long years has he lain
In thy garth, O sad Saint Cleather:
What tears there, bared to weather,
Will cleanse that stain!

Love is long-suffering, brave,
Sweet, prompt, precious as a jewel;
But jealousy is cruel,
Cruel as the grave!

LOST LOVE

I play my sweet old airs—
The airs he knew
When our love was true—
But he does not balk
His determined walk,
And passes up the stairs.

I sing my songs once more,
And presently hear
His footstep near
As if it would stay;
But he goes his way,
And shuts a distant door.

So I wait for another morn,
And another night
In this soul-sick blight;
And I wonder much
As I sit, why such
A woman as I was born!

59 bared to] in what *Hol.* 63 *CP23*] But O, too, Love is cruel, *SC*, *CP19*, *WE*
64 grave! *CP20*] ~. *SC*, *CP19*, *WE*

LOST LOVE. 8–9 ⟨And his step I hear
In the passage near⟩ *Hol.*
13 So] ⟨And⟩ *Hol.* 18 woman] ⟨being⟩ *Hol.*

'MY SPIRIT WILL NOT HAUNT THE MOUND'*

My spirit will not haunt the mound
    Above my breast,
But travel, memory-possessed,
To where my tremulous being found
    Life largest, best.

My phantom-footed shape will go
    When nightfall grays
Hither and thither along the ways
I and another used to know
    In backward days.

And there you'll find me, if a jot
    You still should care
For me, and for my curious air;
If otherwise, then I shall not,
    For you, be there.

WESSEX HEIGHTS*

(1896)

There are some heights in Wessex, shaped as if by a kindly hand
For thinking, dreaming, dying on, and at crises when I stand,
Say, on Ingpen Beacon eastward, or on Wylls-Neck westwardly,
I seem where I was before my birth, and after death may be.

'MY SPIRIT WILL NOT'. *Poetry and Drama*, Dec. 1913
2 Wherein I rest, *PD*   11 find] see *PD*   13 curious] creepy *PD*

WESSEX HEIGHTS. 4 before] ⟨ere⟩ *Hol.*

In the lowlands I have no comrade, not even the lone
man's friend—
Her who suffereth long and is kind; accepts what he is
too weak to mend:
Down there they are dubious and askance; there nobody
thinks as I,
But mind-chains do not clank where one's next neigh-
bour is the sky.

In the towns I am tracked by phantoms having weird
detective ways—
Shadows of beings who fellowed with myself of earlier
days:
They hang about at places, and they say harsh heavy
things—
Men with a wintry sneer, and women with tart dis-
paragings.

Down there I seem to be false to myself, my simple self
that was,
And is not now, and I see him watching, wondering
what crass cause
Can have merged him into such a strange continuator
as this,
Who yet has something in common with himself, my
chrysalis.

I cannot go to the great grey Plain; there's a figure
against the moon,
Nobody sees it but I, and it makes my breast beat out
of tune;
I cannot go to the tall-spired town, being barred by the
forms now passed
For everybody but me, in whose long vision they stand
there fast.

10 with myself] ⟨with myself⟩ with the myself *Hol.* 12 wintry] frigid *SC* 14 what crass cause] ⟨what cause⟩ *Hol.* 17 great] *cap. Hol.* Plain;] ⟨*l.c.*;⟩ *Hol.* 19 tall-spired] ⟨high-spired⟩ *Hol.*

There's a ghost at Yell'ham Bottom chiding loud at the
fall of the night,
There's a ghost in Froom-side Vale, thin lipped and
vague, in a shroud of white,
There is one in the railway-train whenever I do not
want it near,
I see its profile against the pane, saying what I would
not hear.

As for one rare fair woman, I am now but a thought of
hers,
I enter her mind and another thought succeeds me that
she prefers;
Yet my love for her in its fulness she herself even did not
know;
Well, time cures hearts of tenderness, and now I can let
her go.

So I am found on Ingpen Beacon, or on Wylls-Neck to
the west,
Or else on homely Bulbarrow, or little Pilsdon Crest,
Where men have never cared to haunt, nor women have
walked with me,
And ghosts then keep their distance; and I know some
liberty.

IN DEATH DIVIDED

I

I shall rot here, with those whom in their day
You never knew,
And alien ones who, ere they chilled to clay,
Met not my view,
Will in your distant grave-place ever neighbour you.

22 Vale,] ~— *Hol.* 23 it near,] ⟨her there,⟩ *Hol.* 28 time] ⟨God⟩ Time *Hol.* 32 ghosts then] ⟨then ghosts⟩ *Hol.* and I know some] ⟨and I have a sense of⟩; ⟨I've a sense of⟩ *Hol.*

Date ⟨December, 1896.⟩ *Hol.*

II

No shade of pinnacle or tree or tower,
    While earth endures,
Will fall on my mound and within the hour
    Steal on to yours;
One robin never haunt our two green covertures.

III

Some organ may resound on Sunday noons
    By where you lie,
Some other thrill the panes with other tunes
    Where moulder I;
No selfsame chords compose our common lullaby.

IV

The simply-cut memorial at my head
    Perhaps may take
A rustic form, and that above your bed
    A stately make;
No linking symbol show thereon for our tale's sake.

V

And in the monotonous moils of strained, hard-run
    Humanity,
The eternal tie which binds us twain in one
    No eye will see
Stretching across the miles that sever you from me.

189–.

IN DEATH DIVIDED. 6 tower,] ~ *Hol.* 7 endures,] ~ *Hol.* 12 By] ⟨To⟩ *Hol.* 15 chords] ⟨sound⟩ *Hol.* 16 simply-cut] simply graved *Hol.* 17 Perhaps] ⟨Perchance⟩ *Hol.* 18 rustic] Gothic *SC* 19 A classic make; *Hol.*; Be Greek in make; *SC* 20 show thereon] ⟨be engraved⟩ *Hol.* *Date DCM3*

THE PLACE ON THE MAP

I

I look upon the map that hangs by me—
Its shires and towns and rivers lined in varnished
artistry—
And I mark a jutting height
Coloured purple, with a margin of blue sea.

II

—'Twas a day of latter summer, hot and dry;
Ay, even the waves seemed drying as we walked on,
she and I,
By this spot where, calmly quite,
She unfolded what would happen by and by.

III

This hanging map depicts the coast and place,
And re-creates therewith our unforeboded troublous
case
All distinctly to my sight,
And her tension, and the aspect of her face.

IV

Weeks and weeks we had loved beneath that blazing
blue,
Which had lost the art of raining, as her eyes to-day
had too,
While she told what, as by sleight,
Shot our firmament with rays of ruddy hue.

THE PLACE ON THE MAP. *English Review*, Sept. 1913
Subtitle A Poor Schoolmaster's Story. ER
2 lined] ⟨spread⟩ *Hol.* artistry—] ~, *ER, Hol.* 6 walked] ⟨rode⟩ *Hol.* 8 unfolded] informed me *SC, WE* 10 re-creates] adumbrates too *SC14*; resuscitates *SC15* unforeboded] unexpected *SC* 13 blazing] beaming *ER, Hol.* blue,] ~ *Hol.* 14 her eyes to-day] of late her eyes *ER*; her eyes of late *SC14*

V

For the wonder and the wormwood of the whole
Was that what in realms of reason would have joyed
out double soul
Wore a torrid tragic light
Under order-keeping's rigorous control.

VI

So, the map revives her words, the spot, the time,
And the thing we found we had to face before the next
year's prime;
The charted coast stares bright,
And its episode comes back in pantomime.

THE SCHRECKHORN*

(With thoughts of Leslie Stephen)
(*June* 1897)

Aloof, as if a thing of mood and whim;
Now that its spare and desolate figure gleams
Upon my nearing vision, less it seems
A looming Alp-height than a guise of him
Who scaled its horn with ventured life and limb,
Drawn on by vague imaginings, maybe,
Of semblance to his personality
In its quaint glooms, keen lights, and rugged trim.

At his last change, when Life's dull coils unwind,
Will he, in old love, hitherward escape,
And the eternal essence of his mind
Enter this silent adamantine shape,
And his low voicing haunt its slipping snows
When dawn that calls the climber dyes them rose?

20 Under superstition's hideous control. *ER* rigorous] merciless *Hol.*
21 time,] ~ *Hol.* 22 prime;] ~: *Hol.*

THE SCHRECKHORN. F. W. Maitland, *The Life and Letters of Leslie Stephen* (London: 1906)
Headnote Leslie Stephen] L. S. *L & L*; ⟨L. S.⟩ *Hol.*
9 At] —At *L & L*

A SINGER ASLEEP*

(Algernon Charles Swinburne, 1837–1909)

I

In this fair niche above the unslumbering sea,
That sentrys up and down all night, all day,
From cove to promontory, from ness to bay,
The Fates have fitly bidden that he should be
Pillowed eternally.

II

—It was as though a garland of red roses
Had fallen about the hood of some smug nun
When irresponsibly dropped as from the sun,
In fulth of numbers freaked with musical closes,
Upon Victoria's formal middle time
His leaves of rhythm and rhyme.

III

O that far morning of a summer day
When, down a terraced street whose pavements lay
Glassing the sunshine into my bent eyes,
I walked and read with a quick glad surprise
New words, in classic guise,—

IV

The passionate pages of his earlier years,
Fraught with hot sighs, sad laughters, kisses, tears;

A SINGER ASLEEP. *English Review*, April 1910. *MS1* Holmes; *MS2* (*ER*) West Hill Library, Wandsworth, London; *MS3* BL Ashley MS 4467

Title ⟨A South-Coast Nocturne⟩ *MS1*, *MS2* *Headnote* Algernon Charles Swinburne] A. C. S. *MS1*, *MS2*, *ER*; A. C. Swinburne *Hol.*

1 fair niche above] ⟨high niche beside⟩ *MS1*; ⟨recess beside⟩ *MS1*, *MS2* unslumbering] ⟨sleepless⟩ *MS1* sea,] ~ *MS1* 3 ness] ⟨cape⟩ *MS1* 7 about] ⟨upon⟩ *MS1*, *MS2* 8 irresponsibly] ⟨in years faded⟩ *MS1*; ⟨in my primeage⟩ *MS1*, *MS2* sun,] ~ *MS1*, *MS2* 9 numbers] ⟨canzons⟩ *MS1* closes,] ~ *MS1*, *MS2* 10 time] ~⟨,⟩ *Hol.* 12 day] ~⟨,⟩ *MS1* 16 words,] ~ *MS3* guise,—] ~⟨;⟩ *MS1* 17 ⟨That passionate volume⟩ *MS1*, *MS2* 18 kisses,] ⟨bitter⟩ *MS1*, *MS2* tears;] ~⟨!⟩:— *MS1*; ~;— *MS2*

Fresh-fluted notes, yet from a minstrel who
Blew them not naïvely, but as one who knew
Full well why thus he blew.

V

I still can hear the brabble and the roar
At those thy tunes, O still one, now passed through
That fitful fire of tongues then entered new!
Their power is spent like spindrift on this shore;
Thine swells yet more and more.

VI

—His singing-mistress verily was no other
Than she the Lesbian, she the music-mother
Of all the tribe that feel in melodies;
Who leapt, love-anguished, from the Leucadian steep
Into the rambling world-encircling deep
Which hides her where none sees.

VII

And one can hold in thought that nightly here
His phantom may draw down to the water's brim,
And hers come up to meet it, as a dim
Lone shine upon the heaving hydrosphere,
And mariners wonder as they traverse near,
Unknowing of her and him.

VIII

One dreams him sighing to her spectral form:
'O teacher, where lies hid thy burning line;
Where are those songs, O poetess divine
Whose very orts are love incarnadine?'
And her smile back: 'Disciple true and warm,
Sufficient now are thine.' . . .

19 from] ⟨by⟩ *MS1*   25 spindrift on] ⟨wind upon⟩ *MS1*, *MS2*   shore;] ~, *MS1*   27 verily] ⟨surely⟩ *MS1*, *MS2*   no] ⟨none⟩ *MS1*, *MS2*   28 she] ~⟨,⟩ *Hol.*   29 melodies;] ~: *MS1*   37 wonder] ~, *MS3*   38 Unknowing] ⟨Naught knowing⟩ *MS1*, *MS2*   41 divine] ~, *MS1*   42 ⟨Long lost, yet lit with love incarnadine?"⟩ *MS1*; ⟨Whose fragments glow with love incarnadine?"⟩ *MS2*   orts] arts *SC*

IX

So here, beneath the waking constellations,
Where the waves peal their everlasting strains,
And their dull subterrene reverberations
Shake him when storms make mountains of their plains—
Him once their peer in sad improvisations,
And deft as wind to cleave their frothy manes—
I leave him, while the daylight gleam declines
Upon the capes and chines.

Bonchurch, 1910.

A PLAINT TO MAN

When you slowly emerged from the den of Time,
And gained percipience as you grew,
And fleshed you fair out of shapeless slime,

Wherefore, O Man, did there come to you
The unhappy need of creating me—
A form like your own—for praying to?

My virtue, power, utility,
Within my maker must all abide,
Since none in myself can ever be,

One thin as a phasm on a lantern-slide
Shown forth in the dark upon some dim sheet,
And by none but its showman vivified.

'Such a forced device', you may say, 'is meet
For easing a loaded heart at whiles:
Man needs to conceive of a mercy-seat

'Somewhere above the gloomy aisles
Of this wailful world, or he could not bear
The irk no local hope beguiles.'

Date/place om. MS2, ER

A PLAINT TO MAN. *Title* ⟨The Plaint of a Puppet⟩ *Hol.*
10 phasm] shape *SC*

—But since I was framed in your first despair
The doing without me has had no play
In the minds of men when shadows scare;

And now that I dwindle day by day
Beneath the deicide eyes of seers
In a light that will not let me stay,

And to-morrow the whole of me disappears,
The truth should be told, and the fact be faced
That had best been faced in earlier years:

The fact of life with dependence placed
On the human heart's resource alone,
In brotherhood bonded close and graced

With loving-kindness fully blown,
And visioned help unsought, unknown.

1909—10.

GOD'S FUNERAL*

I

I saw a slowly-stepping train—
Lined on the brows, scoop-eyed and bent and hoar—
Following in files across a twilit plain
A strange and mystic form the foremost bore.

II

And by contagious throbs of thought
Or latent knowledge that within me lay
And had already stirred me, I was wrought
To consciousness of sorrow even as they.

GOD'S FUNERAL. *Fortnightly Review*, 1 Mar. 1912. *MS1* Adams
Subtitle An Allegorical Conception/ *Of the present state of Theology FR*; *om. MS1*
2 scoop-eyed] ~, *MS1*, *FR* bent] ~, *MS1*, *FR* 5 thought] ~, *MS1*

III

The fore-borne shape, to my blurred eyes,
At first seemed man-like, and anon to change
To an amorphous cloud of marvellous size,
At times endowed with wings of glorious range.

IV

And this phantasmal variousness
Ever possessed it as they drew along:
Yet throughout all it symboled none the less
Potency vast and loving-kindness strong.

V

Almost before I knew I bent
Towards the moving columns without a word;
They, growing in bulk and numbers as they went,
Struck out sick thoughts that could be overheard:—

VI

'O man-projected Figure, of late
Imaged as we, thy knell who shall survive?
Whence came it we were tempted to create
One whom we can no longer keep alive?

VII

'Framing him jealous, fierce, at first,
We gave him justice as the ages rolled,
Will to bless those by circumstance accurst,
And longsuffering, and mercies manifold.

VIII

'And, tricked by our own early dream
And need of solace, we grew self-deceived,
Our making soon our maker did we deem,
And what we had imagined we believed.

16 vast] ~, *MS1*, *FR* 18 columns] ~, *MS1*, *FR* 22 survive?] ~! *MS1*, *FR* 27 accurst,] ~ *MS1*

IX

'Till, in Time's stayless stealthy swing,
Uncompromising rude reality
Mangled the Monarch of our fashioning,
Who quavered, sank; and now has ceased to be.

X

'So, toward our myth's oblivion,
Darkling, and languid-lipped, we creep and grope
Sadlier than those who wept in Babylon,
Whose Zion was a still abiding hope.

XI

'How sweet it was in years far hied
To start the wheels of day with trustful prayer,
To lie down liegely at the eventide
And feel a blest assurance he was there!

XII

'And who or what shall fill his place?
Whither will wanderers turn distracted eyes
For some fixed star to stimulate their pace
Towards the goal of their enterprise?' . . .

XIII

Some in the background then I saw,
Sweet women, youths, men, all incredulous,
Who chimed: 'This is a counterfeit of straw,
This requiem mockery! Still he lives to us!'

XIV

I could not buoy their faith: and yet
Many I had known: with all I sympathized;
And though struck speechless, I did not forget
That what was mourned for, I, too, long had prized.

36 quavered] quavering *MS1*, *FR* 37 toward] towards *MS1*, *FR*
38 Darkling,] ~ *MS1*, *FR* languid-lipped,] ~ *MS1*, *FR* grope] ~, *MS1*, *FR*, *Hol.* 39 who] ⟨who⟩ that *MS1*; that *FR* 44 feel] bear *MS1*
51 Who chimed as one: "This figure is of straw, *FR*, *SC* 52 to] ⟨for⟩ *Hol.*
53 buoy] prop *FR*, *SC* faith:] ~; *MS1*, *FR* 54 known:] ~; *MS1*, *FR*
56 for,] ~ *MS1*, *FR* long] ⟨once⟩ much *MS1*; once *FR*, *SC*, *WE*

XV

Still, how to bear such loss I deemed
The insistent question for each animate mind,
And gazing, to my growing sight there seemed
A pale yet positive gleam low down behind,

XVI

Whereof, to lift the general night,
A certain few who stood aloof had said,
'See you upon the horizon that small light—
Swelling somewhat?' Each mourner shook his head.

XVII

And they composed a crowd of whom
Some were right good, and many nigh the best. . . .
Thus dazed and puzzled 'twixt the gleam and gloom
Mechanically I followed with the rest.

1908–10.

SPECTRES THAT GRIEVE

'It is not death that harrows us,' they lipped,
'The soundless cell is in itself relief,
For life is an unfenced flower, benumbed and nipped
At unawares, and at its best but brief.'

The speakers, sundry phantoms of the gone,
Had risen like filmy flames of phosphor dye,
As if the palest of sheet lightnings shone
From the sward near me, as from a nether sky.

64 Swelling] ⟨Growing⟩ *MS1* somewhat?'] ~ ?"— *MS1*
Date Begun 1908: finished 1910. *MS1 only*

SPECTRES THAT GRIEVE. *Saturday Review*, 3 Jan. 1914
Title The Plaint of Certain Spectres *SR*
2 is in itself] ⟨is in itself⟩ ⟨brings long desired⟩ *Hol.* 5 the gone,] men gone, *SR*

And much surprised was I that, spent and dead,
They should not, like the many, be at rest,
But stray as apparitions; hence I said,
'Why, having slipped life, hark you back distressed?'

'We are among the few death sets not free,
The hurt, misrepresented names, who come
At each year's brink, and cry to History
To do them justice, or go past them dumb.

'We are stript of rights; our shames lie unredressed,
Our deeds in full anatomy are not shown,
Our words in morsels merely are expressed
On the scriptured page, our motives blurred, unknown.'

Then all these shaken slighted visitants sped
Into the vague, and left me musing there
On fames that well might instance what they had said,
Until the New-Year's dawn strode up the air.

'AH, ARE YOU DIGGING ON MY GRAVE?'

'Ah, are you digging on my grave
    My loved one?—planting rue?'
—'No: yesterday he went to wed
One of the brightest wealth has bred.
"It cannot hurt her now", he said,
    "That I should not be true."'

21 slighted] ill-writ *SR*; ill-vouched *Hol.*

'AH, ARE YOU DIGGING'. *Saturday Review*, 27 Sept. 1913
2 loved] beloved *CP19*   4 One in the prime of lustihead. *SR*; *variant line del. Hol.*

'Then who is digging on my grave?
My nearest dearest kin?'
—'Ah, no; they sit and think, "What use!
What good will planting flowers produce?
No tendance of her mound can loose
Her spirit from Death's gin." '

'But some one digs upon my grave?
My enemy?—prodding sly?'
—'Nay: when she heard you had passed the Gate
That shuts on all flesh soon or late,
She thought you no more worth her hate,
And cares not where you lie.'

'Then, who is digging on my grave?
Say—since I have not guessed!'
—'O it is I, my mistress dear,
Your little dog, who still lives near,
And much I hope my movements here
Have not disturbed your rest?'

'Ah, yes! *You* dig upon my grave . . .
Why flashed it not on me
That one true heart was left behind!
What feeling do we ever find
To equal among human kind
A dog's fidelity!'

'Mistress, I dug upon your grave
To bury a bone, in case
I should be hungry near this spot
When passing on my daily trot.
I am sorry, but I quite forgot
It was your resting-place.'

10 To what will planting flowers conduce? *SR*; *variant line del. Hol.* 35 I quite] I had quite *SR*; ⟨had⟩ *Hol.*

SELF-UNCONSCIOUS*

(Near Bossiney)

Along the way
He walked that day,
Watching shapes that reveries limn,
And seldom he
Had eyes to see
The moment that encompassed him.

Bright yellowhammers
Made mirthful clamours,
And billed long straws with a bustling air,
And bearing their load
Flew up the road
That he followed, alone, without interest there.

From bank to ground
And over and round
They sidled along the adjoining hedge;
Sometimes to the gutter
Their yellow flutter
Would dip from the nearest slatestone ledge.

The smooth sea-line,
With a metal shine,
And flashes of white, and a sail thereon,
He would also descry
With a half-wrapt eye
Between the projects he mused upon.

Yes, round him were these
Earth's artistries,
But specious plans that came to his call
Did most engage
His pilgrimage,
While himself he did not see at all.

SELF-UNCONSCIOUS. *Headnote ME*

3 Watching shapes] ⟨Looking into the forms⟩ ⟨Looking at forms⟩ *Hol.* 6 The life that lay in front of him. *Hol.* 11 Flew up ⟨from⟩ the road. *Hol.* 20 shine,] ~ *Hol.*

Dead now as sherds
Are the yellow birds,
And all that mattered has passed away;
Yet God, the Elf,
Now shows him that self
As he was, and should have been shown, that day.

O it would have been good
Could he then have stood
At a clear-eyed distance, and conned the whole,
But now such vision
Is mere derision,
Nor soothes his body nor saves his soul.

Not much, some may
Incline to say,
To see therein, had it all been seen.
Nay! he is aware
A thing was there
That loomed with an immortal mien.

THE DISCOVERY

I wandered to a crude coast
Like a ghost;
Upon the hills I saw fires—
Funeral pyres
Seemingly—and heard breaking
Waves like distant cannonades that set the land shaking.

32 birds,] ~ *Hol.* 34 Elf,] *l.c. Hol.* 39 clear-eyed] focussed *SC* conned the] ⟨seen him⟩ *Hol.* 45 therein,] in him, *SC14*

THE DISCOVERY. 1 crude] ⟨dark crude⟩ *Hol.* 5 Seemingly—] Seeming— *Hol.* and heard] and I heard *Hol.*

And so I never once guessed
  A Love-nest,
Bowered and candle-lit, lay
  In my way,
Till I found a hid hollow,
Where I burst on her my heart could not but follow.

TOLERANCE

'It is a foolish thing', said I,
'To bear with such, and pass it by;
Yet so I do, I know not why!'

And at each cross I would surmise
That if I had willed not in that wise
I might have spared me many sighs.

But now the only happiness
In looking back that I possess—
Whose lack would leave me comfortless—

Is to remember I refrained
From masteries I might have gained,
And for my tolerance was disdained;

For see, a tomb. And if it were
I had bent and broke, I should not dare
To linger in the shadows there.

7 And I] ⟨And I⟩ And so I *Hol.* 11 found] ⟨plumbed⟩ *Hol.*

TOLERANCE. 4 cross] clash *SC* 5 That if I had acted otherwise *SC* 6 spared] saved *SC* 14 bent] wrenched *Hol.*

BEFORE AND AFTER SUMMER*

I

Looking forward to the spring
One puts up with anything.
On this February day
Though the winds leap down the street,
Wintry scourgings seem but play,
And these later shafts of sleet
—Sharper pointed than the first—
And these later snows—the worst—
Are as a half-transparent blind
Riddled by rays from sun behind.

II

Shadows of the October pine
Reach into this room of mine:
On the pine there swings a bird;
He is shadowed with the tree.
Mutely perched he bills no word;
Blank as I am even is he.
For those happy suns are past,
Fore-discerned in winter last.
When went by their pleasure, then?
I, alas, perceived not when.

AT DAY-CLOSE IN NOVEMBER

The ten hours' light is abating,
    And a late bird wings across,
Where the pines, like waltzers waiting,
    Give their black heads a toss.

BEFORE AND AFTER SUMMER. *New Weekly*, 4 Apr. 1914
3 day *CP*, *WE*, *DCM4*] ~, *NW*, *Hol.*, *SC* 4 Though] ⟨When⟩ *Hol.* leap] ⟨leapt⟩ *Hol.* 9 Are as a] Are a *NW* blind] pane *NW*; ⟨pane⟩ panes *Hol.* 10 Giving on a bright domain. *NW*; ⟨Peeping on a bright champaign.⟩ Riddled by rays from gay champaigns. *Hol.* 13 swings] stands *SC* 17 past,] ~ *Hol.* 20 perceived] ⟨discerned⟩ *Hol.*

AT DAY-CLOSE IN NOVEMBER. *Title* ⟨Autumn Evening⟩ *Hol.*
2 wings] flies *SC*

Beech leaves, that yellow the noon-time,
    Float past like specks in the eye;
I set every tree in my June time,
    And now they obscure the sky.

And the children who ramble through here
    Conceive that there never has been
A time when no tall trees grew here,
    That none will in time be seen.

THE YEAR'S AWAKENING*

How do you know that the pilgrim track
Along the belting zodiac
Swept by the sun in his seeming rounds
Is traced by now to the Fishes' bounds
And into the Ram, when weeks of cloud
Have wrapt the sky in a clammy shroud,
And never as yet a tinct of spring
Has shown in the Earth's apparelling;
    O vespering bird, how do you know,
        How do you know?

How do you know, deep underground,
Hid in your bed from sight and sound,
Without a turn in temperature,
With weather life can scarce endure,
That light has won a fraction's strength,
And day put on some moments' length,
Whereof in merest rote will come,
Weeks hence, mild airs that do not numb;
    O crocus root, how do you know,
        How do you know?

February 1910.

6 past] ⟨now⟩ *Hol.*   12 A time when none will be seen. *SC*, *CP19*

THE YEAR'S AWAKENING. *New Weekly*, 21 Mar. 1914
7–8 *om. NW*   13 turn] change *NW*   17–18 *om. NW*

UNDER THE WATERFALL*

'Whenever I plunge my arm, like this,
In a basin of water, I never miss
The sweet sharp sense of a fugitive day
Fetched back from its thickening shroud of gray.
        Hence the only prime
        And real love-rhyme
        That I know by heart,
        And that leaves no smart,
Is the purl of a little valley fall
About three spans wide and two spans tall
Over a table of solid rock,
And into a scoop of the self-same block;
The purl of a runlet that never ceases
In stir of kingdoms, in wars, in peaces;
With a hollow boiling voice it speaks
And has spoken since hills were turfless peaks.'

'And why gives this the only prime
Idea to you of a real love-rhyme?
And why does plunging your arm in a bowl
Full of spring water, bring throbs to your soul?'

'Well, under the fall, in a crease of the stone,
Though where precisely none ever has known,
Jammed darkly, nothing to show how prized,
And by now with its smoothness opalized,
        Is a drinking-glass:
        For, down that pass
        My lover and I
        Walked under a sky
Of blue with a leaf-wove awning of green,
In the burn of August, to paint the scene,

[*no stanza break*]

UNDER THE WATERFALL. *Title* 〈The glass in the stream〉 *Hol. table of contents*
4 back from] 〈out of〉 *Hol.*   20 〈Full of water like this bring a throb to your soul?"〉 *Hol.*   29 Of spotless blue leaf-veiled with green, *Hol.*   leaf-wove] leaf-woven *SC*

And we placed our basket of fruit and wine
By the runlet's rim, where we sat to dine;
And when we had drunk from the glass together,
Arched by the oak-copse from the weather,
I held the vessel to rinse in the fall,
Where it slipped, and sank, and was past recall,
Though we stooped and plumbed the little abyss
With long bared arms. There the glass still is.
And, as said, if I thrust my arm below
Cold water in basin or bowl, a throe
From the past awakens a sense of that time,
And the glass we used, and the cascade's rhyme.
The basin seems the pool, and its edge
The hard smooth face of the brook-side ledge,
And the leafy pattern of china-ware
The hanging plants that were bathing there.

'By night, by day, when it shines or lours,
There lies intact that chalice of ours,
And its presence adds to the rhyme of love
Persistently sung by the fall above.
No lip has touched it since his and mine
In turns therefrom sipped lovers' wine.'

34 oak-copse] oak-scrub *Hol.* 41 a sense] ⟨the feel⟩ *Hol.* 42 we] both *SC* 46 were bathing] bordered *Hol.* 47 night,] ~ *Hol.* 48 chalice] ⟨glass⟩ *Hol.*

POEMS OF 1912–13*

Veteris vestigia flammae

THE GOING

Why did you give no hint that night
That quickly after the morrow's dawn,
And calmly, as if indifferent quite,
You would close your term here, up and be gone
        Where I could not follow
        With wing of swallow
To gain one glimpse of you ever anon!

        Never to bid good-bye,
        Or lip me the softest call,
Or utter a wish for a word, while I
Saw morning harden upon the wall,
        Unmoved, unknowing
        That your great going
Had place that moment, and altered all.

Why do you make me leave the house
And think for a breath it is you I see
At the end of the alley of bending boughs
Where so often at dusk you used to be;
        Till in darkening dankness
        The yawning blankness
Of the perspective sickens me!

        You were she who abode
        By those red-veined rocks far West,
You were the swan-necked one who rode
Along the beetling Beeny Crest,

THE GOING. 3 quite,] ~ *Hol.*   9 lip] give *SC*   11 wall,] ~ *Hol.* 16 And think for an instant it's you I see *Hol.*   19 Till in creeping dankness *Hol.*

And, reining nigh me,
Would muse and eye me,
While Life unrolled us its very best.

Why, then, latterly did we not speak,
Did we not think of those days long dead,
And ere your vanishing strive to seek
That time's renewal? We might have said,
'In this bright spring weather
We'll visit together
Those places that once we visited.'

Well, well! All's past amend,
Unchangeable. It must go.
I seem but a dead man held on end
To sink down soon. . . . O you could not know
That such swift fleeing
No soul foreseeing—
Not even I—would undo me so!

December 1912.

YOUR LAST DRIVE

Here by the moorway you returned,
And saw the borough lights ahead
That lit your face—all undiscerned
To be in a week the face of the dead,
And you told of the charm of that haloed view
That never again would beam on you.

And on your left you passed the spot
Where eight days later you were to lie,
And be spoken of as one who was not;
Beholding it with a heedless eye
As alien from you, though under its tree
You soon would halt everlastingly.

26 me,] ~ *Hol.* 33 this bright] the next *Hol.* 38 I seem] I am now *Hol.*

YOUR LAST DRIVE. 10 heedless] cursory *SC*

I drove not with you. . . . Yet had I sat
At your side that eve I should not have seen
That the countenance I was glancing at
Had a last-time look in the flickering sheen,
Nor have read the writing upon your face,
'I go hence soon to my resting-place;

'You may miss me then. But I shall not know
How many times you visit me there,
Or what your thoughts are, or if you go
There never at all. And I shall not care.
Should you censure me I shall take no heed
And even your praises no more shall need.'

True: never you'll know. And you will not mind.
But shall I then slight you because of such?
Dear ghost, in the past did you ever find
The thought 'What profit,' move me much?
Yet abides the fact, indeed, the same,—
You are past love, praise, indifference, blame.

December 1912.

THE WALK

You did not walk with me
Of late to the hill-top tree
By the gated ways,
As in earlier days;
You were weak and lame,
So you never came,
And I went alone, and I did not mind,
Not thinking of you as left behind.

24 no more shall] I shall not *SC* 28 ⟨Me one whom consequence influenced much?⟩ ⟨The thought: "What profit?" move me much?⟩ *Hol.*; Me one whom consequence influenced much? *Hol.*, *SC14* 29 Yet the fact indeed remains the same, *SC* 30 are] ⟨have⟩ *Hol.*

THE WALK. 3–4 As in earlier days,
By the gated ways: *Hol.*

I walked up there to-day
Just in the former way:
Surveyed around
The familiar ground
By myself again:
What difference, then?
Only that underlying sense
Of the look of a room on returning thence.

RAIN ON A GRAVE

Clouds spout upon her
Their waters amain
In ruthless disdain,—
Her who but lately
Had shivered with pain
As at touch of dishonour
If there had lit on her
So coldly, so straightly
Such arrows of rain.

One who to shelter
Her delicate head
Would quicken and quicken
Each tentative tread
If drops chanced to pelt her
That summertime spills
In dust-paven rills
When thunder-clouds thicken
And birds close their bills.

10 way:] ~; *Hol., WE*

RAIN ON A GRAVE. *Title* ⟨Rain on her Grave⟩ *Hol.*
2–3 ⟨In ruthless disdain
Their waters amain,—⟩ *Hol.*
10 One] She *SC* 13 tentative] ⟨gingerly⟩ *Hol.*

Would that I lay there
  And she were housed here!
Or better, together
Were folded away there
Exposed to one weather
We both,—who would stray there
When sunny the day there,
  Or evening was clear
  At the prime of the year.

Soon will be growing
  Green blades from her mound,
And daisies be showing
  Like stars on the ground,
Till she form part of them—
Ay—the sweet heart of them,
Loved beyond measure
With a child's pleasure
  All her life's round.

Jan. 31, 1913.

'I FOUND HER OUT THERE'*

I found her out there
On a slope few see,
That falls westwardly
To the salt-edged air,
Where the ocean breaks
On the purple strand,
And the hurricane shakes
The solid land.

22 Were folded] ⟨We both slept⟩ *Hol.* there] ~—*Hol.* 23 weather] ~, *Hol.* 24 ⟨Who often would ⟨⟨stay⟩⟩ stray there⟩ *Hol.* both, —] ~— *Hol.*

'I FOUND HER OUT THERE'. 4 salt-edged] ⟨sharp-edged⟩ salt-edged *Hol.*; sharp-edged *SC14*

I brought her here,
And have laid her to rest
In a noiseless nest
No sea beats near.
She will never be stirred
In her loamy cell
By the waves long heard
And loved so well.

So she does not sleep
By those haunted heights
The Atlantic smites
And the blind gales sweep,
Whence she often would gaze
At Dundagel's famed head,
While the dipping blaze
Dyed her face fire-red;

And would sigh at the tale
Of sunk Lyonnesse,
As a wind-tugged tress
Flapped her cheek like a flail;
Or listen at whiles
With a thought-bound brow
To the murmuring miles
She is far from now.

Yet her shade, maybe,
Will creep underground
Till it catch the sound
Of that western sea
As it swells and sobs
Where she once domiciled,
And joy in its throbs
With the heart of a child.

December 1912

22 famed] far *SC* head,] ~ *Hol.* 27 As] ⟨While⟩ As *Hol.*; While *SC14* 34 creep *Hol.*, *SC15*, *CP*, *WE*] glide *SC14* 39 joy] joys *CP19 only* Date *SP*

WITHOUT CEREMONY

It was your way, my dear,
To vanish without a word
When callers, friends, or kin
Had left, and I hastened in
To rejoin you, as I inferred.

And when you'd a mind to career
Off anywhere—say to town—
You were all on a sudden gone
Before I had thought thereon,
Or noticed your trunks were down.

So, now that you disappear
For ever in that swift style,
Your meaning seems to me
Just as it used to be:
'Good-bye is not worth while!'

LAMENT

How she would have loved
A party to-day!—
Bright-hatted and gloved,
With table and tray
And chairs on the lawn
Her smiles would have shone
With welcomings. . . . But
She is shut, she is shut
        From friendship's spell
        In the jailing shell
        Of her tiny cell.

WITHOUT CEREMONY. 2 vanish] ⟨be gone⟩ ⟨have retired⟩ be gone *Hol.*; be gone *SC* 12 ⟨For all time in the same swift style,⟩ *Hol.* 15 while!'] ~." *Hol.*

LAMENT. 7 With] ⟨With⟩ ⟨Out⟩ *Hol.* 11 tiny] ⟨clodded⟩ *Hol.*

Or she would have reigned
At a dinner to-night
With ardours unfeigned,
And a generous delight;
All in her abode
She'd have freely bestowed
On her guests. . . . But alas,
She is shut under grass
    Where no cups flow,
    Powerless to know
    That it might be so.

And she would have sought
With a child's eager glance
The shy snowdrops brought
By the new year's advance,
And peered in the rime
Of Candlemas-time
For crocuses . . . chanced
It that she were not tranced
    From sights she loved best;
    Wholly possessed
    By an infinite rest!

And we are here staying
Amid these stale things
Who care not for gaying,
And those junketings
That used so to joy her,
And never to cloy her
As us they cloy! . . . But
She is shut, she is shut

14 unfeigned,] ~ *Hol.* 18 guests . . .] ⟨company . . .⟩ *Hol.* 19 ⟨She is shut, she is shut⟩ *Hol.* 22 That it] ⟨Things⟩ ⟨That things⟩ *Hol.* 23 And] ⟨Ay,⟩ *Hol.* 27 rime] ⟨grass⟩ *Hol.* 28 ⟨Of mild Candlemas-time⟩ *Hol.* 29 chanced] ⟨But⟩ *Hol.* 30 ⟨She is shut, she is shut⟩ *Hol.* 31 sights she loved] ⟨sights loved⟩ *Hol.* 34 we] ⟨some⟩ *Hol.* 40 ⟨By frequency. . . . But⟩ *Hol.*

From the cheer of them, dead
To all done and said
In her yew-arched bed.

THE HAUNTER*

He does not think that I haunt here nightly:
How shall I let him know
That whither his fancy sets him wandering
I, too, alertly go?—
Hover and hover a few feet from him
Just as I used to do,
But cannot answer the words he lifts me—
Only listen thereto!

When I could answer he did not say them:
When I could let him know
How I would like to join in his journeys
Seldom he wished to go.
Now that he goes and wants me with him
More than he used to do,
Never he sees my faithful phantom
Though he speaks thereto.

Yes, I companion him to places
Only dreamers know,
Where the shy hares print long paces,
Where the night rooks go;
Into old aisles where the past is all to him,
Close as his shade can do,
Always lacking the power to call to him,
Near as I reach thereto!

42 them,] ⟨it,⟩ *Hol.* 44 her] a *SC* yew-arched] ⟨yew-screened⟩ yew-testered *Hol.*

THE HAUNTER. 3 whither] ⟨when⟩ *Hol.* 7 the words he lifts me—] his words addressed me— *SC* 11 ⟨That I would join in his ⟨⟨boldest⟩⟩ dreamiest journey⟩ *Hol.* 12 ⟨He did not wish to go.⟩ *Hol.* 15 Never he sees] ⟨He sees not⟩ *Hol.* 17 companion] accompany *SC* 19 print long paces,] show their faces, *SC14*; limp long paces, *SC15*

What a good haunter I am, O tell him!
Quickly make him know
If he but sigh since my loss befell him
Straight to his side I go.
Tell him a faithful one is doing
All that love can do
Still that his path may be worth pursuing,
And to bring peace thereto.

THE VOICE*

Woman much missed, how you call to me, call to me,
Saying that now you are not as you were
When you had changed from the one who was all to me,
But as at first, when our day was fair.

Can it be you that I hear? Let me view you, then,
Standing as when I drew near to the town
Where you would wait for me: yes, as I knew you then,
Even to the original air-blue gown!

Or is it only the breeze, in its listlessness
Travelling across the wet mead to me here,
You being ever dissolved to wan wistlessness,
Heard no more again far or near?

25 him!] ~, *Hol.*, *SC* 29 And if it be that at night I am stronger, *SC14* 30 Little harm day can do; *Hol.*; Go, too, by day I do: *SC14* 31 Please, then, keep him in gloom no longer, *SC14* 32 Even ghosts tend thereto! *SC14*

THE VOICE. 1 Woman much missed,] O woman weird, *Hol.* 4 day] ⟨days⟩ *Hol.* 5 view you,] ~ *Hol.* 6 ⟨Standing attent as I came to the town⟩ *Hol.* 7 would wait for] ⟨long waited⟩ *Hol.* 8 air-blue] hat and *Hol.* 11 being ever] ⟨being for ever⟩ *Hol.* dissolved to wan wistlessness, *CP23*] consigned to existlessness, *SC*; dissolved to existlessness, *CP19*, *WE*

Thus I; faltering forward,
Leaves around me falling,
Wind oozing thin through the thorn from norward
And the woman calling.

December 1912.

HIS VISITOR

I come across from Mellstock while the moon wastes weaker
To behold where I lived with you for twenty years and more:
I shall go in the gray, at the passing of the mail-train,
And need no setting open of the long familiar door
As before.

The change I notice in my once own quarters!
A formal-fashioned border where the daisies used to be,
The rooms new painted, and the pictures altered,
And other cups and saucers, and no cozy nook for tea
As with me.

I discern the dim faces of the sleep-wrapt servants;
They are not those who tended me through feeble hours and strong,
But strangers quite, who never knew my rule here,
Who never saw me painting, never heard my softling song
Float along.

So I don't want to linger in this re-decked dwelling,
I feel too uneasy at the contrasts I behold,

13 I;] ⟨with me,⟩ I, *Hol.*
Date om. Hol.

HIS VISITOR. 6 change] ⟨change in⟩ *Hol.* own] old *Hol.* 7 formal-fashioned *CP23*] brilliant budded *SC*, *CP19*, *WE*

And I make again for Mellstock to return here never,
And rejoin the roomy silence, and the mute and manifold
Souls of old.

1913.

A CIRCULAR

As 'legal representative'
I read a missive not my own,
On new designs the senders give
For clothes, in tints as shown.

Here figure blouses, gowns for tea,
And presentation-trains of state,
Charming ball-dresses, millinery,
Warranted up to date.

And this gay-pictured, spring-time shout
Of Fashion, hails what lady proud?
Her who before last year ebbed out
Was costumed in a shroud.

A DREAM OR NO*

Why go to Saint-Juliot? What's Juliot to me?
Some strange necromancy
But charmed me to fancy
That much of my life claims the spot as its key.

18 to] ⟨and⟩ *Hol.* 19 and the mute and manifold] ⟨and submissly re-enfold⟩ where repose the manifold *Hol.* 20 ⟨With the mould.⟩ *Hol.*

A CIRCULAR. 2 own,] ~ *Hol.* 9 spring-time] spring-like *Hol.* 11 ebbed] was *SC* 12 Was costumed in] ⟨Only required⟩ Was folded in *Hol.*

A DREAM OR NO. *Title* ⟨The⟩ A Dream Indeed? *Hol.*
1 ⟨Why journey to Juliot?⟩ ⟨Why go to Saint-Juliot?⟩ Why journey to Juliot? *Hol.* 2 I've been but made fancy *SC14*; I was but made fancy *SC15* 3 By some necromancy *SC*

Yes. I have had dreams of that place in the West,
  And a maiden abiding
  Thereat as in hiding;
Fair-eyed and white-shouldered, broad-browed and brown-tressed,

And of how, coastward bound on a night long ago,
  There lonely I found her,
  The sea-birds around her,
And other than nigh things uncaring to know.

So sweet her life there (in my thought has it seemed)
  That quickly she drew me
  To take her unto me,
And lodge her long years with me. Such have I dreamed.

But nought of that maid from Saint-Juliot I see;
  Can she ever have been here,
  And shed her life's sheen here,
The woman I thought a long housemate with me?

Does there even a place like Saint-Juliot exist?
  Or a Vallency Valley
  With stream and leafed alley,
Or Beeny, or Bos with its flounce flinging mist?

February 1913.

AFTER A JOURNEY

Hereto I come to view a voiceless ghost;
  Whither, O whither will its whim now draw me?

8 brown-tressed, *DCM3*] ~. *all other texts* 13 thought] ⟨dreams⟩ *Hol.*
16 And . . . me.] ⟨And long years abide with her.⟩ And tarry long years with her. *Hol.*
17 maid from Saint-Juliot] ⟨woman of Juliot⟩ *Hol.* 19 here,] ~? *Hol.*
20 The] ⟨That⟩ *Hol.* 21 like Saint-Juliot exist?] ⟨such as Juliot abide?⟩ *Hol.*
24 flounce flinging mist?] ⟨thunderous tide?⟩ *Hol.*
Date 1913 *Hol.*

AFTER A JOURNEY. 1 view a voiceless ghost;] interview a ghost; *SC*
2 Whither,] ~ *Hol.*

Up the cliff, down, till I'm lonely, lost,
And the unseen waters' ejaculations awe me.
Where you will next be there's no knowing,
Facing round about me everywhere,
With your nut-coloured hair,
And gray eyes, and rose-flush coming and going.

Yes: I have re-entered your olden haunts at last;
Through the years, through the dead scenes I have tracked you;
What have you now found to say of our past—
Scanned across the dark space wherein I have lacked you?
Summer gave us sweets, but autumn wrought division?
Things were not lastly as firstly well
With us twain, you tell?
But all's closed now, despite Time's derision.

I see what you are doing: you are leading me on
To the spots we knew when we haunted here together,
The waterfall, above which the mist-bow shone
At the then fair hour in the then fair weather,
And the cave just under, with a voice still so hollow
That it seems to call out to me from forty years ago,
When you were all aglow,
And not the thin ghost that I now frailly follow!

Ignorant of what there is flitting here to see,
The waked birds preen and the seals flop lazily,
Soon you will have, Dear, to vanish from me,
For the stars close their shutters and the dawn whitens hazily.
Trust me, I mind not, though Life lours,
The bringing me here; nay, bring me here again!
I am just the same as when
Our days were a joy, and our paths through flowers.

Pentargan Bay.

4 ejaculations] soliloquies *SC14* 12 Scanned] Viewed *SC* 16 closed] soothed *Hol.* 25 see,] ~ *Hol.* 29 me,] ~ *Hol.* lours,] lowers, *Hol.* 30 The bringing me] The bringing ⟨of⟩ me *Hol.*; The bringing of me *SC14*

A DEATH-DAY RECALLED*

Beeny did not quiver,
  Juliot grew not gray,
Thin Valency's river
  Held its wonted way.
Bos seemed not to utter
  Dimmest note of dirge,
Targan mouth a mutter
  To its creamy surge.

Yet though these, unheeding,
  Listless, passed the hour
Of her spirit's speeding,
  She had, in her flower,
Sought and loved the places—
  Much and often pined
For their lonely faces
  When in towns confined.

Why did not Valency
  In his purl deplore
One whose haunts were whence he
  Drew his limpid store?
Why did Bos not thunder,
  Targan apprehend
Body and breath were sunder
  Of their former friend?

A DEATH-DAY RECALLED. *Title* ⟨A Death-day⟩ *Hol. table of contents* 2 grew] ⟨did⟩ *Hol.* 6 Dimmest] Narrowest *Hol.* 10 Listless,] ⟨Hintless,⟩ *Hol.* 22 apprehend] ~, *Hol.* 23 ⟨Soul and flesh were sunder⟩ *Hol.* breath] *cap. CP*

BEENY CLIFF*

March 1870–*March* 1913

I

O the opal and the sapphire of that wandering western sea,
And the woman riding high above with bright hair flapping free—
The woman whom I loved so, and who loyally loved me.

II

The pale mews plained below us, and the waves seemed far away
In a nether sky, engrossed in saying their ceaseless babbling say,
As we laughed light-heartedly aloft on that clear-sunned March day.

III

A little cloud then cloaked us, and there flew an irised rain,
And the Atlantic dyed its levels with a dull misfeatured stain,
And then the sun burst out again, and purples prinked the main.

IV

—Still in all its chasmal beauty bulks old Beeny to the sky,
And shall she and I not go there once again now March is nigh,
And the sweet things said in that March say anew there by and by?

BEENY CLIFF. 4 pale mews] ⟨white mews⟩ puffins *Hol.* 5 ceaseless] endless *Hol.* 9 again,] ⟨anew,⟩ *Hol.*

V

What if still in chasmal beauty looms that wild weird western shore,
The woman now is—elsewhere—whom the ambling pony bore,
And nor knows nor cares for Beeny, and will laugh there nevermore.

AT CASTLE BOTEREL

As I drive to the junction of lane and highway,
And the drizzle bedrenches the waggonette,
I look behind at the fading byway,
And see on its slope, now glistening wet,
Distinctly yet

Myself and a girlish form benighted
In dry March weather. We climb the road
Beside a chaise. We had just alighted
To ease the sturdy pony's load
When he sighed and slowed.

What we did as we climbed, and what we talked of
Matters not much, nor to what it led,—
Something that life will not be balked of
Without rude reason till hope is dead,
And feeling fled.

It filled but a minute. But was there ever
A time of such quality, since or before,
In that hill's story? To one mind never,
Though it has been climbed, foot-swift, foot-sore,
By thousands more.

13 What if] ⟨Nay. Though⟩ What if *Hol.*; Nay. Though *SC14* shore,] ~⟨,⟩! *Hol.* 15 laugh there] see it *SC*

AT CASTLE BOTEREL. 14 rude reason] ⟨good reason⟩ sore pressure *Hol.* 15 feeling] ⟨spirit⟩ ⟨fancy⟩ *Hol.* 18 To one mind never,] ⟨One mind says never,⟩ ⟨One mind thinks never,⟩ *Hol.* 19 foot-swift, foot-sore,] ⟨of late and yore⟩ ⟨in sun, rain, hoar⟩ *Hol.*

Primaeval rocks form the road's steep border,
And much have they faced there, first and last,
Of the transitory in Earth's long order;
But what they record in colour and cast
Is—that we two passed.

And to me, though Time's unflinching rigour,
In mindless rote, has ruled from sight
The substance now, one phantom figure
Remains on the slope, as when that night
Saw us alight.

I look and see it there, shrinking, shrinking,
I look back at it amid the rain
For the very last time; for my sand is sinking,
And I shall traverse old love's domain
Never again.

March 1913.

PLACES

Nobody says: Ah, that is the place
Where chanced, in the hollow of years ago,
What none of the Three Towns cared to know—
The birth of a little girl of grace—
The sweetest the house saw, first or last;
Yet it was so
On that day long past.

Nobody thinks: There, there she lay
In a room by the Hoe, like the bud of a flower,
And listened, just after the bedtime hour,
To the stammering chimes that used to play
The quaint Old Hundred-and-Thirteenth tune
In Saint Andrew's tower
Night, morn, and noon.

28 phantom] ⟨shadowy⟩ *Hol.*
Place ⟨Boscastle: Cornwall.⟩ *Hol.*

PLACES. 10 hour,] ~ *Hol.*

Nobody calls to mind that here
Upon Boterel Hill, where the waggoners skid,
With cheeks whose airy flush outbid
Fresh fruit in bloom, and free of fear,
She cantered down, as if she must fall
(Though she never did),
To the charm of all.

Nay: one there is to whom these things,
That nobody else's mind calls back,
Have a savour that scenes in being lack,
And a presence more than the actual brings;
To whom to-day is beneaped and stale,
And its urgent clack
But a vapid tale.

Plymouth, *March* 1913.

THE PHANTOM HORSEWOMAN

I

Queer are the ways of a man I know:
He comes and stands
In a careworn craze,
And looks at the sands
And the seaward haze,
With moveless hands
And face and gaze,
Then turns to go . . .
And what does he see when he gazes so?

II

They say he sees as an instant thing
More clear than to-day,
A sweet soft scene
That was once in play

16 waggoners] carters *SC* 19 fall] ~, *Hol.* 20 did),] ~) *Hol.*
22 things,] ~ *Hol.* 23 back,] ~ *Hol.* 26 stale,] ~ *Hol.*

THE PHANTOM HORSEWOMAN. 4 sands] ~, *Hol.*

By that briny green;
Yes, notes alway
Warm, real, and keen,
What his back years bring—
A phantom of his own figuring.

III

Of this vision of his they might say more:
Not only there
Does he see this sight,
But everywhere
In his brain—day, night,
As if on the air
It were drawn rose bright—
Yea, far from that shore
Does he carry this vision of heretofore:

IV

A ghost-girl-rider. And though, toil-tried,
He withers daily,
Time touches her not,
But she still rides gaily
In his rapt thought
On that shagged and shaly
Atlantic spot,
And as when first eyed
Draws rein and sings to the swing of the tide.

1913.

THE SPELL OF THE ROSE

'I mean to build a hall anon,
And shape two turrets there,
And a broad newelled stair,
And a cool well for crystal water;
Yes; I will build a hall anon,
Plant roses love shall feed upon,
And apple trees and pear.'

13 was once *DCM3*] once was *all other texts* *Date om. SC* 27 heretofore:] ~; *Hol.*

He set to build the manor-hall,
And shaped the turrets there,
And the broad newelled stair,
And the cool well for crystal water;
He built for me that manor-hall,
And planted many trees withal,
But no rose anywhere.

And as he planted never a rose
That bears the flower of love,
Though other flowers throve
Some heart-bane moved our souls to sever
Since he had planted never a rose;
And misconceits raised horrid shows,
And agonies came thereof.

'I'll mend these miseries,' then said I,
And so, at dead of night,
I went and, screened from sight,
That nought should keep our souls in severance,
I set a rose-bush. 'This', said I,
'May end divisions dire and wry,
And long-drawn days of blight.'

But I was called from earth—yea, called
Before my rose-bush grew;
And would that now I knew
What feels he of the tree I planted,
And whether, after I was called
To be a ghost, he, as of old,
Gave me his heart anew!

Perhaps now blooms that queen of trees
I set but saw not grow,
And he, beside its glow—

THE SPELL OF THE ROSE. 11 water;] ~: *Hol.* 18 Some heart-bane] A frost-wind *SC* 24 went] ~⟨,⟩ *Hol.* 25 severance,] ~ *Hol.* 29 But—I was called; yea, ghosted—called *Hol.* 32 planted,] ~⟨!⟩ *Hol.* 34 ghost,] ~ *Hol.* 38 glow—] ~, *Hol.*

Eyes couched of the mis-vision that blurred me—
Ay, there beside that queen of trees
He sees me as I was, though sees
Too late to tell me so!

ST. LAUNCE'S REVISITED

Slip back, Time!
Yet again I am nearing
Castle and keep, uprearing
Gray, as in my prime.

At the inn
Smiling nigh, why is it
Not as on my visit
When hope and I were twin?

Groom and jade
Whom I found here, moulder;
Strange the tavern-holder,
Strange the tap-maid.

Here I hired
Horse and man for bearing
Me on my wayfaring
To the door desired.

Evening gloomed
As I journeyed forward
To the faces shoreward,
Till their dwelling loomed.

If again
Towards the Atlantic sea there
I should speed, they'd be there
Surely now as then? . . .

Date ⟨1913⟩ *Hol.*

ST. LAUNCE'S REVISITED. *Title* ⟨At St. Launce's⟩ *Hol.* 2 ⟨I again am nearing⟩ *Hol.* 6 nigh,] close, *SC* 11 Strange ⟨is⟩ the tavern-holder, *Hol.* 14 man] ⟨fly⟩ *Hol.* 16 door] goal *Hol.*

Why waste thought,
When I know them vanished
Under earth; yea, banished
Ever into nought!

WHERE THE PICNIC WAS

Where we made the fire
In the summer time
Of branch and briar
On the hill to the sea,
I slowly climb
Through winter mire,
And scan and trace
The forsaken place
Quite readily.

Now a cold wind blows,
And the grass is gray,
But the spot still shows
As a burnt circle—aye,
And stick-ends, charred,
Still strew the sward
Whereon I stand,
Last relic of the band
Who came that day!

Yes, I am here
Just as last year,
And the sea breathes brine
From its strange straight line
Up hither, the same
As when we four came.

28 nought!] ~⟨!⟩. *Hol.*; ~. *SC*
Date ⟨1913⟩ *Hol.*

WHERE THE PICNIC WAS. 4 sea, *CP*, *WE*, *DCM4*] ~ *Hol.*, *SC*, *SP* 6 mire,] ~ *Hol.*

—But two have wandered far
From this grassy rise
Into urban roar
Where no picnics are,
And one—has shut her eyes
For evermore.

MISCELLANEOUS PIECES

THE WISTFUL LADY

'Love, while you were away there came to me—
From whence I cannot tell—
A plaintive lady pale and passionless,
Who laid her eyes upon me critically,
And weighed me with a wearing wistfulness,
As if she knew me well.'

'I saw no lady of that wistful sort
As I came riding home.
Perhaps she was some dame the Fates constrain
By memories sadder than she can support,
Or by unhappy vacancy of brain,
To leave her roof and roam?'

'Ah, but she knew me. And before this time
I have seen her, lending ear
To my light outdoor words, and pondering each,
Her frail white finger swayed in pantomime,
As if she fain would close with me in speech,
And yet would not come near.

'And once I saw her beckoning with her hand
As I came into sight
At an upper window. And I at last went out;
But when I reached where she had seemed to stand,
And wandered up and down and searched about,
I found she had vanished quite.'

THE WISTFUL LADY. 4 laid] bent *SC* critically,] ~ *Hol.* 15 ⟨To my light words when walking, pondering each,⟩ *Hol.* 17 speech,] ~ *Hol.*

Then thought I how my dead Love used to say,
With a small smile, when she
Was waning wan, that she would hover round
And show herself after her passing day
To any newer Love I might have found,
But show her not to me.

THE WOMAN IN THE RYE

'Why do you stand in the dripping rye,
Cold-lipped, unconscious, wet to the knee,
When there are firesides near?' said I.
'I told him I wished him dead,' said she.

'Yea, cried it in my haste to one
Whom I had loved, whom I well loved still;
And die he did. And I hate the sun,
And stand here lonely, aching, chill;

'Stand waiting, waiting under skies
That blow reproach, the while I see
The rooks sheer off to where he lies
Wrapt in a peace withheld from me!'

THE CHEVAL-GLASS*

Why do you harbour that great cheval-glass
Filling up your narrow room?
You never preen or plume,
Or look in a week at your full-length figure—
Picture of bachelor gloom!

'Well, when I dwelt in ancient England,
Renting the valley farm,
Thoughtless of all heart-harm,

THE WOMAN IN THE RYE. 12 me!'] ~." *Hol.*, *SC*

THE CHEVAL-GLASS. 8 all] ⟨any⟩ *Hol.*

I used to gaze at the parson's daughter,
A creature of nameless charm.

'Thither there came a lover and won her,
Carried her off from my view.
O it was then I knew
Misery of a cast undreamt of—
More than, indeed, my due!

'Then far rumours of her ill-usage
Came, like a chilling breath
When a man languisheth;
Followed by news that her mind lost balance,
And, in a space, of her death.

'Soon sank her father; and next was the auction—
Everything to be sold:
Mid things new and old
Stood this glass in her former chamber,
Long in her use, I was told.

'Well, I awaited the sale and bought it. . . .
There by my bed it stands,
And as the dawn expands
Often I see her pale-faced form there
Brushing her hair's bright bands.

'There, too, at pallid midnight moments
Quick she will come to my call,
Smile from the frame withal
Ponderingly, as she used to regard me
Passing her father's wall.

10 nameless] ⟨light and⟩ ⟨cheer and⟩ *Hol.* 16 'Then] ⟨Soon⟩ *Hol.* ill-usage] ⟨ill-usage⟩ ⟨rough usage⟩ *Hol.* 17 like] ⟨as⟩ *Hol.* 21 ⟨"Vanished her husband; and came the auction;⟩ *Hol.* auction—] ~; *Hol.* 24 Stood this] ⟨There was a⟩ ⟨Stood a tall⟩ *Hol.* former] ⟨sleeping⟩ *Hol.* 26 ⟨"Well, I journeyed that way and bought it. . . .⟩ *Hol.* 29 pale-faced] ⟨fair pale⟩ *Hol.* 30 bright] ⟨bright⟩ ⟨long⟩ *Hol.* bands.] ⟨strands.⟩ *Hol.* 31 pallid midnight] ⟨any mystic⟩ ⟨mystic midnight⟩ *Hol.* 33 ⟨Look in my face withal⟩ *Hol.* 34 ⟨With her great eyes as, times out of counting,⟩ *Hol.* 35 Passing] ⟨When passing⟩ *Hol.*

'So that it was for its revelations
I brought it oversea,
And drag it about with me. . . .
Anon I shall break it and bury its fragments
Where my grave is to be.'

THE RE-ENACTMENT*

Between the folding sea-downs,
In the gloom
Of a wailful wintry nightfall,
When the boom
Of the ocean, like a hammering in a hollow tomb,

Throbbed up the copse-clothed valley
From the shore
To the chamber where I darkled,
Sunk and sore
With gray ponderings why my Loved one had not come before

To salute me in the dwelling
That of late
I had hired to waste a while in—
Dim of date,
Quaint, and remote—wherein I now expectant sate;

On the solitude, unsignalled,
Broke a man
Who, in air as if at home there,
Seemed to scan
Every fire-flecked nook of the apartment span by span.

39 ⟨I shall break it some day and bury its fragments⟩ *Hol.*

THE RE-ENACTMENT. 5 tomb,] ~ *Hol.* 13 ⟨I had sought and made my shelter—⟩ I had hired to while a space in— *Hol.* 14 Dim] Vague *SC* 16 unsignalled,] ~ *Hol.*

A stranger's and no lover's
Eyes were these,
Eyes of a man who measures
What he sees
But vaguely, as if wrapt in filmy phantasies.

Yea, his bearing was so absent
As he stood,
It bespoke a chord so plaintive
In his mood,
That soon I judged he would not wrong my quietude.

'Ah—the supper is just ready!'
Then he said,
'And the years-long-binned Madeira
Flashes red!'
(There was no wine, no food, no supper-table spread.)

'You will forgive my coming,
Lady fair?
I see you as at that time
Rising there,
The self-same curious querying in your eyes and air.

'Yet no. How so? You wear not
The same gown,
Your locks show woful difference,
Are not brown:
What, is it not as when I hither came from town?

'And the place. . . . But you seem other—
Can it be?
What's this that Time is doing
Unto me?
You dwell here, unknown woman? . . . Whereabouts,
then, is she?

23 Eyes] ⟨Those⟩ *Hol.* 30 wrong my quietude.] ⟨mar my solitude.⟩ *Hol.* 31 ready!'] ~," *SC, WE* 33 years-long-binned] ⟨many-years binned⟩ ⟨long-years binned⟩ years-long binned *Hol.*; years'-long binned *SC*; years'-long-binned *CP*, *WE* (*see explanatory note*) 40 air.] ⟨hair.⟩ air. *Hol.*; hair *SC14*

'And the house-things are much shifted.—
Put them where
They stood on this night's fellow;
Shift her chair:
Here was the couch: and the piano should be there.'

I indulged him, verily nerve-strained
Being alone,
And I moved the things as bidden,
One by one,
And feigned to push the old piano where he had shown.

'Aha—now I can see her!
Stand aside:
Don't thrust her from the table
Where, meek-eyed,
She makes attempt with matron-manners to preside.

'She serves me: now she rises,
Goes to play. . . .
But you obstruct her, fill her
With dismay,
And all-embarrassed, scared, she vanishes away!'

And, as 'twere useless longer
To persist,
He sighed, and sought the entry
Ere I wist,
And retreated, disappearing soundless in the mist.

That here some mighty passion
Once had burned,
Which still the walls enghosted,
I discerned,
And that by its strong spell mine might be overturned.

51 house-things] ⟨chattels⟩ *Hol.* 55 and the piano] ⟨the old piano⟩ *Hol.* 60 the old] ⟨my new⟩ ⟨my own⟩ *Hol.* 70 And all-embarrassed, *CP20*, *ME*] And embarrassed, *SC*, *CP19*, *WE* away!'] ~⟨!⟩." *Hol.*

I sat depressed; till, later,
My Love came;
But something in the chamber
Dimmed our flame,—
An emanation, making our due words fall tame,

As if the intenser drama
Shown me there
Of what the walls had witnessed
Filled the air,
And left no room for later passion anywhere.

So came it that our fervours
Did quite fail
Of future consummation—
Being made quail
By the weird witchery of the parlour's hidden tale,

Which I, as years passed, faintly
Learnt to trace,—
One of sad love, born full-winged
In that place
Where the predestined sorrowers first stood face to face.

And as that month of winter
Circles round,
And the evening of the date-day
Grows embrowned,
I am conscious of those presences, and sit spellbound.

There, often—lone, forsaken—
Queries breed
Within me; whether a phantom
Had my heed
On that strange night, or was it some wrecked heart indeed?

85 An] ⟨That⟩ *Hol.* 95 witchery] ⟨glamour⟩ *Hol.* 98 full-winged] ⟨full-fledged⟩ *Hol.*

HER SECRET*

That love's dull smart distressed my heart
He shrewdly learnt to see,
But that I was in love with a dead man
Never suspected he.

He searched for the trace of a pictured face,
He watched each missive come,
And a sheet that seemed like a love-line
Wrought his look lurid and numb.

He dogged my feet to the city street,
He followed me to the sea,
But not to the nigh, still churchyard
Did he dream of following me!

'SHE CHARGED ME'

She charged me with having said this and that
To another woman long years before,
In the very parlour where we sat,—

Sat on a night when the endless pour
Of rain on the roof and the road below
Bent the spring of the spirit more and more. . . .

—So charged she me; and the Cupid's bow
Of her mouth was hard, and her eyes, and her face,
And her white forefinger lifted slow.

Had she done it gently, or shown a trace
That not too curiously would she view
A folly flown ere her reign had place,

HER SECRET. 6 each missive] ⟨the postman⟩ *Hol.* 7 sheet] note *SC* that seemed like] ⟨in the shape of⟩ *Hol.* 8 Made him look frozen and glum. *SC* 11 nigh, still] neighbouring *SC* 12 me! *CP*] ~. *all other texts*

'SHE CHARGED ME'. 2 before,] ~ *Hol.* 4 Sat] ⟨It was⟩ *Hol.* 6 Bent] ⟨Broke⟩ *Hol.* 12 flown] passed *SC* place,] ~ *Hol.*

A kiss might have closed it. But I knew
From the fall of each word, and the pause between,
That the curtain would drop upon us two
Ere long, in our play of slave and queen.

THE NEWCOMER'S WIFE

He paused on the sill of a door ajar
That screened a lively liquor-bar,
For the name had reached him through the door
Of her he had married the week before.

'We called her the Hack of the Parade;
But she was discreet in the games she played;
If slightly worn, she's pretty yet,
And gossips, after all, forget.

'And he knows nothing of her past;
I am glad the girl's in luck at last;
Such ones, though stale to native eyes,
Newcomers snatch at as a prize.'

'Yes, being a stranger he sees her blent
Of all that's fresh and innocent,
Nor dreams how many a love-campaign
She had enjoyed before his reign!'

That night there was the splash of a fall
Over the slimy harbour-wall:
They searched, and at the deepest place
Found him with crabs upon his face.

13 closed] ended *SC*

THE NEWCOMER'S WIFE. 8 ⟨And after all, folk soon forget.⟩ *Hol.* 10 I am] ⟨I'm⟩ *Hol.*

A CONVERSATION AT DAWN*

He lay awake, with a harassed air,
And she, in her cloud of loose lank hair,
Seemed trouble-tried
As the dawn drew in on their faces there.

The chamber looked far over the sea
From a white hotel on a white-stoned quay,
And stepping a stride
He parted the window-drapery.

Above the level horizon spread
The sunrise, firing them foot to head
From its smouldering lair,
And painting their pillows with dyes of red.

'What strange disquiets have stirred you, dear,
This dragging night, with starts in fear
Of me, as it were,
Or of something evil hovering near?'

'My husband, can I have fear of you?
What should one fear from a man whom few,
Or none, had matched
In that late long spell of delays undue!'

He watched her eyes in the heaving sun:
'Then what has kept, O reticent one,
Those lids unlatched—
Anything promised I've not yet done?'

'O it's not a broken promise of yours
(For what quite lightly your lip assures
The due time brings)
That has troubled my sleep, and no waking cures!' . . .

A CONVERSATION AT DAWN. 2 hair,] ~ *Hol.* 25 yours] ~, *Hol.*

'I have shaped my will; 'tis at hand,' said he;
'I subscribe it to-day, that no risk there be
In the hap of things
Of my leaving you menaced by poverty.'

'That a boon provision I'm safe to get,
Signed, sealed by my lord as it were a debt,
I cannot doubt,
Or ever this peering sun be set.'

'But you flung my arms away from your side,
And faced the wall. No month-old bride
Ere the tour be out
In an air so loth can be justified?

'Ah—had you a male friend once loved well,
Upon whose suit disaster fell
And frustrance swift?
Honest you are, and may care to tell.'

She lay impassive, and nothing broke
The stillness other than, stroke by stroke,
The lazy lift
Of the tide below them; till she spoke:

'I once had a friend—a Love, if you will—
Whose wife forsook him, and sank until
She was made a thrall
In a prison-cell for a deed of ill. . . .

'He remained alone; and we met—to love,
But barring legitimate joy thereof
Stood a doorless wall,
Though we prized each other all else above.

33 get,] ~ *Hol.* 34 ⟨Religiously sealed as it were a debt⟩ *Hol.*
52 prison-cell] ⟨prison-house⟩ *Hol.*

'And this was why, though I'd touched my prime,
I put off suitors from time to time—
Yourself with the rest—
Till friends, who approved you, called it crime,

'And when misgivings weighed on me
In my lover's absence, hurriedly,
And much distrest,
I took you. . . . Ah, that such could be! . . .

'Now, saw you when crossing from yonder shore
At yesternoon, that the packet bore
On a white-wreathed bier
A coffined body towards the fore?

'Well, while you stood at the other end,
The loungers talked, and I couldn't but lend
A listening ear,
For they named the dead. 'Twas the wife of my friend.

'He was there, but did not note me, veiled,
Yet I saw that a joy, as of one unjailed,
Now shone in his gaze;
He knew not his hope of me just had failed!

'They had brought her home: she was born in this isle;
And he will return to his domicile,
And pass his days
Alone, and not as he dreamt erstwhile!'

'—So you've lost a sprucer spouse than I!'
She held her peace, as if fain deny
She would indeed
For his pleasure's sake, but could lip no lie.

62 hurriedly,] ⟨over the sea⟩ *Hol.* 69 other] ⟨further⟩ *Hol.*
70 couldn't but] could but *SC*

'One far less formal and plain and slow!'
She let the laconic assertion go
As if of need
She held the conviction that it was so.

'Regard me as his he always should,
He had said, and wed me he vowed he would
In his prime or sere
Most verily do, if ever he could.

'And this fulfilment is now his aim,
For a letter, addressed in my maiden name,
Has dogged me here,
Reminding me faithfully of his claim.

'And it started a hope like a lightning-streak
That I might go to him—say for a week—
And afford you right
To put me away, and your vows unspeak.

'To be sure you have said, as of dim intent,
That marriage is a plain event
Of black and white,
Without any ghost of sentiment,

'And my heart has quailed.—But deny it true
That you will never this lock undo!
No God intends
To thwart the yearning He's father to!'

The husband hemmed, then blandly bowed
In the light of the angry morning cloud.
'So my idyll ends,
And a drama opens!' he mused aloud;

86 laconic] ⟨bitter⟩ *Hol.* 95 here,] ~ *Hol.* 102 plain event] ⟨sacrament⟩ *Hol.* 103 ⟨Nor depth nor height⟩ *Hol.* 104 ⟨Nor any creature can circumvent,⟩ *Hol.* 108 He's] *l.c. Hol.* 109 hemmed,] thought, *Hol.*; sneered, *SC14*

And his features froze. 'You may take it as true
That I will never this lock undo
For so depraved
A passion as that which kindles you!'

Said she: 'I am sorry you see it so;
I had hoped you might have let me go,
And thus been saved
The pain of learning there's more to know.'

'More? What may that be? Gad, I think
You have told me enough to make me blink!
Yet if more remain
Then own it to me. I will not shrink!'

'Well, it is this. As we could not see
That a legal marriage would ever be,
To end our pain
We united ourselves informally;

'And vowed at a chancel-altar nigh,
With book and ring, a lifelong tie;
A contract vain
To the world, but real to Him on High.'

'And you became as his wife?'—'I did.'—
He stood as stiff as a caryatid,
And said, 'Indeed! . . .
No matter. You're mine, whatever you've hid!'

'But is it right! When I only gave
My hand to you in a sweat to save,
Through desperate need
(As I thought), my fame, for I was not brave!'

116 you!'] ~." *SC* 122 me] ⟨one⟩ *Hol.* 126 would] could *SC*
139 need] ~, *Hol.* 140 thought),] ~) *Hol.*

'To save your fame? Your meaning is dim,
For nobody knew of your altar-whim?'
'I mean—I feared
There might be fruit of my tie with him;

'And to cloak it by marriage I'm not the first,
Though, maybe, morally most accurst
Through your unpeered
And strict uprightness. That's the worst!

'While yesterday his worn contours
Convinced me that love like his endures,
And that my troth-plight
Had been his, in fact, and not truly yours.'

'So my lady, you raise the veil by degrees. . . .
I own this last is enough to freeze
The warmest wight!
Now hear the other side, if you please:

'I did say once, though without intent,
That marriage is a plain event
Of black and white,
Whatever may be its sentiment.

'I'll act accordingly, none the less
That you soiled the contract in time of stress,
Thereto induced
By the feared results of your wantonness.

'But the thing is over, and no one knows,
And it's nought to the future what you disclose.
That you'll be loosed
For such an episode, don't suppose!

'No: I'll not free you. And if it appear
There was too good ground for your first fear

156 please:] ~. *Hol.* 157 intent,] ~ *Hol.* 162 contract] ⟨rite⟩ *Hol.*
168 suppose!] ~. *Hol.* 169 And] ⟨E'en⟩ *Hol.*

From your amorous tricks,
I'll father the child. Yes, by God, my dear.

'Even should you fly to his arms, I'll damn
Opinion, and fetch you; treat as sham
Your mutinous kicks,
And whip you home. That's the sort I am!'

She whitened. 'Enough. . . . Since you disapprove
I'll yield in silence, and never move
Till my last pulse ticks
A footstep from the domestic groove.'

'Then swear it,' he said, 'and your king uncrown.'
He drew her forth in her long white gown,
And she knelt and swore.
'Good. Now you may go and again lie down.

'Since you've played these pranks and given no sign,
You shall crave this man of yours; pine and pine
With sighings sore,
'Till I've starved your love for him; nailed you mine!

'I'm a practical man, and want no tears;
You've made a fool of me, it appears;
That you don't again
Is a lesson I'll teach you in future years.'

She answered not, lying listlessly
With her dark dry eyes on the coppery sea,
That now and then
Flung its lazy flounce at the neighbouring quay.

1910.

180a–d ⟨"For really I never knew till now
What a hero my lord was. Nothing can bow
Or bend or lower
A soul so cool! Yes, I'll keep my vow."⟩ *Hol.*

188 mine!] ~. *SC* 193 lying] but lay *SC* 196 at] ⟨by⟩ *Hol.*
Date Autumn: 1910. *Hol.*

A KING'S SOLILOQUY*

On the Night of his Funeral

From the slow march and muffled drum,
And crowds distrest,
And book and bell, at length I have come
To my full rest.

A ten years' rule beneath the sun
Is wound up here,
And what I have done, what left undone,
Figures out clear.

Yet in the estimate of such
It grieves me more
That I by some was loved so much
Than that I bore,

From others, judgment of that hue
Which over-hope
Breeds from a theoretic view
Of regal scope.

For kingly opportunities
Right many have sighed;
How best to bear its devilries
Those learn who have tried!

I have eaten the fat and drunk the sweet,
Lived the life out
From the first greeting glad drum-beat
To the last shout.

What pleasure earth affords to kings
I have enjoyed
Through its long vivid pulse-stirrings
Even till it cloyed.

A KING'S SOLILOQUY. *Title* ⟨The King's Soliloquy⟩ *Hol.* *Subtitle om. Hol.* 12 bore,] ~ *Hol.* 13 others,] ~ *Hol.*

What days of drudgery, nights of stress
Can cark a throne,
Even one maintained in peacefulness,
I too have known.

And so, I think, could I step back
To life again,
I should prefer the average track
Of average men,

Since, as with them, what kingship would
It cannot do,
Nor to first thoughts however good
Hold itself true.

Something binds hard the royal hand,
As all that be,
And it is That has shaped, has planned
My acts and me.

May 1910.

THE CORONATION*

At Westminster, hid from the light of day,
Many who once had shone as monarchs lay.

Edward the Pious, and two Edwards more,
The second Richard, Henrys three or four;

That is to say, those who were called the Third,
Fifth, Seventh, and Eighth (the much self-widowered);

And James the Scot, and near him Charles the Second,
And, too, the second George could there be reckoned.

29 drudgery,] strain, what *SC14* 40 Hold itself] ⟨?Continue?⟩ *Hol.* 41 Something binds] ⟨For what holds⟩ *Hol.* hand,] ~⟨?⟩, *Hol.* 42 ⟨Necessity.⟩ *Hol.* 43 That] ⟨*l.c.*⟩ *Hol.*

THE CORONATION. 6 self-widowered); *DCM4*] ~) *Hol.*; ~), *SC*

Of women, Mary and Queen Elizabeth,
And Anne, all silent in a musing death;

And William's Mary, and Mary, Queen of Scots,
And consort-queens whose names oblivion blots;

And several more whose chronicle one sees
Adorning ancient royal pedigrees.

—Now, as they drowsed on, freed from Life's old thrall,
And heedless, save of things exceptional,

Said one: 'What means this throbbing thudding sound
That reaches to us here from overground;

'A sound of chisels, augers, planes, and saws,
Infringing all ecclesiastic laws?

'And these tons-weight of timber on us pressed,
Unfelt here since we entered into rest?

'Surely, at least to us, being corpses royal,
A meet repose is owing by the loyal?'

'—Perhaps a scaffold!' Mary Stuart sighed,
'If such still be. It was that way I died.'

'—Ods! Far more like', said he the many-wived,
'That for a wedding 'tis this work's contrived.

'Ha-ha! I never would bow down to Rimmon,
But I had a rare time with those six women!'

'Not all at once?' gasped he who loved confession.
'Nay, nay!' said Hal. 'That would have been transgression.'

11 Mary, Queen] Mary Queen *Hol.* 27 "—No, no! . . . Maybe," said he the many-wived, *Hol.* 28 " 'Tis for a wedding that this work's contrived. *Hol.* 32 'Nay, nay!'] "O no!" *Hol.*

'—They build a catafalque here, black and tall,
Perhaps,' mused Richard, 'for some funeral?'

And Anne chimed in: 'Ah, yes: it may be so!'
'Nay!' squeaked Eliza. 'Little you seem to know—

'Clearly 'tis for some crowning here in state,
As they crowned us at our long bygone date;

'Though we'd no such a power of carpentry,
But let the ancient architecture be;

'If I were up there where the parsons sit,
In one of my gold robes, I'd see to it!'

'But you are not,' Charles chuckled. 'You are here,
And never will know the sun again, my dear!'

'Yea,' whispered those whom no one had addressed;
'With slow, sad march, amid a folk distressed,
We were brought here, to take our dusty rest.

'And here, alas, in darkness laid below,
We'll wait and listen, and endure the show. . . .
Clamour dogs kingship; afterwards not so!'

1911.

AQUAE SULIS*

The chimes called midnight, just at interlune,
And the daytime parle on the Roman investigations
Was shut to silence, save for the husky tune
The bubbling waters played near the excavations.

34 mused] ⟨lipped⟩ *Hol.* 44 know] ⟨see⟩ *Hol.* 46 slow,] ~ *Hol.*
50 ⟨Loudly doth Kingship come, and softly go!"⟩ *Hol.*

AQUAE SULIS. 2 parle on] talk of *SC* 3 shut to] checked by *SC*

And a warm air came up from underground,
And the flutter of a filmy shape unsepulchred,
That collected itself, and waited, and looked around:
Nothing was seen, but utterances could be heard:

Those of the Goddess whose shrine was beneath the pile
Of the God with the baldachined altar overhead:
'And what did you win by raising this nave and aisle
Close on the site of the temple I tenanted?

'The notes of your organ have thrilled down out of view
To the earth-clogged wrecks of my edifice many a year,
Though stately and shining once—ay, long ere you
Had set up crucifix and candle here.

'Your priests have trampled the dust of mine without rueing,
Despising the joys of man whom I so much loved,
Though my springs boil on by your Gothic arcades and pewing,
And sculptures crude. . . . Would Jove they could be removed!'

'—Repress, O lady proud, your traditional ires;
You know not by what a frail thread we equally hang;
It is said we are images both—twitched by people's desires;
And that I, as you, fail like a song that men yesterday sang!'

6 And the flutter of *ME*] And a motion, as of *Hol.*; And a flutter, as of *SC*, *CP*, *WE* 9 Goddess *CP23*] *l.c. all other texts* 11 win] get *SC* 15 stately] erect *Hol.* 19 arcades] arch *Hol.* 24 And that I,] And I, *Hol.* as you, fail like *ME*, *CP23*] like you, fail as *SC*, *CP19*, *WE* yesterday] time agone *SC14*

'What—a Jumping-jack you, and myself but a poor
 Jumping-jill,
Now worm-eaten, times agone twitched at Humanity's
 bid?
O I cannot endure it!—But, chance to us whatso there
 will,
Let us kiss and be friends! Come—agree you?'—None
 heard if he did. . . .

And the olden dark hid the cavities late laid bare,
And all was suspended and soundless as before,
Except for a gossamery noise fading off in the air,
And the boiling voice of the waters' medicinal pour.

Bath.

SEVENTY-FOUR AND TWENTY

Here goes a man of seventy-four,
Who sees not what life means for him,
And here another in years a score
Who reads its very figure and trim.

The one who shall walk to-day with me
Is not the youth who gazes far,
But the breezy sire who cannot see
What Earth's ingrained conditions are.

25–8 *om. SC* 29 *preceded by line of spaced dots Hol., SC*

SEVENTY-FOUR AND TWENTY. 6 far,] ~ *Hol.* 7 sire] wight *SC*
8a–d [*centred beneath line 8*]

For I am sick of thinking
 On whither things tend,
And will foster hoodwinking
 Henceforth to the end. *Hol.*

THE ELOPEMENT

'A woman never agreed to it!' said my knowing friend to me.
'That one thing she'd refuse to do for Solomon's mines in fee:
No woman ever will make herself look older than she is.'
I did not answer; but I thought, 'you err there, ancient Quiz.'

It took a rare one, true, to do it; for she was surely rare—
As rare a soul at that sweet time of her life as she was fair.
And urging heart-heaves, too, were strong, for ours was a passionate case,
Yea, passionate enough to lead to freaking with that young face.

I have told no one about it, should perhaps make few believe,
But I think it over now that life looms dull and years bereave,
How blank we stood at our bright wits' end, two blown barks in distress,
How self-regard in her was slain by her large tenderness.

I said: 'The only chance for us in a crisis of this kind
Is going it thorough!'—'Yes,' she calmly breathed. 'Well, I don't mind.'
And we blanched her dark locks ruthlessly: set wrinkles on her brow;
Ay—she was a right rare woman then, whatever she may be now.

THE ELOPEMENT. 3 she is.'] ⟨her years."⟩ *Hol.* 4 ancient Quiz.'] ⟨it appears.⟩ *Hol.* 7 heart-heaves,] motives, *SC* 9 ⟨I have told no one the story; and perhaps few would believe,⟩ *Hol.* it,] ~; *Hol.* 11 blown] frail *SC* 15 wrinkles] ⟨age-lines⟩ *Hol.*

That night we heard a coach drive up, and questions asked below.
'A gent with an elderly wife, sir,' was returned from the bureau.
And the wheels went rattling on, and free at last from public ken
We washed all off in her chamber and restored her youth again.

How many years ago it was! Some fifty can it be
Since that adventure held us, and she played old wife to me?
But in time convention won her, as it wins all women at last,
And now she is rich and respectable, and time has buried the past.

'I ROSE UP AS MY CUSTOM IS'*

I rose up as my custom is
  On the eve of All-Souls' day,
And left my grave for an hour or so
To call on those I used to know
  Before I passed away.

I visited my former Love
  As she lay by her husband's side;
I asked her if life pleased her, now
She was rid of a poet wrung in brow,
  And crazed with the ills he eyed;

Who used to drag her here and there
  Wherever his fancies led,
And point out pale phantasmal things,
And talk of vain vague purposings
  That she discredited.

17 night] ⟨eve⟩ *Hol.* 21 fifty] forty *Hol.*

'I ROSE UP'. 2 All-Souls'] ⟨New Year's⟩ ⟨Midsummer⟩ *Hol.* 8 life pleased her,] ⟨she liked life⟩ *Hol.* 9 brow,] ~ *Hol.* 13 pale] ⟨wan⟩ *Hol.*

She was quite civil, and replied,
  'Old comrade, is that you?
Well, on the whole, I like my life.—
I know I swore I'd be no wife,
  But what was I to do?

'You see, of all men for my sex
  A poet is the worst;
Women are practical, and they
Crave the wherewith to pay their way,
  And slake their social thirst.

'You were a poet—quite the ideal
  That we all love awhile:
But look at this man snoring here—
He's no romantic chanticleer,
  Yet keeps me in good style.

'He makes no quest into my thoughts,
  But a poet wants to know
What one has felt from earliest days,
Why one thought not in other ways,
  And one's Loves of long ago.'

Her words benumbed my fond faint ghost;
  The nightmares neighed from their stalls,
The vampires screeched, the harpies flew,
And under the dim dawn I withdrew
  To Death's inviolate halls.

A WEEK

On Monday night I closed my door,
And thought you were not as heretofore,
And little cared if we met no more.

18 whole,] ~ *Hol.* 31 ⟨"He asks no questions on my thoughts,⟩ *Hol.* 36 ⟨I vanished at the turn of the hour,⟩ *Hol.* faint] frail *SC* 39 dim dawn] ⟨white moon⟩ *Hol.* 40 ⟨To where no sunlight falls.⟩ *Hol.*

I seemed on Tuesday night to trace
Something beyond mere commonplace
In your ideas, and heart, and face.

On Wednesday I did not opine
Your life would ever be one with mine,
Though if it were we should well combine.

On Thursday noon I liked you well,
And fondly felt that we must dwell
Not far apart, whatever befell.

On Friday it was with a thrill
In gazing towards your distant vill
I owned you were my dear one still.

I saw you wholly to my mind
On Saturday—even one who shrined
All that was best of womankind.

As wing-clipt sea-gull for the sea
On Sunday night I longed for thee,
Without whom life were waste to me!

HAD YOU WEPT

Had you wept; had you but neared me with a hazed uncertain ray,
Dewy as the face of the dawn, in your large and luminous eye,
Then would have come back all the joys the tidings had slain that day,
And a new beginning, a fresh fair heaven, have smoothed the things awry.

A WEEK. 12 whatever] ⟨whate'er⟩ whatso *Hol.*

HAD YOU WEPT. 1 hazed] frail *SC* 2 dawn,] ~ *Hol.* 3 tidings] ⟨news⟩ *Hol.*

But you were less feebly human, and no passionate need
for clinging
Possessed your soul to overthrow reserve when I came
near;
Ay, though you suffer as much as I from storms the hours
are bringing
Upon your heart and mine, I never see you shed a tear.

The deep strong woman is weakest, the weak one is the
strong;
The weapon of all weapons best for winning, you have
not used;
Have you never been able, or would you not, through
the evil times and long?
Has not the gift been given you, or such gift have you
refused?
When I bade me not absolve you on that evening or the
morrow,
Why did you not make war on me with those who weep
like rain?
You felt too much, so gained no balm for all your torrid
sorrow,
And hence our deep division, and our dark undying pain.

BEREFT, SHE THINKS SHE DREAMS

I dream that the dearest I ever knew
Has died and been entombed.
I am sure it's a dream that cannot be true,
But I am so overgloomed
By its persistence, that I would gladly
Have quick death take me,
Rather than longer think thus sadly;
So wake me, wake me!

10 winning,] ⟨winning back,⟩ *Hol.* 13 When] ⟨Thus⟩ *Hol.*

BEREFT, SHE THINKS SHE DREAMS. *Title* She thinks she dreams *Hol.*
3 I am sure] ⟨I know⟩ *Hol.* 8 me!] ~. *Hol.*

It has lasted days, but minute and hour
  I expect to get aroused
And find him as usual in the bower
  Where we so happily housed.
Yet stays this nightmare too appalling,
  And like a web shakes me,
And piteously I keep on calling,
  And no one wakes me!

IN THE BRITISH MUSEUM

'What do you see in that time-touched stone,
    When nothing is there
But ashen blankness, although you give it
    A rigid stare?

'You look not quite as if you saw,
    But as if you heard,
Parting your lips, and treading softly
    As mouse or bird.

'It is only the base of a pillar, they'll tell you,
    That came to us
From a far old hill men used to name
    Areopagus.'

—'I know no art, and I only view
    A stone from a wall,
But I am thinking that stone has echoed
    The voice of Paul,

13 too] ⟨so⟩ *Hol.* 14 And] ⟨Which⟩ *Hol.* 15 calling,] ~ *Hol.*

IN THE BRITISH MUSEUM. 1 time-touched] ⟨time-eaten⟩ ⟨time-hardened⟩ *Hol.* 3 although you give] ⟨though you regard⟩ ⟨though you fix on⟩ *Hol.* 4 A] ⟨With⟩ *Hol.* 9 is only the] is the *Hol.* 11 a far old] an old *Hol.*

'Paul as he stood and preached beside it
Facing the crowd,
A small gaunt figure with wasted features,
Calling out loud

'Words that in all their intimate accents
Pattered upon
That marble front, and were wide reflected,
And then were gone.

'I'm a labouring man, and know but little,
Or nothing at all;
But I can't help thinking that stone once echoed
The voice of Paul.'

IN THE SERVANTS' QUARTERS

'Man, you too, aren't you, one of these rough followers of the criminal?
All hanging hereabout to gather how he's going to bear
Examination in the hall.' She flung disdainful glances on
The shabby figure standing at the fire with others there,
Who warmed them by its flare.

'No indeed, my skipping maiden: I know nothing of the trial here,
Or criminal, if so he be.—I chanced to come this way,
And the fire shone out into the dawn, and morning airs are cold now;
I, too, was drawn in part by charms I see before me play,
That I see not every day.'

'Ha, ha!' then laughed the constables who also stood to warm themselves,
The while another maiden scrutinized his features hard,

19 features,] ~ *Hol.* 23 front,] ⟨face⟩ *Hol.* wide] ⟨back⟩ far *Hol.*; far *SC*

IN THE SERVANTS' QUARTERS. *Title* ⟨Humour in the servants' quarters⟩ *Hol.*

As the blaze threw into contrast every line and knot that wrinkled them,
Exclaiming, 'Why, last night when he was brought in by the guard,
You were with him in the yard!'

'Nay, nay, you teasing wench, I say! You know you speak mistakenly.
Cannot a tired pedestrian who has legged it long and far
Here on his way from northern parts, engrossed in humble marketings,
Come in and rest awhile, although judicial doings are
Afoot by morning star?'

'O, come, come!' laughed the constables. 'Why, man, you speak the dialect
He uses in his answers; you can hear him up the stairs.
So own it. We sha'n't hurt ye. There he's speaking now! His syllables
Are those you sound yourself when you are talking unawares,
As this pretty girl declares.'

'And you shudder when his chain clinks!' she rejoined. 'O yes, I noticed it.
And you winced, too, when those cuffs they gave him echoed to us here.
They'll soon be coming down, and you may then have to defend yourself
Unless you hold your tongue, or go away and keep you clear
When he's led to judgment near!'

'No! I'll be damned in hell if I know anything about the man!
No single thing about him more than everybody knows!

17 legged . . . far *CP*, *ME*] ⟨travelled from afar⟩ *Hol.*; footed it afar *SC*, *WE*
18 northern] ⟨northward⟩ *Hol.*
19 although judicial] ⟨albeit some priestly⟩ *Hol.*
23 now!] ~. *Hol.*
27 those cuffs] ⟨that cuff⟩ *Hol.*
30 near!] ~. *Hol.*

Must not I even warm my hands but I am charged with
blasphemies?' . . .
—His face convulses as the morning cock that moment
crows,
And he droops, and turns, and goes.

THE OBLITERATE TOMB*

'More than half my life long
Did they weigh me falsely, to my bitter wrong,
But they all have shrunk away into the silence
Like a lost song.

'And the day has dawned and come
For forgiveness, when the past may hold it dumb
On the once reverberate words of hatred uttered
Half in delirium. . . .

'With folded lips and hands
They lie and wait what next the Will commands,
And doubtless think, if think they can: "Let discord
Sink with Life's sands!"

'By these late years their names,
Their virtues, their hereditary claims,
May be as near defacement at their grave-place
As are their fames.'

—Such thoughts bechanced to seize
A traveller's mind—a man of memories—
As he set foot within the western city
Where had died these

33 Must not I] ⟨Must I not⟩ *Hol.* 35 droops,] stops, *SC*

THE OBLITERATE TOMB. 3 shrunk away] ⟨now dissolved⟩ *Hol.* 4 lost] ⟨sung⟩ *Hol.* 7 once] ⟨long⟩ *Hol.* 11 can:] ~, *Hol.* 12 Sink] ⟨Slip⟩ *Hol.* sands!'] ~⟨!⟩. *Hol.* 17 —Such] Such *Hol.*

Who in their lifetime deemed
Him their chief enemy—one whose brain had schemed
To get their dingy greatness deeplier dingied
And disesteemed.

So, sojourning in their town,
He mused on them and on their once renown,
And said, 'I'll seek their resting-place to-morrow
Ere I lie down,

'And end, lest I forget,
Those ires of many years that I regret,
Renew their names, that men may see some liegeness
Is left them yet.'

Duly next night he went
And sought the church he had known them to frequent,
And wandered, lantern-bearing, in the precincts,
Where they lay pent,

Till by remembrance led
He stood at length beside their slighted bed,
Above which, truly, scarce a line or letter
Could now be read.

'Thus years obliterate
Their graven worth, their chronicle, their date!
At once I'll garnish and revive the record
Of their past state,

'That still the sage may say
In pensive progress here where they decay,
"This stone records a luminous line whose talents
Told in their day."'

23 get] ⟨make⟩ *Hol.* 25 town,] ~*Hol.* 26 mused on them and on] ⟨dreamt of them and of⟩ *Hol.* 29 end,] ⟨mend,⟩ *Hol.* 30 ires] ⟨faults⟩ *Hol.* 32 Is left] ⟨Attends⟩ *Hol.* 33 night] day *SC* 35 And wandered in the precincts, ⟨bent⟩ set on eyeing *Hol.*; And wandered in the precincts, set on eyeing *SC*

While dreaming thus he turned,
For a form shadowed where they lay inurned,
And he beheld a stranger in foreign vesture,
And tropic-burned.

'Sir, I am right pleased to view
That ancestors of mine should interest you,
For I have fared of purpose here to find them. . . .
They are time-worn, true,

'But that's a fault, at most,
Carvers can cure. On the Pacific coast
I have vowed for long that relics of my forbears
I'd trace ere lost,

'And hitherward I come,
Before this same old Time shall strike me numb,
To carry it out.'—'Strange, this is!' said the other;
'What mind shall plumb

'Coincident design!
Though these my father's enemies were and mine,
I nourished a like purpose—to restore them
Each letter and line.'

'Such magnanimity
Is now not needed, sir; for you will see
That since I am here, a thing like this is, plainly,
Best done by me.'

The other bowed, and left,
Crestfallen in sentiment, as one bereft
Of some fair object he had been moved to cherish,
By hands more deft.

49 dreaming] speaking *SC* 51 in foreign vesture,] ⟨foreign tailored⟩ *Hol.* 55 fared] come *SC* of purpose] ⟨expressly⟩ *Hol.* find] trace *SC* 57 fault,] ~ *Hol.* most,] ~ *Hol.* 58 Carvers can] Which cash will *Hol.*; Sculptors can *SC*

And as he slept that night
The phantoms of the ensepulchred stood upright
Before him, trembling that he had set him seeking
Their charnel-site.

And, as unknowing his ruth,
Asked as with terrors founded not on truth
Why he should want them. 'Ha,' they hollowly hackered,
'You come, forsooth,

'By stealth to obliterate
Our graven worth, our chronicle, our date,
That our descendant may not gild the record
Of our past state,

'And that no sage may say
In pensive progress near where we decay:
"This stone records a luminous line whose talents
Told in their day."'

Upon the morrow he went
And to that town and churchyard never bent
His ageing footsteps till, some twelvemonths onward,
An accident

Once more detained him there;
And, stirred by hauntings, he must needs repair
To where the tomb was. Lo, it stood still wasting
In no man's care.

95 till,] ~ *Hol.* onward,] ~ *Hol.* 97 there;] ~ *Hol.*
100a–h
"The travelled man you met
The last time," said the sexton, "has not yet
Appeared again, though wealth he had in plenty.
—Can he forget?

"The architect was hired
And came here on smart summons as desired,
But never the descendant came to tell him
What he required." *SC*

(*Hol.* 100a–h = *SC except* 100a travelled man] ⟨foreigner⟩ *Hol.*; 100d —Can] Can *Hol.*)

And so the tomb remained
Untouched, untended, crumbling, weather-stained,
And though the one-time foe was fain to right it
He still refrained.

'I'll set about it when
I am sure he'll come no more. Best wait till then.'
But so it was that never the kinsman entered
That city again.

Till doubts grew keen
If it had chanced not that the figure seen
Shaped but in dream on that dim doubtful midnight:
Such things had been. . . .

So, the well-meaner died
While waiting tremulously unsatisfied
That no return of the family's foreign scion
Would still betide.

And many years slid by,
And active church-restorers cast their eye
Upon the ancient garth and hoary building
The tomb stood nigh.

And when they had scraped each wall,
Pulled out the stately pews, and smartened all,
'It will be well', declared the spruce churchwarden,
'To overhaul

'And broaden this path where shown;
Nothing prevents it but an old tombstone
Pertaining to a family forgotten,
Of deeds unknown.

107 kinsman] stranger *SC*, *WE*   109–12 *om.* *SC*   110 figure] kinsman *WE*   113 So,] And *SC*   125 where shown;] ⟨o'ergrown;⟩ *Hol.*

'Their names can scarce be read,
Depend on't, all who care for them are dead.'
So went the tomb, whose shards were as path-paving
Distributed.

Over it and about
Men's footsteps beat, and wind and waterspout,
Until the names, aforetime gnawed by weathers,
Were quite worn out.

So that no sage can say
In pensive progress near where they decay,
'This stone records a luminous line whose talents
Told in their day.'

'REGRET NOT ME'

Regret not me;
Beneath the sunny tree
I lie uncaring, slumbering peacefully.

Swift as the light
I flew my faery flight;
Ecstatically I moved, and feared no night.

I did not know
That heydays fade and go,
But deemed that what was would be always so.

I skipped at morn
Between the yellowing corn,
Thinking it good and glorious to be born.

I ran at eves
Among the piled-up sheaves,
Dreaming, 'I grieve not, therefore nothing grieves.'

'REGRET NOT ME'. 1 me;] ~, *Hol.* 12 good and glorious] ⟨joy and jubilance⟩ *Hol.* 14 sheaves,] ~ *Hol.*

Now soon will come
The apple, pear, and plum,
And hinds will sing, and autumn insects hum.

Again you will fare
To cider-makings rare,
And junketings; but I shall not be there.

Yet gaily sing
Until the pewter ring
Those songs we sang when we went gipsying.

And lightly dance
Some triple-timed romance
In coupled figures, and forget mischance;

And mourn not me
Beneath the yellowing tree;
For I shall mind not, slumbering peacefully.

THE RECALCITRANTS*

Let us off and search, and find a place
Where yours and mine can be natural lives,
Where no one comes who dissects and dives
And proclaims that ours is a curious case,
Which its touch of romance can scarcely grace.

You would think it strange at first, but then
Everything has been strange in its time.
When some one said on a day of the prime
He would bow to no brazen god again
He doubtless dazed the mass of men.

21 but] *cap. Hol.* 24 Those songs we] 〈The songs you〉 *Hol.* gipsying.] ~! *SP*

THE RECALCITRANTS. 5 Which] 〈Which〉 That *Hol.*; That *SC*, *WE*

None will see in us a pair whose claims
To righteous judgment we care not making;
Who have doubted if breath be worth the taking,
And have no respect for the current fames
Whence the savour has flown while abide the names.

We have found us already shunned, disdained,
And for re-acceptance have not once striven;
Whatever offence our course has given
The brunt thereof we have long sustained.
Well, let us away, scorned, unexplained.

STARLINGS ON THE ROOF

'No smoke spreads out of this chimney-pot,
The people who lived here have left the spot,
And others are coming who knew them not.

'If you listen anon, with an ear intent,
The voices, you'll find, will be different
From the well-known ones of those who went.'

'Why did they go? Their tones so bland
Were quite familiar to our band;
The comers we shall not understand.'

'They look for a new life, rich and strange;
They do not know that, let them range
Wherever they may, they will get no change.

'They will drag their house-gear ever so far
In their search for a home no miseries mar;
They will find that as they were they are,

11 see in us *CP23*] recognize us as *SC*, *CP19*, *WE*

STARLINGS ON THE ROOF. *Nation*, 18 Oct. 1913. *P1*(*N*) Yale
Headnote (Moving House, Michaelmas) *N*
2 spot,] ~ *Hol.* 9 The] Fresh *N* 10 rich and] ⟨rich and⟩ strenuous, *P1*; strenuous, *N* 13 house-gear] furniture *N*

'That every hearth has a ghost, alack,
And can be but the scene of a bivouac
Till they move their last—no care to pack!'

THE MOON LOOKS IN

I

I have risen again,
And awhile survey
By my chilly ray
Through your window-pane
Your upturned face,
As you think, 'Ah—she
Now dreams of me
In her distant place!'

II

I pierce her blind
In her far-off home:
She fixes a comb,
And says in her mind,
'I start in an hour;
Whom shall I meet?
Won't the men be sweet,
And the women sour!'

THE SWEET HUSSY

In his early days he was quite surprised
When she told him she was compromised

18 *WE*, *CP23*] For a painful halt till the time to pack!" *N*; For a fitful halt till the time to pack!" *Hol.*; Till they move perforce—no time to pack!" *SC*, *CP19*

THE MOON LOOKS IN. 15 sweet,] ~ *Hol.*

THE SWEET HUSSY. 1 his] ⟨his⟩ ⟨my⟩ *Hol.* he] ⟨he⟩ ⟨I⟩ *Hol.* 2 him] ⟨him⟩ me *Hol.*

By meetings and lingerings at his whim,
And thinking not of herself but him;
While she lifted orbs aggrieved and round
That scandal should so soon abound,
(As she had raised them to nine or ten
Of antecedent nice young men):
And in remorse he thought with a sigh,
How good she is, and how bad am I!—
It was years before he understood
That she was the wicked one—he the good.

THE TELEGRAM

'O he's suffering—maybe dying—and I not there to aid,
And smooth his bed and whisper to him! Can I nohow go?
Only the nurse's brief twelve words thus hurriedly conveyed,
As by stealth, to let me know.

'He was the best and brightest!—candour shone upon his brow,
And I shall never meet again a soldier such as he,
And I loved him ere I knew it, and perhaps he's sinking now,
Far, far removed from me!'

—The yachts ride mute at anchor and the fulling moon is fair,
And the giddy folk are strutting up and down the smooth parade,
And in her wild distraction she seems not to be aware
That she lives no more a maid,

3 ⟨By trysts and lingerings to please his whim,⟩ ⟨By trysts and truancies at his whim,⟩ ⟨By coming and going unwarily,⟩ By trysts and lingerings at his whim, *Hol.* 4 him;] ⟨him;⟩ ⟨me;⟩ *Hol.* 5 While she] ⟨And⟩ *Hol.* 8 men):] ~); *Hol.* 9 he] ⟨he⟩ ⟨I⟩ *Hol.* 11 he] ⟨he⟩ ⟨I⟩ *Hol.* 12 he] ⟨he⟩ ⟨I⟩ *Hol.*

THE TELEGRAM. *Harper's Monthly*, Dec. 1913
1 'O he's] "He's *HM* 3 brief twelve words thus] ⟨message, as if⟩ *Hol.* 4 As] ⟨And⟩ *Hol.* 6 soldier such] man so high *HM*, *Hol.*

But has vowed and wived her self to one who blessed the ground she trod
To and from his scene of ministry, and thought her history known
In its last particular to him—aye, almost as to God,
And believed her quite his own.

So rapt her mind's far-off regard she droops as in a swoon,
And a movement of aversion mars her recent spousal grace,
And in silence we two sit here in our waning honeymoon
At this idle watering-place. . . .

What now I see before me is a long lane overhung
With lovelessness, and stretching from the present to the grave.
And I would I were away from this, with friends I knew when young,
Ere a woman held me slave.

THE MOTH-SIGNAL*

(On Egdon Heath)

'What are you still, still thinking,'
He asked in vague surmise,
'That you stare at the wick unblinking
With those deep lost luminous eyes?'

'O, I see a poor moth burning
In the candle-flame,' said she,
'Its wings and legs are turning
To a cinder rapidly.'

13 one who blessed] me who have blessed *HM*, *Hol.* trod] ~, *Hol.* 14 One who wooed her single-heartedly and thought her history known *HM*, *Hol.* 17 So great her absentmindedness she droops as in a swoon, *HM*, *SC* 24 held] called *HM*; ⟨called⟩ *Hol.*
Date (Published 1913.) *Hol.*

THE MOTH-SIGNAL. 1 still,] ~ *Hol.* 4 deep] great *SC*

'Moths fly in from the heather,'
He said, 'now the days decline.'
'I know,' said she. 'The weather,
I hope, will at last be fine.

'I think', she added lightly,
'I'll look out at the door.
The ring the moon wears nightly
May be visible now no more.'

She rose, and, little heeding,
Her life-mate then went on
With his mute and museful reading
In the annals of ages gone.

Outside the house a figure
Came from the tumulus near,
And speedily waxed bigger,
And clasped and called her Dear.

'I saw the pale-winged token
You sent through the crack,' sighed she.
'That moth is burnt and broken
With which you lured out me.

'And were I as the moth is
It might be better far
For one whose marriage troth is
Shattered as potsherds are!'

Then grinned the Ancient Briton
From the tumulus treed with pine:
'So, hearts are thwartly smitten
In these days as in mine!'

18 life-mate] husband *SC* 19 mute and museful *CP23*] attentive *SC*; mute museful *CP19*, *WE* 36 mine!'] ~." *Hol.*

SEEN BY THE WAITS

Through snowy woods and shady
  We went to play a tune
To the lonely manor-lady
  By the light of the Christmas moon.

We violed till, upward glancing
  To where a mirror leaned,
It showed her airily dancing,
  Deeming her movements screened;

Dancing alone in the room there,
  Thin-draped in her robe of night;
Her postures, glassed in the gloom there,
  Were a strange phantasmal sight.

She had learnt (we heard when homing)
  That her roving spouse was dead;
Why she had danced in the gloaming
  We thought, but never said.

THE TWO SOLDIERS

Just at the corner of the wall
  We met—yes, he and I—
Who had not faced in camp or hall
  Since we bade home good-bye,
And what once happened came back—all—
  Out of those years gone by;

And that strange woman whom we knew
  And loved—long dead and gone,

SEEN BY THE WAITS. 7 It showed] We saw *SC*   8 screened;] ~. *Hol.*

THE TWO SOLDIERS. *Title* ⟨A Rencounter⟩ *Hol.*   6 by; *ME*] ~. *all other texts*

Whose poor half-perished residue,
  Tombless and trod, lay yon,
But at this moment to our view
  Rose like a phantom wan!

And in his fixed face I could see,
  Lit by a lurid shine,
The drama re-enact which she
  Had dyed incarnadine
For us, and more. And doubtless he
  Beheld it too in mine.

A start, as at one slightly known,
  And with an indifferent air
We passed, without a sign being shown
  That, as it real were,
A memory-acted scene had thrown
  Its tragic shadow there.

THE DEATH OF REGRET*

I opened my shutter at sunrise,
  And looked at the hill hard by,
And I heartily grieved for the comrade
  Who wandered up there to die.

I let in the morn on the morrow,
  And failed not to think of him then,
As he trod up that rise in the twilight,
  And never came down again.

I undid the shutter a week thence,
  But not until after I'd turned
Did I call back his last departure
  By the upland there discerned.

10 ⟨Lay without stone far yon!⟩ *Hol.* yon, *ME*] ~ ! *all other texts* 12 wan! *ME*] ~. *all other texts*

THE DEATH OF REGRET. 2 looked] ⟨gazed⟩ *Hol.* 11 ⟨Recalled I his final departure⟩ *Hol.*

Uncovering the casement long later,
  I bent to my toil till the gray,
When I said to myself, 'Ah—what ails me,
  To forget him all the day!'

As daily I flung back the shutter
  In the same blank bald routine,
He scarcely once rose to remembrance
  Through a month of my facing the scene.

And ah, seldom now do I ponder
  At the window as heretofore
On the long valued one who died yonder,
  And wastes by the sycamore.

IN THE DAYS OF CRINOLINE

A plain tilt-bonnet on her head
She took the path across the leaze.
—Her spouse the vicar, gardening, said,
'Too dowdy that, for coquetries,
    So I can hoe at ease.'

But when she had passed into the heath,
And gained the wood beyond the flat,
She raised her skirts, and from beneath
Unpinned and drew as from a sheath
    An ostrich-feathered hat.

And where the hat had hung she now
Concealed and pinned the dowdy hood,
And set the hat upon her brow,
And thus emerging from the wood
    Tripped on in jaunty mood.

13 casement] ⟨lattice⟩ *Hol.* 23 long valued] ⟨cheris[hed]⟩ *Hol.*

IN THE DAYS OF CRINOLINE. *Title* ⟨The Vicar's Young Wife⟩ *Hol.* 3 ⟨Her husband, ⟨⟨good-man,⟩⟩ gardening, looked and said,⟩ *Hol.* —Her] Her *Hol.* 5 hoe] ⟨rest⟩ *Hol.* 6 into] ⟨across⟩ *Hol.*

The sun was low and crimson-faced
As two came that way from the town,
And plunged into the wood untraced. . . .
When severally therefrom they paced
The sun had quite gone down.

The hat and feather disappeared,
The dowdy hood again was donned,
And in the gloom the fair one neared
Her home and husband dour, who conned
Calmly his blue-eyed blonde.

'To-day', he said, 'you have shown good sense,
A dress so modest and so meek
Should always deck your goings hence
Alone.' And as a recompense
He kissed her on the cheek.

THE ROMAN GRAVEMOUNDS*

By Rome's dim relics there walks a man,
Eyes bent; and he carries a basket and spade;
I guess what impels him to scrape and scan;
Yea, his dreams of that Empire long decayed.

'Vast was Rome', he must muse, 'in the world's regard,
Vast it looms there still, vast it ever will be;'

17 As] ⟨When⟩ *Hol.* 19 ⟨When flushed therefrom alone she paced⟩ ⟨When soft therefrom apart they paced⟩ When separately therefrom they paced *Hol.* severally] separately *SC* 23 one] ⟨wife⟩ *Hol.* 24 ⟨Her home and spouse, who calmly conned⟩ *Hol.* 25 Calmly his] ⟨His beating⟩ *Hol.*
Date ⟨July. 1911.⟩ *Hol.*

THE ROMAN GRAVEMOUNDS. *English Review*, Dec. 1911. *MS1*, *P1–P3* (*ER*) *Fales*
Title By the Roman Earthworks *MS1*; Among the Roman Earthmounds *P1*; Among the Roman Gravemounds *P2–ER*
1 man,] ~ *Hol.* 2 and he] he *MS1–ER*; ⟨he⟩ *Hol.* and spade;] and ⟨a⟩ spade; *P1* 3 scan;] ~— *MS1–ER* 4 Yea, his] His *MS1–ER* 5 regard,] ~; *MS1–ER* 6 still,] ~; *MS1–ER*

And he stoops as to dig and unmine some shard
Left by those who are held in such memory.

But no; in his basket, see, he has brought
A little white furred thing, stiff of limb,
Whose life never won from the world a thought;
It is this, and not Rome, that is moving him.

And to make it a grave he has come to the spot,
And he delves in the ancient dead's long home;
Their fames, their achievements, the man knows not;
The furred thing is all to him—nothing Rome!

'Here say you that Caesar's warriors lie?—
But my little white cat was my only friend!
Could she but live, might the record die
Of Caesar, his legions, his aims, his end!'

Well, Rome's long rule here is oft and again
A theme for the sages of history,
And the small furred life was worth no one's pen;
Yet its mourner's mood has a charm for me.

November 1910.

THE WORKBOX

'See, here's the workbox, little wife,
  That I made of polished oak.'
He was a joiner, of village life;
  She came of borough folk.

7 dig] ⟨delve⟩ *MS1* 16 him—] ~, *MS1–ER* Rome!] ~. *MS1–ER* 19 but live,] ⟨live⟩ *Hol.* 20 end!'] ~!" . . . *MS1–ER* 23 pen;] ~, *MS1–ER* 24 mood has a charm] view is the view *MS1–ER* mood] ⟨view⟩ *Hol.*
Date Nov. 8, 1910 *MS1*; *om. P1–ER*

THE WORKBOX. 4 She] ⟨And she⟩ *Hol.*

He holds the present up to her
As with a smile she nears
And answers to the profferer,
‘’Twill last all my sewing years!’

‘I warrant it will. And longer too.
’Tis a scantling that I got
Off poor John Wayward’s coffin, who
Died of they knew not what.

‘The shingled pattern that seems to cease
Against your box’s rim
Continues right on in the piece
That’s underground with him.

‘And while I worked it made me think
Of timber’s varied doom;
One inch where people eat and drink,
The next inch in a tomb.

‘But why do you look so white, my dear,
And turn aside your face?
You knew not that good lad, I fear,
Though he came from your native place?’

‘How could I know that good young man,
Though he came from my native town,
When he must have left far earlier than
I was a woman grown?’

‘Ah, no. I should have understood!
It shocked you that I gave

5 holds] ⟨duly hands⟩ *Hol.* 8 sewing] ⟨working⟩ *Hol.* 10 got] ⟨cut⟩ *Hol.* 11 John] ⟨Hugh⟩ *Hol.* 12 ⟨Came from your native spot.⟩ *Hol.* 18 ⟨Of timber and its doom;⟩ *Hol.* 22 ⟨And turn your face aside?⟩ *Hol.* 23 You knew not] ⟨Did you know⟩ *Hol.* 24 ⟨Or sorrow that he died?⟩ *Hol.* 26 ⟨Or sorrow that he died,⟩ *Hol.* 27 ⟨When it all happened earlier than⟩ When he must have left there earlier than *Hol.* far] there *SC* 28 ⟨I reached this countryside?”⟩ *Hol.* grown?’] ~.” *Hol.*

To you one end of a piece of wood
Whose other is in a grave?'

'Don't, dear, despise my intellect,
Mere accidental things
Of that sort never have effect
On my imaginings.'

Yet still her lips were limp and wan,
Her face still held aside,
As if she had known not only John,
But known of what he died.

THE SACRILEGE*

A Ballad-Tragedy
(*Circa* 182–)

Part I

'I have a Love I love too well
Where Dunkery frowns on Exon Moor;
I have a Love I love too well,
To whom, ere she was mine,
"Such is my love for you," I said,
"That you shall have to hood your head
A silken kerchief crimson-red,
Wove finest of the fine."

'And since this Love, for one mad moon,
On Exon Wild by Dunkery Tor,
Since this my Love for one mad moon
Did clasp me as her king,
I snatched a silk-piece red and rare
From off a stall at Priddy Fair,
For handkerchief to hood her hair
When we went gallanting.

37 limp] ⟨weak⟩ ⟨strained⟩ *Hol.*

THE SACRILEGE. *Fortnightly Review*, 1 Nov. 1911

'Full soon the four weeks neared their end
Where Dunkery frowns on Exon Moor;
And when the four weeks neared their end,
And their swift sweets outwore,
I said, "What shall I do to own
Those beauties bright as tulips blown,
And keep you here with me alone
As mine for evermore?"

'And as she drowsed within my van
On Exon Wild by Dunkery Tor—
And as she drowsed within my van,
And dawning turned to day,
She heavily raised her sloe-black eyes
And murmured back in softest wise,
"One more thing, and the charms you prize
Are yours henceforth for aye.

'"And swear I will I'll never go
While Dunkery frowns on Exon Moor
To meet the Cornish Wrestler Joe
For dance and dallyings.
If you'll to yon cathedral shrine,
And finger from the chest divine
Treasure to buy me ear-drops fine,
And richly jewelled rings."

'I said: "I am one who has gathered gear
From Marlbury Downs to Dunkery Tor,
Who has gathered gear for many a year
From mansion, mart and fair;
But at God's house I've stayed my hand,
Hearing within me some command—
Curbed by a law not of the land
From doing damage there!"

18 Moor;] ⟨Tor⟩ *Hol.* 35 Wrestler] *l.c. Hol.* 48 there!"] ∼.' *SC, CP19*

'Whereat she pouts, this Love of mine,
As Dunkery pouts to Exon Moor,
And still she pouts, this Love of mine,
So cityward I go.
But ere I start to do the thing,
And speed my soul's imperilling
For one who is my ravishing
And all the joy I know,

'I come to lay this charge on thee—
On Exon Wild by Dunkery Tor—
I come to lay this charge on thee
With solemn speech and sign:
Should things go ill, and my life pay
For botchery in this rash assay,
You are to take hers likewise—yea,
The month the law takes mine.

'For should my rival, Wrestler Joe,
Where Dunkery frowns on Exon Moor—
My reckless rival, Wrestler Joe,
My Love's bedwinner be,
My rafted spirit would not rest,
But wander weary and distrest
Throughout the world in wild protest:
The thought nigh maddens me!'

Part II

Thus did he speak—this brother of mine—
On Exon Wild by Dunkery Tor,
Born at my birth of mother of mine,
And forthwith went his way
To dare the deed some coming night . . .
I kept the watch with shaking sight,
The moon at moments breaking bright,
At others glooming gray.

50 pouts to] frowns on *SC*, *CP19*
68 bedwinner] possessor *SC*, *CP19*
69 rafted] tortured *SC*, *CP19*

For three full days I heard no sound
Where Dunkery frowns on Exon Moor,
I heard no sound at all around
        Whether his fay prevailed,
Or one more foul the master were,
Till some afoot did tidings bear
How that, for all his practised care,
        He had been caught and jailed.

They had heard a crash when twelve had chimed
By Mendip east of Dunkery Tor,
When twelve had chimed and moonlight climbed;
        They watched, and he was tracked
By arch and aisle and saint and knight
Of sculptured stonework sheeted white
In the cathedral's ghostly light,
        And captured in the act.

Yes; for this Love he loved too well
Where Dunkery sights the Severn shore,
All for this Love he loved too well
        He burst the holy bars,
Seized golden vessels from the chest
To buy her ornaments of the best,
At her ill-witchery's request
        And lure of eyes like stars. . . .

When blustering March confused the sky
In Toneborough Town by Exon Moor,
When blustering March confused the sky
        They stretched him; and he died.
Down in the crowd where I, to see
The end of him, stood silently,
With a set face he lipped to me—
        'Remember.' 'Ay!' I cried.

83 For three full days I heard no sound *FR*   85 more foul] malign *SC, CP19*   were,] ~ *Hol.*   86 bear] ~, *Hol.*   89–96 *om. FR*   89 twelve had] midnight *Hol.*   91 twelve had] midnight *Hol.*   98 On Exon Wild by Dunkery Tor— *FR*   101 golden] silver *FR*   102 best,] ~ *Hol.*   106 Moor,] ~; *Hol.*

By night and day I shadowed her
From Toneborough Deane to Dunkery Tor,
I shadowed her asleep, astir,
　　And yet I could not bear—
Till Wrestler Joe anon began
To figure as her chosen man,
And took her to his shining van—
　　To doom a form so fair!

He made it handsome for her sake—
And Dunkery smiled to Exon Moor—
He made it handsome for her sake,
　　Painting it out and in;
And on the door of apple-green
A bright brass knocker soon was seen,
And window-curtains white and clean
　　For her to sit within.

And all could see she clave to him
As cleaves a cloud to Dunkery Tor,
Yea, all could see she clave to him,
　　And every day I said,
'A pity it seems to part those two
That hourly grow to love more true:
Yet she's the wanton woman who
　　Sent onc to swing till dead!'

That blew to blazing all my hate,
While Dunkery frowned on Exon Moor,
And when the river swelled, her fate
　　Came to her pitilessly. . . .
I dogged her, crying: 'Across that plank
They use as bridge to reach yon bank
A coat and hat lie limp and dank;
　　Your goodman's, can they be?'

115 By night and day I shadowed her; *FR* 126 bright] gay *FR* 134 grow] seem *FR*; ⟨seem⟩ *Hol.* 136 Sent one to his death-bed!" *FR*; ⟨Drove one to his death-bed!"⟩ *Hol.*

She paled, and went, I close behind—
And Exon frowned to Dunkery Tor,
She went, and I came up behind
And tipped the plank that bore
Her, fleetly flitting across to eye
What such might bode. She slid awry;
And from the current came a cry,
A gurgle; and no more.

How that befell no mortal knew
From Marlbury Downs to Exon Moor;
No mortal knew that deed undue
But he who schemed the crime,
Which night still covers. . . . But in dream
Those ropes of hair upon the stream
He sees, and he will hear that scream
Until his judgment-time.

THE ABBEY MASON*

Inventor of the 'Perpendicular' Style of Gothic Architecture

(WITH MEMORIES OF JOHN HICKS, ARCHITECT)

The new-vamped Abbey shaped apace
In the fourteenth century of grace;

(The church which, at an after date,
Acquired cathedral rank and state.)

Panel and circumscribing wall
Of latest feature, trim and tall,

Rose roundabout the Norman core
In prouder pose than theretofore,

155 How that befel no mortal knew *FR*

THE ABBEY MASON. *Harper's Monthly*, Dec. 1912. *MS1* (*HM*) PML
Dedication om. HM, SC
1 new-vamped] new-schemed *HM* 2 grace;] ~. *MS1*

Encasing magically the old
With parpend ashlars manifold.

The trowels rang out, and tracery
Appeared where blanks had used to be.

Men toiled for pleasure more than pay,
And all went smoothly day by day,

Till, in due course, the transept part
Engrossed the master-mason's art.

—Home-coming thence he tossed and turned
Throughout the night till the new sun burned.

'What fearful visions have inspired
These gaingivings?' his wife inquired;

'As if your tools were in your hand
You have hammered, fitted, muttered, planned;

'You have thumped as you were working hard:
I might have found me bruised and scarred.

'What then's amiss? What eating care
Looms nigh, whereof I am unaware?'

He answered not, but churchward went,
Viewing his draughts with discontent;

And fumbled there the livelong day
Till, hollow-eyed, he came away.

—'Twas said, 'The master-mason's ill!'
And all the abbey works stood still.

9 old] ~, *MS1*, *HM* 16 art.] ~. . . . *MS1* 17 —Home-coming] Homecoming *MS1* 20 inquired;] ~: *MS1* 25 amiss? *MS1*, *HM*, *ME*] ~. *SC*, *CP*, *WE* 29 fumbled] fumbling *HM* 30 Till,] ~ *MS1* 31 —'Twas] 'Twas *MS1* 32 abbey] *cap.* *MS1*

Quoth Abbot Wygmore: 'Why, O why
Distress yourself? You'll surely die!'

The mason answered, trouble-torn,
'This long-vogued style is quite outworn!

'The upper archmould nohow serves
To meet the lower tracery curves:

'The ogees bend too far away
To give the flexures interplay.

'This it is causes my distress. . . .
So it will ever be unless

'New forms be found to supersede
The circle when occasions need.

'To carry it out I have tried and toiled,
And now perforce must own me foiled!

'Jeerers will say: "Here was a man
Who could not end what he began!"'

—So passed that day, the next, the next;
The abbot scanned the task, perplexed;

The townsmen mustered all their wit
To fathom how to compass it,

But no raw artistries availed
Where practice in the craft had failed. . . .

—One night he tossed, all open-eyed,
And early left his helpmeet's side.

41 distress. . . .] ~; *MS1* 42 be] ~, *MS1*, *HM* 46 And now I needs must own me foiled. *HM* 48 began!"'] ~.'" *MS1* 49 —So] So *MS1* 50 abbot] *cap. MS1 and so throughout poem* 54 failed. . . .] ~, *MS1*

Scattering the rushes of the floor
He wandered from the chamber door

And sought the sizing pile, whereon
Struck dimly a cadaverous dawn

Through freezing rain, that drenched the board
Of diagram-lines he last had scored—

Chalked phantasies in vain begot
To knife the architectural knot—

In front of which he dully stood,
Regarding them in hopeless mood.

He closelier looked; then looked again:
The chalk-scratched draught-board faced the rain,

Whose icicled drops deformed the lines
Innumerous of his lame designs,

So that they streamed in small white threads
From the upper segments to the heads

Of arcs below, uniting them
Each by a stalactitic stem.

—At once, with eyes that struck out sparks,
He adds accessory cusping-marks,

Then laughs aloud. The thing was done
So long assayed from sun to sun. . . .

57 of] on *MS1* 61 Through rain that drenched the diagram-board *HM*; *variant line del. Hol.* 62 Of diagram-lines] Of tentative lines *HM*; ⟨Of tentative lines⟩ ⟨To tentative lines⟩ *Hol.* 67 again:] ~ *Hol.* 68 chalk-scratched] huge black *MS1* 69 icicled drops] drops had so *HM* 70 designs,] ~ *MS1*, *HM*, *Hol.* 71 So that they] That they had *HM* 75 —At] At *MS1* 78 So long assayed] That he had essayed *MS1*; So long essayed *HM*

—Now in his joy he grew aware
Of one behind him standing there,

And, turning, saw the abbot, who
The weather's whim was watching too.

Onward to Prime the abbot went,
Tacit upon the incident.

—Men now discerned as days revolved
The ogive riddle had been solved;

Templates were cut, fresh lines were chalked
Where lines had been defaced and balked,

And the work swelled and mounted higher,
Achievement distancing desire;

Here jambs with transoms fixed between,
Where never the like before had been—

There little mullions thinly sawn
Where meeting circles once were drawn.

'We knew', men said, 'the thing would go
After his craft-wit got aglow,

'And, once fulfilled what he has designed,
We'll honour him and his great mind!'

When matters stood thus poised awhile,
And all surroundings shed a smile,

79 —Now in his joy] Now, in his joy, *MS1*, *HM* 81 And,] ~ *MS1* turning,] ~ *MS1* 83 went,] ~ *MS1* 84 incident.] ~. . . . *MS1*, *HM* 89 higher,] ~ *MS1* 97 designed,] ~ *MS1* 98 We'll honour such a magic mind." *MS1*; ~!" *HM* 99 awhile,] ~ *MS1* 100 smile,] ~ *MS1*

The master-mason on an eve
Homed to his wife and seemed to grieve. . . .

—'The abbot spoke to me to-day:
He hangs about the works alway.

'He knows the source as well as I
Of the new style men magnify.

'He said: "You pride yourself too much
On your creation. Is it such?

'"Surely the hand of God it is
That conjured so, and only His!—

'"Disclosing by the frost and rain
Forms your invention chased in vain;

'"Hence the devices deemed so great
You copied, and did not create."

'I feel the abbot's words are just,
And that all thanks renounce I must.

'Can a man welcome praise and pelf
For hatching art that hatched itself? . . .

'So, I shall own the deft design
Is Heaven's outshaping, and not mine.'

'What!' said she. 'Praise your works ensure
To throw away, and quite obscure

'Your beaming and benificent star?
Better you leave things as they are!

101 -mason] ~, *MS1* eve] ~, *MS1* 102 wife] ~, *MS1*, *HM* 106 men] folk *MS1* 110 His!—] *l.c.* *MS1*, *Hol.* 111 frost and] wash of *HM* 118 itself? . . .] ~?— *MS1* 120 mine.'] ~."— *MS1*, *HM*

'Why, think awhile. Had not your zest
In your lovèd craft curtailed your rest—

'Had you not gone there ere the day
The sun had melted all away!'

—But, though his good wife argued so,
The mason let the people know

That not unaided sprang the thought
Whereby the glorious fane was wrought,

But that by frost when dawn was dim
The method was disclosed to him.

'Yet,' said the townspeople thereat,
''Tis your own doing, even with that!'

But he—chafed, childlike, in extremes—
The temperament of men of dreams—

Aloofly scrupled to admit
That he did aught but borrow it,

And diffidently made request
That with the abbot all should rest.

—As none could doubt the abbot's word,
Or question what the church averred,

The mason was at length believed
Of no more count than he conceived,

And soon began to lose the fame
That late had gathered round his name. . . .

127 day] ~, *MS1*, *HM* 128 The rain had scoured the lines away!" *HM* 129 —But,] —~ *MS1*, *HM*, *Hol.* so,] ~ *MS1*, *Hol.* 133 frost] storm, *HM*; rain *Hol.* dim] ~, *MS1* 142 rest.] ~.— *MS1* 143 —As] As *MS1* 144 church] *cap.* *MS1*, *HM*, *Hol.*

—Time passed, and like a living thing
The pile went on embodying,

And workmen died, and young ones grew,
And the old mason sank from view

And Abbots Wygmore and Staunton went
And Horton sped the embellishment.

But not till years had far progressed
Chanced it that, one day, much impressed,

Standing within the well-graced aisle,
He asked who first conceived the style;

And some decrepit sage detailed
How, when invention nought availed,

The cloud-cast waters in their whim
Came down, and gave the hint to him

Who struck each arc, and made each mould;
And how the abbot would not hold

As sole begetter him who applied
Forms the Almighty sent as guide;

And how the master lost renown,
And wore in death no artist's crown.

—Then Horton, who in inner thought
Had more perceptions than he taught,

Replied: 'Nay; art can but transmute;
Invention is not absolute;

152 view] ~, *MS1*　　153 went] ~, *MS1*, *HM*　　154 embellishment.] ~.— *MS1*　　157 well-graced] screen-graced *HM*

'Things fail to spring from nought at call,
And art-beginnings most of all.

'He did but what all artists do,
Wait upon Nature for his cue.'

—'Had you been here to tell them so
Lord Abbot, sixty years ago,

'The mason, now long underground,
Doubtless a different fate had found.

'He passed into oblivion dim,
And none knew what became of him!

'His name? 'Twas of some common kind
And now has faded out of mind.'

The abbot: 'It shall not be hid!
I'll trace it.' . . . But he never did.

—When longer yet dank death had wormed
The brain wherein the style had germed

From Gloucester church it flew afar—
The style called Perpendicular.—

To Winton and to Westminster
It ranged, and grew still beautifuller:

From Solway Frith to Dover Strand
Its fascination starred the land,

176 Nature] *l.c. MS1, HM* cue.'] ~."— *MS1* 177 so] ~, *MS1, HM* 181 dim,] ~ *Hol.* 183 kind] ~, *MS1, HM* 184 now has] now it has *HM* mind.'] ~." . . . *MS1, HM, Hol.* 185 abbot: *HM, Hol.*] *cap. MS1, SC, CP, WE* 186 it.' . . .] ~.— *MS1, HM*; ~." *Hol.* did.] ~.— *MS1* 188 germed] ~, *MS1, HM* 189 church] *cap. MS1, HM* flew] spread *MS1* 190 Perpendicular.—] "~."— *MS1, HM* 192 beautifuller:] ~; *MS1, HM* 193 Strand] *l.c. Hol.*

Not only on cathedral walls
But upon courts and castle halls.

Till every edifice in the isle
Was patterned to no other style,

And till, long having played its part,
The curtain fell on Gothic art.

—Well: when in Wessex on your rounds,
Take a brief step beyond its bounds,

And enter Gloucester: seek the quoin
Where choir and transept interjoin,

And, gazing at the forms there flung
Against the sky by one unsung—

The ogee arches transom-topped,
The tracery-stalks by spandrels stopped,

Petrified lacework—lightly lined
On ancient massiveness behind—

Muse that some minds so modest be
As to renounce fame's fairest fee,

(Like him who crystallized on this spot
His visionings, but lies forgot,

And many a mediaeval one
Whose symmetries salute the sun)

While others boom a baseless claim,
And upon nothing rear a name.

199 part,] ~ *Hol.* 200 art.] ~.... *MS1*, *HM* 201 rounds,] ~ *MS1*, *Hol.* 205 there flung] ~— *MS1*; so famed, *HM* 206 Charmed from the rock by one unsung— *MS1*; Charmed from the stone by one unnamed—*HM* 207 arches] ~, *MS1* 209 lacework—] ~, *MS1*, *HM* 212 fee,] ~ *MS1*, *HM* 217 boom] blow *MS1* claim,] ~ *Hol.* 218 And out of nothing carve a name. *HM*

THE JUBILEE OF A MAGAZINE

(To the Editor)

Yes; your up-dated modern page—
All flower-fresh, as it appears—
Can claim a time-tried lineage,

That reaches backward fifty years
(Which, if but short for sleepy squires,
Is much in magazines' careers).

—Here, on your cover, never tires
The sower, reaper, thresher, while
As through the seasons of our sires

Each wills to work in ancient style
With seedlip, sickle, share and flail,
Though modes have since moved many a mile!

The steel-roped plough now rips the vale,
With cog and tooth the sheaves are won,
Wired wheels drum out the wheat like hail;

But if we ask, what has been done
To unify the mortal lot
Since your bright leaves first saw the sun,

Beyond mechanic furtherance—what
Advance can rightness, candour, claim?
Truth bends abashed, and answers not.

THE JUBILEE OF A MAGAZINE. *Cornhill*, Jan. 1910

Title An Impromptu to the Editor *C*; ⟨"The Cornhill's" Jubilee⟩ *Hol.* *Dedication om. C*; *del. Hol.*

2 flower-fresh] fancy-fresh *C* 3 lineage,] ~ *Hol.* 6 much] long *C* 9 through] in *C* 15 And wire-works hurls the wheat like hail; *C*

Despite your volumes' gentle aim
To straighten visions wry and wrong,
Events jar onward much the same!

—Had custom tended to prolong,
As on your golden page engrained,
Old processes of blade and prong,

And best invention been retained
For high crusades to lessen tears
Throughout the race, the world had gained! . . .
But too much, this, for fifty years.

THE SATIN SHOES

'If ever I walk to church to wed,
As other maidens use,
And face the gathered eyes,' she said,
'I'll go in satin shoes!'

She was as fair as early day
Shining on meads unmown,
And her sweet syllables seemed to play
Like flute-notes softly blown.

The time arrived when it was meet
That she should be a bride;
The satin shoes were on her feet,
Her father was at her side.

23 To lift the mists, let truth be seen, *C* wrong,] ~ *Hol.* 24 Pragmatic wiles go on the same, *C*

24a–c Though I admit that there have been
Large conquests of the wry and wrong
Effected by your magazine. *C*

28 best] men's *C*

THE SATIN SHOES. *Harper's Monthly*, Jan. 1910
Subtitle A Quiet Tragedy *HM*
1 to church] forth *HM*; ⟨forth⟩ *Hol.* 5 She] (~ *HM* 8 blown.] ~.) *HM*

They stood within the dairy door,
And gazed across the green;
The church loomed on the distant moor,
But rain was thick between.

'The grass-path hardly can be stepped,
The lane is like a pool!'—
Her dream is shown to be inept,
Her wish they overrule.

'To go forth shod in satin soft
A coach would be required!'
For thickest boots the shoes were doffed—
Those shoes her soul desired. . . .

All day the bride, as overborne,
Was seen to brood apart,
And that the shoes had not been worn
Sat heavy on her heart.

From her wrecked dream, as months flew on,
Her thought seemed not to range.
'What ails the wife?' they said anon,
'That she should be so strange?' . . .

Ah—what coach comes with furtive glide—
A coach of closed-up kind?
It comes to fetch the last year's bride,
Who wanders in her mind.

She strove with them, and fearfully ran
Stairward with one low scream:
'Nay—coax her', said the madhouse man,
'With some old household theme.'

12 Her father at her side. *HM*; ⟨Her father was beside.⟩ *Hol.* 16 But rain-streams fell between. *HM* thick] ⟨thick⟩ ⟨dense⟩ *Hol.* 17 "The grass will drench, even lightly stepped, *HM*; *variant line del. Hol.* grass-path] ⟨wet path⟩ *Hol.* 18 lane] road *HM*; ⟨road⟩ *Hol.* 23 For boots the satin shoes were doffed— *HM*; *variant line del. Hol.* 24 desired. . . .] ~. *HM* 25 overborne,] one down borne, *HM*; ⟨one down borne,⟩ *Hol.* 33 Ah—] "Ah— *HM* 34 kind?] ~?" *HM* 35 It] "~ *HM* 36 mind.] ~." *HM*

'If you will go, dear, you must fain
 Put on those shoes—the pair
Meant for your marriage, which the rain
 Forbade you then to wear.'

She clapped her hands, flushed joyous hues;
 'O yes—I'll up and ride
If I am to wear my satin shoes
 And be a proper bride!'

Out then her little foot held she,
 As to depart with speed;
The madhouse man smiled pleasantly
 To see the wile succeed.

She turned to him when all was done,
 And gave him her thin hand,
Exclaiming like an enraptured one,
 'This time it will be grand!'

She mounted with a face elate,
 Shut was the carriage door;
They drove her to the madhouse gate,
 And she was seen no more. . . .

Yet she was fair as early day
 Shining on meads unmown,
And her sweet syllables seemed to play
 Like flute-notes softly blown.

EXEUNT OMNES*

I

Everybody else, then, going,
And I still left where the fair was? . . .

55 An enraptured] a raptured *HM*

EXEUNT OMNES. *Title* ⟨Epilogue⟩ *Hol.*

Much have I seen of neighbour loungers
Making a lusty showing,
Each now past all knowing.

II

There is an air of blankness
In the street and the littered spaces;
Thoroughfare, steeple, bridge and highway
Wizen themselves to lankness;
Kennels dribble dankness.

III

Folk all fade. And whither,
As I wait alone where the fair was?
Into the clammy and numbing night-fog
Whence they entered hither.
Soon one more goes thither!

June 2, 1913.

A POET

Attentive eyes, fantastic heed,
Assessing minds, he does not need,
Nor urgent writs to sup or dine,
Nor pledges in the rosy wine.

For loud acclaim he does not care
By the august or rich or fair,
Nor for smart pilgrims from afar,
Curious on where his hauntings are.

4 lusty showing,] brave outshowing, *Hol.* 15 *ME*, *CP23*] ⟨Soon soon I follow thither.⟩ Soon do I follow thither. *Hol.*; Soon do I follow thither! *SC*, *CP19*, *WE*

A POET. *Title* ⟨The Poet⟩ *Hol.*
4 rosy] roseate *SC*

But soon or later, when you hear
That he has doffed this wrinkled gear,
Some evening, at the first star-ray,
Come to his graveside, pause and say:

'Whatever his message—glad or grim—
Two bright-souled women clave to him';
Stand and say that while day decays;
It will be word enough of praise.

July 1914.

10 gear,] ~⟨—⟩ *Hol.* 13 ⟨"Whatever message his to tell,⟩ *Hol.*; "Whatever the message his to tell, *Hol.*, *SC* 14 bright-souled] ⟨spotless⟩ thoughtful *Hol.*; thoughtful *SC14* clave to him';] loved him well." *SC* 15 while day decays;] amid the dim: *SC* 16 It will be praise enough for him. *SC*

Date om. Hol.

SATIRES OF CIRCUMSTANCE
IN FIFTEEN GLIMPSES*

(*First published April 1911*)

I

AT TEA

The kettle descants in a cozy drone,
And the young wife looks in her husband's face,
And then at her guest's, and shows in her own
Her sense that she fills an envied place;
And the visiting lady is all abloom,
And says there was never so sweet a room.

And the happy young housewife does not know
That the woman beside her was first his choice,
Till the fates ordained it could not be so. . . .
Betraying nothing in look or voice
The guest sits smiling and sips her tea,
And he throws her a stray glance yearningly.

II

IN CHURCH

'And now to God the Father,' he ends,
And his voice thrills up to the topmost tiles:

SATIRES OF CIRCUMSTANCE. *Fortnightly Review*, 1 Apr. 1911
IN FIFTEEN GLIMPSES] In Twelve Scenes *FR*; In ⟨Sixteen⟩ Fifteen Glimpses *Hol.* *First . . . 1911*] *om. SC*

I. AT TEA. *Fortnightly Review*, 1 Apr. 1911
8 first his] his first *FR*; ⟨his first⟩ *Hol.*

II. IN CHURCH. *Fortnightly Review*, 1 Apr. 1911
1 he ends,] ends he, *FR*

Each listener chokes as he bows and bends,
And emotion pervades the crowded aisles.
Then the preacher glides to the vestry-door,
And shuts it, and thinks he is seen no more.

The door swings softly ajar meanwhile,
And a pupil of his in the Bible class,
Who adores him as one without gloss or guile,
Sees her idol stand with a satisfied smile
And re-enact at the vestry-glass
Each pulpit gesture in deft dumb-show
That had moved the congregation so.

III

BY HER AUNT'S GRAVE*

'Sixpence a week', says the girl to her lover,
'Aunt used to bring me, for she could confide
In me alone, she vowed. 'Twas to cover
The cost of her headstone when she died.
And that was a year ago last June;
I've not yet fixed it. But I must soon.'

'And where is the money now, my dear?'
'O, snug in my purse . . . Aunt was *so* slow
In saving it—eighty weeks, or near.' . . .
'Let's spend it,' he hints. 'For she won't know.
There's a dance to-night at the Load of Hay.'
She passively nods. And they go that way.

3 and bends,] his knee, *FR*　　5 to] through *FR*　　8 pupil] lover *FR*
9 *om. FR*

III. BY HER AUNT'S GRAVE. *Fortnightly Review*, 1 Apr. 1911
6 I've not yet put it here. I must soon." *FR*; *variant line del. Hol.*　　7 now, my dear?'] now?" asks he. *FR*; now⟨?⟩, my Dear?" *Hol.*　　9 weeks, or near.' . . .] weeks!" says she. . . . *FR*

IV

IN THE ROOM OF THE BRIDE-ELECT*

'Would it had been the man of our wish!'
Sighs her mother. To whom with vehemence she
In the wedding-dress—the wife to be—
'Then why were you so mollyish
As not to insist on him for me!'
The mother, amazed: 'Why, dearest one,
Because you pleaded for this or none!'

'But Father and you should have stood out strong!
Since then, to my cost, I have lived to find
That you were right and that I was wrong;
This man is a dolt to the one declined. . . .
Ah!—here he comes with his button-hole rose.
Good God—I must marry him I suppose!'

V

AT A WATERING-PLACE

They sit and smoke on the esplanade,
The man and his friend, and regard the bay
Where the far chalk cliffs, to the left displayed,
Smile sallowly in the decline of day.
And saunterers pass with laugh and jest—
A handsome couple among the rest.

'That smart proud pair', says the man to his friend,
'Are to marry next week. . . . How little he thinks

IV. IN THE ROOM OF THE BRIDE-ELECT. *Fortnightly Review*, 1 Apr. 1911
3 *om. FR* 12 comes . . . rose.] comes. Well—'tis too late now, *FR*; comes. Well—it's too late now, *Hol.* 13 And I must marry him anyhow!" *FR*, *Hol.*

V. AT A WATERING-PLACE. *Fortnightly Review*, 1 Apr. 1911
4 Smile sallowly] Glow ochreous *FR*

That dozens of days and nights on end
I have stroked her neck, unhooked the links
Of her sleeve to get at her upper arm. . . .
Well, bliss is in ignorance: what's the harm!'

VI

IN THE CEMETERY*

'You see those mothers squabbling there?'
Remarks the man of the cemetery.
'One says in tears, "'*Tis mine lies here!*"
Another, "*Nay, mine, you Pharisee!*"
Another, "*How dare you move my flowers*
And put your own on this grave of ours!"
But all their children were laid therein
At different times, like sprats in a tin.

'And then the main drain had to cross,
And we moved the lot some nights ago,
And packed them away in the general foss
With hundreds more. But their folks don't know,
And as well cry over a new-laid drain
As anything else, to ease your pain!'

VII

OUTSIDE THE WINDOW

'My stick!' he says, and turns in the lane
To the house just left, whence a vixen voice
Comes out with the firelight through the pane,
And he sees within that the girl of his choice
Stands rating her mother with eyes aglare
For something said while he was there.

VI. IN THE CEMETERY. *Fortnightly Review*, 1 Apr. 1911
5–6 *om. FR*   8 times,] hours, *FR*

VII. OUTSIDE THE WINDOW. *Fortnightly Review*, 1 Apr. 1911

'At last I behold her soul undraped!'
Thinks the man who had loved her more than himself;
'My God!—'tis but narrowly I have escaped.—
My precious porcelain proves it delf.'
His face has reddened like one ashamed,
And he steals off, leaving his stick unclaimed.

VIII

IN THE STUDY*

He enters, and mute on the edge of a chair
Sits a thin-faced lady, a stranger there,
A type of decayed gentility;
And by some small signs he well can guess
That she comes to him almost breakfastless.

'I have called—I hope I do not err—
I am looking for a purchaser
Of some score volumes of the works
Of eminent divines I own,—
Left by my father—though it irks
My patience to offer them.' And she smiles
As if necessity were unknown;
'But the truth of it is that oftenwhiles
I have wished, as I am fond of art,
To make my rooms a little smart,
And these old books are so in the way.'
And lightly still she laughs to him,
As if to sell were a mere gay whim,
And that, to be frank, Life were indeed
To her not vinegar and gall,
But fresh and honey-like; and Need
No household skeleton at all.

VIII. IN THE STUDY. 4 well can guess] ⟨seems to see⟩ *Hol.* 5 ⟨That as yet no breakfast has tasted she.⟩ *Hol.* 11 patience] ⟨ease⟩ *Hol.* 15 smart,] ~⟨."⟩, *Hol.*; ~." *SC* 16 *om. SC*; *Hol. = established text except* so] much 18 to sell] ⟨it all⟩ ⟨this thought⟩ *Hol.* gay] ⟨light⟩ *Hol.*

IX

AT THE ALTAR-RAIL

'My bride is not coming, alas!' says the groom,
And the telegram shakes in his hand. 'I own
It was hurried! We met at a dancing-room
When I went to the Cattle-Show alone,
And then, next night, where the Fountain leaps,
And the Street of the Quarter-Circle sweeps.

'Ay, she won me to ask her to be my wife—
'Twas foolish perhaps!—to forsake the ways
Of the flaring town for a farmer's life.
She agreed. And we fixed it. Now she says:
"*It's sweet of you, dear, to prepare me a nest,*
But a swift, short, gay life suits me best.
What I really am you have never gleaned;
I had eaten the apple ere you were weaned."'

X

IN THE NUPTIAL CHAMBER

'O that mastering tune!' And up in the bed
Like a lace-robed phantom springs the bride;
'And why?' asks the man she had that day wed,
With a start, as the band plays on outside.
'It's the townsfolks' cheery compliment
Because of our marriage, my Innocent.'

'O but you don't know! 'Tis the passionate air
To which my old Love waltzed with me,

IX. AT THE ALTAR-RAIL. *Fortnightly Review*, 1 Apr. 1911
7 wife—] ~. *Hol.*

X. IN THE NUPTIAL CHAMBER. *Fortnightly Review*, 1 Apr. 1911
1 mastering tune!' *Hol.*, *WE*, *CP23*] ~?" *SC*, *CP19*; soul-stabbing tune!" *FR*

And I swore as we spun that none should share
My home, my kisses, till death, save he!
And he dominates me and thrills me through,
And it's he I embrace while embracing you!'

XI

IN THE RESTAURANT

'But hear. If you stay, and the child be born,
It will pass as your husband's with the rest,
While, if we fly, the teeth of scorn
Will be gleaming at us from east to west;
And the child will come as a life despised;
I feel an elopement is ill-advised!'

'O you realize not what it is, my dear,
To a woman! Daily and hourly alarms
Lest the truth should out. How can I stay here,
And nightly take him into my arms!
Come to the child no name or fame,
Let's go, and face it, and bear the shame.'

XII

AT THE DRAPER'S

'I stood at the back of the shop, my dear,
But you did not perceive me.
Well, when they deliver what you were shown
I shall know nothing of it, believe me!'

XI. IN THE RESTAURANT. *Fortnightly Review*, 1 Apr. 1911
5 life] thing *FR* 8 hourly] nightly *FR*; ⟨nightly⟩ *Hol.* 10 nightly] smile and *FR*; ⟨at his will⟩ *Hol.* 11 fame,] ~ *FR*, *Hol.* 12 Let's *DCM3*] Let us *all other texts*

XII. AT THE DRAPER'S. *Saturday Review*, 16 May 1914
Title How he looked in at the draper's *SR*
1 stood] was *SR* 4 *I* shall not know it, believe me!" *SR*

And he coughed and coughed as she paled and said,
'O, I didn't see you come in there—
Why couldn't you speak?'—'Well, I didn't. I left
That you should not notice I'd been there.

'You were viewing some lovely things. "*Soon required*
For a widow, of latest fashion";
And I knew 'twould upset you to meet the man
Who had to be cold and ashen

'And screwed in a box before they could dress you
"*In the last new note in mourning*",
As they defined it. So, not to distress you,
I left you to your adorning.'

XIII

ON THE DEATH-BED*

'I'll tell—being past all praying for—
Then promptly die. . . . He was out at the war,
And got some scent of the intimacy
That was under way between her and me;
And he stole back home, and appeared like a ghost
One night, at the very time almost
That I reached her house. Well, I shot him dead,
And secretly buried him. Nothing was said.

'The news of the battle came next day;
He was scheduled missing. I hurried away,
Got out there, visited the field,
And sent home word that a search revealed

6 'O,] "Why— *SR* 9 things.] robes; *SR*; robes. *Hol.* 10 *latest*] *next month's SR* fashion';] ~'. *Hol.* 11 upset you] be awkward *SR* 13 they] you *SR* 14 *note in*] *note of SR* 15 they] you *SR*

XIII. ON THE DEATH-BED. *Title* ⟨At the Death-bed⟩ ⟨From the Death-bed⟩ *Hol.* *Hol. omits quotation marks*
1 being] ⟨since⟩ *Hol.* 2 Then] ⟨And⟩ *Hol.*

He was one of the slain; though, lying alone
And stript, his body had not been known.

'But she suspected. I lost her love,
Yea, my hope of earth, and of Heaven above;
And my time's now come, and I'll pay the score,
Though it be burning for evermore.'

XIV

OVER THE COFFIN

They stand confronting, the coffin between,
His wife of old, and his wife of late,
And the dead man whose they both had been
Seems listening aloof, as to things past date.
—'I have called,' says the first. 'Do you marvel or not?'
'In truth,' says the second, 'I do—somewhat.'

'Well, there was a word to be said by me! . . .
I divorced that man because of you—
It seemed I must do it, boundenly;
But now I am older, and tell you true,
For life is little, and dead lies he;
I would I had let alone you two!
And both of us, scorning parochial ways,
Had lived like the wives in the patriarchs' days.'

XV

IN THE MOONLIGHT

'O lonely workman, standing there
In a dream, why do you stare and stare
At her grave, as no other grave there were?

16 Yea,] ⟨And⟩ *Hol.*

XIV. OVER THE COFFIN. *Fortnightly Review*, 1 Apr. 1911
1 stand] ~⟨,⟩ *Hol.*

'If your great gaunt eyes so importune
Her soul by the shine of this corpse-cold moon,
Maybe you'll raise her phantom soon!'

'Why, fool, it is what I would rather see
Than all the living folk there be;
But alas, there is no such joy for me!'

'Ah—she was one you loved, no doubt,
Through good and evil, through rain and drought,
And when she passed, all your sun went out?'

'Nay: she was the woman I did not love,
Whom all the others were ranked above,
Whom during her life I thought nothing of.'

XV. IN THE MOONLIGHT. 4 great gaunt] hopeless *SP*
Date 1910 *Hol.*

MOMENTS OF VISION
AND
MISCELLANEOUS VERSES

CONTENTS

FINALE—

MOMENTS OF VISION

That mirror
Which makes of men a transparency,
Who holds that mirror
And bids us such a breast-bare spectacle see
Of you and me?

That mirror
Whose magic penetrates like a dart,
Who lifts that mirror
And throws our mind back on us, and our heart,
Until we start?

That mirror
Works well in these night hours of ache;
Why in that mirror
Are tincts we never see ourselves once take
When the world is awake?

That mirror
Can test each mortal when unaware;
Yea, that strange mirror
May catch his last thoughts, whole life foul or fair,
Glassing it—where?

THE VOICE OF THINGS

Forty Augusts—aye, and several more—ago,
When I paced the headlands loosed from dull employ,
The waves huzza'd like a multitude below,
In the sway of an all-including joy
Without cloy.

MOMENTS OF VISION. *MS1* HRC

4 breast-bare *CP23*] shudderful *Hol.*; ⟨shudderful⟩ *MS1*; breast-bared *MV*, *CP19*, *WE* 14 tincts] tints *Hol.* 15 the world is] ⟨men are⟩ *Hol.*; ⟨the world is⟩ ⟨men are⟩ *MS1* 20 Glassing] Reflecting *MV17*

THE VOICE OF THINGS. 1 Augusts—] years— *MV17* 2 loosed] free *Hol.*

Blankly I walked there a double decade after,
When thwarts had flung their toils in front of me,
And I heard the waters wagging in a long ironic laughter
At the lot of men, and all the vapoury
Things that be.

Wheeling change has set me again standing where
Once I heard the waves huzza at Lammas-tide;
But they supplicate now—like a congregation there
Who murmur the Confession—I outside,
Prayer denied.

'WHY BE AT PAINS?'

(Wooer's Song)

Why be at pains that I should know
You sought not me?
Do breezes, then, make features glow
So rosily?
Come, the lit port is at our back,
And the tumbling sea;
Elsewhere the lampless uphill track
To uncertainty!

O should not we two waifs join hands?
I am alone,
You would enrich me more than lands
By being my own.
Yet, though this facile moment flies,
Close is your tone,
And ere to-morrow's dewfall dries
I plough the unknown.

7 toils] shapes *Hol.*

'WHY BE AT PAINS?'. 1 that I should] ⟨that I should⟩ ⟨to let me⟩ *Hol.* 26 Elsewhere] ⟨In front⟩ *Hol.* 16 plough] seek *Hol.*

'WE SAT AT THE WINDOW'*

(Bournemouth, 1875)

We sat at the window looking out,
And the rain came down like silken strings
That Swithin's day. Each gutter and spout
Babbled unchecked in the busy way
    Of witless things:
Nothing to read, nothing to see
Seemed in that room for her and me
    On Swithin's day.

We were irked by the scene, by our own selves; yes,
For I did not know, nor did she infer
How much there was to read and guess
By her in me, and to see and crown
    By me in her.
Wasted were two souls in their prime,
And great was the waste, that July time
    When the rain came down.

AFTERNOON SERVICE AT MELLSTOCK*

(*Circa* 1850)

On afternoons of drowsy calm
  We stood in the panelled pew,
Singing one-voiced a Tate-and-Brady psalm
  To the tune of 'Cambridge New'.

'WE SAT AT THE WINDOW'. 2 And the rain] ⟨And rain⟩ *Hol.* 9 ⟨Yes; we were irked at its nothingness,⟩ We were irked by the scene, by each other; yes, *Hol.* 12 see] ⟨see⟩ ⟨prize⟩ *Hol.*

AFTERNOON SERVICE. 3 one-voiced] full-voiced *MV17*

We watched the elms, we watched the rooks,
The clouds upon the breeze,
Between the whiles of glancing at our books,
And swaying like the trees.

So mindless were those outpourings!—
Though I am not aware
That I have gained by subtle thought on things
Since we stood psalming there.

AT THE WICKET-GATE

There floated the sounds of church-chiming,
But no one was nigh,
Till there came, as a break in the loneness,
Her father, she, I.
And we slowly moved on to the wicket,
And downlooking stood,
Till anon people passed, and amid them
We parted for good.

Greater, wiser, may part there than we three
Who parted there then,
But never will Fates colder-featured
Hold sway there again.
Of the churchgoers through the still meadows
No single one knew
What a play was played under their eyes there
As thence we withdrew.

5 elms,] ⟨clouds,⟩ *Hol.* 6 clouds] ~, *Hol.* breeze,] ~ *Hol.*
9 mindless] ⟨simple⟩ *Hol.* 11 subtle thought on] ⟨thought on subtler⟩ *Hol.*

AT THE WICKET-GATE. 1 floated] echoed *MV17* 5 on] up *MV17*
11 Fates colder-featured] ⟨dooms darker-featured⟩ *Hol.* Fates] *l.c.* *Hol.*
12 Hold sway] Be sealed *Hol.*; Nod nay *MV17* 16 ⟨What a thing was done⟩ *Hol.*

IN A MUSEUM

I

Here's the mould of a musical bird long passed from light,
Which over the earth before man came was winging;
There's a contralto voice I heard last night,
That lodges in me still with its sweet singing.

II

Such a dream is Time that the coo of this ancient bird
Has perished not, but is blent, or will be blending
Mid visionless wilds of space with the voice that I heard,
In the full-fugued song of the universe unending.

Exeter.

APOSTROPHE TO AN OLD PSALM TUNE*

I met you first—ah, when did I first meet you?
When I was full of wonder, and innocent,
Standing meek-eyed with those of choric bent,
While dimming day grew dimmer
In the pulpit-glimmer.

Much riper in years I met you—in a temple
Where summer sunset streamed upon our shapes,
And you spread over me like a gauze that drapes,
And flapped from floor to rafters,
Sweet as angels' laughters.

But you had been stripped of some of your old vesture
By Monk, or another. Now you wore no frill,
And at first you startled me. But I knew you still,
Though I missed the minim's waver,
And the dotted quaver.

IN A MUSEUM. 1 Here's] ⟨There's⟩ *Hol.* 4 lodges] lingers *Hol.* 5 coo] ⟨voice⟩ *Hol.* 7 visionless] fathomless *Hol.* 8 full-fugued] general *Hol.*

APOSTROPHE. 3 of choric bent,] whose voices blent, *Hol.* 5 pulpit-glimmer.] candle-glimmer. *MV17* 14 minim's] crotchet's *Hol.*

I grew accustomed to you thus. And you hailed me
Through one who evoked you often. Then at last
Your raiser was borne off, and I mourned you had passed
From my life with your late outsetter;
Till I said, ''Tis better!'

But you waylaid me. I rose and went as a ghost goes,
And said, eyes-full: 'I'll never hear it again!
It is overmuch for scathed and memoried men
When sitting among strange people
Under their steeple.'

Now, a new stirrer of tones calls you up before me
And wakes your speech, as she of Endor did
(When sought by Saul who, in disguises hid,
Fell down on the earth to hear it)
Samuel's spirit.

So, your quired oracles beat till they make me tremble
As I discern your mien in the old attire,
Here in these turmoiled years of belligerent fire
Living still on—and onward, maybe,
Till Doom's great day be!

Sunday, August 13, 1916.

AT THE WORD 'FAREWELL'*

She looked like a bird from a cloud
On the clammy lawn,
Moving alone, bare-browed
In the dim of dawn.
The candles alight in the room
For my parting meal
Made all things withoutdoors loom
Strange, ghostly, unreal.

26 stirrer] ⟨waker⟩ *Hol.* me] ~, *Hol.* 27 wakes] ⟨makes⟩ *Hol.* did] ~, *Hol.*

AT THE WORD 'FAREWELL'. *SP* (1916)
2 clammy] ⟨sloping⟩ *Hol.* 4 dawn. *Hol., ME*] ~, *MV, CP, WE*

The hour itself was a ghost,
And it seemed to me then
As of chances the chance furthermost
I should see her again.
I beheld not where all was so fleet
That a Plan of the past
Which had ruled us from birthtime to meet
Was in working at last:

No prelude did I there perceive
To a drama at all,
Or foreshadow what fortune might weave
From beginnings so small;
But I rose as if quicked by a spur
I was bound to obey,
And stepped through the casement to her
Still alone in the gray.

'I am leaving you. . . . Farewell!' I said,
As I followed her on
By an alley bare boughs overspread;
'I soon must be gone!'
Even then the scale might have been turned
Against love by a feather,
—But crimson one cheek of hers burned
When we came in together.

FIRST SIGHT OF HER AND AFTER*

A day is drawing to its fall
I had not dreamed to see;
The first of many to enthrall
My spirit, will it be?
Or is this eve the end of all
Such new delight for me?

16 Was accomplished at last. *MV17* 25 Farewell!'] ~," *Hol.* said,] ~ *Hol.* 31 —But] But ⟨—⟩ *Hol.*
Date ⟨1913⟩ *Hol.*

FIRST SIGHT OF HER. *SP* (1916).
Title The Return from First Beholding Her *SP* The Day of First Sight *MV17*

I journey home: the pattern grows
  Of moonshades on the way:
'Soon the first quarter, I suppose,'
  Sky-glancing travellers say;
I realize that it, for those,
  Has been a common day.

THE RIVAL*

I determined to find out whose it was—
The portrait he looked at so, and sighed;
Bitterly have I rued my meanness
  And wept for it since he died!

I searched his desk when he was away,
And there was the likeness—yes, my own!
Taken when I was the season's fairest,
  And time-lines all unknown.

I smiled at my image, and put it back,
And he went on cherishing it, until
I was chafed that he loved not the me then living,
  But that past woman still.

Well, such was my jealousy at last,
I destroyed that face of the former me;
Could you ever have dreamed the heart of woman
  Would work so foolishly!

HEREDITY*

I am the family face;
Flesh perishes, I live on,

10 say;] ~. *Hol.*

THE RIVAL. 7 fairest,] beauty, *MV17* 8 time-lines] crows'-feet *Hol.* 15 Could you ever have believed a woman *MV17* 16 work] act *MV17*

Projecting trait and trace
Through time to times anon,
And leaping from place to place
Over oblivion.

The years-heired feature that can
In curve and voice and eye
Despise the human span
Of durance—that is I;
The eternal thing in man,
That heeds no call to die.

'YOU WERE THE SORT THAT MEN FORGET'

You were the sort that men forget;
Though I—not yet!—
Perhaps not ever. Your slighted weakness
Adds to the strength of my regret!

You'd not the art—you never had
For good or bad—
To make men see how sweet your meaning,
Which, visible, had charmed them glad.

You would, by words inept let fall,
Offend them all,
Even if they saw your warm devotion
Would hold your life's blood at their call.

You lacked the eye to understand
Those friends offhand
Whose mode was crude, though whose dim purport
Outpriced the courtesies of the bland.

HEREDITY. 7 years-heired] family *MV17* 8 curve] gait *Hol.*

'YOU WERE THE SORT'. 5 You'd] You had *MV17* 7 meaning,] meanings, *Hol.* 9 fall,] ~ *Hol.* 13 eye] art *MV17*; grasp *PE* 15 purport] meaning *MV17* 16 Outpriced] Surpassed *MV17*

I am now the only being who
Remembers you
It may be. What a waste that Nature
Grudged soul so dear the art its due!

SHE, I, AND THEY

I was sitting,
She was knitting,
And the portraits of our fore-folk hung around;
When there struck on us a sigh;
'Ah—what is that?' said I:
'Was it not you?' said she. 'A sigh did sound.'

I had not breathed it,
Nor the night-wind heaved it,
And how it came to us we could not guess;
And we looked up at each face
Framed and glazed there in its place,
Still hearkening; but thenceforth was silentness.

Half in dreaming,
'Then its meaning',
Said we, 'must be surely this; that they repine
That we should be the last
Of stocks once unsurpassed,
And unable to keep up their sturdy line.'

1916.

NEAR LANIVET, 1872*

There was a stunted handpost just on the crest,
Only a few feet high:

SHE, I, AND THEY. 3 ⟨forefathers hung round;⟩ *Hol.* 7 breathed] ⟨breathed⟩ heaved *Hol.* 8 Nor the night wind breathed it, *Hol.*; Nor the hearth-smoke wreathed it, *MV17* 10 And] ⟨Till⟩ *Hol.*
Date August 1. 1916 *Hol.*

She was tired, and we stopped in the twilight-time for her rest,
At the crossways close thereby.

She leant back, being so weary, against its stem,
And laid her arms on its own,
Each open palm stretched out to each end of them,
Her sad face sideways thrown.

Her white-clothed form at this dim-lit cease of day
Made her look as one crucified
In my gaze at her from the midst of the dusty way,
And hurriedly 'Don't,' I cried.

I do not think she heard. Loosing thence she said,
As she stepped forth ready to go,
'I am rested now.—Something strange came into my head;
I wish I had not leant so!'

And wordless we moved onward down from the hill
In the west cloud's murked obscure,
And looking back we could see the handpost still
In the solitude of the moor.

'It struck her too,' I thought, for as if afraid
She heavily breathed as we trailed;
Till she said, 'I did not think how 'twould look in the shade,
When I leant there like one nailed.'

I, lightly: 'There's nothing in it. For *you*, anyhow!'
—'O I know there is not,' said she . . .

NEAR LANIVET. 3 rest,] ~ *Hol.* 4 close thereby.] it stood by. *MV17* 7 Each open palm] With open hands *Hol.*; Each open hand *MV17* each end of them,] the end of them; *Hol.* 8 Her sad face] ⟨And her face was⟩ Her wan face *Hol.* 9 cease] end *MV17* 11 In my gaze] ⟨As I gazed⟩ *Hol.* 16 ⟨I wish it had not been so!"⟩ ⟨I wish I had not done so!"⟩ *Hol.* 23 shade,] ~ *Hol.* 24 like] ⟨as⟩ *Hol.*

'Yet I wonder . . . If no one is bodily crucified now,
In spirit one may be!'

And we dragged on and on, while we seemed to see
In the running of Time's far glass
Her crucified, as she had wondered if she might be
Some day.—Alas, alas!

JOYS OF MEMORY

When the spring comes round, and a certain day
Looks out from the brume by the eastern copsetrees
And says, Remember,
I begin again, as if it were new,
A day of like date I once lived through,
Whiling it hour by hour away;
So shall I do till my December,
When spring comes round.

I take my holiday then and my rest
Away from the dun life here about me,
Old hours re-greeting
With the quiet sense that bring they must
Such throbs as at first, till I house with dust,
And in the numbness my heartsome zest
For things that were, be past repeating
When spring comes round.

TO THE MOON

'What have you looked at, Moon,
In your time,

27 'Yet . . . If] ⟨"Yet twas strange. For if⟩ *Hol.*
Tailnote ⟨From an old note⟩ *Hol.*

JOYS OF MEMORY. 2 brume] cloud *Hol.* 5 A day of like date] The life of that date *MV17* 11 re-greeting] ~⟨,⟩ *Hol.* 13 house with] sink to *Hol.* 14 numbness] silence *Hol.* heartsome] ⟨mental⟩ *Hol.*

TO THE MOON. *Title* ⟨Questions to the Moon⟩ *Hol.*

Now long past your prime?'
'O, I have looked at, often looked at
Sweet, sublime,
Sore things, shudderful, night and noon
In my time.'

'What have you mused on, Moon,
In your day,
So aloof, so far away?'
'O, I have mused on, often mused on
Growth, decay,
Nations alive, dead, mad, aswoon,
In my day!'

'Have you much wondered, Moon,
On your rounds,
Self-wrapt, beyond Earth's bounds?'
'Yea, I have wondered, often wondered
At the sounds
Reaching me of the human tune
On my rounds.'

'What do you think of it, Moon,
As you go?
Is Life much, or no?'
'O, I think of it, often think of it
As a show
God ought surely to shut up soon,
As I go.'

COPYING ARCHITECTURE IN AN OLD MINSTER*

(Wimborne)

How smartly the quarters of the hour march by
That the jack-o'-clock never forgets;

4 often] ⟨looked at,⟩ *Hol.* 6 Sore] Small *Hol.* 11 often] ⟨mused on,⟩ *Hol.* 13 mad,] ⟨maddened,⟩ *Hol.* 18 often] ⟨wondered,⟩ *Hol.* 25 often] ⟨think of it,⟩ *Hol.* 27 God ought] ⟨That ought⟩ God ought *Hol.*; God means *MV17*

Ding-dong; and before I have traced a cusp's eye,
Or got the true twist of the ogee over,
A double ding-dong ricochetts.

Just so did he clang here before I came,
And so will he clang when I'm gone
Through the Minster's cavernous hollows—the same
Tale of hours never more to be will he deliver
To the speechless midnight and dawn!

I grow to conceive it a call to ghosts,
Whose mould lies below and around.
Yes; the next 'Come, come,' draws them out from their posts,
And they gather, and one shade appears, and another,
As the eve-damps creep from the ground.

See—a Courtenay stands by his quatrefoiled tomb,
And a Duke and his Duchess near;
And one Sir Edmund in columned gloom,
And a Saxon king by the presbytery chamber;
And shapes unknown in the rear.

Maybe they have met for a parle on some plan
To better ail-stricken mankind;
I catch their cheepings, though thinner than
The overhead creak of a passager's pinion
When leaving land behind.

Or perhaps they speak to the yet unborn,
And caution them not to come

COPYING ARCHITECTURE. 4 ⟨Or got the true curve of the ogee over, its⟩ *Hol.* over,] ⟨upholding,⟩ *Hol.* 5 A double] ⟨Twice⟩ *Hol.* 9 hours] ⟨hours⟩ ⟨quarters⟩ *Hol.* deliver] ⟨deliver here⟩ *Hol.* 10 ⟨Loud to the midnight and dawn.⟩ *Hol.* dawn!] ~. *MV17* 14 another,] ⟨another one,⟩ ⟨another shade⟩ *Hol.* 15 ⟨Creeping like damps from the ground.⟩ *Hol.* 17 near;] ~, *Hol.* 19 presbytery chamber;] ⟨door of the presbytery;⟩ ⟨steps of the presbytery;⟩ *Hol.* 20 ⟨Also dim forms in the rear.⟩ *Hol.* 24 passager's] puffin's *Hol.*

To a world so ancient and trouble-torn,
Of foiled intents, vain lovingkindness,
And ardours chilled and numb.

They waste to fog as I stir and.stand,
And move from the arched recess,
And pick up the drawing that slipped from my hand,
And feel for the pencil I dropped in the cranny
In a moment's forgetfulness.

TO SHAKESPEARE*

After Three Hundred Years

Bright baffling Soul, least capturable of themes,
Thou, who display'dst a life of commonplace,
Leaving no intimate word or personal trace
Of high design outside the artistry
Of thy penned dreams,
Still shalt remain at heart unread eternally.

Through human orbits thy discourse to-day,
Despite thy formal pilgrimage, throbs on
In harmonies that cow Oblivion,
And, like the wind, with all-uncared effect
Maintain a sway
Not fore-desired, in tracks unchosen and unchecked.

And yet, at thy last breath, with mindless note
The borough clocks but samely tongued the hour,
The Avon just as always glassed the tower,

TO SHAKESPEARE. *Fortnightly Review*, 1 June 1916; Israel Gollancz, ed., *Book of Homage to Shakespeare* (Oxford: 1916); *FEH* (1916). *MS1* BL Ashley MS 3343; *MS2 Written into Sydney Cockerell's facsimile of first folio*

1 Bright baffling] ⟨Daemonic⟩ *Hol.* 7 to-day,] ~ *MS2* 9 cow] ⟨break⟩ *Hol.* 14 but samely] as usual *FR*, *BHS*, *FEH*, *MS1*; ⟨as usual⟩ *Hol.*; in sameness *Hol.*, *MV17* 15 The Avon idled past the garth and tower, *BHS*; *variant line del. Hol.*

Thy age was published on thy passing-bell
But in due rote
With other dwellers' deaths accorded a like knell.

And at the strokes some townsman (met, maybe,
And thereon queried by some squire's good dame
Driving in shopward) may have given thy name,
With, 'Yes, a worthy man and well-to-do;
Though, as for me,
I knew him but by just a neighbour's nod, 'tis true.

'I' faith, few knew him much here, save by word,
He having elsewhere led his busier life;
Though to be sure he left with us his wife.'
—'Ah, one of the tradesmen's sons, I now recall. . .
Witty, I've heard. . . .
We did not know him. . . . Well, good-day. Deatn
comes to all.'

So, like a strange bright bird we sometimes find
To mingle with the barn-door brood awhile,
Then vanish from their homely domicile—
Into man's poesy, we wot not whence,
Flew thy strange mind,
Lodged there a radiant guest, and sped for ever thence.

1916.

18 dwellers' deaths] native men's *FR*, *FEH*, *MS1*; men's that year *BHS*; ⟨men's that year⟩ *Hol.* 22 'Yes,] ~ *MS2* 25 word,] ~ *MS1* 31 So—like a strange bright-pinioned bird we find *FR*, *BHS*, *FEH* 33 their] ⟨the⟩ *Hol.* 34 wot] weet *BHS* whence,] ~ *Hol.*
Date February 14, 1916. *FR*, *BHS*, *FEH*, *MS1*, *Hol.*

QUID HIC AGIS?*

I

When I weekly knew
An ancient pew,
And murmured there
The forms of prayer
And thanks and praise
In the ancient ways,
And heard read out
During August drought
That chapter from Kings
Harvest-time brings;
—How the prophet, broken
By griefs unspoken,
Went heavily away
To fast and to pray,
And, while waiting to die,
The Lord passed by,
And a whirlwind and fire
Drew nigher and nigher,
And a small voice anon
Bade him up and be gone,—
I did not apprehend
As I sat to the end
And watched for her smile
Across the sunned aisle,
That this tale of a seer
Which came once a year
Might, when sands were heaping,
Be like a sweat creeping,
Or in any degree
Bear on her or on me!

QUID HIC AGIS?. *Spectator*, 19 Aug. 1916; *FEH* (1916). *TS* (*FEH*) Purdy
Title In Time of Slaughter *S*; "When I weekly knew" *FEH*, *Hol.*
7 heard] ~, *Hol.* 10 The Trinity-time brings; *S* 17 And a] And *S* and fire] of fire *FEH* 24 sunned] south *S*, *FEH*, *Hol.* 25 tale *MV17*, *CP23*] theme *MV19*, *CP19*, *WE* 30 Bear on her and me. *S* me!] ~. *Hol.*, *MV17*

II

When later, by chance
Of circumstance,
It befel me to read
On a hot afternoon
At the lectern there
The selfsame words
As the lesson decreed,
To the gathered few
From the hamlets near—
Folk of flocks and herds
Sitting half aswoon,
Who listened thereto
As women and men
Not overmuch
Concerned at such—
So, like them then,
I did not see
What drought might be
With me, with her,
As the Kalendar
Moved on, and Time
Devoured our prime.

III

But now, at last,
When our glory has passed,
And there is no smile
From her in the aisle,

31–46 *S condenses as follows*: When later I stood
By the chancel-rood
On a hot afternoon,
And read the same words
To the gathered few—
Those of flocks and herds
Sitting half aswoon,
Who listened thereto
As women and men
Detached—even then

36–7 *transposed FEH* 48 drought might] drought there might *S*
54 glory] sun *S*, *FEH*, *Hol.* 55–60 *om. S*

But where it once shone
A marble, men say,
With her name thereon
Is discerned to-day;
And spiritless
In the wilderness
I shrink from sight
And desire the night,
(Though, as in old wise,
I might still arise,
Go forth, and stand
And prophesy in the land),
I feel the shake
Of wind and earthquake,
And consuming fire
Nigher and nigher,
And the voice catch clear,
'What doest thou here?'

The Spectator: 1916.

ON A MIDSUMMER EVE

I idly cut a parsley stalk,
And blew therein towards the moon;
I had not thought what ghosts would walk
With shivering footsteps to my tune.

I went, and knelt, and scooped my hand
As if to drink, into the brook,
And a faint figure seemed to stand
Above me, with the bygone look.

I lipped rough rhymes of chance, not choice,
I thought not what my words might be;
There came into my ear a voice
That turned a tenderer verse for me.

Tailnote om. Hol.; date only FEH

ON A MIDSUMMER EVE. *SP* (1916)
3 had] ⟨did⟩ *Hol.*

TIMING HER

(Written to an old folk-tune)

Lalage's coming:
Where is she now, O?
Turning to bow, O,
And smile, is she,
Just at parting,
Parting, parting,
As she is starting
To come to me?

Where is she now, O,
Now, and now, O,
Shadowing a bough, O,
Of hedge or tree
As she is rushing,
Rushing, rushing,
Gossamers brushing
To come to me?

Lalage's coming;
Where is she now, O;
Climbing the brow, O,
Of hills I see?
Yes, she is nearing,
Nearing, nearing,
Weather unfearing
To come to me.

Near is she now, O,
Now, and now, O;
Milk the rich cow, O,
Forward the tea;
Shake the down bed for her,
Linen sheets spread for her,

TIMING HER. 10 Now, O, now, O, *MV17* 15 Gossamers brushing] ⟨Gossamers brushing⟩ Gossamer-brushing *Hol.* 26 Now, O, now, O; *MV17*

Drape round the head for her
Coming to me.

Lalage's coming,
She's nearer now, O,
End anyhow, O,
To-day's husbandry!
Would a gilt chair were mine,
Slippers of vair were mine,
Brushes for hair were mine
Of ivory!

What will she think, O,
She who's so comely,
Viewing how homely
A sort are we!
Nothing resplendent,
No prompt attendant,
Not one dependent
Pertaining to me!

Lalage's coming;
Where is she now, O?
Fain I'd avow, O,
Full honestly
Nought here's enough for her,
All is too rough for her,
Even my love for her
Poor in degree.

She's nearer now, O,
Still nearer now, O,
She 'tis, I vow, O,
Passing the lea.

34 *CP23*] Nearer is she now, O, *MV*, *CP19*, *WE*; Nearer is now, O, *ME* 36 To-day's] ⟨All⟩ *Hol.* 37 mine,] ⟨ready,⟩ *Hol.* 38 mine,] ⟨ready,⟩ *Hol.* 39 mine] ⟨ready⟩ *Hol.* 44 A sort] ⟨Here⟩ *Hol.* 53 here's] ⟨is⟩ *Hol.* 54 is] ⟨here's⟩ *Hol.* 57 *ME*, *CP23*] Nearer is she now, O, *MV*, *CP19*, *WE* 58 *ME*, *CP23*] Now, O, now, O, *MV17*; Now, and now, O, *MV19*, *CP19*, *WE* 59 'tis, *DCM3*] it is, *all other texts*

Rush down to meet her there,
Call out and greet her there,
Never a sweeter there
Crossed to me!

Lalage's come; aye,
Come is she now, O! . . .
Does Heaven allow, O,
A meeting to be?
Yes, she is here now,
Here now, here now,
Nothing to fear now,
Here's Lalage!

BEFORE KNOWLEDGE*

When I walked roseless tracks and wide,
Ere dawned your date for meeting me,
O why did you not cry Halloo
Across the stretch between, and say:

'We move, while years as yet divide,
On closing lines which—though it be
You know me not nor I know you—
Will intersect and join some day!'

Then well I had borne
Each scraping thorn;
But the winters froze,
And grew no rose;
No bridge bestrode
The gap at all;
No shape you showed,
And I heard no call!

BEFORE KNOWLEDGE. 2 dawned] ⟨came⟩ *Hol.* 4 Across the stretch] ⟨Over the years⟩ *Hol.* 5 while years] ⟨though miles⟩ *Hol.* 6 though] ⟨if⟩ *Hol.* 13 bridge] bond *Hol.*

THE BLINDED BIRD*

So zestfully canst thou sing?
And all this indignity,
With God's consent, on thee!
Blinded ere yet a-wing
By the red-hot needle thou,
I stand and wonder how
So zestfully thou canst sing!

Resenting not such wrong,
Thy grievous pain forgot,
Eternal dark thy lot,
Groping thy whole life long,
After that stab of fire;
Enjailed in pitiless wire;
Resenting not such wrong!

Who hath charity? This bird.
Who suffereth long and is kind,
Is not provoked, though blind
And alive ensepulchred?
Who hopeth, endureth all things?
Who thinketh no evil, but sings?
Who is divine? This bird.

'THE WIND BLEW WORDS'

The wind blew words along the skies,
  And these it blew to me
Through the wide dusk: 'Lift up your eyes,
  Behold this troubled tree,
Complaining as it sways and plies;
  It is a limb of thee.

THE BLINDED BIRD. 8 such] ⟨this⟩ *Hol.* 14 such] ⟨this⟩ *Hol.*

'THE WIND BLEW WORDS'. 2 ⟨These did it blow to me⟩ *Hol.* 4 troubled] writhing *Hol.*

'Yea, too, the creatures sheltering round—
  Dumb figures, wild and tame,
Yea, too, thy fellows who abound—
  Either of speech the same
Or far and strange—black, dwarfed, and browned,
  They are stuff of thy own frame.'

I moved on in a surging awe
  Of inarticulateness
At the pathetic Me I saw
  In all his huge distress,
Making self-slaughter of the law
  To kill, break, or suppress.

THE FADED FACE*

How was this I did not see
Such a look as here was shown
Ere its womanhood had blown
Past its first felicity?—
That I did not know you young,
    Faded Face,
        Know you young!

Why did Time so ill bestead
That I heard no voice of yours
Hail from out the curved contours
Of those lips when rosy red;
Weeted not the songs they sung,
    Faded Face,
        Songs they sung!

18 break,] bind, *MV17*

THE FADED FACE. 3 Ere its] ⟨When its⟩ ⟨Ere your⟩ *Hol.* 4 Past its] ⟨In a⟩ *Hol.* 6 Face,] ⟨*l.c.*⟩ *Hol.* 10 out] 'twixt *Hol.* 12 Weeted] Listed *MV*, *CP19*, *WE* 13 Face,] ⟨*l.c.*⟩ *Hol.*

By these blanchings, blooms of old,
And the relics of your voice—
Leavings rare of rich and choice
From your early tone and mould—
Let me mourn,—aye, over-wrung,
    Faded Face,
        Over-wrung!

THE RIDDLE

I

Stretching eyes west
Over the sea,
Wind foul or fair,
Always stood she
Prospect-impressed;
Solely out there
Did her gaze rest,
Never elsewhere
Seemed charm to be.

II

Always eyes east
Ponders she now—
As in devotion—
Hills of blank brow
Where no waves plough.
Never the least
Room for emotion
Drawn from the ocean
Does she allow.

15 By your picture as of old, *Hol.* 18 ⟨From your tone and from your mould—⟩ *Hol.* 19 mourn,—] ⟨mourn,⟩ die,— *Hol.* over-wrung, *Clark*] overwrung, *MV*, *WE*; sorrow-wrung, *CP* 20 Face,] ⟨*l.c.*⟩ *Hol.* 21 Over-wrung! *Clark*] Overwrung! *MV*, *WE*; Sorrow-wrung! *CP*

THE RIDDLE. 5 ⟨Beauty-impressed;⟩ *Hol.* 9 ⟨Charm seemed to be.⟩ *Hol.* 11 ⟨Ponders she now—⟩ She ponders now *Hol.* 12 devotion—] ~⟨—⟩ *Hol.*; ~, *MV17*

THE DUEL*

'I am here to time, you see;
The glade is well-screened—eh?—against alarm;
Fit place to vindicate by my arm
The honour of my spotless wife,
Who scorns your libel upon her life
In boasting intimacy!

'"All hush-offerings you'll spurn,
My husband. Two must come; one only go,"
She said. "That he'll be you I know;
To faith like ours Heaven will be just,
And I shall abide in fullest trust
Your speedy glad return."'

'Good. Here am also I;
And we'll proceed without more waste of words
To warm your cockpit. Of the swords
Take your choice. I shall thereby
Feel that on me no blame can lie,
Whatever Fate accords.'

So stripped they there, and fought,
And the swords clicked and scraped, and the onsets sped;
Till the husband fell; and his shirt was red
With streams from his heart's hot cistern. Nought
Could save him now; and the other, wrought
Maybe to pity, said:

'Why did you urge on this?
Your wife assured you; and 't had better been
That you had let things pass, serene
In confidence of long-tried bliss,
Holding there could be nought amiss
In what my words might mean.'

THE DUEL. 15 warm] ⟨test⟩ *Hol.* 29 there] ⟨it⟩ *Hol.* 30 ⟨That words of mine could mean."⟩ *Hol.*

Then, seeing nor ruth nor rage
Could move his foeman more—now Death's deaf thrall—
He wiped his steel, and, with a call
Like turtledove to dove, swift broke
Into the copse, where under an oak
His horse cropt, held by a page.

'All's over, Sweet,' he cried
To the wife, thus guised; for the young page was she.
''Tis as we hoped and said 'twould be.
He never guessed. . . . We mount and ride
To where our love can reign uneyed.
He's clay, and we are free.'

AT MAYFAIR LODGINGS*

How could I be aware,
The opposite window eyeing
As I lay listless there,
That through its blinds was dying
One I had rated rare
Before I had set me sighing
For another more fair?

Had the house-front been glass,
My vision unobscuring,
Could aught have come to pass
More happiness-insuring
To her, loved as a lass
When spouseless, all-alluring?
I reckon not, alas!

32 more—now] ⟨longer,⟩ *Hol.* 33 steel,] ⟨sword,⟩ *Hol.* 37 cried] ⟨said⟩ *Hol.* 42 clay,] dust, *MV17*

AT MAYFAIR LODGINGS. *Title* ⟨At Lodgings in London⟩ *Hol.* 3 ⟨Listless, as I sat there,⟩ *Hol.* lay] sat *Hol.* 4 was] lay *Hol.* 5 rated] ⟨held as⟩ *Hol.* 10 ⟨Could I have brought to pass⟩ *Hol.* 11 More] ⟨Aught⟩ *Hol.* 12 ⟨That might have made her as⟩ *Hol.*

So, the square window stood,
Steadily night-long shining
In my close neighbourhood,
Who looked forth undivining
That soon would go for good
One there in pain reclining,
Unpardoned, unadieu'd.

Silently screened from view
Her tragedy was ending
That need not have come due
Had she been less unbending.
How near, near were we two
At that last vital rending,—
And neither of us knew!

TO MY FATHER'S VIOLIN

Does he want you down there
In the Nether Glooms where
The hours may be a dragging load upon him,
As he hears the axle grind
Round and round
Of the great world, in the blind
Still profound
Of the night-time? He might liven at the sound
Of your string, revealing you had not forgone him.

In the gallery west the nave,
But a few yards from his grave,
Did you, tucked beneath his chin, to his bowing
Guide the homely harmony
Of the quire
Who for long years strenuously—
Son and sire—
Caught the strains that at his fingering low or higher
From your four thin threads and eff-holes came outflowing.

TO MY FATHER'S VIOLIN. *Title* ⟨To My Father's Fiddle⟩ *Hol.*
2 ⟨In the nether world shades, where⟩ *Hol.* 14 quire] ~⟨,⟩ *Hol.*
15 Who] ⟨Who⟩ Which *Hol.*

And, too, what merry tunes
He would bow at nights or noons
That chanced to find him bent to lute a measure,
When he made you speak his heart
As in dream,
Without book or music-chart,
On some theme
Elusive as a jack-o'-lanthorn's gleam,
And the psalm of duty shelved for trill of pleasure.

Well, you can not, alas,
The barrier overpass
That screens him in those Mournful Meads hereunder,
Where no fiddling can be heard
In the glades
Of silentness, no bird
Thrills the shades;
Where no viol is touched for songs or serenades,
No bowing wakes a congregation's wonder.

He must do without you now,
Stir you no more anyhow
To yearning concords taught you in your glory;
While, your strings a tangled wreck,
Once smart drawn,
Ten worm-wounds in your neck,
Purflings wan
With dust-hoar, here alone I sadly con
Your present dumbness, shape your olden story.

1916.

THE STATUE OF LIBERTY

This statue of Liberty, busy man,
Here erect in the city square,

19–27 *om. Hol.* 30 those] the *Hol.* Mournful Meads] ⟨Mournful Fields⟩ ⟨Bloomless Fields⟩ *Hol.* 41 smart drawn,] ⟨tight-drawn,⟩ ⟨up-drawn,⟩ tight-drawn, *Hol.* 42 Ten] ⟨Seven⟩ *Hol.* worm-wounds] worm-holes *MV17* 44 dust-hoar,] dust-films, *Hol.*

I have watched while your scrubbings, this early morning,
Strangely wistful,
And half tristful,
Have turned her from foul to fair;

With your bucket of water, and mop, and brush,
Bringing her out of the grime
That has smeared her during the smokes of winter
With such glumness
In her dumbness,
And aged her before her time.

You have washed her down with motherly care—
Head, shoulders, arm, and foot,
To the very hem of the robes that drape her—
All expertly
And alertly,
Till a long stream, black with soot,

Flows over the pavement to the road,
And her shape looms pure as snow:
I read you are hired by the City guardians—
May be yearly,
Or once merely—
To treat the statues so?

'Oh, I'm not hired by the Councilmen
To cleanse the statues here.
I do this one as a self-willed duty,
Not as paid to,
Or at all made to,
But because the doing is dear.'

THE STATUE OF LIBERTY. 3 scrubbings,] ⟨labours,⟩ *Hol.* 6 turned her] ⟨changed it⟩ *Hol.* fair;] ~, *Hol.* 8 Bringing her out of] ⟨Scrubbing away⟩ *Hol.* 9 smeared] ⟨made⟩ *Hol.* 10 With such glumness] ⟨So uncomely⟩ *Hol.* 11 In her dumbness,] ⟨Gazing dumbly,⟩ *Hol.* 15 hem] ⟨skirts⟩ skirt *Hol.* 27 this one as] ⟨this as⟩ *Hol.* 30 But because] ⟨Because⟩ *Hol.*

Ah, then I hail you brother and friend!
Liberty's knight divine.
What you have done would have been my doing,
Yea, most verily,
Well, and thoroughly,
Had but your courage been mine!

'Oh I care not for Liberty's mould,
Liberty charms not me;
What's Freedom but an idler's vision,
Vain, pernicious,
Often vicious,
Of things that cannot be!

'Memory it is that brings me to this—
Of a daughter—my one sweet own.
She grew a famous carver's model,
One of the fairest
And of the rarest:—
She sat for the figure as shown.

'But alas, she died in this distant place
Before I was warned to betake
Myself to her side! . . . And in love of my darling,
In love of the fame of her,
And the good name of her,
I do this for her sake.'

Answer I gave not. Of that form
The carver was I at his side;

37 mould,] ⟨shape—,⟩ *Hol.* 39 vision,] ⟨dreaming,⟩ *Hol.* 41 ⟨Often as vicious,⟩ *Hol.* 44 sweet] ⟨poor⟩ *Hol.* 45 grew] ⟨was⟩ *Hol.* 47 rarest:—] ~ ;— *Hol.*

48a–f ⟨"Alas for her calling. It suited her not;
She learnt ways sinister;
And—died . . . And tendance of this her image he[re]
With some gladness,
Though in sadness,
I give for love of her."⟩ *Hol.*

56 carver] ⟨sculptor⟩ *Hol.*

His child, my model, held so saintly,
Grand in feature,
Gross in nature,
In the dens of vice had died.

THE BACKGROUND AND THE FIGURE*

(Lover's Ditty)

I think of the slope where the rabbits fed,
Of the periwinks' rockwork lair,
Of the fuchsias ringing their bells of red—
And the something else seen there.

Between the blooms where the sod basked bright,
By the bobbing fuchsia trees,
Was another and yet more eyesome sight—
The sight that richened these.

I shall seek those beauties in the spring,
When the days are fit and fair,
But only as foils to the one more thing
That also will flower there!

THE CHANGE

Out of the past there rises a week—
Who shall read the years O!—
Out of the past there rises a week
Enringed with a purple zone.
Out of the past there rises a week
When thoughts were strung too thick to speak,
And the magic of its lineaments remains with me alone.

57 held] ⟨deemed⟩ *Hol.* 58 Grand] ⟨Fair⟩ *Hol.*

THE BACKGROUND AND THE FIGURE. 7 yet more eyesome] culminating *MV17* 8 richened] gloried *Hol.* 12 there!] ~. *Hol.*, *MV17*

THE CHANGE. 2 read] ⟨know⟩ *Hol.*

In that week there was heard a singing—
  Who shall spell the years, the years!—
In that week there was heard a singing,
  And the white owl wondered why.
In that week, yea, a voice was ringing,
And forth from the casement were candles flinging
Radiance that fell on the deodar and lit up the path
      thereby.

Could that song have a mocking note?—
  Who shall unroll the years O!—
Could that song have a mocking note
  To the white owl's sense as it fell?
Could that song have a mocking note
As it trilled out warm from the singer's throat,
And who was the mocker and who the mocked when
      two felt all was well?

In a tedious trampling crowd yet later—
  Who shall bare the years, the years!—
In a tedious trampling crowd yet later,
  When silvery singings were dumb;
In a crowd uncaring what time might fate her,
Mid murks of night I stood to await her,
And the twanging of iron wheels gave out the signal that
      she was come.

She said with a travel-tired smile—
  Who shall lift the years O!—
She said with a travel-tired smile,
  Half scared by scene so strange;

9 spell] ⟨know⟩ *Hol.* the years, the years!—] the years O!— *MV17* 12 In that week there was heard a singing, *MV17* 14 deodar] fuchsia-trees *Hol.* 16 unroll] ⟨know⟩ *Hol.* 22 tedious trampling] ⟨dull and dreary⟩ *Hol.* crowd yet] crowd, far *MV17* 23 bare] ⟨know⟩ *Hol.* the years, the years!—] the years O!— *MV17* 24 tedious trampling] ⟨dull and dreary⟩ *Hol.* crowd yet] crowd, far *MV17* 26 In a ⟨dull and dreary⟩ tedious trampling crowd, far later, *Hol.*; In a tedious trampling crowd, far later, *MV17* 27 Mid murks of night] In the filmy night *Hol.*; In the murky night *MV17* 30 lift] ⟨know⟩ *Hol.*

She said, outworn by mile on mile,
The blurred lamps wanning her face the while,
'O Love, I am here; I am with you!' . . . Ah, that there should have come a change!

O the doom by someone spoken—
Who shall unseal the years, the years!—
O the doom that gave no token,
When nothing of bale saw we:
O the doom by someone spoken,
O the heart by someone broken,
The heart whose sweet reverberances are all time leaves to me.

Jan.–Feb. 1913.

SITTING ON THE BRIDGE*

(Echo of an old song)

Sitting on the bridge
Past the barracks, town and ridge,
At once the spirit seized us
To sing a song that pleased us—
As 'The Fifth' were much in rumour;
It was 'Whilst I'm in the humour,
Take me, Paddy, will you now?'
And a lancer soon drew nigh,
And his Royal Irish eye
Said, 'Willing, faith, am I,
O, to take you anyhow, dears,
To take you anyhow.'

33 She said with a travel-tired smile, *MV17* 34 blurred] fogged *Hol.* 37 unseal] ⟨know⟩ *Hol.* the years, the years!—] the years O!— *MV17* 38 O the doom by someone spoken *MV17* 39 we:] ~! *Hol.*

SITTING ON THE BRIDGE. *Headnote* (*An old air echoed*) *Hol.*
2 Between the town and ridge, *Hol.* 5 A song then much in rumour; *Hol.* 8 lancer soon drew] soldier drew *Hol.*; lancer drew *MV17* 9 And the corner of his eye *Hol.* 10 Said "Willing quite am I, *Hol.*

But, lo!—dad walking by,
Cried, 'What, you lightheels! Fie!
Is this the way you roam
And mock the sunset gleam?'
And he marched us straightway home,
Though we said, 'We are only, daddy,
Singing, "Will you take me, Paddy?"'
—Well, we never saw from then,
If we sang there anywhen,
The soldier dear again,
Except at night in dream-time,
Except at night in dream.

Perhaps that soldier's fighting
In a land that's far away,
Or he may be idly plighting
Some foreign hussy gay;
Or perhaps his bones are whiting
In the wind to their decay! . . .
Ah!—does he mind him how
The girls he saw that day
On the bridge, were sitting singing
At the time of curfew-ringing,
'Take me, Paddy; will you now, dear?
Paddy, will you now?'

Grey's Bridge.

THE YOUNG CHURCHWARDEN

When he lit the candles there,
And the light fell on his hand,

13 ⟨But daddy walked by,⟩ But daddy, walking by, *Hol.* 14 ⟨And cried: "What, you girls! Fie!⟩ Cried: "What, you light girls! Fie! *Hol.* 19 Paddy?"'] ~'."— *Hol.* 20 —Well,] ⟨And⟩ Well, *Hol.* 27 idly] lightly *Hol.* 30 In a graveless decay! . . . *MV17* 36 Paddy,] ~ *Hol.* *Place om. Hol.*

THE YOUNG CHURCHWARDEN. *Title* ⟨At an Evening Service⟩ *Hol.* *Headnote* August 14. 1870 *Hol.*

And it trembled as he scanned
Her and me, his vanquished air
Hinted that his dream was done,
And I saw he had begun
　　To understand.

When Love's viol was unstrung,
Sore I wished the hand that shook
Had been mine that shared her book
While that evening hymn was sung,
His the victor's, as he lit
Candles where he had bidden us sit
　　With vanquished look.

Now her dust lies listless there,
His afar from tending hand,
What avails the victory scanned?
Does he smile from upper air:
'Ah, my friend, your dream is done;
And 'tis *you* who have begun
　　To understand!'

'I TRAVEL AS A PHANTOM NOW'

I travel as a phantom now,
For people do not wish to see
In flesh and blood so bare a bough
　　As Nature makes of me.

And thus I visit bodiless
Strange gloomy households often at odds,
And wonder if Man's consciousness
　　Was a mistake of God's.

3 he] ⟨I⟩ *Hol.* 4 Her and me, his] ⟨Book and him whose⟩ *Hol.* 6 And I saw] ⟨I perceived⟩ *Hol.* 15 Now] ~, *Hol.* listless] ⟨yonder⟩ ⟨nigh out⟩ *Hol.* 16 hand,] ~; *Hol.* 19 'Ah,] ⟨"Now,⟩ *Hol.* 20 And] ⟨Yea,⟩ *Hol.*

'I TRAVEL'. 4 As Nature makes me. *Hol.* 6 gloomy] ⟨gloomy⟩ ⟨various⟩ *Hol.* often] ⟨often⟩ ⟨some⟩ *Hol.*

And next I meet you, and I pause,
And think that if mistake it were,
As some have said, O then it was
One that I well can bear!

1915.

LINES

TO A MOVEMENT IN MOZART'S E-FLAT SYMPHONY*

Show me again the time
When in the Junetide's prime
We flew by meads and mountains northerly!—
Yea, to such freshness, fairness, fulness, fineness, freeness,
Love lures life on.

Show me again the day
When from the sandy bay
We looked together upon the pestered sea!—
Yea, to such surging, swaying, sighing, swelling, shrinking,
Love lures life on.

Show me again the hour
When by the pinnacled tower
We eyed each other and feared futurity!—
Yea, to such bodings, broodings, beatings, blanchings, blessings,
Love lures life on.

Show me again just this:
The moment of that kiss

LINES. *Title* MOVEMENT] ⟨MINUET⟩ *Hol.*
4 to] with *Hol.* 7 bay] ⟨way⟩ *Hol.* 8 pestered] ⟨burnished⟩ capricious *Hol.* 9 to] with *Hol.* 14 to] with *Hol.*

Away from the prancing folk, by the strawberry-tree!—
Yea, to such ratheness, rareness, ripeness, richness,
rashness,
Love lures life on.

Begun November 1898.

'IN THE SEVENTIES'*

'Qui deridetur ab amico suo sicut ego.'—Job.

In the seventies I was bearing in my breast,
Penned tight,
Certain starry thoughts that threw a magic light
On the worktimes and the soundless hours of rest
In the seventies; aye, I bore them in my breast
Penned tight.

In the seventies when my neighbours—even my friend—
Saw me pass,
Heads were shaken, and I heard the words, 'Alas,
For his onward years and name unless he mend!'
In the seventies, when my neighbours and my friend
Saw me pass.

In the seventies those who met me did not know
Of the vision
That immuned me from the chillings of misprision
And the damps that choked my goings to and fro
In the seventies; yea, those nodders did not know
Of the vision.

In the seventies nought could darken or destroy it,
Locked in me,
Though as delicate as lamp-worm's lucency;

18 strawberry-tree!—] 〈arching tree:〉 *Hol.* 19 to] with *Hol.* ratheness, . . . rashness, *DCM3*] rashness, ratheness, rareness, ripeness, richness, *all other texts* Date om. *Hol.*

'IN THE SEVENTIES'. 15 That immuned] 〈That had immuned〉 *Hol.* 16 〈And the choking fens of〉 *Hol.* 21 lamp-worm's lucency;] eve-worm's radiancy; *Hol.*

Neither mist nor murk could weaken or alloy it
In the seventies!—could not darken or destroy it,
Locked in me.

THE PEDIGREE

I

I bent in the deep of night
Over a pedigree the chronicler gave
As mine; and as I bent there, half-unrobed,
The uncurtained panes of my window-square let in the watery light
Of the moon in its old age:
And green-rheumed clouds were hurrying past where mute and cold it globed
Like a drifting dolphin's eye seen through a lapping wave.

II

So, scanning my sire-sown tree,
And the hieroglyphs of this spouse tied to that,
With offspring mapped below in lineage,
Till the tangles troubled me,
The branches seemed to twist into a seared and cynic face
Which winked and tokened towards the window like a Mage
Enchanting me to gaze again thereat.

III

It was a mirror now,
And in it a long perspective I could trace
Of my begetters, dwindling backward each past each
All with the kindred look,

22 ⟨Neither moth nor rust could tarnish or alloy it⟩ *Hol.*

THE PEDIGREE. 1 in] at *Hol.* 6 green-rheumed] greenish *Hol.* 7 drifting dolphin's] dying fish's *Hol.*; dying dolphin's *MV17* 18 kindred] family *MV17*

Whose names had since been inked down in their place
On the recorder's book,
Generation and generation of my mien, and build, and brow.

IV

And then did I divine
That every heave and coil and move I made
Within my brain, and in my mood and speech,
Was in the glass portrayed
As long forestalled by their so making it;
The first of them, the primest fuglemen of my line,
Being fogged in far antiqueness past surmise and reason's reach.

V

Said I then, sunk in tone,
'I am merest mimicker and counterfeit!—
Though thinking, *I am I*,
And what I do I do myself alone.'
—The cynic twist of the page thereat unknit
Back to its normal figure, having wrought its purport wry,
The Mage's mirror left the window-square,
And the stained moon and drift retook their places there.

1916.

HIS HEART

A WOMAN'S DREAM

At midnight, in the room where he lay dead
Whom in his life I had never clearly read,
I thought if I could peer into that citadel
His heart, I should at last know full and well

19 since been] long stood *Hol.* 30 'I am merest mimicker] "I'm ⟨a⟩ mere continuator *Hol.*; I am mere continuator *MV17* 36 And moon and drifting cloud retook their places there. *Hol.*

What hereto had been known to him alone,
Despite our long sit-out of years foreflown,
'And if', I said, 'I do this for his memory's sake,
It would not wound him, even if he could wake.'

So I bent over him. He seemed to smile
With a calm confidence the whole long while
That I, withdrawing his heart, held it and, bit by bit,
Perused the unguessed things found written on it.

It was inscribed like a terrestrial sphere
With quaint vermiculations close and clear—
His graving. Had I known, would I have risked the stroke
Its reading brought, and my own heart nigh broke!

Yes, there at last, eyes opened, did I see
His whole sincere symmetric history;
There were his truth, his simple singlemindedness,
Strained, maybe, by time's storms, but there no less.

There were the daily deeds from sun to sun
In blindness, but good faith, that he had done;
There were regrets, at instances wherein he swerved
(As he conceived) from cherishings I had deserved.

There were old hours all figured down as bliss—
Those spent with me—(how little had I thought this!)
There those when, at my absence, whether he slept or
waked,
(Though I knew not 'twas so!) his spirit ached.

There that when we were severed, how day dulled
Till time joined us anew, was chronicled:
And arguments and battlings in defence of me
That heart recorded clearly and ruddily.

HIS HEART. 8 would] ⟨will⟩ *Hol.* even if he could] ⟨since he will not⟩ *Hol.* 15 graving.] ⟨penning⟩ *Hol.* 23 he swerved] he had swerved *Hol.*

I put it back, and left him as he lay
While pierced the morning pink and then the gray
Into each dreary room and corridor around,
Where I shall wait, but his step will not sound.

WHERE THEY LIVED

Dishevelled leaves creep down
Upon that bank to-day,
Some green, some yellow, and some pale brown;
The wet bents bob and sway;
The once warm slippery turf is sodden
Where we laughingly sat or lay.

The summerhouse is gone,
Leaving a weedy space;
The bushes that veiled it once have grown
Gaunt trees that interlace,
Through whose lank limbs I see too clearly
The nakedness of the place.

And where were hills of blue,
Blind drifts of vapour blow,
And the names of former dwellers few,
If any, people know,
And instead of a voice that called, 'Come in, Dears,'
Time calls, 'Pass below!'

THE OCCULTATION*

When the cloud shut down on the morning shine,
And darkened the sun,
I said, 'So ended that joy of mine
Years back begun.'

36 wait, but his step] ⟨wait a step that⟩ ⟨wait, but his step⟩ wait a step that *Hol.*

WHERE THEY LIVED. 1 creep] come *MV17* 6 laughingly] ⟨laughing⟩ *Hol.* 8 space;] ~, *Hol.* 11 lank limbs] ⟨bare stems⟩ *Hol.*; flayed fingers *Hol.*, *MV17* 13 blue,] ~ *Hol.* 18 Time calls,] ⟨The years call,⟩ *Hol.* *Date* ⟨March 1913.⟩ ⟨Oct. 1913.⟩ *Hol.*

But day continued its lustrous roll
    In upper air;
And did my late irradiate soul
    Live on somewhere?

LIFE LAUGHS ONWARD

Rambling I looked for an old abode
Where, years back, one had lived I knew;
Its site a dwelling duly showed,
    But it was new.

I went where, not so long ago,
The sod had riven two breasts asunder;
Daisies throve gaily there, as though
    No grave were under.

I walked along a terrace where
Loud children gambolled in the sun;
The figure that had once sat there
    Was missed by none.

Life laughed and moved on unsubdued,
I saw that Old succumbed to Young:
'Twas well. My too regretful mood
    Died on my tongue.

THE PEACE-OFFERING

It was but a little thing,
Yet I knew it meant to me
Ease from what had given a sting
To the very birdsinging
    Latterly.

THE OCCULTATION. 5 its lustrous roll] on to its goal *Hol.* 7 late] ⟨lost⟩ *Hol.*

LIFE LAUGHS ONWARD. 2 Where,] ~ *Hol.* back,] ~ *Hol.*

But I would not welcome it;
And for all I then declined
O the regrettings infinite
When the night-processions flit
Through the mind!

'SOMETHING TAPPED'

Something tapped on the pane of my room
When there was never a trace
Of wind or rain, and I saw in the gloom
My weary Belovéd's face.

'O I am tired of waiting,' she said,
'Night, morn, noon, afternoon;
So cold it is in my lonely bed,
And I thought you would join me soon!'

I rose and neared the window-glass,
But vanished thence had she:
Only a pallid moth, alas,
Tapped at the pane for me.

August 1913.

THE WOUND*

I climbed to the crest,
And, fog-festooned,
The sun lay west
Like a crimson wound:

THE PEACE-OFFERING. 6 it;] ~, *Hol.* 10 the] my *Hol.*

'SOMETHING TAPPED'. *Date* 1913. *Hol.*

THE WOUND. *Sphere*, 27 May 1916; *SP* (1916)

Like that wound of mine
  Of which none knew,
For I'd given no sign
  That it pierced me through.

A MERRYMAKING IN QUESTION

'I will get a new string for my fiddle,
  And call to the neighbours to come,
And partners shall dance down the middle
  Until the old pewter-wares hum:
  And we'll sip the mead, cyder, and rum!'

From the night came the oddest of answers:
  A hollow wind, like a bassoon,
And headstones all ranged up as dancers,
  And cypresses droning a croon,
  And gurgoyles that mouthed to the tune.

'I SAID AND SANG HER EXCELLENCE'

(Fickle Lover's Song)

I said and sang her excellence:
  They called it laud undue.
      (Have your way, my heart, O!)
Yet what was homage far above
The plain deserts of my olden Love
  Proved verity of my new.

A MERRYMAKING IN QUESTION. *Sphere*, 27 May 1916; *SP* (1916)
9 croon,] ~ *Hol.* 10 And crossbones that clicked to the tune. *S* mouthed to] ⟨gushed to⟩ *Hol.*; gushed to *SP*

'She moves a sylph in picture-land,
  Where nothing frosts the air:'
      (Have your way, my heart, O!)
'To all winged pipers overhead
She is known by shape and song,' I said,
  Conscious of licence there.

I sang of her in a dim old hall
  Dream-built too fancifully,
      (Have your way, my heart, O!)
But lo, the ripe months chanced to lead
My feet to such a hall indeed,
  Where stood the very She.

Strange, startling, was it then to learn
  I had glanced down unborn time,
      (Have your way, my heart, O!)
And prophesied, whereby I knew
That which the years had planned to do
  In warranty of my rhyme.

By Rushy-Pond.

A JANUARY NIGHT*

(1879)

The rain smites more and more,
The east wind snarls and sneezes;
Through the joints of the quivering door
    The water wheezes.

The tip of each ivy-shoot
Writhes on its neighbour's face;
There is some hid dread afoot
    That we cannot trace.

'I SAID AND SANG'. 7 picture-land,] ~ *Hol.* 19 startling,] ~ *Hol.*

A JANUARY NIGHT. 1 smites] beats *Hol.* 5 tip] point *MV17*

Is it the spirit astray
Of the man at the house below
Whose coffin they took in to-day?
    We do not know.

A KISS

By a wall the stranger now calls his,
Was born of old a particular kiss,
Without forethought in its genesis;
Which in a trice took wing on the air.
And where that spot is nothing shows:
    There ivy calmly grows,
    And no one knows
    What a birth was there!

That kiss is gone where none can tell—
Not even those who felt its spell:
It cannot have died; that know we well.
Somewhere it pursues its flight,
One of a long procession of sounds
    Travelling aethereal rounds
    Far from earth's bounds
    In the infinite.

THE ANNOUNCEMENT

They came, the brothers, and took two chairs
    In their usual quiet way;
And for a time we did not think
    They had much to say.

A KISS. 1 ⟨By the garden wall where the stranger is⟩ By the wall where now the stranger is *Hol.*   8 there!] ~. *Hol.*, *MV17*

THE ANNOUNCEMENT. *Headnote* ⟨January 1879⟩ *Hol.*
4 much] ⟨aught⟩ *Hol.*

And they began and talked awhile
Of ordinary things,
Till spread that silence in the room
A pent thought brings.

And then they said: 'The end has come.
Yes: it has come at last.'
And we looked down, and knew that day
A spirit had passed.

THE OXEN*

Christmas Eve, and twelve of the clock.
'Now they are all on their knees,'
An elder said as we sat in a flock
By the embers in hearthside ease.

We pictured the meek mild creatures where
They dwelt in their strawy pen,
Nor did it occur to one of us there
To doubt they were kneeling then.

So fair a fancy few would weave
In these years! Yet, I feel,
If someone said on Christmas Eve,
'Come; see the oxen kneel

'In the lonely barton by yonder coomb
Our childhood used to know,'
I should go with him in the gloom,
Hoping it might be so.

1915.

8 A pent] ⟨Which pent⟩ *Hol.*; Which a pent *Hol.*, *MV17*

THE OXEN. *Times*, 24 Dec. 1915; *SP* (1916). *MS1* [*see explanatory notes*]
9 would weave] believe *T* 10 years!] ~. *MS1* 11 Eve,] ~ *MS1*
15 gloom,] ~ *Hol.*
Date om. MV17

THE TRESSES

'When the air was damp
It made my curls hang slack
As they kissed my neck and back
While I footed the salt-aired track
I loved to tramp.

'When it was dry
They would roll up crisp and tight
As I went on in the light
Of the sun, which my own sprite
Seemed to outvie.

'Now I am old;
And have not one gay curl
As I had when a girl
For dampness to unfurl
Or sun uphold!'

THE PHOTOGRAPH

The flame crept up the portrait line by line
As it lay on the coals in the silence of night's profound,
And over the arm's incline,
And along the marge of the silkwork superfine,
And gnawed at the delicate bosom's defenceless round.

Then I vented a cry of hurt, and averted my eyes,
The spectacle was one that I could not bear,
To my deep and sad surprise;
But, compelled to heed, I again looked furtive-wise
Till the flame had eaten her breasts, and mouth, and hair.

THE TRESSES. 2 curls] ⟨hair⟩ *Hol.* 4 I footed] footing *Hol.* salt-aired] ⟨breezy⟩ *Hol.*

THE PHOTOGRAPH. 4 marge] edge *MV17* 5 gnawed at] ⟨into⟩ *Hol.* 6 hurt,] ⟨pain⟩ *Hol.*

'Thank God, she is out of it now!' I said at last,
In a great relief of heart when the thing was done
That had set my soul aghast,
And nothing was left of the picture unsheathed from the past
But the ashen ghost of the card it had figured on.

She was a woman long hid amid packs of years,
She might have been living or dead; she was lost to my sight,
And the deed that had nigh drawn tears
Was done in a casual clearance of life's arrears;
But I felt as if I had put her to death that night! . . .

. . . .

—Well; she knew nothing thereof did she survive,
And suffered nothing if numbered among the dead;
Yet—yet—if on earth alive
Did she feel a smart, and with vague strange anguish strive?
If in heaven, did she smile at me sadly and shake her head?

ON A HEATH*

I could hear a gown-skirt rustling
Before I could see her shape,
Rustling through the heather
That wove the common's drape,
On that evening of dark weather
When I hearkened, lips agape.

And the town-shine in the distance
Did but baffle here the sight,

12 thing was done] ⟨whole was gone⟩ *Hol.* 16 amid packs] ⟨in the gray⟩ *Hol.* 18 deed] ⟨act⟩ *Hol.* drawn] ⟨touched⟩ *Hol.* 24 smart, and with vague] smart—with a vague *Hol.* 25 smile at me sadly] ⟨smile sadly⟩ *Hol.*

ON A HEATH. 4 wove] formed *MV17*

And then a voice flew forward:
  'Dear, is't you? I fear the night!'
And the herons flapped to norward
  In the firs upon my right.

There was another looming
  Whose life we did not see;
There was one stilly blooming
  Full nigh to where walked we;
There was a shade entombing
  All that was bright of me.

AN ANNIVERSARY*

It was at the very date to which we have come,
  In the month of the matching name,
When, at a like minute, the sun had upswum,
  Its couch-time at night being the same.
And the same path stretched here that people now follow,
  And the same stile crossed their way,
And beyond the same green hillock and hollow
  The same horizon lay;
And the same man pilgrims now hereby who pilgrimed here that day.

Let so much be said of the date-day's sameness;
  But the tree that neighbours the track,
And stoops like a pedlar afflicted with lameness,
  Knew of no sogged wound or wind-crack.

9 flew] came *MV17* 10 'Dear, is't you?] ⟨"You, dear?⟩ *Hol.*; "Are you there? *Hol.*, *MV17* 14 life] build *MV17* 15 one stilly] a flower *Hol.*; one meekly *MV17* 16 In close propinquity; *MV17*

AN ANNIVERSARY. 1 was at] ⟨was at⟩ ⟨was here at⟩ *Hol.* we have] ⟨we now have⟩ *Hol.* 2 ⟨And also in the month of this name,⟩ *Hol.* 3 minute,] ⟨second,⟩ *Hol.* 4 couch-time] ⟨couch-time⟩ bed-time *Hol.* 6 stile] stiles *Hol.* 9 pilgrims now hereby] passes now thereby *Hol.*; passes now hereby *MV17* pilgrimed here] passed thereby *Hol.*; passed hereby *MV17* 13 Had no waterlogged wound or wind-crack. *MV17*

And the joints of that wall were not enshrouded
With mosses of many tones,
And the garth up afar was not overcrowded
With a multitude of white stones,
And the man's eyes then were not so sunk that you saw the socket-bones.

Kingston-Maurward Ewelease.

'BY THE RUNIC STONE'

(Two who became a story)

By the Runic Stone
They sat, where the grass sloped down,
And chattered, he white-hatted, she in brown,
Pink-faced, breeze-blown.

Rapt there alone
In the transport of talking so
In such a place, there was nothing to let them know
What hours had flown.

And the die thrown
By them heedlessly there, the dent
It was to cut in their encompassment,
Were, too, unknown.

It might have strown
Their zest with qualms to see,
As in a glass, Time toss their history
From zone to zone!

14 joints *ME*, *CP23*] stones *MV*, *CP19*, *WE* that] the *Hol.* 16 up afar] on the hill *Hol.*
Place om. Hol.

'BY THE RUNIC STONE'. *Subtitle om. MV17*
2 grass] ⟨green⟩ *Hol.* 6 transport] newness *MV17* 10 ⟨Then by them there, the dent⟩ *Hol.* 11 encompassment,] ⟨environment,⟩ *Hol.*

THE PINK FROCK*

'O my pretty pink frock,
I shan't be able to wear it!
Why is he dying just now?
I can hardly bear it!

'He might have contrived to live on;
But they say there's no hope whatever:
And must I shut myself up,
And go out never?

'O my pretty pink frock,
Puff-sleeved and accordion-pleated!
He might have passed in July,
And not so cheated!'

TRANSFORMATIONS

Portion of this yew
Is a man my grandsire knew,
Bosomed here at its foot:
This branch may be his wife,
A ruddy human life
Now turned to a green shoot.

These grasses must be made
Of her who often prayed,
Last century, for repose;
And the fair girl long ago
Whom I vainly tried to know
May be entering this rose.

THE PINK FROCK. 11 passed in] ⟨made it⟩ *Hol.* 12 And none been cheated!" *Hol.*; And me uncheated!" *MV17*; And me not cheated!" *PE*

TRANSFORMATIONS. *Title* ⟨In a Churchyard⟩ *Hol.* 2 grandsire] ⟨father⟩ *Hol.* 3 Bosomed here] ⟨Embosomed⟩ *Hol.* 4 may be] maybe *MV17* wife,] ~,— *Hol.* 11 vainly *ME*] often *MV, CP, WE*

So, they are not underground,
But as nerves and veins abound
In the growths of upper air,
And they feel the sun and rain,
And the energy again
That made them what they were!

IN HER PRECINCTS*

Her house looked cold from the foggy lea,
And the square of each window a dull black blur
Where showed no stir:
Yes, her gloom within at the lack of me
Seemed matching mine at the lack of her.

The black squares grew to be squares of light
As the eveshade swathed the house and lawn,
And viols gave tone;
There was glee within. And I found that night
The gloom of severance mine alone.

Kingston-Maurward Park.

THE LAST SIGNAL*

(*Oct.* 11, 1886)

A MEMORY OF WILLIAM BARNES

Silently I footed by an uphill road
That led from my abode to a spot yew-boughed;
Yellowly the sun sloped low down to westward,
And dark was the east with cloud.

14 nerves] films *Hol.*

IN HER PRECINTS. 7 As dusk increased round the house and lawn, *Hol.* *Place om. Hol.*

THE LAST SIGNAL. *Dedication* In Memoriam William Barnes *Hol.*

Then, amid the shadow of that livid sad east,
Where the light was least, and a gate stood wide,
Something flashed the fire of the sun that was facing it,
Like a brief blaze on that side.

Looking hard and harder I knew what it meant—
The sudden shine sent from the livid east scene;
It meant the west mirrored by the coffin of my friend there,
Turning to the road from his green,

To take his last journey forth—he who in his prime
Trudged so many a time from that gate athwart the land!
Thus a farewell to me he signalled on his grave-way,
As with a wave of his hand.

Winterborne-Came Path.

THE HOUSE OF SILENCE

'That is a quiet place—
That house in the trees with the shady lawn.'
'—If, child, you knew what there goes on
You would not call it a quiet place.
Why, a phantom abides there, the last of its race,
And a brain spins there till dawn.'

'But I see nobody there,—
Nobody moves about the green,
Or wanders the heavy trees between.'
'—Ah, that's because you do not bear
The visioning powers of souls who dare
To pierce the material screen.

5 amid *CP23*] below *MV*, *CP19*, *WE* 7 Something flashed the fire *ME*, *CP23*] Flashed a reflection *MV17*; Flashed back the fire *MV19*, *CP19*, *WE* 11 It meant the west] 'Twas the west *Hol.*; It meant the sun *MV17* *Place om. Hol.*

THE HOUSE OF SILENCE. *Strand*, Oct. 1924 [*facsimile of MS1*]. *MS1* DCM
10 do not bear] ⟨are not aware⟩ *MS1* 11 ⟨Of the eyes of souls who inhabit ⟨⟨there⟩⟩ where⟩ *MS1* 12 ⟨Wondrous things have been.⟩ *MS1*

'Morning, noon, and night,
Mid those funereal shades that seem
The uncanny scenery of a dream,
Figures dance to a mind with sight,
And music and laughter like floods of light
Make all the precincts gleam.

'It is a poet's bower,
Through which there pass, in fleet arrays,
Long teams of all the years and days,
Of joys and sorrows, of earth and heaven,
That meet mankind in its ages seven,
An aeon in an hour.'

GREAT THINGS

Sweet cyder is a great thing,
A great thing to me,
Spinning down to Weymouth town
By Ridgeway thirstily,
And maid and mistress summoning
Who tend the hostelry:
O cyder is a great thing,
A great thing to me!

The dance it is a great thing,
A great thing to me,
With candles lit and partners fit
For night-long revelry;

17 ⟨And laughter comes like a flood of light,⟩ *MS1* 18 Make] ⟨And⟩ *MS1* 20 fleet] long *MS1*, *Hol.* 21 Long teams] Processions *MS1*, *Hol.* 23 its] his *MS1*, *Hol.*, *MV17* seven,] ~— *MS1* 24 An aeon] ⟨A universe⟩ *MS1*

GREAT THINGS. 3 Vamping down to Budmouth town *Hol.* 9 The dance it] ⟨Dancing⟩ *Hol.* thing,] ~ *Hol.* 12 night-long] ⟨any⟩ *Hol.* revelry;] ~. *Hol.*

And going home when day-dawning
  Peeps pale upon the lea:
O dancing is a great thing,
  A great thing to me!

Love is, yea, a great thing,
  A great thing to me,
When, having drawn across the lawn
  In darkness silently,
A figure flits like one a-wing
  Out from the nearest tree:
O love is, yes, a great thing,
  A great thing to me!

Will these be always great things,
  Great things to me? . . .
Let it befall that One will call,
  'Soul, I have need of thee':
What then? Joy-jaunts, impassioned flings,
  Love, and its ecstasy,
Will always have been great things,
  Great things to me!

THE CHIMES*

That morning when I trod the town
The twitching chimes of long renown
    Played out to me
The sweet Sicilian sailors' tune,
And I knew not if late or soon
    My day would be:

24 *MV17*, *ME*, *CP23*] Aye, greatest thing to me! *MV19*, *CP19*, *WE* 26 Great *MV17*, *ME*, *CP23*] Greatest *MV19*, *CP19*, *WE* me? . . .] ~? *Hol.* 27 Let] Will *Hol.* 28 thee':] ~"? . . . *Hol.* 32 Great *MV17*, *ME*, *CP23*] Greatest *MV19*, *CP19*, *WE*

THE CHIMES. 1 when I trod] I walked up *MV17* 6 be:] ~; *Hol.*

A day of sunshine beryl-bright
And windless; yea, think as I might,
I could not say,
Even to within years' measure, when
One would be at my side who then
Was far away.

When hard utilitarian times
Had stilled the sweet Saint-Peter's chimes
I learnt to see
That bale may spring where blisses are,
And one desired might be afar
Though near to me.

THE FIGURE IN THE SCENE*

It pleased her to step in front and sit
Where the cragged slope was green,
While I stood back that I might pencil it
With her amid the scene.
Till it gloomed and rained;
But I kept on, despite the drifting wet
That fell and stained
My draught, leaving for curious quizzings yet
The blots engrained.

And thus I drew her there alone,
Seated amid the gauze
Of moisture, hooded, only her outline shown,
With rainfall marked across.

7 beryl-bright] ⟨silver-bright⟩ *Hol.*

THE FIGURE IN THE SCENE. 2 cragged] ⟨cliff⟩ *Hol.* 3 stood] ⟨stayed⟩ *Hol.* 5 And then it rained; *Hol.* 8 leaving] ⟨and leaves⟩ *Hol.* quizzings] ⟨notice⟩ *Hol.* 12 hooded,] ⟨cloaked,⟩ *Hol.* 13 rainfall] rain-lines *MV17*

—Soon passed our stay;
Yet her rainy form is the Genius still of the spot,
Immutable, yea,
Though the place now knows her no more, and has known her not
Ever since that day.

From and old note.

'WHY DID I SKETCH'*

Why did I sketch an upland green,
And put the figure in
Of one on the spot with me?—
For now that one has ceased to be seen
The picture waxes akin
To a wordless irony.

If you go drawing on down or cliff
Let no soft curves intrude
Of a woman's silhouette,
But show the escarpments stark and stiff
As in utter solitude;
So shall you half forget.

Let me sooner pass from sight of the sky
Than again on a thoughtless day
Limn, laugh, and sing, and rhyme
With a woman sitting near, whom I
Paint in for love, and who may
Be called hence in my time!

From an old note.

14 ⟨'Twas but a stay;⟩ *Hol.* —Soon] ~ *Hol.* 15 Yet her rainy form] ⟨Of minutes in the rain⟩ ⟨Yet her form⟩ *Hol.* Genius] ⟨*l.c.*⟩ *Hol.* 16 ⟨As pictured, yea,⟩ *Hol.*

'WHY DID I SKETCH'. 1 an upland] ⟨a cliff-side⟩ *Hol.* 7 down] ⟨crag⟩ *Hol.* 15 Limn,] Sketch, *MV17* 17 love, and who] ⟨love, who⟩ *Hol.*

CONJECTURE*

If there were in my kalendar
No Emma, Florence, Mary,
What would be my existence now—
A hermit's?—wanderer's weary?—
How should I live, and how
Near would be death, or far?

Could it have been that other eyes
Might have uplit my highway?
That fond, sad, retrospective sight
Would catch from this dim byway
Prized figures different quite
From those that now arise?

With how strange aspect would there creep
The dawn, the night, the daytime,
If memory were not what it is
In song-time, toil, or pray-time.—
O were it else than this,
I'd pass to pulseless sleep!

THE BLOW

That no man schemed it is my hope—
Yea, that it fell by will and scope
Of That Which some enthrone,
And for whose meaning myriads grope.

For I would not that of my kind
There should, of his unbiased mind,
Have been one known
Who such a stroke could have designed;

CONJECTURE. 8 Might] ⟨Would⟩ *Hol.* 11 Prized figures] ⟨Past phantoms⟩ Past figures *Hol.* 13 creep] come *Hol.* 16 toil,] say, *Hol.* time.—] ~ !— *Hol.* 17 ⟨Were ghosts not this, and this⟩ Well, were it not as this, *Hol.* 18 ⟨I would be dead and dumb!⟩; I'd have me dead and dumb. *Hol.*

THE BLOW. 7 ⟨Have been a single one known⟩ ⟨Have been even one known⟩ *Hol.*

Since it would augur works and ways
Below the lowest that man assays
To have hurled that stone
Into the sunshine of our days!

And if it prove that no man did,
And that the Inscrutable, the Hid,
Was cause alone
Of this foul crash our lives amid,

I'll go in due time, and forget
In some deep graveyard's oubliette
The thing whereof I groan,
And cease from troubling; thankful yet

Time's finger should have stretched to show
No aimful author's was the blow
That swept us prone,
But the Immanent Doer's That doth not know,

Which in some age unguessed of us
May lift Its blinding incubus,
And see, and own:
'It grieves me I did thus and thus!'

LOVE THE MONOPOLIST

(Young Lover's Reverie)

The train draws forth from the station-yard,
And with it carries me.
I rise, and stretch out, and regard
The platform left, and see
An airy slim blue form there standing,
And know that it is she.

10 man] ⟨mind⟩ *Hol.* 11 To have hurled] To hurl *Hol.* 23 That swept] ⟨Which left⟩ *Hol.* 24 Doer's That] ⟨Doer who⟩ Doer That *Hol.* doth] does *MV17* 26 ⟨May lift Its incubus,⟩ *Hol.*

While with strained vision I watch on,
The figure turns round quite
To greet friends gaily; then is gone. . . .
The import may be slight,
But why remained she not hard gazing
Till I was out of sight?

'O do not chat with others there,'
I brood. 'They are not I.
O strain your thoughts as if they were
Gold bands between us; eye
All neighbour scenes as so much blankness
Till I again am by!

'A troubled soughing in the breeze
And the sky overhead
Let yourself feel; and shadeful trees,
Ripe corn, and apples red,
Read as things barren and distasteful
While we are separated!

'When I come back uncloak your gloom,
And let in lovely day;
Then the long dark as of the tomb
Can well be thrust away
With sweet things I shall have to practise,
And you will have to say!'

Begun 1871: *finished*——.

AT MIDDLE-FIELD GATE IN FEBRUARY*

The bars are thick with drops that show
As they gather themselves from the fog

LOVE THE MONOPOLIST. 9 gaily; ⟨smiling;⟩ *Hol.* 14 I brood.] I feel. *Hol.* 18 by!] ⟨nigh!⟩ *Hol.* 21 shadeful] ⟨in the⟩ *Hol.* 22 apples] poppies *Hol.* 25 your] ⟨the⟩ *Hol.* 27 Then] ⟨So⟩ *Hol.* 28 Can well be] ⟨We then will⟩ *Hol.*

AT MIDDLE-FIELD GATE. *Title* Middle-Field] ⟨Middle-Hill⟩ *Hol.*

Like silver buttons ranged in a row,
And as evenly spaced as if measured, although
They fall at the feeblest jog.

They load the leafless hedge hard by,
And the blades of last year's grass,
While the fallow ploughland turned up nigh
In raw rolls clammy and clogging lie—
Too clogging for feet to pass.

How dry it was on a far-back day
When straws hung the hedge and around,
When amid the sheaves in amorous play
In curtained bonnets and light array
Bloomed a bevy now underground!

Bockhampton Lane.

THE YOUTH WHO CARRIED A LIGHT

I saw him pass as the new day dawned,
Murmuring some musical phrase;
Horses were drinking and floundering in the pond,
And the tired stars thinned their gaze;
Yet these were not the spectacles at all that he conned,
But an inner one, giving out rays.

Such was the thing in his eye, walking there,
The very and visible thing,
A close light, displacing the gray of the morning air,
And the tokens that the dark was taking wing;
And was it not the radiance of a purpose rare
That might ripe to its accomplishing?

3 buttons] ⟨nail-heads⟩ *Hol.* ranged] set *MV17* 4 And as] ⟨As⟩ *Hol.* evenly] equally *MV17* 8 fallow ploughland] arable ridges *MV17* 9 raw rolls,] brown lines, *MV17* 11 far-back] ⟨certain⟩ *Hol.* 12 hung] draped *Hol.* 15 Bloomed] Moved *MV17*
Place om. Hol.

THE YOUTH. *Aberdeen University Review*, Feb. 1916
1 dawned,] ~ *Hol.* 8 very] real *AUR*

What became of that light? I wonder still its fate!
    Was it quenched ere its full apogee?
Did it struggle frail and frailer to a beam emaciate?
    Did it thrive till matured in verity?
Or did it travel on, to be a new young dreamer's freight,
    And thence on infinitely?

1915.

THE HEAD ABOVE THE FOG

    Something do I see
Above the fog that sheets the mead,
A figure like to life indeed,
Moving along with spectre-speed,
    Seen by none but me.

    O the vision keen!—
Tripping along to me for love
As in the flesh it used to move,
Only its hat and plume above
    The evening fog-fleece seen.

    In the day-fall wan,
When nighted birds break off their song,
Mere ghostly head it skims along,
Just as it did when warm and strong,
    Body seeming gone.

    Such it is I see
Above the fog that sheets the mead—
Yea, that which once could breathe and plead!—
Skimming along with spectre-speed
    To a last tryst with me.

14 ere its full] at its very *MV17*   17 ⟨Or did it pass elsewhere, to make a new young soul elate,⟩ *Hol.*
Date om. Hol., AUR

THE HEAD ABOVE THE FOG. 6 keen!—] ~, *MV17*   10 evening] filmy *MV17*   fog-fleece] fog-layer *Hol.*

OVERLOOKING THE RIVER STOUR*

The swallows flew in the curves of an eight
Above the river-gleam
In the wet June's last beam:
Like little crossbows animate
The swallows flew in the curves of an eight
Above the river-gleam.

Planing up shavings of crystal spray
A moor-hen darted out
From the bank thereabout,
And through the stream-shine ripped his way;
Planing up shavings of crystal spray
A moor-hen darted out.

Closed were the kingcups; and the mead
Dripped in monotonous green,
Though the day's morning sheen
Had shown it golden and honeybee'd;
Closed were the kingcups; and the mead
Dripped in monotonous green.

And never I turned my head, alack,
While these things met my gaze
Through the pane's drop-drenched glaze,
To see the more behind my back. . . .
O never I turned, but let, alack,
These less things hold my gaze!

THE MUSICAL BOX*

Lifelong to be
Seemed the fair colour of the time;
That there was standing shadowed near

OVERLOOKING THE RIVER STOUR. *Title* ⟨Overlooking the Stour⟩ *Hol.* *Headnote* ⟨(1877.)⟩ *Hol.*

1 curves] shape *Hol.* 5 curves] shape *Hol.* 7 of crystal] made of *MV17* 11 of crystal] made of *MV17* 16 golden] ⟨yellowed⟩ *Hol.*

A spirit who sang to the gentle chime
Of the self-struck notes, I did not hear,
        I did not see.

        Thus did it sing
To the mindless lyre that played indoors
As she came to listen for me without:
'O value what the nonce outpours—
This best of life—that shines about
        Your welcoming!'

        I had slowed along
After the torrid hours were done,
Though still the posts and walls and road
Flung back their sense of the hot-faced sun,
And had walked by Stourside Mill, where broad
        Stream-lilies throng.

        And I descried
The dusky house that stood apart,
And her, white-muslined, waiting there
In the porch with high-expectant heart,
While still the thin mechanic air
        Went on inside.

        At whiles would flit
Swart bats, whose wings, be-webbed and tanned,
Whirred like the wheels of ancient clocks:
She laughed a hailing as she scanned
Me in the gloom, the tuneful box
        Intoning it.

        Lifelong to be
I thought it. That there watched hard by

THE MUSICAL BOX. 8 lyre] ⟨shape⟩ *Hol.* 9 me] ⟨us⟩ *Hol.* 13 I] ⟨We⟩ *Hol.* 17 had] ⟨we⟩ *Hol.* Stourside Mill,] way of the mill, *Hol.* 19 I] ⟨we⟩ *Hol.* 26 ⟨Swart bats whose webbed and skinny vans⟩ ⟨Swart bats whose clammy wings and tanned,⟩ *Hol.* 27 wheels] fly *MV17* 28 a] ⟨her⟩ *Hol.* 29 Me] ⟨Us⟩ *Hol.*

A spirit who sang to the indoor tune,
'O make the most of what is nigh!'
I did not hear in my dull soul-swoon—
I did not see.

ON STURMINSTER FOOT-BRIDGE*

(Onomatopoeic)

Reticulations creep upon the slack stream's face
When the wind skims irritably past,
The current clucks smartly into each hollow place
That years of flood have scrabbled in the pier's sodden base;
The floating-lily leaves rot fast.

On a roof stand the swallows ranged in wistful waiting rows,
Till they arrow off and drop like stones
Among the eyot-withies at whose foot the river flows;
And beneath the roof is she who in the dark world shows
As a lattice-gleam when midnight moans.

ROYAL SPONSORS*

'The king and the queen will stand to the child;
'Twill be handed down in song;
And it's no more than their deserving,
With my lord so faithful at Court so long,
And so staunch and strong.

33 tune,] ~ *Hol.*

ON STURMINSTER FOOT-BRIDGE. *Title* On Stourcastle Foot-bridge *Hol.* *Headnote CP23*] 〈(1877.)〉 *Hol.*
5 floating-lily] 〈waterlily〉 *Hol.* 6 ranged in wistful waiting rows,] equidistantly in rows, *MV17* 8 foot] roots *MV17* 9 in the] 〈in a〉 *Hol.* 10 As a lattice-gleam] 〈Like a white light〉 As a lamp-light *Hol.*

ROYAL SPONSORS. 3 deserving,] ~ *Hol.* 5 staunch] 〈stout〉 *Hol.*

'O never before was known such a thing!
'Twill be a grand time for all;
And the beef will be a whole-roast bullock,
And the servants will have a feast in the hall,
And the ladies a ball.

'While from Jordan's stream by a traveller,
In a flagon of silver wrought,
And by caravan, stage-coach, wain, and waggon
A precious trickle has been brought,
Clear as when caught.'

The morning came. To the park of the peer
The royal couple bore;
And the font was filled with the Jordan water,
And the household awaited their guests before
The carpeted door.

But when they went to the silk-lined cot
The child was found to have died.
'What's now to be done? We can disappoint not
The king and queen!' the family cried
With eyes spread wide.

'Even now they approach the chestnut-drive!
The service must be read.'
'Well, since we can't christen the child alive,
By God we shall have to christen him dead!'
The marquis said.

Thus, breath-forsaken, a corpse was taken
To the private chapel—yea—

8 whole-roast] whole-roasted *MV17* 11 ⟨While on Jordan's banks a traveller,⟩ *Hol.* 12 ⟨The clearest trickle has sought,⟩ *Hol.* 14 ⟨A dip from the precious trickle has brought,⟩ *Hol.* 15 Clear] ⟨Cool⟩ *Hol.* 19 awaited] ⟨waited⟩ *Hol.* 21 silk-lined] ⟨quaint oak⟩ *Hol.* 23 We can disappoint not] ⟨How shall disappoint we⟩ *Hol.* 24 queen!'] ~?" *Hol.* 26 chestnut-drive!] ~!⟨"⟩— *Hol.* 27 The] ⟨"⟩The *Hol.* read.'] ~, *Hol.* 28 'Well,] ⟨And⟩ *Hol.* alive,] ⟨alive, why⟩ *Hol.*

And the king knew not, nor the queen, God wot,
That they answered for one returned to clay
At the font that day.

OLD FURNITURE*

I know not how it may be with others
Who sit amid relics of householdry
That date from the days of their mothers' mothers,
But well I know how it is with me
Continually.

I see the hands of the generations
That owned each shiny familiar thing
In play on its knobs and indentations,
And with its ancient fashioning
Still dallying:

Hands behind hands, growing paler and paler,
As in a mirror a candle-flame
Shows images of itself, each frailer
As it recedes, though the eye may frame
Its shape the same.

On the clock's dull dial a foggy finger,
Moving to set the minutes right
With tentative touches that lift and linger
In the wont of a moth on a summer night,
Creeps to my sight.

On this old viol, too, fingers are dancing—
As whilom—just over the strings by the nut,

33 king] ⟨queen⟩ *Hol.* not,] ~ *Hol.*

OLD FURNITURE. 1 I know not] I don't know *Hol.* 16 finger,] ~ *Hol.* 19 wont] way *Hol.* night,] ~ *Hol.* 20 to] on *MV17* 22 ⟨Over the strings below the nut,⟩ My father's—just over the strings by the nut, *Hol.*

The tip of a bow receding, advancing
In airy quivers, as if it would cut
The plaintive gut.

And I see a face by that box for tinder,
Glowing forth in fits from the dark,
And fading again, as the linten cinder
Kindles to red at the flinty spark,
Or goes out stark.

Well, well. It is best to be up and doing,
The world has no use for one to-day
Who eyes things thus—no aim pursuing!
He should not continue in this stay,
But sink away.

A THOUGHT IN TWO MOODS*

I saw it—pink and white—revealed
Upon the white and green;
The white and green was a daisied field,
The pink and white Ethleen.

And as I looked it seemed in kind
That difference they had none;
The two fair bodiments combined
As varied miens of one.

23 a] ⟨a⟩ his *Hol.* 25 plaintive] ⟨plaintive⟩ plaining *Hol.*
26–30 ⟨And⟩ From each curled eff-hole the ghosts of ditties
Incanted there by his skill in his prime
Quaver in whispers the pangs and pities
They once could language, and in their time
Would daily chime. *Hol.*
31 best] ⟨time⟩ *Hol.* be up and doing,] ⟨up and be doing,⟩ *Hol.* 32 world has] ⟨world's⟩ *Hol.* 34 not continue] ⟨cease continuing⟩ ⟨continue not⟩ *Hol.* 35 But] ⟨And⟩ *Hol.*

A THOUGHT IN TWO MOODS. *Title* ⟨One Thought in Two Moods⟩ *Hol.*
4 Ethleen.] my queen. *Hol.* 7 bodiments] spectacles *Hol.* 8 ⟨Mosaic-like in one.⟩ As corporate parts of one. *Hol.*

A sense that, in some mouldering year,
  As one they both would lie,
Made me move quickly on to her
  To pass the pale thought by.

She laughed and said: 'Out there, to me,
  You looked so weather-browned,
And brown in clothes, you seemed to be
  Made of the dusty ground!'

THE LAST PERFORMANCE*

'I am playing my oldest tunes,' declared she,
    'All the old tunes I know,—
Those I learnt ever so long ago.'
—Why she should think just then she'd play them
    Silence cloaks like snow.

When I returned from the town at nightfall
    Notes continued to pour
As when I had left two hours before:
'It's the very last time,' she said in closing;
    'From now I play no more.'

A few morns onward found her fading,
    And, as her life outflew,
I thought of her playing her tunes right through;
And I felt she had known of what was coming,
    And wondered how she knew.

1912.

9 ⟨A prescience that, in some far year,⟩ *Hol.* 10 To one they would be wrought, *Hol.* 12 To kill the pallid thought. *Hol.* 15 brown in clothes,] ⟨stood so still,⟩ *Hol.* 16 ground!'] ~." *Hol.*

THE LAST PERFORMANCE. 7 Notes] ⟨Her notes⟩ *Hol.* 9 closing;] ⟨pausing;⟩ *Hol.* 11 fading,] dying, *Hol.* 13 ⟨I thought of the tunes she had played right through;⟩ ⟨I thought of how she had played right through;⟩ I thought of her playing her repertory through; *Hol.* 14 felt] ⟨saw⟩ *Hol.*
Date ⟨From old notes, 1912.⟩ *Hol.*

'YOU ON THE TOWER'

I

'You on the tower of my factory—
What do you see up there?
Do you see Enjoyment with wide wings
Advancing to reach me here?'
—'Yea; I see Enjoyment with wide wings
Advancing to reach you here.'

II

'Good. Soon I'll come and ask you
To tell me again thereon. . . .
Well, what is he doing now? Hoi, there!'
—'He still is flying on.'
'Ah, waiting till I have full-finished.
Good. Tell me again anon. . . .

III

'Hoi, Watchman! I'm here. When comes he?
Between my sweats I am chill.'
—'Oh, you there, working still?
Why, surely he reached you a time back,
And took you miles from your mill?
He duly came in his winging,
And now he has passed out of view.
How can it be that you missed him?
He brushed you by as he flew.'

THE INTERLOPER*

'And I saw the figure and visage of Madness seeking for a home.'

There are three folk driving in a quaint old chaise,
And the cliff-side track looks green and fair;

'YOU ON THE TOWER'. 2 there?] ~?⟨"⟩ *Hol.* 5 —'Yea;] ~— *Hol.* 11 'Ah,] "Ah— *Hol.* 15 working] asking *MV17*

THE INTERLOPER. *Subtitle* ⟨One who ought not to be there.⟩ *Hol.* *Epigraph CP23* 1 quaint old chaise,] ⟨basket-chaise,⟩ *Hol.* 2 green] ⟨quaint⟩ *Hol.*

I view them talking in quiet glee
As they drop down towards the puffins' lair
By the roughest of ways;
But another with the three rides on, I see,
Whom I like not to be there!

No: it's not anybody you think of. Next
A dwelling appears by a slow sweet stream
Where two sit happy and half in the dark:
They read, helped out by a frail-wick'd gleam,
Some rhythmic text;
But one sits with them whom they don't mark,
One I'm wishing could not be there.

No: not whom you knew and name. And now
I discern gay diners in a mansion-place,
And the guests dropping wit—pert, prim, or choice,
And the hostess's tender and laughing face,
And the host's bland brow;
But I cannot help hearing a hollow voice,
And I'd fain not hear it there.

No: it's not from the stranger you met once. Ah,
Yet a goodlier scene than that succeeds;
People on a lawn—quite a crowd of them. Yes,
And they chatter and ramble as fancy leads;
And they say, 'Hurrah!'
To a blithe speech made; save one, mirthless,
Who ought not to be there.

3 view] see *Hol.* 6 But] ⟨And⟩ *Hol.* 7 Whom I like] ⟨One who ought⟩ *Hol.* there!] ~. *Hol.* 11 frail-wick'd gleam,] candle-gleam, *Hol.* 13 But] ⟨And⟩ *Hol.* 15 ⟨No: it's not the one you knew and name.⟩ No: it's not one you knew and name. And now *Hol.* 17 ⟨And the guests dropping wit in a friendly voice,⟩ *Hol.* pert,] ⟨petty,⟩ *Hol.* 20 voice,] ⟨noise,⟩ *Hol.* 22 stranger] person *Hol.* 23 Yet a] ⟨An even⟩ *Hol.* 25 ramble as] ramble ⟨round about⟩ as *Hol.* 27 mirthless,] shadowless, *MV17*; unwatched, *MV19* 28 Who] ⟨One who⟩ *Hol.*

Nay: it's not the pale Form your imagings raise,
That waits on us all at a destined time,
It is not the Fourth Figure the Furnace showed;
O that it were such a shape sublime
In these latter days!
It is that under which best lives corrode;
Would, would it could not be there!

LOGS ON THE HEARTH*

A Memory of a Sister

The fire advances along the log
Of the tree we felled,
Which bloomed and bore striped apples by the peck
Till its last hour of bearing knelled.

The fork that first my hand would reach
And then my foot
In climbings upward inch by inch, lies now
Sawn, sapless, darkening with soot.

Where the bark chars is where, one year,
It was pruned, and bled—
Then overgrew the wound. But now, at last,
Its growings all have stagnated.

My fellow-climber rises dim
From her chilly grave—
Just as she was, her foot near mine on the bending limb,
Laughing, her young brown hand awave.

December 1915.

29 ⟨No; it's not the pale figure your imaging draws,⟩ *Hol.* Nay:] No; *Hol.* Form] *l.c. Hol.* 30 ⟨That waits upon us all at a late or early time,⟩ *Hol.* 31 Fourth Figure] ⟨gaunt shape⟩ *Hol.* 32 ⟨In especial when they falter past their prime,⟩ *Hol.* 34 best] ⟨men's⟩ *Hol.*

LOGS ON THE HEARTH. *Headnote om. MV17*
2 felled,] ~⟨—⟩ *Hol.*; ~ *MV17* 2a, 6a, 10a, 14a ⟨Ah, the time O!—⟩ That time O!— *Hol.*; That time O!— *MV17* 3 Which bloomed] ⟨That grew⟩ *Hol.* 10 bled—] ~⟨,⟩— *Hol.*

THE SUNSHADE

Ah—it's the skeleton of a lady's sunshade,
  Here at my feet in the hard rock's chink,
  Merely a naked sheaf of wires!—
  Twenty years have gone with their livers and diers
  Since it was silked in its white or pink.

Noonshine riddles the ribs of the sunshade,
  No more a screen from the weakest ray;
  Nothing to tell us the hue of its dyes,
  Nothing but rusty bones as it lies
  In its coffin of stone, unseen till to-day.

Where is the woman who carried that sunshade
  Up and down this seaside place?—
  Little thumb standing against its stem,
  Thoughts perhaps bent on a love-stratagem,
  Softening yet more the already soft face!

Is the fair woman who carried that sunshade
  A skeleton just as her property is,
  Laid in the chink that none may scan?
  And does she regret—if regret dust can—
  The vain things thought when she flourished this?

Swanage Cliffs.

THE AGEING HOUSE

When the walls were red
That now are seen
To be overspread
With a mouldy green,

THE SUNSHADE. 3 a naked] a ⟨bare⟩ naked *Hol.* 11 sunshade] ~⟨?⟩ *Hol.* 12 ⟨Where is the hand that held it in place?—⟩ *Hol.* this seaside] this ⟨gay⟩ seaside *Hol.* 13 stem,] ~— *Hol.* 14 love-stratagem,] ~— *Hol.* 15 face!] ~? *Hol.* 16 the fair] not the *MV17* 18 Laid] ⟨Lying⟩ *Hol.* *Place Swanage. Hol.*

A fresh fair head
Would often lean
From the sunny casement
And scan the scene,
While blithely spoke the wind to the little sycamore tree.

But storms have raged
Those walls about,
And the head has aged
That once looked out;
And zest is suaged
And trust grows doubt,
And slow effacement
Is rife throughout,
While fiercely girds the wind at the long-limbed sycamore tree!

THE CAGED GOLDFINCH

Within a churchyard, on a recent grave,
I saw a little cage
That jailed a goldfinch. All was silence save
Its hops from stage to stage.

There was inquiry in its wistful eye,
And once it tried to sing;
Of him or her who placed it there, and why,
No one knew anything.

THE AGEING HOUSE. 9 to] in *Hol.* the little sycamore] the sycamore *MV17* 15 grows] is *MV* 17 Is rife] Proceeds *MV17* throughout,] ~ *Hol.* 18 the long-limbed sycamore] the sycamore *MV17* tree!] ~. *Hol.*

THE CAGED GOLDFINCH. 3 jailed] prisoned *Hol.*
8a–d True, a woman was found drowned the day ensuing,
And some at times averred
The grave to be her false one's, who when wooing
Gave her the bird. *MV17*
(*Hol.* = *MV17 except* 8a True,] But *Hol.*)

AT MADAME TUSSAUD'S IN VICTORIAN YEARS

'That same first fiddler who leads the orchéstra to-night
Here fiddled four decades of years ago;
He bears the same babe-like smile of self-centred delight,
Same trinket on watch-chain, same ring on the hand with the bow.

'But his face, if regarded, is woefully wanner, and drier,
And his once dark beard has grown straggling and gray;
Yet a blissful existence he seems to have led with his lyre,
In a trance of his own, where no wearing or tearing had sway.

'Mid these wax figures, who nothing can do, it may seem
That to do but a little thing counts a great deal;
To be watched by kings, councillors, queens, may be flattering to him—
With their glass eyes longing they too could wake notes that appeal.'

. . . .

Ah, but he played staunchly—that fiddler—whoever he was,
With the innocent heart and the soul-touching string:
May he find the Fair Haven! For did he not smile with good cause?
Yes; gamuts that graced forty years'-flight were not a small thing!

AT MADAME TUSSAUD'S. *Title* ⟨At Madame Tussaud's and later⟩ At Madame Tussaud's in Victorian Times *Hol.*
2 four decades of years] a quarter of a century *Hol.* 3 bears] wears *Hol.*
5 "But to come to the flesh. It is wanner, more ploughshared, and drier, *Hol.*
6 has grown straggling and gray;] ⟨is gone ashen and gray;⟩ has grown whited and stray; *Hol.* 7 led] had *MV17* 8 where no] ⟨from which all⟩ *Hol.* 12 As if they wished *they* could make notes that sigh, wail, and appeal." *Hol.* they too] that they *MV17* 13 staunchly—] well— *Hol.*
16 Yea; what he gave forth forty seasons was not a small thing! *Hol.*

THE BALLET

They crush together—a rustling heap of flesh—
Of more than flesh, a heap of souls; and then
They part, enmesh,
And crush together again,
Like the pink petals of a too sanguine rose
Frightened shut just when it blows.

Though all alike in their tinsel livery,
And indistinguishable at a sweeping glance,
They muster, maybe,
As lives wide in irrelevance;
A world of her own has each one underneath,
Detached as a sword from its sheath.

Daughters, wives, mistresses; honest or false, sold, bought;
Hearts of all sizes; gay, fond, gushing, or penned,
Various in thought
Of lover, rival, friend;
Links in a one-pulsed chain, all showing one smile,
Yet severed so many a mile!

THE FIVE STUDENTS*

The sparrow dips in his wheel-rut bath,
The sun grows passionate-eyed,
And boils the dew to smoke by the paddock-path;
As strenuously we stride,—
Five of us; dark He, fair He, dark She, fair She, I,
All beating by.

THE BALLET. 2 souls;] ⟨hearts;⟩ *Hol.* 5 too sanguine rose] ⟨quick-opened rose,⟩ sanguine rose *Hol.* 9 muster,] ⟨enmix,⟩ *Hol.* 10 ⟨London, America, France;⟩ *Hol.* 12 Detached] ⟨Distant⟩ *Hol.* 13 honest or false, sold, bought;] ⟨honest, wronged, subtle, sold;⟩ *Hol.* 17 a one-pulsed] ⟨one snake-like⟩ one serpentine *Hol.*; a one-impulsed *MV17*

THE FIVE STUDENTS. 3 smoke] ⟨smoke⟩ fumes *Hol.* 4 strenuously] ⟨stoutly on⟩ *Hol.*

The air is shaken, the high-road hot,
Shadowless swoons the day,
The greens are sobered and cattle at rest; but not
We on our urgent way,—
Four of us; fair She, dark She, fair He, I are there,
But one—elsewhere.

Autumn moulds the hard fruit mellow,
And forward still we press
Through moors, briar-meshed plantations, clay-pits yellow,
As in the spring hours—yes,
Three of us; fair He, fair She, I, as heretofore,
But—fallen one more.

The leaf drops: earthworms draw it in
At night-time noiselessly,
The fingers of birch and beech are skeleton-thin,
And yet on the beat are we,—
Two of us; fair She, I. But no more left to go
The track we know.

Icicles tag the church-aisle leads,
The flag-rope gibbers hoarse,
The home-bound foot-folk wrap their snow-flaked heads,
Yet I still stalk the course,—
One of us. . . . Dark and fair He, dark and fair She, gone:
The rest—anon.

9 sobered] darkened *MV17* 12 But] ⟨And⟩ *Hol.* 21 skeleton-thin,] ⟨filigree-thin,⟩ *Hol.* 30 ⟨The rest—anon.⟩ Somewhither yon. *Hol.*

30a–l

And what do they say in that yon Pale Land
Who trod the track with me,
If there they dwell, and watch, and understand?
They murmur, it may be,
"All of us—how we strode, as still does that lean thrall
For nought at all!"

The Years may add: "Peace; know ye not,
Life's ashy track hence eyeing,
That though gilt Vanity called your eyes somewhat,
And ye were torn in trying,
All of you, while you panted, saw aureola'd far
Heaven's central star?" *Hol.*

THE WIND'S PROPHECY*

I travel on by barren farms,
And gulls glint out like silver flecks
Against a cloud that speaks of wrecks,
And bellies down with black alarms.
I say: 'Thus from my lady's arms
I go; those arms I love the best!'
The wind replies from dip and rise,
'Nay; toward her arms thou journeyest.'

A distant verge morosely gray
Appears, while clots of flying foam
Break from its muddy monochrome,
And a light blinks up far away.
I sigh: 'My eyes now as all day
Behold her ebon loops of hair!'
Like bursting bonds the wind responds,
'Nay, wait for tresses flashing fair!'

From tides the lofty coastlines screen
Come smitings like the slam of doors,
Or hammerings on hollow floors,
As the swell cleaves through caves unseen.
Say I: 'Though broad this wild terrene,
Her city home is matched of none!'
From the hoarse skies the wind replies:
'Thou shouldst have said her sea-bord one.'

The all-prevailing clouds exclude
The one quick timorous transient star;
The waves outside where breakers are
Huzza like a mad multitude.

THE WIND'S PROPHECY. 2 glint] shine *Hol.* 4 black alarms.] ⟨threatening storms.⟩ *Hol.* 7 dip] vale *Hol.* 8 journeyest.'] ~⟨!⟩." *Hol.* 13 all day] ⟨alway⟩ *Hol.* 14 loops] locks *Hol.* 17 coastlines *WE*] ⟨coast-cliffs⟩ *Hol.*; coastlands *Hol.*, *MV*, *CP* 18 smitings] noises *Hol.* 20 cleaves through] dives up *Hol.* 21 ⟨Say I: "Though far from her I have been,⟩ *Hol.* wild terrene,] royal mesne, *Hol.* 23 hoarse] loud *Hol.* replies:] ~; *Hol.* 24 'Thou shouldst have said] ⟨"Thy meaning is⟩ *Hol.*

'Where the sun ups it, mist-imbued,'
I cry, 'there reigns the star for me!'
The wind outshrieks from points and peaks:
'Here, westward, where it downs, mean ye!'

Yonder the headland, vulturine,
Snores like old Skrymer in his sleep,
And every chasm and every steep
Blackens as wakes each pharos-shine.
'I roam, but one is safely mine,'
I say. 'God grant she stay my own!'
Low laughs the wind as if it grinned:
'Thy Love is one thou'st not yet known.'

Rewritten from an old copy.

DURING WIND AND RAIN

They sing their dearest songs—
He, she, all of them—yea,
Treble and tenor and bass,
  And one to play;
With the candles mooning each face. . . .
  Ah, no; the years O!
How the sick leaves reel down in throngs!

They clear the creeping moss—
Elders and juniors—aye,
Making the pathways neat
  And the garden gay;

29 ups it] rises *Hol.* mist-imbued,'] ⟨silver-hued,"⟩ *Hol.* 30 reigns] shines *Hol.* 32 downs,] sets, *Hol.* ye!'] ~." *Hol.* 34 old Skrymer] a giant *MV17* 36 Blackens as ⟨spreads the⟩ wakes each lighthouse-shine. *Hol.* 37 roam,] ⟨stray,⟩ *Hol.* mine,'] ~⟨!⟩," *Hol.* 38 stay] ⟨stand⟩ *Hol.* 40 thou'st] ⟨thou hast⟩ *Hol.*
Tailnote ⟨Rewritten from old notes.⟩ *Hol.*

DURING WIND AND RAIN. 2 —yea,] —yea *Hol.* 7 How the sick leaves reel] ⟨The sickened leaves drop⟩ *Hol.* 9 aye,] yea, *MV17* 10 Making] ⟨Shaping⟩ *Hol.*

And they build a shady seat. . . .
  Ah, no; the years, the years;
See, the white storm-birds wing across.

They are blithely breakfasting all—
Men and maidens—yea,
Under the summer tree,
  With a glimpse of the bay,
While pet fowl come to the knee. . . .
  Ah, no; the years O!
And the rotten rose is ript from the wall.

They change to a high new house,
He, she, all of them—aye,
Clocks and carpets and chairs
  On the lawn all day,
And brightest things that are theirs. . . .
  Ah, no; the years, the years;
Down their carved names the rain-drop ploughs.

HE PREFERS HER EARTHLY

This after-sunset is a sight for seeing,
Cliff-heads of craggy cloud surrounding it.
  —And dwell you in that glory-show?
You may; for there are strange strange things in being,
    Stranger than I know.

Yet if that chasm of splendour claim your presence
Which glows between the ash cloud and the dun,
  How changed must be your mortal mould!
Changed to a firmament-riding earthless essence
    From what you were of old:

13 Ah, no; the years O! *MV17*   14 See, the] ⟨The⟩ ⟨How the⟩ *Hol.* the white *CP23*] the webbed white *MV*, *CP19*, *WE*   across.] ~⟨!⟩. *Hol.* 19 fowl] birds *MV17*   21 And the] ⟨And the⟩ ⟨The⟩ *Hol.*   And the wind-whipt creeper lets go the wall. *Hol.*   23 aye,] yea, *MV17*   27 Ah, no; the years O! *MV17*   28 ⟨On their chiselled names the lichen grows.⟩ *Hol.* carved *CP23*] chiselled *MV*, *CP19*, *WE*

HE PREFERS HER EARTHLY. *Title* He prefers the earthly *Hol.*

All too unlike the fond and fragile creature
Then known to me. . . . Well, shall I say it plain?
I would not have you thus and there,
But still would grieve on, missing you, still feature
You as the one you were.

THE DOLLS

'Whenever you dress me dolls, mammy,
Why do you dress them so,
And make them gallant soldiers,
When never a one I know;
And not as gentle ladies
With frills and frocks and curls,
As people dress the dollies
Of other little girls?'

Ah—why did she not answer:—
'Because your mammy's heed
Is always gallant soldiers,
As well may be, indeed.
One of them was your daddy,
His name I must not tell;
He's not the dad who lives here,
But one I love too well.'

MOLLY GONE*

No more summer for Molly and me;
There is snow on the tree,
And the blackbirds plump large as the rooks are, almost,
And the water is hard
Where they used to dip bills at the dawn ere her figure was lost
To these coasts, now my prison close-barred.

THE DOLLS. 4 know;] ~, *Hol.*

MOLLY GONE. 1 me;] ~, *Hol.* 2 tree,] ~ *Hol.* 3 plump] seem *Hol.* 5 at] in *Hol.* 6 my] a *Hol.*

No more planting by Molly and me
Where the beds used to be
Of sweet-william; no training the clambering rose
By the framework of fir
Now bowering the pathway, whereon it swings gaily and blows
As if calling commendment from her.

No more jauntings by Molly and me
To the town by the sea,
Or along over Whitesheet to Wynyard's green Gap,
Catching Montacute Crest
To the right against Sedgmoor, and Corton-Hill's far-distant cap,
And Pilsdon and Lewsdon to west.

No more singing by Molly to me
In the evenings when she
Was in mood and in voice, and the candles were lit,
And past the porch-quoin
The rays would spring out on the laurels; and dumbledores hit
On the pane, as if wishing to join.

Where, then, is Molly, who's no more with me?
—As I stand on this lea,
Thinking thus, there's a many-flamed star in the air,
That tosses a sign
That her glance is regarding its face from her home, so that there
Her eyes may have meetings with mine.

13 jauntings] ⟨outings⟩ *Hol.* 22 ⟨And I stood by the quoin,⟩ *Hol.* 23 The rays] ⟨And the rays⟩ *Hol.* spring] shine *MV17* 27 many-flamed] many-rayed *MV17* 28 tosses] twinkles *Hol.*; flickers *MV17* 29 home,] ⟨nook,⟩ *Hol.*

A BACKWARD SPRING

The trees are afraid to put forth buds,
And there is timidity in the grass;
The plots lie gray where gouged by spuds,
    And whether next week will pass
Free of sly sour winds is the fret of each bush
    Of barberry waiting to bloom.

Yet the snowdrop's face betrays no gloom,
And the primrose pants in its heedless push,
Though the myrtle asks if it's worth the fight
    This year with frost and rime
    To venture one more time
On delicate leaves and buttons of white
From the selfsame bough as at last year's prime,
And never to ruminate on or remember
What happened to it in mid-December.

April 1917.

LOOKING ACROSS*

I

It is dark in the sky,
And silence is where
Our laughs rang high;
And recall do I
That One is out there.

II

The dawn is not nigh,
And the trees are bare,
And the waterways sigh
That a year has drawn by,
And Two are out there.

A BACKWARD SPRING. 3 gouged] broken *MV17* 12 buttons] buds *MV17*

LOOKING ACROSS. 3 We said Good-bye; *MV17* 9 drawn] gone *Hol.*

III

The wind drops to die
Like the phantom of Care
Too frail for a cry,
And heart brings to eye
That Three are out there.

IV

This Life runs dry
That once ran rare
And rosy in dye,
And fleet the days fly,
And Four are out there.

V

Tired, tired am I
Of this earthly air,
And my wraith asks: Why,
Since these calm lie,
Are not Five out there?

December 1915.

AT A SEASIDE TOWN IN 1869*

(Young Lover's Reverie)

I went and stood outside myself,
    Spelled the dark sky
    And ship-lights nigh,
And grumbling winds that passed thereby.

Then next inside myself I looked,
    And there, above
    All, shone my Love,
That nothing matched the image of.

14 And it's in my mind's eye *MV17* 19 fleet] quick *Hol.* 23 asks:] ~; *Hol.* 24 Since these have passed by, *MV17* calm *ME*, *CP23*] calmly *MV19*, *CP19*, *WE*

AT A SEASIDE TOWN. *Title* At a Seaside Town, 1869 *Hol.*

Beyond myself again I ranged;
  And saw the free
  Life by the sea,
And folk indifferent to me.

O 'twas a charm to draw within
  Thereafter, where
  But she was; care
For one thing only, her hid there!

But so it chanced, without myself
  I had to look,
  And then I took
More heed of what I had long forsook:

The boats, the sands, the esplanade,
  The laughing crowd;
  Light-hearted, loud
Greetings from some not ill-endowed;

The evening sunlit cliffs, the talk,
  Hailings and halts,
  The keen sea-salts,
The band, the Morgenblätter Waltz.

Still, when at night I drew inside
  Forward she came,
  Sad, but the same
As when I first had known her name.

Then rose a time when, as by force,
  Outwardly wooed
  By contacts crude,
Her image in abeyance stood. . . .

9 Beyond] ⟨Without⟩ *Hol.* ranged;] went; *Hol.* 10 ⟨Again to see⟩ *Hol.* 13 draw] go *Hol.* 17 without] ⟨outside⟩ *Hol.* 20 forsook:] ~. *Hol.*, *MV* 24 ill-endowed;] ~: *Hol.*, *MV* 28 Morgenblätter] *italics, cancelled Hol.* Waltz.] *l.c. Hol.* 32 name.] ~⟨!⟩. *Hol.* 33 force,] ~ *Hol.*

At last I said: This outside life
　　Shall not endure;
　　I'll seek the pure
Thought-world, and bask in her allure.

Myself again I crept within,
　　Scanned with keen care
　　The temple where
She'd shone, but could not find her there.

I sought and sought. But O her soul
　　Has not since thrown
　　Upon my own
One beam! Yea, she is gone, is gone.

From an old note.

THE GLIMPSE*

She sped through the door
And, following in haste,
And stirred to the core,
I entered hot-faced;
But I could not find her,
No sign was behind her.
'Where is she?' I said:
—'Who?' they asked that sat there;
'Not a soul's come in sight.'
—'A maid with red hair.'
—'Ah.' They paled. 'She is dead.
People see her at night,
But you are the first
On whom she has burst
In the keen common light.'

41 crept] went *Hol.* 42 keen] ⟨much⟩ *Hol.* 44 shone,] ⟨been,⟩ *Hol.* 48 beam!] ⟨shine!⟩ beam. *Hol.*

THE GLIMPSE. 11 dead.] ~. . . . *MV17*

It was ages ago,
When I was quite strong:
I have waited since,—O,
I have waited so long!
—Yea, I set me to own
The house, where now lone
I dwell in void rooms
Booming hollow as tombs!
But I never come near her,
Though nightly I hear her.
And my cheek has grown thin
And my hair has grown gray
With this waiting therein;
But she still keeps away!

THE PEDESTRIAN*

An Incident of 1883

'Sir, will you let me give you a ride?
Nox venit, and the heath is wide.'
—My phaeton-lantern shone on one
    Young, fair, even fresh,
    But burdened with flesh:
A leathern satchel at his side,
His breathings short, his coat undone.

'Twas as if his corpulent figure slopped
With the shake of his walking when he stopped,
And, though the night's pinch grew acute,
    He wore but a thin
    Wind-thridded suit,
Yet well-shaped shoes for walking in,
Artistic beaver, cane gold-topped.

22 ⟨In the empty rooms⟩ *Hol.* 26 And] ⟨Till⟩ *Hol.* 28 ⟨For her coming again⟩ *Hol.*

THE PEDESTRIAN. 2 The night gets dense, the heath is wide." *MV17* 3 phaeton-lantern] ⟨waggon-lantern⟩ *Hol.* 5 flesh:] ~; *Hol.* 8 'Twas] ⟨It seem⟩ *Hol.* 12 Wind-thridded] Alpaca *Hol.* 14 beaver,] garments, *MV17*

'Alas, my friend,' he said with a smile,
'I am daily bound to foot ten mile—
Wet, dry, or dark—before I rest.
        Six months to live
        My doctors give
Me as my prospect here, at best,
Unless I vamp my sturdiest!'

His voice was that of a man refined,
A man, one well could feel, of mind,
Quite winning in its musical ease;
        But in mould maligned
        By some disease;
And I asked again. But he shook his head;
Then, as if more were due, he said:—

'A student was I—of Schopenhauer,
Kant, Hegel,—and the fountained bower
Of the Muses, too, knew my regard:
        But ah—I fear me
        The grave gapes near me! . . .
Would I could this gross sheath discard,
And rise an ethereal shape, unmarred!'

How I remember him!—his short breath,
His aspect, marked for early death,
As he dropped into the night for ever;
        One caught in his prime
        Of high endeavour;
From all philosophies soon to sever
Through an unconscienced trick of Time!

16 foot] walk *Hol.* 24 ease;] ~, *Hol.* 25 But in mould] ⟨In form⟩ But in form *Hol.* 27 And I asked again.] ⟨I asked once more.⟩ *Hol.* 28 ⟨At my further proffers. "No," he said.⟩ And, as if more were due, then said:— *Hol.* 30 fountained] rosier *Hol.* 34 sheath] ⟨flesh⟩ *Hol.* 42 ⟨Under some scurvy trick of Time!⟩ *Hol.*

'WHO'S IN THE NEXT ROOM?'

'Who's in the next room?—who?
I seemed to see
Somebody in the dawning passing through,
Unknown to me.'
'Nay: you saw nought. He passed invisibly.'

'Who's in the next room?—who?
I seem to hear
Somebody muttering firm in a language new
That chills the ear.'
'No: you catch not his tongue who has entered there.'

'Who's in the next room?—who?
I seem to feel
His breath like a clammy draught, as if it drew
From the Polar Wheel.'
'No: none who breathes at all does the door conceal.'

'Who's in the next room?—who?
A figure wan
With a message to one in there of something due?
Shall I know him anon?'
'Yea he; and he brought such; and you'll know him anon.'

AT A COUNTRY FAIR*

At a bygone Western country fair
I saw a giant led by a dwarf
With a red string like a long thin scarf;
How much he was the stronger there
The giant seemed unaware.

And then I saw that the giant was blind,
And the dwarf a shrewd-eyed little thing;

The giant, mild, timid, obeyed the string
As if he had no independent mind,
Or will of any kind.

Wherever the dwarf decided to go
At his heels the other trotted meekly,
(Perhaps—I know not—reproaching weakly)
Like one Fate bade that it must be so,
Whether he wished or no.

Various sights in various climes
I have seen, and more I may see yet,
But that sight never shall I forget,
And have thought it the sorriest of pantomimes,
If once, a hundred times!

THE MEMORIAL BRASS: 186–

'Why do you weep there, O sweet lady,
Why do you weep before that brass?—
(I'm a mere student sketching the mediaeval)
Is some late death lined there, alas?—
Your father's? . . . Well, all pay the debt that paid he!'

'Young man, O must I tell!—My husband's! And under
His name I set mine, and my *death*!—
Its date left vacant till my heirs should fill it,
Stating me faithful till my last breath.'
—'Madam, that you are a widow wakes my wonder!'

AT A COUNTRY FAIR. 8 mild, timid,] ⟨mild, and timid,⟩ *Hol.* 13 ⟨(Perhaps—though I know not—reproaching meekly)⟩ *Hol.* 14 ⟨Like one to whom Fate said: It must be so,⟩ *Hol.* it] *cap. Hol.* 15 ⟨Whether you wsh or no.⟩ *Hol.* 19 sorriest] ⟨sorest⟩ *Hol.*

THE MEMORIAL BRASS. 3 student] ⟨architect⟩ *Hol.* 4 Is] —Is *Hol.* lined] ⟨writ⟩ *Hol.* 6 And under] ⟨Under⟩ *Hol.* 7 *death*!—] ∼— *Hol.* 8 Its] ⟨The⟩ *Hol.* it,] ∼ *Hol.* 9 As his grieved widow's, at my last breath." *Hol.* faithful] his *MV17*

'O wait! For last month I—re-married!
    And now I fear 'twas a deed amiss.
We've just come home. And I am sick and saddened
    At what the new one will say to this;
And will he think—think that I should have tarried?

    'I may add, surely,—with no wish to harm him—
    That he's a temper—yes, I fear!
And when he comes to church next Sunday morning,
    And sees that written . . . O dear, O dear!'
—'Madam, I swear your beauty will disarm him!'

HER LOVE-BIRDS

When I looked up at my love-birds
    That Sunday afternoon,
    There was in their tiny tune
A dying fetch like broken words,
When I looked up at my love-birds
    That Sunday afternoon.

When he, too, scanned the love-birds
    On entering there that day,
    'Twas as if he had nought to say
Of his long journey citywards,
When he, too, scanned the love-birds,
    On entering there that day.

11 'O wait!] ⟨"That's it!⟩ *Hol.* 14 At what he'll say when he sees this; *MV17* this;] ~: *Hol.* 17 That he's] He has *MV17* 19 And sees that] ⟨My death there⟩ *Hol.*

HER LOVE-BIRDS. *Title* ⟨The Love-Birds⟩ *Hol.*

[*Hol. is in direct address, with open double quotation marks at the beginning of each stanza, and closing quotation marks at the end of the last line.*]

1 my] ⟨the⟩ *Hol.* 2 That] ⟨On that⟩ *Hol.* 4 fetch] fall *Hol.* 5 my] ⟨the⟩ *Hol.* 6 That] ⟨On that⟩ *Hol.* 8 On entering] ⟨As he entered⟩ *Hol.* 10 ⟨Of his journey to the land of herds,⟩ *Hol.* long] ⟨lengthened⟩ *Hol.* 11 love-birds,] ~ *Hol.* 12 On entering] ⟨As he entered⟩ *Hol.*

And billed and billed the love-birds,
As 'twere in fond despair
At the stress of silence where
Had once been tones in tenor thirds,
And billed and billed the love-birds
As 'twere in fond despair.

O, his speech that chilled the love-birds,
And smote like death on me,
As I learnt what was to be,
And knew my life was broke in sherds!
O, his speech that chilled the love-birds,
And smote like death on me!

PAYING CALLS

I went by footpath and by stile
Beyond where bustle ends,
Strayed here a mile and there a mile
And called upon some friends.

On certain ones I had not seen
For years past did I call,
And then on others who had been
The oldest friends of all.

It was the time of midsummer
When they had used to roam;
But now, though tempting was the air,
I found them all at home.

I spoke to one and other of them
By mound and stone and tree
Of things we had done ere days were dim,
But they spoke not to me.

13 love-birds,] ~ *Hol.* 14 in fond] in ⟨a⟩ fond *Hol.* 18 in fond] in ⟨a⟩ fond *Hol.* 20 me,] ~! *Hol.* 22 sherds!] ~. *Hol.*

PAYING CALLS. *SP* (1916) 14 mound] path *MV17*

THE UPPER BIRCH-LEAVES

Warm yellowy-green
In the blue serene,
How they skip and sway
On this autumn day!
They cannot know
What has happened below,—
That their boughs down there
Are already quite bare,
That their own will be
When a week has passed,—
For they jig as in glee
To this very last.

But no; there lies
At times in their tune
A note that cries
What at first I fear
I did not hear:
'O we remember
At each wind's hollo—
Though life holds yet—
We go hence soon,
For 'tis November;
—But that *you* follow
You may forget!'

'IT NEVER LOOKS LIKE SUMMER'*

'It never looks like summer here
    On Beeny by the sea.'
But though she saw its look as drear,
    Summer it seemed to me.

THE UPPER BIRCH-LEAVES. *Title* The Upper Leaves *Hol.*
2 serene,] bright sheen, *Hol.* 7 their] ⟨the⟩ *Hol.* 11 jig] trill *Hol.*
23 *you*] *rom. CP*

'IT NEVER LOOKS'. 3 But though to her its look was drear, *MV17*

It never looks like summer now
Whatever weather's there;
But ah, it cannot anyhow,
On Beeny or elsewhere!

Boscastle,
March 8, 1913.

EVERYTHING COMES

'The house is bleak and cold
Built so new for me!
All the winds upon the wold
Search it through for me;
No screening trees abound,
And the curious eyes around
Keep on view for me.'

'My Love, I am planting trees
As a screen for you
Both from winds, and eyes that tease
And peer in for you.
Only wait till they have grown,
No such bower will be known
As I mean for you.'

'Then I will bear it, Love,
And will wait,' she said.
—So, with years, there grew a grove.
'Skill how great!' she said.
'As you wished, Dear?'—'Yes, I see!
But—I'm dying; and for me
'Tis too late,' she said.

7 But ah,] But then *MV17* 8 elsewhere!] ~. *Hol.* *Place/date* Boscastle / ⟨Saturday⟩ / 8 March: 1913. *Hol.*

EVERYTHING COMES. 3 All the] All *Hol.* 19 "⟨Just as⟩ As you wished?"—"It is, I see! *Hol.* 21 too late,'] *ital. Hol.*

THE MAN WITH A PAST

There was merry-making
When the first dart fell
As a heralding,—
Till grinned the fully bared thing,
And froze like a spell—
Like a spell.

Innocent was she,
Innocent was I,
Too simple we!
Before us we did not see,
Nearing, aught wry—
Aught wry!

I can tell it not now,
It was long ago;
And such things cow;
But that is why and how
Two lives were so—
Were so.

Yes, the years matured,
And the blows were three
That time ensured
On her, which she dumbly endured;
And one on me—
One on me.

HE FEARS HIS GOOD FORTUNE*

There was a glorious time
At an epoch of my prime;

THE MAN WITH A PAST. 3 ⟨As from a wing,—⟩ *Hol.* 4 bared] seen *Hol.* 24 me.] ~! *Hol.*

HE FEARS HIS GOOD FORTUNE. *MS1* Adams
MS1 omits all quotation marks

Mornings beryl-bespread,
And evenings golden-red;
    Nothing gray:
And in my heart I said,
'However this chanced to be,
It is too full for me,
Too rare, too rapturous, rash,
Its spell must close with a crash
    Some day!'

The radiance went on
Anon and yet anon,
And sweetness fell around
Like manna on the ground.
    'I've no claim',
Said I, 'to be thus crowned:
I am not worthy this:—
Must it not go amiss?—
Well . . . let the end foreseen
Come duly!—I am serene.'
    —And it came.

HE WONDERS ABOUT HIMSELF*

No use hoping, or feeling vext,
Tugged by a force above or under
Like some fantocine, much I wonder
What I shall find me doing next!

3 beryl-bespread,] ⟨gem-bespread,⟩ *MS1*   4 golden-red;] gold and red; *MS1*, *Hol.*   5 gray:] ~; *MS1*   8 full] ⟨good⟩ *MS1*   10 ⟨The end must come with a crash⟩ *MS1*
16–22 ⟨I exclaim
O why does such abound?
And am I worthy this?—
Must it not go amiss?—
The end I have foreseen;
⟨⟨Well—⟩⟩ Let it come; I am serene. . . .
Well, it came.⟩ *MS1*

HE WONDERS ABOUT HIMSELF. 2 Tugged] ⟨Driven⟩ *Hol.*   3 some fantocine,] ⟨an automaton,⟩ *Hol.*   4 me] ⟨myself⟩ *Hol.*

Shall I be rushing where bright eyes be?
Shall I be suffering sorrows seven?
Shall I be watching the stars of heaven,
Thinking one of them looks like thee?

Part is mine of the general Will,
Cannot my share in the sum of forces
Bend a digit creature-courses,
And a fair desire fulfil?

Nov. 1893.

JUBILATE*

'The very last time I ever was here,' he said,
'I saw much less of the quick than I saw of the dead.'
—He was a man I had met with somewhere before,
But how or when I now could recall no more.

'The hazy mazy moonlight at one in the morning
Spread out as a sea across the frozen snow,
Glazed to live sparkles like the great breastplate adorning
The priest of the Temple, with Urim and Thummim aglow.

'The yew-tree arms, glued hard to the stiff stark air,
Hung still in the village sky as theatre-scenes
When I came by the churchyard wall, and halted there
At a shut-in sound of fiddles and tambourines.

10 forces *Hol.*, *DCM3*] ⟨forces⟩ ⟨sources⟩ *Hol.*; sources *all other texts* 11 creature-courses, *Hol.*, *DCM3*] ⟨Nature's courses⟩ ⟨the poise of forces,⟩ *Hol.*; the poise of forces, *all other texts* 12 fair] fain *Hol.*

JUBILATE. 4 now] ⟨then⟩ *Hol.* 6 Spread] ⟨Shone⟩ *Hol.* 7 ⟨Which was glazed and sparkled like the breastplate adorning⟩ *Hol.* 8 ⟨The priest of the tabernacle that one reads of, you know.⟩ *Hol.* 9 stiff stark] ⟨frosty⟩ *Hol.* 10 still] ⟨stiff⟩ *Hol.* village] ⟨churchyard⟩ *Hol.* 11 the churchyard wall,] ⟨Mellstock Ridge⟩ *Hol.*

'And as I stood harkening, dulcimers, hautboys, and shawms,
And violoncellos, and a three-stringed double-bass,
Joined in, and were intermixed with a singing of psalms;
And I looked over at the dead men's dwelling-place.

'Through the shine of the slippery snow I now could see,
As it were through a crystal roof, a great company
Of the dead minueting in stately step underground
To the tune of the instruments I had before heard sound.

'It was "Eden New", and dancing they sang in a chore,
"We are out of it all!—yea, in Little-Ease cramped no more!"
And their shrouded figures pacing with joy I could see
As you see the stage from the gallery. And they had no heed of me.

'And I lifted my head quite dazed from the churchyard wall
And I doubted not that it warned I should soon have my call.
But—' . . . Then in the ashes he emptied the dregs of his cup,
And onward he went, and the darkness swallowed him up.

HE REVISITS HIS FIRST SCHOOL*

I should not have shown in the flesh,
I ought to have gone as a ghost;

13 stood harkening,] ⟨got nearer,⟩ *Hol.* 16 over at] ⟨over the wall at⟩ ⟨over into⟩ *Hol.* 18 crystal] glass *Hol.* a great] quite a great *Hol.* 19 minueting in stately step] allemanding without shoes *Hol.* 20 tune] ⟨notes⟩ *Hol.* 21 'It was "Eden New",] ⟨The⟩ "It was 'Wilton New,' *Hol.* 22 ⟨'Heigho, my hearts, we can suffer on earth no more!'⟩ 'We are out of it all!—we can suffer on earth no more!' *Hol.* 23 pacing] whirling *Hol.* 26 That for weeks thereafter marked my chin with a gall. . . . *Hol.* 27 But—'] Yes". . . . *Hol.*

HE REVISITS HIS FIRST SCHOOL. 1 shown] gone *Hol.*

It was awkward, unseemly almost,
Standing solidly there as when fresh,
Pink, tiny, crisp-curled,
My pinions yet furled
From the winds of the world.

After waiting so many a year
To wait longer, and go as a sprite
From the tomb at the mid of some night
Was the right, radiant way to appear;
Not as one wanzing weak
From life's roar and reek,
His rest still to seek:

Yea, beglimpsed through the quaint quarried glass
Of green moonlight, by me greener made,
When they'd cry, perhaps, 'There sits his shade
In his olden haunt—just as he was
When in Walkingame he
Conned the grand Rule-of-Three
With the bent of a bee.'

But to show in the afternoon sun,
With an aspect of hollow-eyed care,
When none wished to see me come there,
Was a garish thing, better undone.
Yes; wrong was the way;
But yet, let me say,
I may right it—some day.

'I THOUGHT, MY HEART'*

I thought, my Heart, that you had healed
Of those sore smartings of the past,

11 right,] ⟨true,⟩ ⟨rare,⟩ *Hol.* radiant] ⟨beauteous⟩ *Hol.* 12 wanzing] growing *Hol.* 14 seek:] ~. *Hol.* 15 beglimpsed] in gleams *Hol.* 21 Assiduously. *Hol.* 22 show] go *Hol.* 27 ⟨But let me yet say,⟩ *Hol.* 28 it—some] it some *Hol.*

'I THOUGHT, MY HEART'. Ruth Head, *Pages from the Works of Thomas Hardy* (London: 1922). *MS1* DCM [*first two stanzas only*]; *MS2* Adams [*third stanza only*]
2 sore] ⟨keen⟩ *MS1*

And that the summers had oversealed
All mark of them at last.
But closely scanning in the night
I saw them standing crimson-bright
Just as she made them:
Nothing could fade them;
Yea, I can swear
That there they were—
They still were there!

Then the Vision of her who cut them came,
And looking over my shoulder said,
'I am sure you deal me all the blame
For those sharp smarts and red;
But meet me, dearest, to-morrow night,
In the churchyard at the moon's half-height,
And so strange a kiss
Shall be mine, I wis,
That you'll cease to know
If the wounds you show
Be there or no!'

7 them:] ~; *MS1*   10 were—] ~, *MS1*   11 there!] ~. *Hol.*
12 ⟨And the double of her who made them came,⟩ *MS1*   Then] ⟨But⟩ *MS1*
15 sharp] ⟨keen⟩ *MS1*   18 so strange] ⟨such⟩ *MS1*
20–2
⟨That you will swear
With heart laid bare
No wounds are there."⟩ *MS1*
22 no!'] ~." *MS1*, *Hol.*
22a–k
That kiss so strange, so stark, I'll take
When the world sleeps sound, and no noise will scare,
And a moon-touch whitens each stone and stake;
Yes; I will meet her there—
Just at the time she calls "*to-morrow,*"
But I call "*after the shut of sorrow*"—
And with her dwell—
Inseparable
With cease of pain,
And frost and rain,
And life's inane. *MS2* [*see explanatory notes*]
22c a] ⟨the⟩ *MS2*.   stake;] ~, *Hol.*   22e–f *no ital. Hol.*
22g dwell—] ~, *Hol.*   22h Her parallel *Hol.*, *PWTH*; ⟨Her parallel⟩ *MS2*
22i With cease] In quit *Hol.*; In cease *PWTH*; ⟨In⟩ With cease *MS2*   22j frost] ~, *Hol.*   22k life's] *cap. Hol.*

FRAGMENT

At last I entered a long dark gallery,
Catacomb-lined; and ranged at the side
Were the bodies of men from far and wide
Who, motion past, were nevertheless not dead.

'The sense of waiting here strikes strong;
Everyone's waiting, waiting, it seems to me;
What are you waiting for so long?—
What is to happen?' I said.

'O we are waiting for one called God,' said they,
'(Though by some the Will, or Force, or Laws;
And, vaguely, by some, the Ultimate Cause;)
Waiting for him to see us before we are clay.
Yes; waiting, waiting, for God *to know it*.' . . .
'To know what?' questioned I.
'To know how things have been going on earth and
below it:
It is clear he must know some day.'
I thereon asked them why.
'Since he made us humble pioneers
Of himself in consciousness of Life's tears,
It needs no mighty prophecy
To tell that what he could mindlessly show
His creatures, he himself will know.

'By some still close-cowled mystery
We have reached feeling faster than he,
But he will overtake us anon,
If the world goes on.'

FRAGMENT. 1 last I] last ⟨in⟩ I *Hol.* 4 motion past,] motionless, *MV17* 5 strikes] ⟨is⟩ *Hol.* 10 ⟨"(Though some call him Will, Force, or Laws;⟩ *Hol.* 11 And vaguely, by some,] ⟨And some, in⟩ ⟨And vaguely some⟩ *Hol.* 19 Life's] men's *Hol.* 23 close-cowled] close-cloaked *Hol.*

MIDNIGHT ON THE GREAT WESTERN*

In the third-class seat sat the journeying boy,
    And the roof-lamp's oily flame
Played down on his listless form and face,
Bewrapt past knowing to what he was going,
        Or whence he came.

In the band of his hat the journeying boy
    Had a ticket stuck; and a string
Around his neck bore the key of his box,
That twinkled gleams of the lamp's sad beams
        Like a living thing.

What past can be yours, O journeying boy
    Towards a world unknown,
Who calmly, as if incurious quite
On all at stake, can undertake
        This plunge alone?

Knows your soul a sphere, O journeying boy,
    Our rude realms far above,
Whence with spacious vision you mark and mete
This region of sin that you find you in,
        But are not of?

HONEYMOON-TIME AT AN INN

At the shiver of morning, a little before the false dawn,
    The moon was at the window-square,
  Deedily brooding in deformed decay—
  The curve hewn off her cheek as by an adze;
At the shiver of morning a little before the false dawn
    So the moon looked in there.

MIDNIGHT ON THE GREAT WESTERN. 3 Played] Shone *Hol.* 4 Bewrapt] ⟨Bedulled⟩ *Hol.* 7 string] ~⟨,⟩ *Hol.* 11 boy] ~⟨,⟩ *Hol.* 13 incurious] indifferent *MV17* 14 On] To *MV17* 18 mark] measure *Hol.*

HONEYMOON-TIME AT AN INN. 3 decay—] ~, *Hol.*

Her speechless eyeing reached across the chamber,
Where lay two souls opprest,
One a white lady sighing, 'Why am I sad!'
To him who sighed back, 'Sad, my Love, am I!'
And speechlessly the old moon conned the chamber,
And these two reft of rest.

While their large-pupilled vision swept the scene there,
Nought seeming imminent,
Something fell sheer, and crashed, and from the floor
Lay glittering at the pair with a shattered gaze,
While their large-pupilled vision swept the scene there,
And the many-eyed thing outleant.

With a start they saw that it was an old-time pier-glass
Which had stood on the mantel near,
Its silvering blemished,—yes, as if worn away
By the eyes of the countless dead who had smirked at it
Ere these two ever knew that old-time pier-glass
And its vague and vacant leer.

As he looked, his bride like a moth skimmed forth, and kneeling
Quick, with quivering sighs,
Gathered the pieces under the moon's sly ray,
Unwitting as an automaton what she did;
Till he entreated, hasting to where she was kneeling,
'Let it stay where it lies!'

'Long years of sorrow this means!' breathed the lady
As they retired. 'Alas!'
And she lifted one pale hand across her eyes.
'Don't trouble, Love; it's nothing,' the bridegroom said.
'Long years of sorrow for us!' murmured the lady,
'Or ever this evil pass!'

17 ⟨While shone the moon unmoved upon the scene there,⟩ *Hol.* 19 With a] In their *Hol.* 21 Its silvering] ⟨Its silver⟩ Quicksilver *Hol.* 27 sly] ⟨slant⟩ *Hol.* 28 Unwitting] Unconscious *MV17* 31 breathed] said *MV17* 33 pale] small *Hol.*

And the Spirits Ironic laughed behind the wainscot,
    And the Spirits of Pity sighed.
  'It's good', said the Spirits Ironic, 'to tickle their minds
  With a portent of their wedlock's after-grinds.'
And the Spirits of Pity sighed behind the wainscot,
    'It's a portent we cannot abide!

'More, what shall happen to prove the truth of the
        portent?'
    —'Oh; in brief, they will fade till old,
  And their loves grow numbed ere death, by the cark
        of care.'
  —'But nought see we that asks for portents there?—
'Tis the lot of all.'—'Well, no less true is a portent
    That it fits all mortal mould.'

THE ROBIN

When up aloft
I fly and fly,
I see in pools
The shining sky,
And a happy bird
Am I, am I!

When I descend
Towards their brink
I stand, and look,
And stoop, and drink,
And bathe my wings,
And chink and prink.

When winter frost
Makes earth as steel

39 tickle] ⟨move⟩ *Hol.* 40 their] ⟨their⟩ ⟨wildgoose⟩ *Hol.* after-grinds.'] after-woes." *Hol.*

THE ROBIN. 2 ⟨I fly, I fly,⟩ *Hol.* 6 I!] ~. *Hol.*

I search and search
But find no meal,
And most unhappy
Then I feel.

But when it lasts,
And snows still fall,
I get to feel
No grief at all,
For I turn to a cold stiff
Feathery ball!

'I ROSE AND WENT TO ROU'TOR TOWN'*

(She, alone)

I rose and went to Rou'tor Town
With gaiety and good heart,
And ardour for the start,
That morning ere the moon was down
That lit me off to Rou'tor Town
With gaiety and good heart.

When sojourn soon at Rou'tor Town
Wrote sorrows on my face,
I strove that none should trace
The pale and gray, once pink and brown,
When sojourn soon at Rou'tor Town
Wrote sorrows on my face.

The evil wrought at Rou'tor Town
On him I'd loved so true
I cannot tell anew:

21–2 ⟨I soon escape
My troubles all,⟩ *Hol.*

'I ROSE AND WENT'. *Headnote om. MV17*
2 heart,] ~ *Hol.*
14–15 ⟨To thoughts I'd cherished well
'Tis not in me to tell:⟩ *Hol.*

But nought can quench, but nought can drown
The evil wrought at Rou'tor Town
On him I'd loved so true!

THE NETTLES

This, then, is the grave of my son,
Whose heart she won! And nettles grow
Upon his mound; and she lives just below.

How he upbraided me, and left,
And our lives were cleft, because I said
She was hard, unfeeling, caring but to wed.

Well, to see this sight I have fared these miles,
And her firelight smiles from her window there,
Whom he left his mother to cherish with tender care!

It is enough. I'll turn and go;
Yes, nettles grow where lone lies he,
Who spurned me for seeing what he could not see.

IN A WAITING-ROOM

On a morning sick as the day of doom
With the drizzling gray
Of an English May,
There were few in the railway waiting-room.
About its walls were framed and varnished
Pictures of liners, fly-blown, tarnished.
The table bore a Testament
For travellers' reading, if suchwise bent.

18 ⟨To thoughts I'd cherished well!⟩ *Hol.*

IN A WAITING-ROOM. 1 sick] ⟨sad⟩ *Hol.*

I read it on and on,
And, thronging the Gospel of Saint John,
Were figures—additions, multiplications—
By some one scrawled, with sundry emendations;
Not scoffingly designed,
But with an absent mind,—
Plainly a bagman's counts of cost,
What he had profited, what lost;
And whilst I wondered if there could have been
Any particle of a soul
In that poor man at all,
To cypher rates of wage
Upon that printed page,
There joined in the charmless scene
And stood over me and the scribbled book
(To lend the hour's mean hue
A smear of tragedy too)
A soldier and wife, with haggard look
Subdued to stone by strong endeavour;
And then I heard
From a casual word
They were parting as they believed for ever.

But next there came
Like the eastern flame
Of some high altar, children—a pair—
Who laughed at the fly-blown pictures there.
'Here are the lovely ships that we,
Mother, are by and by going to see!
When we get there it's 'most sure to be fine,
And the band will play, and the sun will shine!'

It rained on the skylight with a din
As we waited and still no train came in;
But the words of the child in the squalid room
Had spread a glory through the gloom.

10 thronging] mixed with *Hol.* 20 cypher] ⟨figure⟩ *Hol.* 22 charmless] dreary *MV17* 23 book] ~, *Hol.* 33 Of some high altar] Of morning in April, *MV17* 40 in;] ~, *Hol.* 41 ⟨But a glory had been brought into the room⟩ *Hol.* 42 ⟨By the faith of the child amid the gloom.⟩ *Hol.*

THE CLOCK-WINDER

It is dark as a cave,
Or a vault in the nave
When the iron door
Is closed, and the floor
Of the church relaid
With trowel and spade.

But the parish-clerk
Cares not for the dark
As he winds in the tower
At a regular hour
The rheumatic clock,
Whose dilatory knock
You can hear when praying
At the day's decaying,
Or at any lone while
From a pew in the aisle.

Up, up from the ground
Around and around
In the turret stair
He clambers, to where
The wheelwork is,
With its tick, click, whizz,
Reposefully measuring
Each day to its end
That mortal men spend
In sorrowing and pleasuring.
Nightly thus does he climb
To the trackway of Time.

Him I followed one night
To this place without light,
And, ere I spoke, heard
Him say, word by word,

THE CLOCK-WINDER. *Hol. has first 28 lines only*
21 wheelwork] machinery *MV17* 23 Reposefully] Deliberately *MV17*

At the end of his winding,
The darkness unminding:—

'So I wipe out one more,
My Dear, of the sore
Sad days that still be,
Like a drying Dead Sea,
Between you and me!'

Who she was no man knew:
He had long borne him blind
To all womankind;
And was ever one who
Kept his past out of view.

OLD EXCURSIONS*

'What's the good of going to Ridgeway,
Cerne, or Sydling Mill,
Or to Yell'ham Hill,
Blithely bearing Casterbridge-way
As we used to do?
She will no more climb up there,
Or be visible anywhere
In those haunts we knew.'

But to-night, while walking weary,
Near me seemed her shade,
Come as 'twere to upbraid
This my mood in deeming dreary
Scenes that used to please;
And, if she did come to me,
Still solicitous, there may be
Good in going to these.

OLD EXCURSIONS. *MS1* DCM
first stanza not in quotation marks MS1, Hol.
2 Sydling] Sutton *MS1, Hol.* 4 Casterbridge-way] ~, *MS1*
6 there,] ~ *Hol.* 9 to-night,] ~ *MS1, Hol.* weary,] ~ *MS1, Hol.*

So, I'll care to roam to Ridgeway,
Cerne, or Sydling Mill,
Or to Yell'ham Hill,
Blithely bearing Casterbridge-way
As we used to do,
Since her phasm may flit out there,
And may greet me anywhere
In those haunts we knew.

April 1913.

THE MASKED FACE

I found me in a great surging space,
At either end a door,
And I said: 'What is this giddying place,
With no firm-fixéd floor,
That I knew not of before?'
'It is Life,' said a mask-clad face.

I asked: 'But how do I come here,
Who never wished to come;
Can the light and air be made more clear,
The floor more quietsome,
And the doors set wide? They numb
Fast-locked, and fill with fear.'

The mask put on a bleak smile then,
And said, 'O vassal-wight,
There once complained a goosequill pen
To the scribe of the Infinite
Of the words it had to write
Because they were past its ken.'

17 So,] ~ *MS1* 18 Sydling] Sutton *MS1*, *Hol.* 22 If her phantom flits out there, *Hol.*; If her ⟨spirit⟩ phantom flits out there, *MS1* 23 greet] meet *MS1*, *Hol.*

THE MASKED FACE. 4 floor,] ~⟨?⟩, *Hol.* 5 That I've never seen before?" *Hol.* 8 come;] ~, *Hol.*

IN A WHISPERING GALLERY*

That whisper takes the voice
Of a Spirit's compassionings,
Close, but invisible,
And throws me under a spell
At the kindling vision it brings;
And for a moment I rejoice,
And believe in transcendent things
That would mould from this muddy earth
A spot for the splendid birth
Of everlasting lives,
Whereto no night arrives;
And from this gaunt gallery
A tabernacle of worth
On this drab-aired afternoon,
When you can barely see
Across its hazed lacune
If opposite aught there be
Of fleshed humanity
Wherewith I may commune;
Or if the voice so near
Be a soul's voice floating here.

THE SOMETHING THAT SAVED HIM

It was when
Whirls of thick waters laved me
Again and again,
That something arose and saved me;
Yea, it was then.

IN A WHISPERING GALLERY. 1 takes] seems *Hol.* 2 Of a Spirit's compassionings, *ME*, *CP23*] Of a Spirit, speaking to me, *MV*, *CP19*, *WE* 8 mould from] make of *MV17* 10 lives,] ~ *Hol.* 11 arrives;] ~, *Hol.* 12 And this gaunt gray gallery *MV17*, *CP* 14 drab-aired] drab-fogged *Hol.* 15 barely] scarcely *Hol.*

In that day
Unseeing the azure went I
On my way,
And to white winter bent I,
Knowing no May.

Reft of renown,
Under the night clouds beating
Up and down,
In my needfulness greeting
Cit and clown.

Long there had been
Much of a murky colour
In the scene,
Dull prospects meeting duller;
Nought between.

Last, there loomed
A closing-in blind alley,
Though there boomed
A feeble summons to rally
Where it gloomed.

The clock rang;
The hour brought a hand to deliver;
I upsprang,
And looked back at den, ditch and river,
And sang.

THE ENEMY'S PORTRAIT

He saw the portrait of his enemy, offered
At auction in a street he journeyed nigh,
That enemy, now late dead, who in his lifetime
Had injured deeply him the passer-by.

THE SOMETHING THAT SAVED HIM. 14 needfulness] wistfulness *MV17*, *WE* 27 ⟨Something arose to deliver;⟩ *Hol.* 29 ⟨And looked back, safe, at the river,⟩ *Hol.* 30 ⟨And I sang.⟩ *Hol.*

THE ENEMY'S PORTRAIT. 1 enemy,] ~ *Hol.*

'To get that picture, pleased be God, I'll try,
And utterly destroy it; and no more
Shall be inflicted on man's mortal eye
A countenance so sinister and sore!'

And so he bought the painting. Driving homeward,
'The frame will come in useful,' he declared,
'The rest is fuel.' On his arrival, weary,
Asked what he bore with him, and how he fared,
He said he had bid for a picture, though he cared
For the frame only: on the morrow he
Would burn the canvas, which could well be spared,
Seeing that it portrayed his enemy.

Next day some other duty found him busy:
The foe was laid his face against the wall;
But on the next he set himself to loosen
The straining-strips. And then a casual call
Prevented his proceeding therewithal;
And thus the picture waited, day by day,
Its owner's pleasure, like a wretched thrall,
Until a month and more had slipped away.

And then upon a morn he found it shifted,
Hung in a corner by a servitor.
'Why did you take on you to hang that picture?
You know it was the frame I bought it for.'
'It stood in the way of every visitor,
And I just hitched it there.'—'Well, it must go:
I don't commemorate men whom I abhor.
Remind me 'tis to do. The frame I'll stow.'

But things become forgotten. In the shadow
Of the dark corner hung it by its string,
And there it stayed—once noticed by its owner,
Who said, 'Ah me—I must destroy that thing!'

8 ⟨A countenance of memories so sore!"⟩ *Hol.* 9 homeward,] ~ *Hol.* 12 bore] brought *Hol.* 13 bid for] bought *Hol.* 20 straining-strips.] ⟨straining-frame.⟩ *Hol.* 36 'Ah me—] "Dear me— *MV17*; ~⟨!⟩— *Hol.*

But when he died, there, none remembering,
It hung, till moved to prominence, as one sees;
And comers pause and say, examining,
'Strange, I thought they were bitterest enemies?'

IMAGININGS

She saw herself a lady
With fifty frocks in wear,
And rolling wheels, and rooms the best,
And faithful maidens' care,
And open lawns and shady
For weathers warm or drear.

She found herself a striver,
All liberal gifts debarred,
With days of gloom, and movements stressed,
And early visions marred,
And got no man to wive her
But one whose lot was hard.

Yet in the moony night-time
She steals to stile and lea
During his heavy slumberous rest
When homecome wearily,
And dreams of some blest bright-time
She knows can never be.

40 *ME*] "I thought they were the bitterest enemies?" *all other texts*

IMAGININGS. 2 ⟨With velvet shoes to wear,⟩ *Hol.* 5 and] ⟨or⟩ *Hol.* 6 warm] ⟨clear⟩ *Hol.* 8 All] ⟨With⟩ *Hol.* 14 ⟨She stole to lawn and lea⟩ *Hol.* 15 During] ⟨Amid⟩ *Hol.* 17 dreams] ⟨dreamt⟩ *Hol.* 18 knows can] ⟨knew could⟩ *Hol.*

ON THE DOORSTEP

The rain imprinted the step's wet shine
With target-circles that quivered and crossed
As I was leaving this porch of mine;
When from within there swelled and paused
        A song's sweet note;
    And back I turned, and thought,
        'Here I'll abide.'

The step shines wet beneath the rain,
Which prints its circles as heretofore;
I watch them from the porch again,
But no song-notes within the door
        Now call to me
    To shun the dripping lea;
        And forth I stride.

Jan. 1914

SIGNS AND TOKENS

Said the red-cloaked crone
In a whispered moan:

'The dead man was limp
When laid in his chest;
Yea, limp; and why
But to signify
That the grave will crimp
Ere next year's sun
Yet another one
Of those in that house—
It may be the best—
For its endless drowse!'

ON THE DOORSTEP. *Title* ⟨Staying and Going⟩ *Hol.* 3 was leaving] ⟨looked out from⟩ *Hol.* 4 When] ⟨While⟩ *Hol.* 6 And back I turned,] ⟨And I turned,⟩ *Hol.* 9 prints] ⟨shapes⟩ *Hol.* 11 no song-notes] ⟨songster notes⟩ *Hol.* 12 to] ⟨not⟩ *Hol.* 13 To shun] ⟨From⟩ *Hol.*

SIGNS AND TOKENS. 2 moan:] tone: *Hol.*

Said the brown-shawled dame
To confirm the same:

'And the slothful flies
On the rotting fruit
Have been seen to wear
While crawling there
Crape scarves, by eyes
That were quick and acute;
As did those that had pitched
On the cows by the pails,
And with flaps of their tails
Were far away switched.'

Said the third in plaid,
Each word being weighed:

'And trotting does
In the park, in the lane,
And just outside
The shuttered pane,
Have also been heard—
Quick feet as light
As the feet of a sprite—
And the wise mind knows
What things may betide
When such has occurred.'

Cried the black-craped fourth,
Cold faced as the north:

'O, though giving such
Some head-room, I smile
At your falterings
When noting those things
Round your domicile!

13 the] ⟨a⟩ *Hol.* 25 the] ⟨a⟩ *Hol.* 28 park,] ⟨field,⟩ *Hol.*
37 the] ⟨a⟩ *Hol.* 43 Round] In *Hol.*

For what, what can touch
One whom, riven of all
That makes life gay,
No hints can appal
Of more takings away!'

PATHS OF FORMER TIME

No; no;
It must not be so:
They are the ways we do not go.

Still chew
The kine, and moo
In the meadows we used to wander through;

Still purl
The rivulets and curl
Towards the weirs with a musical swirl;

Haymakers
As in former years
Rake rolls into heaps that the pitchfork rears;

Wheels crack
On the turfy track
The waggon pursues with its toppling pack.

'Why then shun—
Since summer's not done—
All this because of the lack of one?'

Had you been
Sharer of that scene
You would not ask while it bites in keen

PATHS OF FORMER TIME. *Title* ⟨The Old Paths⟩ *Hol.*
20 Sharer] ⟨A sharer⟩ *Hol.* 21 bites in] lingers *Hol.*

Why it is so
We can no more go
By the summer paths we used to know!

1913.

THE CLOCK OF THE YEARS*

'A spirit passed before my face; the hair of my flesh stood up.'

And the Spirit said,
'I can make the clock of the years go backward,
But am loth to stop it where you will.'
And I cried, 'Agreed
To that. Proceed:
It's better than dead!'

He answered, 'Peace';
And called her up—as last before me;
Then younger, younger she freshed, to the year
I first had known
Her woman-grown,
And I cried, 'Cease!—

'Thus far is good—
It is enough—let her stay thus always!'
But alas for me. He shook his head:
No stop was there;
And she waned child-fair,
And to babyhood.

Still less in mien
To my great sorrow became she slowly,
And smalled till she was nought at all
In his checkless griff;
And it was as if
She had never been.

Date ⟨Copied from notes of 1912–13.⟩ *Hol.*

THE CLOCK OF THE YEARS. *Title* ⟨The Clock of Time⟩ *Hol.*
2 of the years] ⟨of years⟩ *Hol.* 9 freshed,] grew, *MV17*
11 woman-grown,] ⟨full my own,⟩ *Hol.*

'Better', I plained,
'She were dead as before! The memory of her
Had lived in me; but it cannot now!'
And coldly his voice:
'It was your choice
To mar the ordained.'

1916.

AT THE PIANO

A woman was playing,
A man looking on;
And the mould of her face,
And her neck, and her hair,
Which the rays fell upon
Of the two candles there,
Sent him mentally straying
In some fancy-place
Where pain had no trace.

A cowled Apparition
Came pushing between;
And her notes seemed to sigh,
And the lights to burn pale,
As a spell numbed the scene.
But the maid saw no bale,
And the man no monition;
And Time laughed awry,
And the Phantom hid nigh.

25 ⟨"Better," said I,⟩ *Hol.* 27 Had lived] ⟨Could live⟩ *Hol.*
28 coldly] again *Hol.*; sternly *MV17*

AT THE PIANO. 3 mould] ⟨bend⟩ *Hol.* face,] ~ *Hol.* 4 neck,] ~ *Hol.*
10 Apparition] ⟨*l.c.*⟩ *Hol.* 14 ⟨A spell numbing the scene.⟩ *Hol.*
18 hid nigh.] ⟨passed by.⟩ *Hol.*

THE SHADOW ON THE STONE

I went by the Druid stone
That broods in the garden white and lone,
And I stopped and looked at the shifting shadows
That at some moments fall thereon
From the tree hard by with a rhythmic swing,
And they shaped in my imagining
To the shade that a well-known head and shoulders
Threw there when she was gardening.

I thought her behind my back,
Yea, her I long had learned to lack,
And I said: 'I am sure you are standing behind me,
Though how do you get into this old track?'
And there was no sound but the fall of a leaf
As a sad response; and to keep down grief
I would not turn my head to discover
That there was nothing in my belief.

Yet I wanted to look and see
That nobody stood at the back of me;
But I thought once more: 'Nay, I'll not unvision
A shape which, somehow, there may be.'
So I went on softly from the glade,
And left her behind me throwing her shade,
As she were indeed an apparition—
My head unturned lest my dream should fade.

Begun 1913: *finished* 1916.

THE SHADOW ON THE STONE. 2 broods] stands *MV17* white and lone,] ⟨all alone,⟩ *Hol.* 4 fall thereon *ME, CP23*] ⟨fall thereon⟩ ⟨there are strown⟩ *Hol.*; there are thrown *Hol.*, *MV*, *CP19*, *WE* 7 a] ⟨the⟩ *Hol.* 14 As a sad] ⟨By way of⟩ *Hol.* 17 ⟨Then⟩ I felt I must look to see *Hol.* 23 ⟨And entered into the dusk of the boscage,⟩ *Hol.*
Date ⟨From old notes, 1913.⟩ ⟨From an old note, 1913.⟩ *Hol.*

IN THE GARDEN*

(M. H.)

We waited for the sun
To break its cloudy prison
(For day was not yet done,
And night still unbegun)
Leaning by the dial.

After many a trial—
We all silent there—
It burst as new-arisen,
Shading its finger where
Time travelled at that minute.

Little saw we in it,
But this much I know,
Of lookers on that shade,
Her towards whom it made
Soonest had to go.

1915.

THE TREE AND THE LADY*

I have done all I could
For that lady I knew! Through the heats I have shaded her,
Drawn to her songsters when summer has jaded her,
Home from the heath or the wood.

At the mirth-time of May,
When my shadow first lured her, I'd donned my new bravery
Of greenth: 'twas my all. Now I shiver in slavery,
Icicles grieving me gray.

IN THE GARDEN. *Dedication om. Hol.*
8 ⟨Burst it as new-risen,⟩ *Hol.* 9 Throwing a shade to where *MV17*, *CP*

THE TREE AND THE LADY. 2 Through the] Throughout *Hol.* 5 At] ⟨In⟩ *Hol.* of] ⟨in⟩ *Hol.* 7 greenth:] green: *Hol.*

Plumed to every twig's end
I could tempt her chair under me. Much did I treasure her
During those days she had nothing to pleasure her;
Mutely she used me as friend.

I'm a skeleton now,
And she's gone, craving warmth. The rime sticks like a skin to me;
Through me Arcturus peers; Nor'lights shoot into me;
Gone is she, scorning my bough!

AN UPBRAIDING

Now I am dead you sing to me
The songs we used to know,
But while I lived you had no wish
Or care for doing so.

Now I am dead you come to me
In the moonlight, comfortless;
Ah, what would I have given alive
To win such tenderness!

When you are dead, and stand to me
Not differenced, as now,
But like again, will you be cold
As when we lived, or how?

THE YOUNG GLASS-STAINER*

'These Gothic windows, how they wear me out
With cusp and foil, and nothing straight or square,
Crude colours, leaden borders roundabout,
And fitting in Peter here, and Matthew there!

AN UPBRAIDING. 6 In the moonlight,] ⟨In moonlight,⟩ *Hol.* 9 stand to me] ⟨we shall be⟩ *Hol.*

THE YOUNG GLASS-STAINER. 4 ⟨And fitting ⟨⟨Christ⟩⟩ Luke in ⟨⟨there⟩⟩ here, and John in there!⟩ *Hol.*

'What a vocation! Here do I draw now
The abnormal, loving the Hellenic norm;
Martha I paint, and dream of Hera's brow,
Mary, and think of Aphrodite's form.'

Nov. 1893.

LOOKING AT A PICTURE ON AN ANNIVERSARY*

But don't you know it, my dear,
    Don't you know it,
That this day of the year
(What rainbow-rays embow it!)
We met, strangers confessed,
    But parted—blest?

Though at this query, my dear,
    There in your frame
Unmoved you still appear,
You must be thinking the same,
But keep that look demure
    Just to allure.

And now at length a trace
    I surely vision
Upon that wistful face
Of old-time recognition,
Smiling forth, 'Yes, as you say,
    It is the day.'

For this one phase of you
    Now left on earth
This great date must endue
With pulsings of rebirth!—
I see them vitalize
    Those two deep eyes!

LOOKING AT A PICTURE. *Title* a] ⟨her⟩ *Hol.*
19 phase] shape *Hol.* 22 pulsings of] ⟨omens of its⟩ *Hol.* rebirth!—] ~?— *MV, CP* 23 them] ⟨it⟩ *Hol.*

But if this face I con
  Does not declare
Consciousness living on
Still in it, little I care
To live myself, my dear,
  Lone-labouring here!

Spring 1913.

THE CHOIRMASTER'S BURIAL*

He often would ask us
That, when he died,
After playing so many
To their last rest,
If out of us any
Should here abide,
And it would not task us,
We would with our lutes
Play over him
By his grave-brim
The psalm he liked best—
The one whose sense suits
'Mount Ephraim'—
And perhaps we should seem
To him, in Death's dream,
Like the seraphim.

As soon as I knew
That his spirit was gone
I thought this his due,
And spoke thereupon.

30 ⟨In loneliness here!⟩ *Hol.*
Date ⟨March,⟩ 1913. *Hol.*

THE CHOIRMASTER'S BURIAL. *Title* ⟨The Choirmaster's Funeral⟩ *Hol.*
12 sense] ⟨mood⟩ *Hol.*

'I think', said the vicar,
'A read service quicker
Than viols out-of-doors
In these frosts and hoars.
That old-fashioned way
Requires a fine day,
And it seems to me
It had better not be.'

Hence, that afternoon,
Though never knew he
That his wish could not be,
To get through it faster
They buried the master
Without any tune.

But 'twas said that, when
At the dead of next night
The vicar looked out,
There struck on his ken
Thronged roundabout,
Where the frost was graying
The headstoned grass,
A band all in white
Like the saints in church-glass,
Singing and playing
The ancient stave
By the choirmaster's grave.

Such the tenor man told
When he had grown old.

23 viols] a hymn *Hol.* 30 never] ⟨nought of it⟩ *Hol.* 47 tenor] treble *MV17*

THE MAN WHO FORGOT*

At a lonely cross where bye-roads met
  I sat upon a gate;
I saw the sun decline and set,
  And still was fain to wait.

A trotting boy passed up the way
  And roused me from my thought;
I called to him, and showed where lay
  A spot I shyly sought.

'A summer-house fair stands hidden where
  You see the moonlight thrown;
Go, tell me if within it there
  A lady sits alone.'

He half demurred, but took the track,
  And silence held the scene;
I saw his figure rambling back;
  I asked him if he had been.

'I went just where you said, but found
  No summer-house was there:
Beyond the slope 'tis all bare ground;
  Nothing stands anywhere.

'A man asked what my brains were worth;
  The house, he said, grew rotten,
And was pulled down before my birth,
  And is almost forgotten!'

My right mind woke, and I stood dumb;
  Forty years' frost and flower
Had fleeted since I'd used to come
  To meet her in that bower.

THE MAN WHO FORGOT. [*Hol. is in direct address, with open double quotation marks at the beginning of each stanza, and closing quotation marks at the end of the last line.*]

8 A neighbouring spot I sought. *Hol.* 9 summer-house fair stands] ⟨summer-house stands⟩ *Hol.* 25 dumb;] numb; *Hol.*

WHILE DRAWING IN A CHURCHYARD*

'It is sad that so many of worth,
Still in the flesh,' soughed the yew,
'Misjudge their lot whom kindly earth
Secludes from view.

'They ride their diurnal round
Each day-span's sum of hours
In peerless ease, without jolt or bound
Or ache like ours.

'If the living could but hear
What is heard by my roots as they creep
Round the restful flock, and the things said there,
No one would weep.'

'"Now set among the wise,"
They say: "Enlarged in scope,
That no God trumpet us to rise
We truly hope."'

I listened to his strange tale
In the mood that stillness brings,
And I grew to accept as the day wore pale
That show of things.

WHILE DRAWING IN A CHURCHYARD. *Title* ⟨While Drawing Architecture in a Churchyard⟩ *Hol.*
1 worth,] ~ *Hol.* 11 flock,] ⟨graves,⟩ *Hol.* 12 ⟨They would not weep."⟩ *Hol.* 14 say:] ⟨state:⟩ *Hol.* 15 ⟨That none will trumpet us to rise⟩ That no official trump call *Rise*! *Hol.* God *ME*, *CP23*] *l.c.* *MV*, *CP19*, *WE* 20 show] view *MV17*

'FOR LIFE I HAD NEVER CARED GREATLY'

For Life I had never cared greatly,
As worth a man's while;
Peradventures unsought,
Peradventures that finished in nought,
Had kept me from youth and through manhood till lately
Unwon by its style.

In earliest years—why I know not—
I viewed it askance;
Conditions of doubt,
Conditions that leaked slowly out,
May haply have bent me to stand and to show not
Much zest for its dance.

With symphonies soft and sweet colour
It courted me then,
Till evasions seemed wrong,
Till evasions gave in to its song,
And I warmed, until living aloofly loomed duller
Than life among men.

Anew I found nought to set eyes on,
When, lifting its hand,
It uncloaked a star,
Uncloaked it from fog-damps afar,
And showed its beams burning from pole to horizon
As bright as a brand.

And so, the rough highway forgetting,
I pace hill and dale
Regarding the sky,
Regarding the vision on high,
And thus re-illumed have no humour for letting
My pilgrimage fail.

'FOR LIFE I HAD NEVER CARED GREATLY'. 1 greatly,] ~ *Hol.* 3 Peradventures] Adventures *Hol.* 4 Peradventures] Adventures *Hol.* 5 through] ⟨till⟩ *Hol.* 17 loomed] seemed *Hol.* 25 forgetting,] ~ *Hol.* 26 pace] pad *Hol.*

POEMS OF WAR AND PATRIOTISM*

'MEN WHO MARCH AWAY'*

(SONG OF THE SOLDIERS)

What of the faith and fire within us
        Men who march away
        Ere the barn-cocks say
        Night is growing gray,
Leaving all that here can win us;
What of the faith and fire within us
        Men who march away?

Is it a purblind prank, O think you,
        Friend with the musing eye,
        Who watch us stepping by
        With doubt and dolorous sigh?
Can much pondering so hoodwink you!
Is it a purblind prank, O think you,
        Friend with the musing eye?

Nay. We well see what we are doing,
        Though some may not see—
        Dalliers as they be—
        England's need are we;

'MEN WHO MARCH AWAY'. *Times*, 9 Sept. 1914; *Times Literary Supplement*, 10 Sept. 1914; *New York Times*, 10 Sept. 1914; *SP* (1916). *MS1* Eton; *MS2* HRC; *SCHol.* = *TLS* cutting, corrected by Hardy [*see explanatory notes*]

Title Song of the Soldiers *T*, *NYT* *Subtitle om. MS2*

2 away] ~, *MS1* 5 *DCM2*, *MV*, *CP*, *WE*] To hazards whence no tears can win us; *T*, *NYT*, *MS1*, *SC*, *SP*; *variant line del. MVHol.* can] could *MS2* 9 eye,] ~ *MS1*, *MS2* 11 doubt] doubts *NYT* 15 Nay. We] Nay; we *MVHol.* well see] see well *T*, *NYT*; ⟨see well⟩ *MS1*, *SCHol.* doing,] ~ *MS2*, *DCM2* 16 see—] ~, *MS2*, *DCM2* 17 be—] ~!— *T*; may be *NYT*; ~⟨!⟩—*SCHol.*; ~.—*MS1*, *MVHol.*; ~: *MS2*; ~; *DCM2* 18 we;] ~: *MS1*

Her distress would leave us rueing:
Nay. We well see what we are doing,
Though some may not see!

In our heart of hearts believing
Victory crowns the just,
And that braggarts must
Surely bite the dust,
Press we to the field ungrieving,
In our heart of hearts believing
Victory crowns the just.

Hence the faith and fire within us
Men who march away
Ere the barn-cocks say
Night is growing gray,
Leaving all that here can win us;
Hence the faith and fire within us
Men who march away.

September 5, 1914.

HIS COUNTRY*

He travels southward, and looks around;

I journeyed from my native spot
Across the south sea shine,
And found that people in hall and cot
Laboured and suffered each his lot
Even as I did mine.

19 leave] set *T*, *NYT*; ⟨set⟩ *MS1*, *SCHol.* 20 Nay. We] Nay; we *MVHol.* well see] see well *T*, *NYT*; ⟨see well⟩ *MS1*, *SCHol.* we are] we're *NYT* 26 Press] March *T*, *NYT*; ⟨March⟩ *MS1*, *SCHol.* ungrieving,] ~ *MVHol.* 33 *DCM2*, *MV*, *CP*, *WE*] To hazards whence no tears can win us; *T*, *NYT*, *MS1*, *SC*, *SP*; *variant line del.* *MVHol.* can] could *MS2* 35 away.] ~! *MVHol.*
Date om. *T*, *NYT*

HIS COUNTRY. 5 As did myself and mine. *Hol.*

and cannot discover the boundary

Thus noting them in meads and marts
It did not seem to me
That my dear country with its hearts,
Minds, yearnings, worse and better parts,
Had ended with the sea.

of his native country;

I further and further went anon,
As such I still surveyed,
And further yet—yea, on and on,
And all the men I looked upon
Had heart-strings fellow-made.

or where his duties to his fellow-creatures end;

I traced the whole terrestrial round,
Homing the other side;
Then said I, 'What is there to bound
My denizenship? It seems I have found
Its scope to be world-wide.'

nor who are his enemies.

I asked me: 'Whom have I to fight,
And whom have I to dare,
And whom to weaken, crush, and blight?
My country seems to have kept in sight
On my way everywhere.'

1913.

ENGLAND TO GERMANY IN 1914*

'O England, may God punish thee!'
—Is it that Teuton genius flowers

6 Thus] ⟨So,⟩ *Hol.* 11 anon,] ~ *Hol.* 17 Homing] ⟨And up⟩ And back *Hol.* *marginal gloss*: end;] ~. *Hol.*

25a–e
"Ah, you deceive you by such pleas!"
Said one with pitying eye.
"Foreigners—not like us—are these;
Stretch country-love beyond the seas?—
Too Christian!"—"Strange," said I. *MV17*

But he is set right by a wise man who pities his blindness.

(*Hol.* = *MV17* *except* 25e No never!"—"Ah," said I.)

ENGLAND TO GERMANY. *FEH* (1917)
Title England to Germany *FEH*

Only to breathe malignity
Upon its friend of earlier hours?
—We have eaten your bread, you have eaten ours,
We have loved your burgs, your pines' green moan,
Fair Rhine-stream, and its storied towers;
Your shining souls of deathless dowers
Have won us as they were our own:

We have nursed no dreams to shed your blood,
We have matched your might not rancorously,
Save a flushed few whose blatant mood
You heard and marked as well as we
To tongue not in their country's key;
But yet you cry with face aflame,
'O England, may God punish thee!'
And foul in onward history,
And present sight, your ancient name.

Autumn 1914.

ON THE BELGIAN EXPATRIATION

I dreamt that people from the Land of Chimes
Arrived one autumn morning with their bells,
To hoist them on the towers and citadels
Of my own country, that the musical rhymes

Rung by them into space at meted times
Amid the market's daily stir and stress,
And the night's empty star-lit silentness,
Might solace souls of this and kindred climes.

6 We have loved your cities, landscapes lone, *FEH*; We have loved your cities, ⟨landscapes⟩ forest lone, *Hol.* 8 souls] ones *FEH*; ⟨ones⟩ *Hol.* 12 flushed few] few fools, *FEH*, *Hol.* 13 heard and marked] recognized *FEH*; ⟨recognized⟩ read and marked *Hol.* 14 tongue] ring *FEH*, *Hol.*

ON THE BELGIAN EXPATRIATION. Hall Caine, ed., *King Albert's Book* (London: 1914)
Title Sonnet on the Belgian Expatriation *KAB*
5 Rung] ⟨Rolled⟩ *Hol.* meted] measured *KAB*, *MV17*

Then I awoke; and lo, before me stood
The visioned ones, but pale and full of fear;
From Bruges they came, and Antwerp, and Ostend,

No carillons in their train. Foes of mad mood
Had shattered these to shards amid the gear
Of ravaged roof, and smouldering gable-end.

October 18, 1914.

AN APPEAL TO AMERICA ON BEHALF OF THE BELGIAN DESTITUTE*

Seven millions stand
Emaciate, in that ancient Delta-land:—
We here, full-charged with our own maimed and dead,
And coiled in throbbing conflicts slow and sore,
Can poorly soothe these ails unmerited
Of souls forlorn upon the facing shore!—
Where naked, gaunt, in endless band on band
Seven millions stand.

No man can say
To your great country that, with scant delay,
You must, perforce, ease them in their loud need:
We know that nearer first your duty lies;
But—is it much to ask that you let plead
Your lovingkindness with you—wooing-wise—
Albeit that aught you owe, and must repay,
No man can say?

December 1914.

12 Foes of mad mood] Vicissitude *KAB* 13 Had left these tinkling to the invader's ear, *KAB* 14 Of ravaged roof,] And ravaged street, *KAB*
Date om. KAB

AN APPEAL TO AMERICA. *New York Times*, 4 Jan. 1915; *FEH* (1917). *TS* (*NYT*) Fales
Title to] ⟨of⟩ *Hol.*
5 poorly soothe] soothe how slight *TS*, *T*; ⟨soothe how slight⟩ *Hol.*

THE PITY OF IT*

I walked in loamy Wessex lanes, afar
From rail-track and from highway, and I heard
In field and farmstead many an ancient word
Of local lineage like 'Thu bist', 'Er war',

'Ich woll', 'Er sholl', and by-talk similar,
Nigh as they speak who in this month's moon gird
At England's very loins, thereunto spurred
By gangs whose glory threats and slaughters are.

Then seemed a Heart crying: 'Whosoever they be
At root and bottom of this, who flung this flame
Between kin folk kin tongued even as are we,

'Sinister, ugly, lurid, be their fame;
May their familiars grow to shun their name,
And their brood perish everlastingly.'

April 1915.

IN TIME OF WARS AND TUMULTS

'Would that I'd not drawn breath here!' some one said,
'To stalk upon this stage of evil deeds,
Where purposelessly month by month proceeds
A play so sorely shaped and blood-bespread.'

THE PITY OF IT. *Fortnightly Review*, 1 Apr. 1915; *Dorset Year-book* (1916–17); *FEH* (1917). *MS1* HRC

4 lineage] ~, *MS1* 5 by-talk] ⟨small talk⟩ *MS1* 6 Nigh] Even *FR*, *MS1*, *MV17*, *DYB*, *CP19* this] each *DYB* 12 lurid,] ~ *MS1* 14 brood *CP*] breed *all other texts*

Date om. FR, *DYB*; 1915 *MS1*; February 1915 *FEH*, *Hol.*; April 1915./("*Fortnightly Review.*") *MV17*

IN TIME OF WARS AND TUMULTS. *Sphere*, 24 Nov. 1917

Title In the Time of War and Tumults *S*

3 month by month] year by year *Hol.*

Yet had his spark not quickened, but lain dead
To the gross spectacles of this our day,
And never put on the proffered cloak of clay,
He had but known not things now manifested;

Life would have swirled the same. Morns would have dawned
On the uprooting by the night-gun's stroke
Of what the yester noonshine brought to flower;

Brown martial brows in dying throes have wanned
Despite his absence; hearts no fewer been broke
By Empery's insatiate lust of power.

1915.

IN TIME OF 'THE BREAKING OF NATIONS'*

I

Only a man harrowing clods
  In a slow silent walk
With an old horse that stumbles and nods
  Half asleep as they stalk.

II

Only thin smoke without flame
  From the heaps of couch-grass;
Yet this will go onward the same
  Though Dynasties pass.

8 known not *Hol.*, *MV19*, *CP*, *WE*] not known *S*, *MV17* 11 noonshine brought] sunlight made *Hol.* 13 fewer been] ⟨bruised and⟩ *Hol.* 14 ⟨By monarchism's unnatural greed of power.⟩ *Hol.*
Date om. S

IN TIME OF 'THE BREAKING OF NATIONS'. *Saturday Review*, 29 Jan. 1916; *SP* (1916). *MS1* Bancroft; *MS2* Eton
Headnote (Jer. LI. 20.) *MS1*, *MS2*
1 man] hind *MS1* 6 couch-grass;] couch grass: *MS1*, *MS2*, *SP*
7 onward] on just *SR*

III

Yonder a maid and her wight
  Come whispering by:
War's annals will cloud into night
  Ere their story die.

1915.

CRY OF THE HOMELESS*

After the Prussian Invasion of Belgium

'Instigator of the ruin—
  Whichsoever thou mayst be
Of the masterful of Europe
  That contrived our misery—
Hear the wormwood-worded greeting
  From each city, shore, and lea
    Of thy victims:
  "Conqueror, all hail to thee!"

'Yea: "All hail!" we grimly shout thee
  That wast author, fount, and head
Of these wounds, whoever proven
  When our times are throughly read.
"May thy loved be slighted, blighted,
  And forsaken," be it said
    By thy victims,
  "And thy children beg their bread!"

11 cloud] fade *MS1*, *SR*, *Hol.*, *SP*
Date om. MS1, *SR*, *SP*; 1915/("*Saturday Review.*") *MV17*

CRY OF THE HOMELESS. Edith Wharton, ed., *The Book of the Homeless* (New York and London: 1916); *FEH* (1917). *MS1* (*BH*) LC
Headnote om. MS1 *text not set within quotation marks MS1*, *BH*
2 mayst] mayest *FEH* 3 masterful] mastering minds *MS1*, *BH*
8 "Conqueror,] "Enemy, *MS1*, *BH* 13 "May thy dearest ones be blighted *MS1*, *BH*

'Nay: a richer malediction!—
  Rather let this thing befall
In time's hurling and unfurling
  On the night when comes thy call;
That compassion dew thy pillow
  And bedrench thy senses all
    For thy victims,
  Till death dark thee with his pall.'

August 1915.

BEFORE MARCHING AND AFTER*

(In Memoriam F.W.G.)

  Orion swung southward aslant
  Where the starved Egdon pine-trees had thinned,
  The Pleiads aloft seemed to pant
  With the heather that twitched in the wind;
But he looked on indifferent to sights such as these,
Unswayed by love, friendship, home joy or home sorrow,
And wondered to what he would march on the morrow.

  The crazed household-clock with its whirr
  Rang midnight within as he stood,
  He heard the low sighing of her
  Who had striven from his birth for his good;
But he still only asked the spring starlight, the breeze,
What great thing or small thing his history would borrow
From that Game with Death he would play on the morrow.

17 Nay: too much the malediction.—*MS1*, *BH* richer] lesser *FEH* 19 In the unfurling of the future, *MS1*, *BH* time's] *cap. FEH* 20 call;] ~: *MS1* 22 bedrench] absorb *MV17*, *CP19*

BEFORE MARCHING AND AFTER. *Fortnightly Review*, 1 Oct. 1915; *SP* (1916). *MS1*, *MS2*, HRC; *TS* Fales

2 ⟨Where the old Egdon pines starved and thinned,⟩ *MS1* 6 ⟨Regardless of love, friends, home-joy and home sorrow,⟩ *MS1* or] ⟨and⟩ *MS2* 7 wondered] ⟨marvelled⟩ *MS1* 10 sighing] ⟨sighings⟩ *MS1*

When the heath wore the robe of late summer,
And the fuchsia-bells, hot in the sun,
Hung red by the door, a quick comer
Brought tidings that marching was done
For him who had joined in that game over-seas
Where Death stood to win, though his name was to borrow
A brightness therefrom not to fade on the morrow.

September 1915.

'OFTEN WHEN WARRING'

Often when warring for he wist not what,
An enemy-soldier, passing by one weak,
Has tendered water, wiped the burning cheek,
And cooled the lips so black and clammed and hot;

Then gone his way, and maybe quite forgot
The deed of grace amid the roar and reek;
Yet larger vision than loud arms bespeak
He there has reached, although he has known it not.

For natural mindsight, triumphing in the act
Over the throes of artificial rage,
Has thuswise muffled victory's peal of pride,
Rended to ribands policy's specious page
That deals but with evasion, code, and pact,
And war's apology wholly stultified.

1915.

16 in] ⟨with⟩ *MS1* 19 game] *cap. MS1, MS2, FR* 20 win,] ~ ; *MS1, MS2* name was to] memory would *FR, SP* 21 brightness] ⟨glory⟩ *MS1* fade] die *FR, SP*

'OFTEN WHEN WARRING'. *Sphere*, 10 Nov. 1917
7 loud arms bespeak] the tongue can speak *MV17, CP19* 8 there] thus *S* 9 mindsight,] ⟨judgment,⟩ *Hol.* 11 thuswise] thereby *MV17*
Date om. S

THEN AND NOW*

When battles were fought
With a chivalrous sense of Should and Ought,
In spirit men said,
'End we quick or dead,
Honour is some reward!
Let us fight fair—for our own best or worst;
So, Gentlemen of the Guard,
Fire first!'

In the open they stood,
Man to man in his knightlihood:
They would not deign
To profit by a stain
On the honourable rules,
Knowing that practise perfidy no man durst
Who in the heroic schools
Was nurst.

But now, behold, what
Is warfare wherein honour is not!
Rama laments
Its dead innocents:
Herod breathes: 'Sly slaughter
Shall rule! Let us, by modes once called accurst,
Overhead, under water,
Stab first.'

1915.

THEN AND NOW. *Times*, 11 July 1917
2 Should and Ought,] *l.c. T, Hol.* 18 Is war with those where honour is not! *T*; *variant line del. Hol.* 21 Herod breathes:] Herod howls: *T*; ⟨Herod howls:⟩ Despots nod: *Hol.* 22 Shall rule!] Rules now! *T*; ⟨?Is tow'rd!?⟩ ⟨Shall rule now!⟩ *Hol.*
Date om. T; Written 1915: published 1917. *Hol.*; *Written* 1915: *published in* "*The Times*," 1917. *MV17*

A CALL TO NATIONAL SERVICE*

Up and be doing, all who have a hand
To lift, a back to bend. It must not be
In times like these that vaguely linger we
To air our vaunts and hopes; and leave our land

Untended as a wild of weeds and sand.
—Say, then, 'I come!' and go, O women and men
Of palace, ploughshare, easel, counter, pen;
That scareless, scathless, England still may stand.

Would years but let me stir as once I stirred
At many a dawn to take the forward track,
And with a stride plunged on to enterprize,

I now would speed like yester wind that whirred
Through yielding pines; and serve with never a slack,
So loud for promptness all around outcries!

March 1917.

THE DEAD AND THE LIVING ONE*

The dead woman lay in her first night's grave,
And twilight fell from the clouds' concave,
And those she had asked to forgive forgave.

The woman passing came to a pause
By the heaped white shapes of wreath and cross,
And looked upon where the other was.

A CALL TO NATIONAL SERVICE. *Times* and *Morning Post*, 12 Mar. 1917; *FEH* (1917). *TS* (*MP*) Adams
Title om. T; For National Service *MP*, *TS*; ⟨For National Service⟩ *Hol.*
8 It will enray your name to dates unscanned. *T*, *MP*, *TS*; *variant line del. Hol.*
13 yielding] breaking *T*, *MP*, *TS*; ⟨breaking⟩ *Hol.*
Signed, *Hol.*

THE DEAD AND THE LIVING ONE. *Sphere*, 25 Dec. 1915. *P1* (*S*) Berg
2 clouds'] sky's *S*; ⟨sky's⟩ *Hol.*

And as she mused there thus spoke she:
'Never your countenance did I see,
But you've been a good good friend to me!'

Rose a plaintive voice from the sod below:
'O woman whose accents I do not know,
What is it that makes you approve me so?'

'O dead one, ere my soldier went,
I heard him saying, with warm intent,
To his friend, when won by your blandishment:

'"I would change for that lass here and now!
And if I return I may break my vow
To my present Love, and contrive somehow

'"To call my own this new-found pearl,
Whose eyes have the light, whose lips the curl,
I always have looked for in a girl!"

'—And this is why that by ceasing to be—
Though never your countenance did I see—
You prove you a good good friend to me;

'And I pray each hour for your soul's repose
In gratitude for your joining those
No lover will clasp when his campaigns close.'

Away she turned, when arose to her eye
A martial phantom of gory dye,
That said, with a thin and far-off sigh:

'O sweetheart, neither shall I clasp you,
For the foe this day has pierced me through,
And sent me to where she is. Adieu!—

10 Rose] Came *MV*, *CP19* sod] grave *S* 29 martial] soldier's *S*; ⟨soldier's⟩ *Hol.* 32 through,] ~ *Hol.* 33 is.] ~.⟨—⟩ *Hol.*

'And forget not when the night-wind's whine
Calls over this turf where her limbs recline,
That it travels on to lament by mine.'

There was a cry by the white-flowered mound,
There was a laugh from underground,
There was a deeper gloom around.

1915.

A NEW YEAR'S EVE IN WAR TIME*

I

Phantasmal fears,
And the flap of the flame,
And the throb of the clock,
And a loosened slate,
And the blind night's drone,
Which tiredly the spectral pines intone!

II

And the blood in my ears
Strumming always the same,
And the gable-cock
With its fitful grate,
And myself, alone.

III

The twelfth hour nears
Hand-hid, as in shame;
I undo the lock,
And listen, and wait
For the Young Unknown.

34–9 *om. S* 35 recline,] decline, *MV*
Date 1915/("*The Sphere.*") *MV17*

A NEW YEAR'S EVE. *Sphere*, 6 Jan. 1917; *FEH* (1917). *P1* (*FEH*) Adams
6 Which] While *S* intone!] ~. *Hol.* 11 myself,] ourselves, *FEH*

IV

In the dark there careers—
As if Death astride came
To numb all with his knock—
A horse at mad rate
Over rut and stone.

V

No figure appears,
No call of my name,
No sound but 'Tic-toc'
Without check. Past the gate
It clatters—is gone.

VI

What rider it bears
There is none to proclaim;
And the Old Year has struck,
And, scarce animate,
The New makes moan.

VII

Maybe that 'More Tears!—
More Famine and Flame—
More Severance and Shock!'
Is the order from Fate
That the Rider speeds on
To pale Europe; and tiredly the pines intone.

1915–1916.

21a While tiredly the spectral pines intone. *S* 23 my] our *S* 36 That he carries to prone *FEH*; *variant line del. Hol.* speeds] bears *S*, *Hol.* 37 To] And *FEH*; ⟨And⟩ *Hol.*
Date 1916 *Hol.*; January 1917 *S*, *FEH*

'I MET A MAN'*

I met a man when night was nigh,
Who said, with shining face and eye
Like Moses' after Sinai:—

'I have seen the Moulder of Monarchies,
Realms, peoples, plains and hills,
Sitting upon the sunlit seas!—
And, as He sat, soliloquies
Fell from Him like an antiphonic breeze
That pricks the waves to thrills.

'Meseemed that of the maimed and dead
Mown down upon the globe,—
Their plenteous blooms of promise shed
Ere fruiting-time—His words were said,
Sitting against the western web of red
Wrapt in His crimson robe.

'And I could catch them now and then:
—"Why let these gambling clans
Of human Cockers, pit liege men
From mart and city, dale and glen,
In death-mains, but to swell and swell again
Their swollen All-Empery plans,

'"When a mere nod (if my malign
Compeer but passive keep)
Would mend that old mistake of mine
I made with Saul, and ever consign
All Lords of War whose sanctuaries enshrine
Liberticide, to sleep?

'I MET A MAN'. *Fortnightly Review*, 1 Feb. 1917; *FEH* (1917). *P1* (*FEH*, ll. 1–21) Adams

7 He] It *FR*, *FEH*; ⟨It⟩ *Hol.* 8 Fell from It like a fitful lyric breeze *FR*; *variant line del. P1*, *Hol.* Him] It *FEH* 13 His] Its *FR*, *FEH*; ⟨Its⟩ *Hol.* 14 web] webs *FR*; ⟨webs⟩ *P1* 15 His] Its *FR*, *FEH*; ⟨Its⟩ *Hol.* 17 gambling] dominant *FR*; ⟨dominant⟩ *P1*, *Hol.* 22 mere] fleet *FR*; ⟨fleet⟩ *Hol.* malign] *cap. FR*, *FEH*, *Hol.* 26 All Lords of war with scutcheoned Rights-Divine *FR*; *variant line del. Hol.* 27 Liberticide,] Of Liberticide, *FR*; ⟨Of⟩ Liberticide, *Hol.*

'"With violence the lands are spread
Even as in Israel's day,
And it repenteth me I bred
Chartered armipotents lust-led
To feuds. . . . Yea, grieves my heart, as then I said,
To see their evil way!"

—'The utterance grew, and flapped like flame,
And further speech I feared;
But no Celestial tongued acclaim,
And no huzzas from earthlings came,
And the heavens mutely masked as 'twere in shame
Till daylight disappeared.'

Thus ended he as night rode high—
The man of shining face and eye,
Like Moses' after Sinai.

1916.

'I LOOKED UP FROM MY WRITING'

I looked up from my writing,
And gave a start to see,
As if rapt in my inditing,
The moon's full gaze on me.

Her meditative misty head
Was spectral in its air,
And I involuntarily said,
'What are you doing there?'

'Oh, I've been scanning pond and hole
And waterway hereabout
For the body of one with a sunken soul
Who has put his life-light out.

31 Caste-mad armipotents court-fed *FR*; *variant line del. Hol.* 32 To feuds] For feud *FR*; ⟨For feud⟩ *Hol.* 36 acclaim,] ~ *Hol.*

'I LOOKED UP'. 3 inditing,] ~ *Hol.* 11 sunken] ⟨heavy⟩ *Hol.*

'Did you hear his frenzied tattle?
It was sorrow for his son
Who is slain in brutish battle,
Though he has injured none.

'And now I am curious to look
Into the blinkered mind
Of one who wants to write a book
In a world of such a kind.'

Her temper overwrought me,
And I edged to shun her view,
For I felt assured she thought me
One who should drown him too.

15 brutish] booming *Hol.*

FINALE

THE COMING OF THE END*

How it came to an end!
The meeting afar from the crowd,
And the love-looks and laughters unpenned,
The parting when much was avowed,
How it came to an end!

It came to an end;
Yes, the outgazing over the stream,
With the sun on each serpentine bend,
Or, later, the luring moon-gleam;
It came to an end.

It came to an end,
The housebuilding, furnishing, planting,
As if there were ages to spend
In welcoming, feasting, and jaunting;
It came to an end.

It came to an end,
That journey of one day a week:
('It always goes on,' said a friend,
'Just the same in bright weathers or bleak;')
But it came to an end.

'*How* will come to an end
This orbit so smoothly begun,
Unless some convulsion attend?'
I often said. 'What will be done
When it comes to an end?'

THE COMING OF THE END. 21 '*How*] *rom. Hol.*

Well, it came to an end
Quite silently—stopped without jerk;
Better close no prevision could lend;
Working out as One planned it should work
Ere it came to an end.

AFTERWARDS

When the Present has latched its postern behind my tremulous stay,
And the May month flaps its glad green leaves like wings,
Delicate-filmed as new-spun silk, will the neighbours say,
'He was a man who used to notice such things'?

If it be in the dusk when, like an eyelid's soundless blink,
The dewfall-hawk comes crossing the shades to alight
Upon the wind-warped upland thorn, a gazer may think,
'To him this must have been a familiar sight'.

If I pass during some nocturnal blackness, mothy and warm,
When the hedgehog travels furtively over the lawn,
One may say, 'He strove that such innocent creatures should come to no harm,
But he could do little for them; and now he is gone'.

If, when hearing that I have been stilled at last, they stand at the door,
Watching the full-starred heavens that winter sees,
Will this thought rise on those who will meet my face no more,
'He was one who had an eye for such mysteries'?

AFTERWARDS. 1 When night has closed its shutters on my dismantled day, *Hol.* 2 wings,] ~ *Hol.* 3 will] ⟨with⟩ *Hol.* neighbours] people *MV17* 4 such] these *Hol.* 7 wind-warped] nibbled *Hol.* a gazer may] will a gazer *MV17* 8 sight'.] ~"? *MV17* 9 pass during] ⟨go during⟩ ⟨pass amid⟩ *Hol.* 10 When] ⟨And⟩ *Hol.* 11 One may say,] Will they say, *MV17* come to no] not come to *Hol.* 12 gone'.] ~"? *MV* 16 mysteries'?] ~." *Hol.*

And will any say when my bell of quittance is heard in
    the gloom,
  And a crossing breeze cuts a pause in its outrollings,
Till they swell again, as they were a new bell's boom,
  'He hears it not now, but used to notice such things'?

17 bell of quittance] parting bell *Hol.* 18 ⟨And a crossing breeze makes a blank in its utterings,⟩ *Hol.* 19 they swell] ⟨it rise⟩ *Hol.*; they rise *Hol.*, *MV*, *CP* they were] ⟨it were⟩ *Hol.* 20 not now,] ⟨not,⟩ *Hol.* things'?] ~." *Hol.*

LATE LYRICS AND EARLIER
WITH MANY OTHER VERSES

CONTENTS

APOLOGY*

About half the verses that follow were written quite lately. The rest are older, having been held over in MS. when past volumes were published, on considering that these would contain a sufficient number of pages to offer readers at one time, more especially during the distractions of the war. The unusually far back poems to be found here are, however, but some that were overlooked in gathering previous collections. A freshness in them, now unattainable, seemed to make up for their inexperience and to justify their inclusion. A few are dated; the dates of others are not discoverable.

The launching of a volume of this kind in neo-Georgian days by one who began writing in mid-Victorian, and has published nothing to speak of for some years, may seem to call for a few words of excuse or explanation. Whether or no, readers may feel assured that a new book is submitted to them with great hesitation at so belated a date. Insistent practical reasons, however, among which were requests from some illustrious men of letters who are in sympathy with my productions, the accident that several of the poems have already seen the light, and that dozens of them have been lying about for years, compelled the course adopted, in spite of the natural disinclination of a writer whose works have been so frequently regarded askance by a pragmatic section here and there, to draw attention to them once more.

I do not know that it is necessary to say much on the contents of the book, even in deference to suggestions that will be mentioned presently. I believe that those readers who care for my poems at all—readers to whom no passport is required—will care for this new instalment of them, perhaps the last, as much as for any that have preceded them.

APOLOGY. *Title* Preface *Hol. table of contents*
1 verses that follow] ⟨following verses⟩ *Hol.* 10 dated;] ~ : *Hol.* 15 submitted] ⟨presented⟩ *Hol.* 23 pragmatic section] ⟨section here⟩ section of opinion here *Hol.* 27 mentioned] explained *Hol.*

Moreover, in the eyes of a less friendly class the pieces, though a very mixed collection indeed, contain, so far as I am able to see, little or nothing in technic or teaching that can be considered a Star-Chamber matter, or so much as agitating to a ladies' school; even though, to use Wordsworth's observation in his Preface to *Lyrical Ballads*, such readers may suppose 'that by the act of writing in verse an author makes a formal engagement that he will gratify certain known habits of association: that he not only thus apprises the reader that certain classes of ideas and expressions will be found in his book, but that others will be carefully excluded'.

It is true, nevertheless, that some grave, positive, stark, delineations are interspersed among those of the passive, lighter, and traditional sort presumably nearer to stereotyped tastes. For—while I am quite aware that a thinker is not expected, and, indeed, is scarcely allowed, now more than heretofore, to state all that crosses his mind concerning existence in this universe, in his attempts to explain or excuse the presence of evil and the incongruity of penalizing the irresponsible—it must be obvious to open intelligences that, without denying the beauty and faithful service of certain venerable cults, such disallowance of 'obstinate questionings' and 'blank misgivings' tends to a paralysed intellectual stalemate. Heine observed nearly a hundred years ago that the soul has her eternal rights; that she will not be darkened by statutes, nor lullabied by the music of bells. And what is today, in allusions to the present author's pages, alleged to be 'pessimism' is, in truth, only such 'questionings' in the exploration of reality, and is the first step twoards the soul's betterment, and the body's also.

If I may be forgiven for quoting my own old words, let me repeat what I printed in this relation more than twenty years ago, and wrote much earlier, in a poem entitled 'In Tenebris':

31 Moreover,] ⟨And even⟩ *Hol.* a less friendly] ⟨the cooler⟩ *Hol.* 32 contain,] may contain, *Hol.* 35 school; even though,] ⟨school, though⟩ *Hol.* observation] phrase *Hol.* 36 such readers may suppose] ⟨they may hold⟩ *Hol.* 36–41 ⟨"that by the act of writing in verse an author not only apprizes the reader that certain classes of ideas and expressions will be found in his book, but that others will be carefully excluded."⟩ *Hol.* 42 stark,] ⟨what may be called stark,⟩ *Hol.* 51–2 certain venerable] ⟨the old⟩ certain old *Hol.* 60 and the body's] ⟨and body's⟩ *Hol.*

If way to the Better there be, it exacts a full look at the Worst:

that is to say, by the exploration of reality, and its frank recognition stage by stage along the survey, with an eye to the best consummation possible: briefly, evolutionary meliorism. But it is called pessimism nevertheless; under which word, expressed with condemnatory emphasis, it is regarded by many as some pernicious new thing (though so old as to underlie the Gospel scheme, and even to permeate the Greek drama); and the subject is charitably left to decent silence, as if further comment were needless.

Happily there are some who feel such Levitical passing-by to be, alas, by no means a permanent dismissal of the matter; that comment on where the world stands is very much the reverse of needless in these disordered years of our prematurely afflicted century: that amendment and not madness lies that way. And looking down the future these few hold fast to the same: that whether the human and kindred animal races survive till the exhaustion or destruction of the globe, or whether these races perish and are succeeded by others before that conclusion comes, pain to all upon it, tongued or dumb, shall be kept down to a minimum by loving-kindness, operating through scientific knowledge, and actuated by the modicum of free will conjecturally possessed by organic life when the mighty necessitating forces—unconscious or other—that have 'the balancings of the clouds', happen to be in equilibrium, which may or may not be often.

To conclude this question I may add that the argument of the so-called optimists is neatly summarized in a stern pronouncement against me by my friend Mr. Frederic Harrison in a late essay of his, in the words: 'This view of life is not mine'. The solemn declaration does not seem to me to be so annihilating to the said 'view' (really a series of fugitive impressions which I have never tried to co-ordinate) as is complacently assumed. Surely it embodies a too human fallacy

65 frank] full *Hol.* 66 survey,] journey, *Hol.* 67 possible:] ~; *Hol.* 69 condemnatory] terminative *Hol.* 69–72 regarded . . . subject is] *om. Hol.* 71 Gospel scheme,] Christian idea, *LL22a* 75 matter;] ~, *Hol.* 79 future these few] whole long future they *Hol.* same:] ~; *Hol.* 86 mighty] ⟨huge⟩ *Hol.* 87–8 that have . . . clouds',] *om. Hol.*

quite familiar in logic. Next, a knowing reviewer, apparently a Roman Catholic young man, speaks, with some rather gross instances of the *suggestio falsi* in his whole article, of 'Mr. Hardy refusing consolation', the 'dark gravity of his ideas', and so on. When a Positivist and a Romanist agree there must be something wonderful in it, which should make a poet sit up. But . . . O that 'twere possible!

I would not have alluded in this place or anywhere else to such casual personal criticisms—for casual and unreflecting they must be—but for the satisfaction of two or three friends in whose opinion a short answer was deemed desirable, on account of the continual repetition of these criticisms, or more precisely, quizzings. After all, the serious and truly literary inquiry in this connection is: Should a shaper of such stuff as dreams are made on disregard considerations of what is customary and expected, and apply himself to the real function of poetry, the application of ideas to life (in Matthew Arnold's familiar phrase)? This bears more particularly on what has been called the 'philosophy' of these poems—usually reproved as 'queer'. Whoever the author may be that undertakes such application of ideas in this 'philosophic' direction—where it is specially required—glacial judgments must inevitably fall upon him amid opinion whose arbiters largely decry individuality, to whom *ideas* are oddities to smile at, who are moved by a yearning the reverse of that of the Athenian inquirers on Mars Hill; and stiffen their features not only at sound of a new thing, but at a restatement of old things in new terms. Hence should anything of this sort in the following adumbrations seem 'queer'—should any of them seem to good Panglossians to embody strange and disrespectful conceptions

98–9 Next, . . . man,] ⟨An apparently Roman-Catholic young man⟩; A knowing young man, apparently a Roman-Catholic, *Hol.* 99–100 with . . . article,] too, in a recent periodical *Hol.* 100 his whole article,] his article, *LL* 101 and so on.] and so on, with sportive pity. *Hol.* 102 Romanist] Catholic *LL* 110 precisely,] ⟨truly⟩ *Hol.* 114 life (in] ~, ~ *Hol.* 115 phrase)?] ~. *Hol.* 120 arbiters largely decry] ⟨arbiters decry⟩ *Hol.* 121 to whom *ideas* are oddities to smile at, who] *om. Hol.* 123 and] who *Hol.* 126 'queer'—] "queer" (to use again the favourite word of ⟨one of my critics⟩ a critic)— *Hol.* 127 Panglossians] philistines *Hol.*

of this best of all possible worlds, I apologize; but cannot help it.

Such divergences, which, though piquant for the nonce, it would be affectation to say are not saddening and discouraging likewise, may, to be sure, arise sometimes from superficial aspect only, writer and reader seeing the same thing at different angles. But in palpable cases of divergence they arise, as already said, whenever a serious effort is made towards that which the authority I have cited—who would now be called old-fashioned, possibly even parochial—affirmed to be what no good critic could deny as the poet's province, the application of ideas to life. One might shrewdly guess, by the by, that in such recommendation the famous writer may have overlooked the cold-shouldering results upon an enthusiastic disciple that would be pretty certain to follow his putting the high aim in practice and have forgotten the disconcerting experience of Gil Blas with the Archbishop.

To add a few more words to what has already taken up too many, there is a contingency liable to miscellanies of verse that I have never seen mentioned, so far as I can remember; I mean the chance little shocks that may be caused over a book of various character like the present and its predecessors by the juxtaposition of unrelated, even discordant, effusions; poems perhaps years apart in the making, yet facing each other. An odd result of this has been that dramatic anecdotes of a satirical and humorous intention following verse in graver voice, have been read as misfires because they raise the smile that they were intended to raise, the journalist, deaf to the sudden change of key, being unconscious that he is laughing with the

128–9 best . . . help it.] life, so they must. *Hol.* 130–3 Such . . . writer] ⟨Such regrettable divergences, which, though piquant and amusing for the nonce, it would be affectation to say are not saddening and discouraging too, may, to be sure, lie sometimes in appearance only, owing to writer⟩ *Hol.* 130 divergences] ⟨divergences of vision,⟩ *Hol.* 132 likewise,] too, *Hol.* 143 practice] ~, *Hol.* 146 verse] ⟨verse like this⟩ *Hol.* 152 this has] this, more grievous to the author than little shocks, has *Hol.* 153 intention following] ⟨intention—such as "Royal Sponsors"—following⟩ *Hol.*; intention (such, *e.g.*, as "Royal Sponsors") following *LL* 154 misfires] failures *Hol.* 155–6 deaf to the sudden change of key,] blind to the sudden change, *Hol.*

author and not at him. I admit that I did not foresee such contingencies as I ought to have done, and that people might not perceive when the tone altered. But the difficulties of arranging the themes in a graduated kinship of moods would have been so great that irrelation was almost unavoidable with efforts so diverse. I must trust for right note-catching to those finely-touched spirits who can divine without half a whisper, whose intuitiveness is proof against all the accidents of inconsequence. In respect of the less alert, however, should any one's train of thought be thrown out of gear by a consecutive piping of vocal reeds in jarring tonics, without a semiquaver's rest between, and be led thereby to miss the writer's aim and meaning in one out of two contiguous compositions, I shall deeply regret it.

Having at last, I think, finished with the personal points that I was recommended to notice, I will forsake the immediate object of this Preface; and, leaving *Late Lyrics* to whatever fate it deserves, digress for a few moments to more general considerations. The thoughts of any man of letters concerned to keep poetry alive cannot but run uncomfortably on the precarious prospects of English verse at the present day. Verily the hazards and casualties surrounding the birth and setting forth of almost every modern creation in numbers are ominously like those of one of Shelley's paper-boats on a windy lake. And a forward conjecture scarcely permits the hope of a better time, unless men's tendencies should change. So indeed of all art, literature, and 'high thinking' nowadays. Whether owing to the barbarizing of taste in the younger minds by the dark madness of the late war, the unabashed cultivation of selfishness in all classes, the plethoric growth of knowledge simultaneously with the stunting of wisdom, 'a degrading thirst after outrageous stimulation' (to quote Wordsworth again), or from any other cause, we seem threatened with a new Dark Age.

159 tone] key *Hol.* 164–5 against . . . inconsequence.] ⟨against inconsequence.⟩ *Hol.* 166–7 a consecutive piping] ⟨an abrupt sounding⟩ an abrupt succession *Hol.* 168 thereby] ⟨in consequence⟩ *Hol.* 169 one out of] ⟨one of⟩ *Hol.* 171 last,] last ⟨done with⟩ *Hol.* that] ⟨to which⟩ *Hol.* 174 to] to ⟨a⟩ *Hol.* 182 tendencies should change.] ⟨instincts change.⟩ *Hol.* 184–5 dark madness] curse *Hol.*

I formerly thought, like other much exercised writers, that so far as literature was concerned a partial cause might be impotent or mischievous criticism; the satirizing of individuality, the lack of whole-seeing in contemporary estimates of poetry and kindred work, the knowingness affected by junior reviewers, the overgrowth of meticulousness in their peerings for an opinion, as if it were a cultivated habit in them to scrutinize the tool-marks and be blind to the building, to hearken for the key-creaks and be deaf to the diapason, to judge the landscape by a nocturnal exploration with a flash-lantern. In other words, to carry on the old game of sampling the poem or drama by quoting the worst line or worst passage only, in ignorance or not of Coleridge's proof that a versification of any length neither can be nor ought to be all poetry; of reading meanings into a book that its author never dreamt of writing there. I might go on interminably.

But I do not now think any such temporary obstructions to be the cause of the hazard, for these negligences and ignorances, though they may have stifled a few true poets in the run of generations, disperse like stricken leaves before the wind of next week, and are no more heard of again in the region of letters than their writers themselves. No: we may be convinced that something of the deeper sort mentioned must be the cause.

In any event poetry, pure literature in general, religion—I include religion, in its essential and undogmatic sense, because

190 other much exercised] so many roughly handled *LL* 200 words,] ~ *Hol.* 202 in ignorance or not of] when well acquainted with *Hol.* 205 there.] there. ⟨Carelessness, too, I adduced, (of which might be given one curious instance; the statement that my verse is bad, the writer being a novice, and my prose good, the writer being an old hand thereat; when by reference to dates it could be seen that he has written verse thirty years, and prose about twentyfive at the outside).⟩ Carelessness, too, I adduced, (of which might be given one curiously iterated instance; the statement that this writer's verse is bad, he being a novice of the eleventh hour therein: his prose good, he being a practised hand at it; when by reference to dates it could be seen that he has written verse thirty years, and prose twentyfive at the outside): *Hol.* interminably.] indefinitely. *Hol.* 206–7 But . . . for] ⟨But I do not think so now, for⟩ *Hol.* 208 true] good *Hol.* 215 religion . . . because *WE*] religion because *LL22a*, *22b*; religion, in its undogmatic sense, because *LL22c*, *CP23*

poetry and religion touch each other, or rather modulate into each other; are, indeed, often but different names for the same thing—these, I say, the visible signs of mental and emotional life, must like all other things keep moving, becoming; even though at present, when belief in witches of Endor is displacing the Darwinian theory and 'the truth that shall make you free', men's minds appear, as above noted, to be moving backwards rather than on. I speak somewhat sweepingly, and should except many thoughtful writers in verse and prose; also men in certain worthy but small bodies of various denominations, and perhaps in the homely quarter where advance might have been the very least expected a few years back—the English Church—if one reads it rightly as showing evidence of 'removing those things that are shaken', in accordance with the wise Epistolary recommendation to the Hebrews. For since the historic and once august hierarchy of Rome some generation ago lost its chance of being the religion of the future by doing otherwise, and throwing over the little band of New Catholics who were making a struggle for continuity by applying the principle of evolution to their own faith, joining hands with modern science, and outflanking the hesitating English instinct towards liturgical restatement (a flank march which I at the time quite expected to witness, with the gathering of many millions of waiting agnostics into its fold); since then, one may ask, what other purely English establishment than the Church of sufficient dignity and footing, with such strength of old association, such scope for transmutability, such architectural spell, is left in this country to keep the shreds of morality together?

220 witches of Endor] ⟨Endor witches⟩ *Hol.* 222 above] ⟨just⟩ *Hol.* 223–4 I . . . men] I speak, of course, somewhat sweepingly, and should except many isolated minds; also the minds of men *LL22a, 22b* 228 if one . . . showing] ⟨since it has shown⟩ *Hol.* 230 Epistolary] ⟨Apostolic⟩ *Hol.* 231 historic and once august] ⟨great historic⟩ *Hol.* generation] ⟨thirty years⟩ *Hol.* 233–4 New Catholics] Neo-Catholics *Hol.*; neo-Catholics *LL22a, 22b* 237 restatement] reform *LL22a, 22b* 239 many] tens of *Hol.* 240–3 establishment . . . spell,] establishment of sufficient dignity and footing, and with such strength of old association, *Hol.*; establishment than the Church, of sufficient dignity and footing, and with such strength of old association, such architectural spell, *LL22a, 22b*

It may indeed be a forlorn hope, a mere dream, that of an alliance between religion, which must be retained unless the world is to perish, and complete rationality, which must come, unless also the world is to perish, by means of the interfusing effect of poetry—'the breath and finer spirit of all knowledge; the impassioned expression of science', as it was defined by an English poet who was quite orthodox in his ideas. But if it be true, as Comte argued, that advance is never in a straight line, but in a looped orbit, we may, in the aforesaid ominous moving backward, be doing it *pour mieux sauter*, drawing back for a spring. I repeat that I forlornly hope so, notwithstanding the supercilious regard of hope by Schopenhauer, von Hartmann, and other philosophers down to Einstein who have my respect. But one dares not prophesy. Physical, chronological, and other contingencies keep me in these days from critical studies and literary circles

> Where once we held debate, a band
> Of youthful friends, on mind and art

(if one may quote Tennyson in this century). Hence I cannot know how things are going so well as I used to know them, and the aforesaid limitations must quite prevent my knowing henceforward.

I have to thank the editors and owners of *The Times*, *Fortnightly*, *Mercury*, and other periodicals in which a few of the poems have appeared for kindly assenting to their being reclaimed for collected publication.

T. H.

February 1922.

245 may indeed] may *LL*, *CP* 254 *pour mieux sauter*,] *mieux sauter*, *Hol.* 256–7 hope by . . . respect.] ⟨hope by philosophers I respect.⟩ ⟨hope by Schopenhauer and other philosophers down to Einstein.⟩ hope by Schopenhauer and other philosphers. *Hol.* 263 century).] ⟨twentieth century.⟩ century of "free verse"). *Hol.*; century of free verse). *LL* 267–8 owners . . . in which] owners of periodicals in which *Hol.* 269 kindly assenting] assenting *Hol.*

WEATHERS

I

This is the weather the cuckoo likes,
  And so do I;
When showers betumble the chestnut spikes,
  And nestlings fly:
And the little brown nightingale bills his best,
And they sit outside at 'The Travellers' Rest',
And maids come forth sprig-muslin drest,
And citizens dream of the south and west,
  And so do I.

II

This is the weather the shepherd shuns,
  And so do I;
When beeches drip in browns and duns,
  And thresh, and ply;
And hill-hid tides throb, throe on throe,
And meadow rivulets overflow,
And drops on gate-bars hang in a row,
And rooks in families homeward go,
  And so do I.

THE MAID OF KEINTON MANDEVILLE*

(A Tribute to Sir H. Bishop)

I hear that maiden still
Of Keinton Mandeville
Singing, in flights that played
As wind-wafts through us all,

WEATHERS. *Good Housekeeping* (London), May 1922
5 bills] sings *Hol.*, *GH* 13 thresh,] ⟨toss,⟩ *Hol.* 14 ⟨And from the sea strange noises blow,⟩ And from the sea throbs throe on throe, *Hol.* hill-hid] distant *GH*

THE MAID OF KEINTON MANDEVILLE. *Athenaeum*, 30 Apr. 1920. *TS*, *P1*, *P2* (*A*) Berg
Headnote (A tribute to Sir Henry Bishop on the sixty-fifth anniversary of his death: April 30, 1855.) *A*
3 in] ⟨of⟩ *Hol.*

Till they made our mood a thrall
To their aery rise and fall,
'Should he upbraid!'

Rose-necked, in sky-gray gown,
From a stage in Stower Town
Did she sing, and singing smile
As she blent that dexterous voice
With the ditty of her choice,
And banished our annoys
Thereawhile.

One with such song had power
To wing the heaviest hour
Of him who housed with her.
Who did I never knew
When her spoused estate ondrew,
And her warble flung its woo
In his ear.

Ah, she's a beldame now,
Time-trenched on cheek and brow,
Whom I once heard as a maid
From Keinton Mandeville
Of matchless scope and skill
Sing, with smile and swell and trill,
'Should he upbraid!'

1915 *or* 1916.

SUMMER SCHEMES*

When friendly summer calls again,
Calls again
Her little fifers to these hills,
We'll go—we two—to that arched fane

7 upbraid!'] ~." *Hol., LL22a, 22b* 14 ⟨There awhile.⟩ *Hol.* 15 Such song, such sleight, were power *TS*; ⟨sleight⟩ lure *P1*; lure *A* with such song] ⟨with song⟩ *Hol.* 16 wing] fledge *A* 19 spoused] ⟨espoused⟩ *P1* 22 a beldame] an ancient *A*; ⟨an ancient⟩ *Hol.* 26 scope] vein *TS*; ⟨vein⟩ mood *P1*; ⟨mood⟩ mien *P2*; mien *A*
Date om. A

Of leafage where they prime their bills
Before they start to flood the plain
With quavers, minims, shakes, and trills.
    '—We'll go,' I sing; but who shall say
    What may not chance before that day!

And we shall see the waters spring,
        Waters spring
From chinks the scrubby copses crown;
And we shall trace their oncreeping
To where the cascade tumbles down
And sends the bobbing growths aswing,
And ferns not quite but almost drown.
    '—We shall,' I say; but who may sing
    Of what another moon will bring!

EPEISODIA

I

Past the hills that peep
Where the leaze is smiling,
On and on beguiling
Crisply-cropping sheep;
Under boughs of brushwood
Linking tree and tree
In a shade of lushwood,
    There caressed we!

II

Hemmed by city walls
That outshut the sunlight,
In a foggy dun light,
Where the footstep falls

SUMMER SCHEMES. 10 spring,] ~; *Hol.*

EPEISODIA. 9 city] ⟨heavy⟩ *Hol.*   10 outshut] ⟨outfaced⟩ *Hol.*

With a pit-pat wearisome
In its cadency
On the flagstones drearisome,
There pressed we!

III

Where in wild-winged crowds
Blown birds show their whiteness
Up against the lightness
Of the clammy clouds;
By the random river
Pushing to the sea,
Under bents that quiver,
There shall rest we.

FAINTHEART IN A RAILWAY TRAIN*

At nine in the morning there passed a church,
At ten there passed me by the sea,
At twelve a town of smoke and smirch,
At two a forest of oak and birch,
And then, on a platform, she:

A radiant stranger, who saw not me.
I said, 'Get out to her do I dare?'
But I kept my seat in my search for a plea,
And the wheels moved on. O could it but be
That I had alighted there!

15 drearisome, *Hol.*, *WE*] ~ *LL*, *CP* 17 wild-winged] ⟨wet-wild⟩ *Hol.* 18 Blown birds] ⟨Stormbirds⟩ *Hol.* 20 clammy] ⟨dripping⟩ *Hol.* clouds;] ~, *Hol.* 23 ⟨With a plunge and quiver,⟩ *Hol.* quiver, *Hol.*, *WE*] ~ *LL*, *CP* 24 *WE*, *DCM3*] There rest we. *LL*, *CP*

FAINTHEART IN A RAILWAY TRAIN. *London Mercury*, Jan. 1920. *MS1* (*LM*) Colby
Title A Glimpse from the Train *MS1*, *LM*
5 she:] ~. *MS1* 6 Her I could see, though she saw not me: *MS1*, *LM* radiant] matchless *Hol.* 7 said, *WE*, *DCM3*] queried, *LM*, *LL*, *CP*

AT MOONRISE AND ONWARDS

I thought you a fire
On Heath-Plantation Hill,
Dealing out mischief the most dire
To the chattels of men of hire
There in their vill.

But by and by
You turned a yellow-green,
Like a large glow-worm in the sky;
And then I could descry
Your mood and mien.

How well I know
Your furtive feminine shape!
As if reluctantly you show
You nude of cloud, and but by favour throw
Aside its drape....

—How many a year
Have you kept pace with me,
Wan Woman of the waste up there,
Behind a hedge, or the bare
Bough of a tree!

No novelty are you,
O Lady of all my time,
Veering unbid into my view
Whether I near Death's mew,
Or Life's top cyme!

AT MOONRISE AND ONWARDS. 2 Heath-Plantation] Heron-Plantation *LL22a, 22b* 10 mood] ⟨shape⟩ *Hol.* 12 Your] ⟨That⟩ *Hol.* 13 ⟨As if reluctant in its show⟩ *Hol.* 14 ⟨You'd not, forever so,⟩ *Hol.* 15 ⟨Be seen in drape . . .⟩ *Hol.* 18 Woman] ⟨*l.c.*⟩ *Hol.* 22 Lady] ⟨*l.c.*⟩ *Hol.* 24 near] ⟨neared⟩ *Hol.*

THE GARDEN SEAT

Its former green is blue and thin,
And its once firm legs sink in and in;
Soon it will break down unaware,
Soon it will break down unaware.

At night when reddest flowers are black
Those who once sat thereon come back;
Quite a row of them sitting there,
Quite a row of them sitting there.

With them the seat does not break down,
Nor winter freeze them, nor floods drown,
For they are as light as upper air,
They are as light as upper air!

BARTHÉLÉMON AT VAUXHALL*

François Hippolite Barthélémon, first-fiddler at Vauxhall Gardens, composed what was probably the most popular morning hymn-tune ever written. It was formerly sung, full-voiced, every Sunday in most churches, to Bishop Ken's words, but is now seldom heard.

He said: 'Awake my soul, and with the sun,' . . .
And paused upon the bridge, his eyes due east,
Where was emerging like a full-robed priest
The irradiate globe that vouched the dark as done.

THE GARDEN SEAT. 10 winter] ⟨does frost⟩ *Hol.* 11 upper] ⟨skiey⟩ *Hol.* 12 upper] ⟨skiey⟩ *Hol.*

BARTHÉLÉMON AT VAUXHALL. *Times*, 23 July 1921

Headnote ⟨Barthélémon, first-fiddler at Vauxhall Gardens, is said to have been the composer of what was probably the most popular hymn-tune ever written. It was formerly sung every Sunday in most churches, to Ken's words, but is now silenced for reasons unknown. The circumstances of the following lines have no claim to be more than supposititious.⟩ *Hol.* heard.] heard. To-day is the anniversary of his death in 1808. The circumstances of the following lines have no claim to be more than supposititious. *T*

It lit his face— the weary face of one
Who in the adjacent gardens charged his string,
Nightly, with many a tuneful tender thing,
Till stars were weak, and dancing hours outrun.

And then were threads of matin music spun
In trial tones as he pursued his way:
'This is a morn', he murmured, 'well begun:
This strain to Ken will count when I am clay!'

And count it did; till, caught by echoing lyres,
It spread to galleried naves and mighty quires.

'I SOMETIMES THINK'*

(For F. E. H.)

I sometimes think as here I sit
    Of things I have done,
Which seemed in doing not unfit
    To face the sun:
Yet never a soul has paused a whit
    On such—not one.

There was that eager strenuous press
    To sow good seed;
There was that saving from distress
    In the nick of need;
There were those words in the wilderness:
    Who cared to heed?

Yet can this be full true, or no?
    For one did care,
And, spiriting into my house, to, fro,
    Like wind on the stair,
Cares still, heeds all, and will, even though
    I may despair.

7 thing,] ~ *Hol.*

'I SOMETIMES THINK'. 5 has paused] ⟨will pause⟩ *Hol.* 10 nick] ⟨hour⟩ *Hol.*

JEZREEL*

On its Seizure by the English under Allenby,
September 1918

Did they catch as it were in a Vision at shut of the day—
When their cavalry smote through the ancient Esdraelon
Plain,
And they crossed where the Tishbite stood forth in his
enemy's way—
His gaunt mournful Shade as he bade the King haste off
amain?

On war-men at this end of time—even on Englishmen's
eyes—
Who slay with their arms of new might in that long-ago
place,
Flashed he who drove furiously? . . . Ah, did the phantom
arise
Of that queen, of that proud Tyrian woman who painted
her face?

Faintly marked they the words 'Throw her down!' from
the Night eerily,
Spectre-spots of the blood of her body on some rotten
wall?
And the thin note of pity that came: 'A King's daughter
is she,'
As they passed where she trodden was once by the
chargers' footfall?

Could such be the hauntings of men of to-day, at the cease
Of pursuit, at the dusk-hour, ere slumber their senses
could seal?

JEZREEL. *Times*, 27 Sept. 1918; *FEH* (1919). *TS*, *P1* (*FEH*) Buffalo
Headnote om. T, *FEH*, *Hol.*
4 King] *l.c. T*, *FEH* 9 Faintly marked] Faint-marked *T*, *FEH* from the Night *DCM1*, *DCM3*] rise from Time *T*, *FEH*; rise from Night *LL*, *CP*, *WE*
11 King's] *l.c. T*, *FEH*

Enghosted seers, kings—one on horseback who asked 'Is it
peace?'. . .
Yea, strange things and spectral may men have beheld in
Jezreel!

September 24, 1918.

A JOG-TROT PAIR

Who were the twain that trod this track
So many times together
Hither and back,
In spells of certain and uncertain weather?

Commonplace in conduct they
Who wandered to and fro here
Day by day:
Two that few dwellers troubled themselves to know here.

The very gravel-path was prim
That daily they would follow:
Borders trim:
Never a wayward sprout, or hump, or hollow.

Trite usages in tamest style
Had tended to their plighting.
'It's just worth while,
Perhaps,' they had said. 'And saves much sad good-
nighting.'

And petty seemed the happenings
That ministered to their joyance:
Simple things,
Onerous to satiate souls, increased their buoyance.

15 kings] *cap. Hol.* asked] asks *T, FEH* peace?' . . .] ~?" *Hol.* 16 in] at *TS*; ⟨at⟩ *P1*
Date om. T; 25 September 1918. *FEH*

A JOG-TROT PAIR. 7 day:] ~; *Hol.* 12 sprout,] growth *Hol.* hump,] ~ *Hol.* 24 cleverest, smartest,] ⟨richest, wisest,⟩ *Hol.*

Who could those common people be,
Of days the plainest, barest?
They were we;
Yes; happier than the cleverest, smartest, rarest.

'THE CURTAINS NOW ARE DRAWN'*

(Song)

I

The curtains now are drawn,
And the spindrift strikes the glass,
Blown up the jaggèd pass
By the surly salt sou'-west,
And the sneering glare is gone
Behind the yonder crest,
While she sings to me:
'O the dream that thou art my Love, be it thine,
And the dream that I am thy Love, be it mine,
And death may come, but loving is divine.'

II

I stand here in the rain,
With its smite upon her stone,
And the grasses that have grown
Over women, children, men,
And their texts that 'Life is vain';
But I hear the notes as when
Once she sang to me:
'O the dream that thou art my Love, be it thine,
And the dream that I am thy Love, be it mine,
And death may come, but loving is divine.'

1913.

'THE CURTAINS NOW'. *Headnote* ⟨Song: Major and Minor⟩ *Hol.*
I] I ⟨Major⟩ *Hol.* 3 the jaggèd pass] ⟨across the grass⟩ *Hol.*; the jagged pass *Hol.*, *LL22a*, *22b* 4 sou'-west,] ⟨north-west,⟩ *Hol.* 5 sneering] ⟨pallid⟩ *Hol.* 8 art] are *Hol.* II] II ⟨Minor⟩ *Hol.* 12 stone,] ~ *Hol.* 15 their texts] ⟨I read⟩ *Hol.*

'ACCORDING TO THE MIGHTY WORKING'*

I

When moiling seems at cease
In the vague void of night-time,
And heaven's wide roomage stormless
Between the dusk and light-time,
And fear at last is formless,
We call the allurement Peace.

II

Peace, this hid riot, Change,
This revel of quick-cued mumming,
This never truly being,
This evermore becoming,
This spinner's wheel onfleeing
Outside perception's range.

1917.

'I WAS NOT HE'

(Song)

I was not he—the man
Who used to pilgrim to your gate,
At whose smart step you grew elate,
And rosed, as maidens can,
For a brief span.

It was not I who sang
Beside the keys you touched so true
With note-bent eyes, as if with you
It counted not whence sprang
The voice that rang. . . .

'ACCORDING TO THE MIGHTY WORKING'. *Athenaeum*, 4 Apr. 1919. *TS*, *P1*, *P2* Berg *Title* ⟨Transmutation⟩ *TS* 1 at] to *TS* 3 And earth's high arch is stormless *TS*; And heavens lamped roomage stormless *P1* 4 dusk] dark *TS*, *P1* 6 allurement] picture *TS* Peace] *l.c.* *TS*, *P1* 8 quick-cued] wordless *TS* 10 evermore] steadfastly *TS* 12 Outside] Past all *TS* perception's] conception's *P1*, *P2*, *A*; ⟨conception's⟩ *Hol.*

'I WAS NOT HE'. 3 smart] ⟨quick⟩ *Hol.*

Yet though my destiny
It was to miss your early sweet,
You still, when turned to you my feet,
Had sweet enough to be
A prize for me!

THE WEST-OF-WESSEX GIRL*

A very West-of-Wessex girl,
As blithe as blithe could be,
Was once well-known to me,
And she would laud her native town,
And hope and hope that we
Might sometime study up and down
Its charms in company.

But never I squired my Wessex girl
In jaunts to Hoe or street
When hearts were high in beat,
Nor saw her in the marbled ways
Where market-people meet
That in her bounding early days
Were friendly with her feet.

Yet now my West-of-Wessex girl,
When midnight hammers slow
From Andrew's, blow by blow,
As phantom draws me by the hand
To the place—Plymouth Hoe—
Where side by side in life, as planned,
We never were to go!

Begun in Plymouth, *March* 1913.

THE WEST-OF-WESSEX GIRL. 2 ⟨As fair as fair could be,⟩ *Hol.* 15 girl,] ~⟨—⟩, *Hol.* 16 ⟨When twelve is hammered slow⟩ *Hol.* 17 ⟨From Andrew's tower below,—⟩ *Hol.* 18 draws] ⟨leads⟩ *Hol.*

WELCOME HOME

Back to my native place
Bent upon returning,
Bosom all day burning
To be where my race
Well were known, 'twas keen with me
There to dwell in amity.

Folk had sought their beds,
But I hailed: to view me
Under the moon, out to me
Several pushed their heads,
And to each I told my name,
Plans, and that therefrom I came.

'Did you? . . . Ah, 'tis true,'
Said they, 'back a long time,
Here had spent his young time,
Some such man as you . . .
Good-night.' The casement closed again,
And I was left in the frosty lane.

GOING AND STAYING*

I

The moving sun-shapes on the spray,
The sparkles where the brook was flowing,
Pink faces, plightings, moonlit May,
These were the things we wished would stay;
But they were going.

WELCOME HOME. 1 Back to *WE, DCM3*] To *LL, CP* 5 keen with *WE, DCM3*] ⟨borne on⟩ planned by *Hol.*; much with *LL, CP* 9 out] ⟨quick⟩ *Hol.* 12 Plans,] ⟨My plans,⟩ *Hol.* 13 ⟨"Ah, did you? Well, 'tis true⟩ *Hol.* 14 Said they, *WE, DCM3*] ⟨I once heard,⟩ ⟨One said,⟩ *Hol.*; I once heard, *Hol., LL, CP* 15 Here had spent] ⟨Lived here in⟩ ⟨Here had spent⟩ ⟨Here spent⟩ *Hol.* 18 frosty] ⟨moonlit⟩ *Hol.*

GOING AND STAYING. *London Mercury*, Nov. 1919. *MS1* (*LM*) Eton; *P1* (*LM*) Colby *stanzas not numbered, third stanza om. MS1, P1, LM*
3 May,] ~,— *MS1*

II

Seasons of blankness as of snow,
The silent bleed of a world decaying,
The moan of multitudes in woe,
These were the things we wished would go;
But they were staying.

III

Then we looked closelier at Time,
And saw his ghostly arms revolving
To sweep off woeful things with prime,
Things sinister with things sublime
Alike dissolving.

READ BY MOONLIGHT

I paused to read a letter of hers
By the moon's cold shine,
Eyeing it in the tenderest way,
And edging it up to catch each ray
Upon her light-penned line.
I did not know what years would flow
Of her life's span and mine
Ere I read another letter of hers
By the moon's cold shine!

I chance now on the last of hers,
By the moon's cold shine;
It is the one remaining page
Out of the many shallow and sage
Whereto she set her sign.
Who could foresee there were to be
Such missives of pain and pine
Ere I should read this last of hers
By the moon's cold shine!

READ BY MOONLIGHT. 1 paused] ⟨tried⟩ *Hol.* 3 tenderest] ⟨closest⟩ *Hol.* 4 catch] ⟨throw⟩ *Hol.* 10 ⟨I chance now on⟩ ⟨I now unfold⟩ *Hol.* 16 Such missives] ⟨Letters⟩ *Hol.*; Such letters *Hol.*, *LL22a*, *22b*

AT A HOUSE IN HAMPSTEAD*

Sometime the Dwelling of John Keats

O Poet, come you haunting here
Where streets have stolen up all around,
And never a nightingale pours one
Fuil-throated sound?

Drawn from your drowse by the Seven famed Hills,
Thought you to find all just the same
Here shining, as in hours of old,
If you but came?

What will you do in your surprise
At seeing that changes wrought in Rome
Are wrought yet more on the misty slope
One time your home?

Will you wake wind-wafts on these stairs?
Swing the doors open noisily?
Show as an umbraged ghost beside
Your ancient tree?

Or will you, softening, the while
You further and yet further look,
Learn that a laggard few would fain
Preserve your nook? . . .

—Where the Piazza steps incline,
And catch late light at eventide,
I once stood, in that Rome, and thought,
''Twas here he died.'

AT A HOUSE IN HAMPSTEAD. *John Keats Memorial Volume* (London: 1921). *MS1* (*JK*) BL Ashley MS 3351

2 stolen] crept *MS1*, *JK*; ⟨crept⟩ *Hol.* 3 one] ⟨now⟩ *MS1* 5 the Seven famed Hills,] ⟨Rome's gaunt gate,⟩ the far Gaunt Gate, *MS1*, *JK*; ⟨the far gaunt Gate,⟩ ⟨the famed Seven Hills,⟩ *Hol.* 7 hours] ⟨times⟩ ⟨days⟩ hours *MS1*; days *JK* 11 slope] hill *MS1*, *JK*; ⟨hill⟩ *Hol.* 15 an umbraged] ⟨?uneased?⟩ ⟨an umbraged⟩ a troubled *MS1*; a troubled *JK* 22 eventide,] ~ *MS1*

I drew to a violet-sprinkled spot,
Where day and night a pyramid keeps
Uplifted its white hand, and said,
''Tis there he sleeps.'

Pleasanter now it is to hold
That here, where sang he, more of him
Remains than where he, tuneless, cold,
Passed to the dim.

July 1920.

A WOMAN'S FANCY

'Ah, Madam; you've indeed come back here?
'Twas sad—your husband's so swift death,
And you away! You shouldn't have left him:
It hastened his last breath.'

'Dame, I am not the lady you think me;
I know not her, nor know her name;
I've come to lodge here—a friendless woman;
My health my only aim.'

She came; she lodged. Wherever she rambled
They held her as no other than
The lady named; and told how her husband
Had died a forsaken man.

So often did they call her thuswise
Mistakenly, by that man's name,
So much did they declare about him,
That his past form and fame

25 drew] ⟨drew⟩ ⟨went⟩ *MS1*; ⟨went⟩ *Hol.* Date om. *JK* 31 Remains] ~, *MS1*

A WOMAN'S FANCY. 2 so swift] ⟨sudden⟩ *Hol.* 11 told how] ⟨said⟩ *Hol.*

Grew on her, till she pitied his sorrow
  As if she truly had been the cause—
Yea, his deserter; and came to wonder
    What mould of man he was.

'Tell me my history!' would exclaim she;
  '*Our* history,' she said mournfully.
'But *you* know, surely, Ma'am?' they would answer,
    Much in perplexity.

Curious, she crept to his grave one evening,
  And a second time in the dusk of the morrow;
Then a third time, with crescent emotion
    Like a bereaved wife's sorrow.

No gravestone rose by the rounded hillock;
  —'I marvel why this is?' she said.
—'He had no kindred, Ma'am, but you near.'
    —She set a stone at his head.

She learnt to dream of him, and told them:
  'In slumber often uprises he,
And says: "I am joyed that, after all, Dear,
    You've not deserted me!"'

At length died too this kinless woman,
  As he had died she had grown to crave;
And at her dying she besought them
    To bury her in his grave.

Such said, she had paused; until she added:
  'Call me by his name on the stone,
As I were, first to last, his dearest,
    Not she who left him lone!'

And this they did. And so it became there
  That, by the strength of a tender whim,
The stranger was she who bore his name there,
    Not she who wedded him.

19 came] ⟨grew⟩ *Hol.* 20 mould] make *Hol.* 25 crept] ⟨went⟩ *Hol.* 27 crescent] ⟨a crescent⟩ *Hol.* 29 rose by] ⟨marked⟩ *Hol.* 32 a stone at] ⟨one above⟩ *Hol.*

HER SONG

I sang that song on Sunday,
To witch an idle while,
I sang that song on Monday,
As fittest to beguile;
I sang it as the year outwore,
And the new slid in;
I thought not what might shape before
Another would begin.

I sang that song in summer,
All unforeknowingly,
To him as a new-comer
From regions strange to me:
I sang it when in afteryears
The shades stretched out,
And paths were faint; and flocking fears
Brought cup-eyed care and doubt.

Sings he that song on Sundays
In some dim land afar,
On Saturdays, or Mondays,
As when the evening star
Glimpsed in upon his bending face
And my hanging hair,
And time untouched me with a trace
Of soul-smart or despair?

A WET AUGUST

Nine drops of water bead the jessamine,
And nine-and-ninety smear the stones and tiles:
—'Twas not so in that August—full-rayed, fine—
When we lived out-of-doors, sang songs, strode miles.

HER SONG. 1 Sunday,] ~ *Hol.* 15 faint;] ⟨dim,⟩ ~, *Hol.* 17 Sings] ⟨Hums⟩ *Hol.* 18 dim land] ⟨green glade⟩ *Hol.* 21 face] ~, *Hol.*, *CP*

A WET AUGUST. 4 strode] ⟨?leazed?⟩ ⟨roved⟩ *Hol.*

Or was there then no noted radiancy
Of summer? Were dun clouds, a dribbling bough,
Gilt over by the light I bore in me,
And was the waste world just the same as now?

It can have been so: yea, that threatenings
Of coming down-drip on the sunless gray,
By the then golden chances seen in things
Were wrought more bright than brightest skies to-day.

1920.

THE DISSEMBLERS

'It was not you I came to please,
  Only myself,' flipped she;
'I like this spot of phantasies,
  And thought you far from me.'
But O, he was the secret spell
  That led her to the lea!

'It was not she who shaped my ways,
  Or works, or thoughts,' he said.
'I scarcely marked her living days,
  Or missed her much when dead.'
But O, his joyance knew its knell
  When daisies hid her head!

TO A LADY PLAYING AND SINGING IN THE MORNING

Joyful lady, sing!
And I will lurk here listening,

6 dribbling] ⟨dripping⟩ *Hol.* 7 Gilt] ⟨clothed⟩ *Hol.* 8 waste] ⟨wide⟩ *Hol.* 10 down-drip] ⟨downpour⟩ *Hol.* 11 By the then] ⟨By such ?⟩ *Hol.* golden . . . things] possibilities in things *LL22a, 22b*

THE DISSEMBLERS. *Title* The Evaders *Hol.*
2 flipped] ⟨said⟩ *Hol.*

Though nought be done, and nought begun,
And work-hours swift are scurrying.

Sing, O lady, still!
Aye, I will wait each note you trill,
Though duties due that press to do
This whole day long I unfulfil.

'—It is an evening tune;
One not designed to waste the noon,'
You say. I know: time bids me go—
For daytide passes too, too soon!

But let indulgence be,
This once, to my rash ecstasy:
When sounds nowhere that carolled air
My idled morn may comfort me!

'A MAN WAS DRAWING NEAR TO ME'*

On that gray night of mournful drone,
Apart from aught to hear, to see,
I dreamt not that from shires unknown
In gloom, alone,
By Halworthy,
A man was drawing near to me.

I'd no concern at anything,
No sense of coming pull-heart play;
Yet, under the silent outspreading
Of even's wing
Where Otterham lay,
A man was riding up my way.

TO A LADY PLAYING. 4 swift are] ⟨swiftly⟩ *Hol.* scurrying.] ~⟨!⟩. *Hol.* 8 unfulfil.] ~⟨!⟩. *Hol.* 10 not designed] undesigned *Hol.*

'A MAN WAS DRAWING NEAR TO ME'. *Headnote* ⟨(Woman's Song)⟩ *Hol.* 9 ⟨Yet, through the silent darkening⟩ *Hol.* 11 ⟨Out Otterham way,⟩ *Hol.*

I thought of nobody—not of one,
But only of trifles—legends, ghosts—
Though, on the moorland dim and dun
　　That travellers shun
　　About these coasts,
The man had passed Tresparret Posts.

There was no light at all inland,
Only the seaward pharos-fire,
Nothing to let me understand
　　That hard at hand
　　By Hennett Byre
The man was getting nigh and nigher.

There was a rumble at the door,
A draught disturbed the drapery,
And but a minute passed before,
　　With gaze that bore
　　My destiny,
The man revealed himself to me.

THE STRANGE HOUSE

(Max Gate, AD 2000)

'I hear the piano playing—
　Just as a ghost might play.'
'—O, but what are you saying?
　There's no piano to-day;
Their old one was sold and broken;
　Years past it went amiss.'
'—I heard it, or shouldn't have spoken:
　　A strange house, this!

THE STRANGE HOUSE. 2 ⟨Just as she used to play."⟩ *Hol.* Just] ⟨Light⟩ *Hol.*
4–6 ⟨It is never touched to-day;
Some of its wires are broken;
Some of its keys amiss."⟩ *Hol.*

'I catch some undertone here,
  From someone out of sight.'
'—Impossible; we are alone here,
  And shall be through the night.'
'—The parlour-door—what stirred it?'
  '—No one: no soul's in range.'
'—But, anyhow, I heard it,
    And it seems strange!

'Seek my own room I cannot—
  A figure is on the stair!'
'—What figure? Nay, I scan not
  Anyone lingering there.
A bough outside is waving,
  And that's its shade by the moon.'
'—Well, all is strange! I am craving
    Strength to leave soon.'

'—Ah, maybe you've some vision
  Of showings beyond our sphere;
Some sight, sense, intuition
  Of what once happened here?
The house is old; they've hinted
  It once held two love-thralls,
And they may have imprinted
    Their dreams on its walls?

'They were—I think 'twas told me—
  Queer in their works and ways;
The teller would often hold me
  With weird tales of those days.
Some folk can not abide here,
  But we—we do not care
Who loved, laughed, wept, or died here,
    Knew joy, or despair.'

10 someone *Hol.*] some one *all printed texts* 20 Anyone *Hol.*] Any one *all printed texts* 24 leave] ⟨go⟩ *Hol.* 26 showings] ⟨shows⟩ *Hol.* 32 dreams] ⟨history⟩ ⟨mood⟩ *Hol.* 40 ⟨Or loved here to despair."⟩ *Hol.*

'AS 'TWERE TO-NIGHT'

(Song)

As 'twere to-night, in the brief space
Of a far eventime,
My spirit rang achime
At vision of a girl of grace;
As 'twere to-night, in the brief space
Of a far eventime.

As 'twere at noontide of to-morrow
I airily walked and talked,
And wondered as I walked
What it could mean, this soar from sorrow;
As 'twere at noontide of to-morrow
I airily walked and talked.

As 'twere at waning of this week
Broke a new life on me;
Trancings of bliss to be
In some dim dear land soon to seek;
As 'twere at waning of this week
Broke a new life on me!

THE CONTRETEMPS

A forward rush by the lamp in the gloom,
And we clasped, and almost kissed;
But she was not the woman whom
I had promised to meet in the thawing brume
On that harbour-bridge; nor was I he of her tryst.

'AS 'TWERE TO-NIGHT'. 2 far] ⟨spring⟩ *Hol.* 6 far] ⟨spring⟩ *Hol.* 10 sorrow;] ~, *Hol.* 12 I airily] ⟨When thus I⟩ *Hol.* 13 waning] ⟨passage⟩ *Hol.* 17 waning] ⟨passage⟩ *Hol.* 18 ⟨So broke new life on me!⟩ *Hol.*

THE CONTRETEMPS. 5 that] ⟨that⟩ ⟨the⟩ *Hol.*

So loosening from me swift she said:
  'O why, why feign to be
The one I had meant!—to whom I have sped
To fly with, being so sorrily wed!'
—'Twas thus and thus that she upbraided me.

My assignation had struck upon
  Some others' like it, I found.
And her lover rose on the night anon;
And then her husband entered on
The lamplit, snowflaked, sloppiness around.

'Take her and welcome, man!' he cried:
  'I wash my hands of her.
I'll find me twice as good a bride!'
—All this to me, whom he had eyed,
'Twas clear, as his wife's planned deliverer.

And next the lover: 'Little I knew,
  Madam, you had a third!
Kissing here in my very view!'
—Husband and lover then withdrew.
I let them; and I told them not they erred.

Why not? Well, there faced she and I—
  Two strangers who'd kissed, or near,
Chancewise. To see stand weeping by
A woman once embraced, will try
The tension of a man the most austere.

So it began; and I was young,
  She pretty, by the lamp,
As flakes came waltzing down among
The waves of her clinging hair, that hung
Heavily on her temples, dark and damp.

6 swift] ⟨quick⟩ *Hol.*
8 I had meant!—] ⟨of my choice!—⟩ *Hol.*
12 like it,] ⟨rocks,⟩ *Hol.*
20 'Twas clear, *DCM3*] Plainly, *all other texts*
27 Two] ⟨The⟩ *Hol.*
34 ⟨The twinings of her hair, that hung⟩ *Hol.*
35 dark] ⟨limp⟩ ⟨pale⟩ *Hol.*

And there alone still stood we two;
She one cast off for me,
Or so it seemed: while night ondrew,
Forcing a parley what should do
We twain hearts caught in one catastrophe.

In stranded souls a common strait
Wakes latencies unknown,
Whose impulse may precipitate
A life-long leap. The hour was late,
And there was the Jersey boat with its funnel agroan.

'Is wary walking worth much pother?'
It grunted, as still it stayed.
'One pairing is as good as another
Where all is venture! Take each other,
And scrap the oaths that you have aforetime made.'...

—Of the four involved there walks but one
On earth at this late day.
And what of the chapter so begun?
In that odd complex what was done?
Well; happiness comes in full to none:
Let peace lie on lulled lips: I will not say.

Weymouth.

A GENTLEMAN'S EPITAPH ON HIMSELF AND A LADY, WHO WERE BURIED TOGETHER*

I dwelt in the shade of a city,
She far by the sea,
With folk perhaps good, gracious, witty;
But never with me.

43 ⟨That a life's leap precipitate⟩ *Hol.* 44 ⟨The snow was raw, the hour was late,⟩ *Hol.* 45 funnel agroan.] ⟨steamy groan.⟩ *Hol.* 51 ⟨Of the four involved⟩ ⟨—When later⟩ *Hol.* 54 odd] queer *Hol.*

A GENTLEMAN'S EPITAPH. 1 shade] *cap. Hol.*

Her form on the ballroom's smooth flooring
I never once met,
To guide her with accents adoring
Through Weippert's 'First Set.'

I spent my life's seasons with pale ones
In Vanity Fair,
And she enjoyed hers among hale ones
In salt-smelling air.

Maybe she had eyes of deep colour,
Maybe they were blue,
Maybe as she aged they got duller;
That never I knew.

She may have had lips like the coral,
But I never kissed them,
Saw pouting, nor curling in quarrel,
Nor sought for, nor missed them.

Not a word passed of love all our lifetime,
Between us, nor thrill;
We'd never a husband-and-wife time,
For good or for ill.

Yet as one dust, through bleak days and vernal,
Lie I and lies she,
This never-known lady, eternal
Companion to me!

THE OLD GOWN

(Song)

I have seen her in gowns the brightest,
Of azure, green, and red,
And in the simplest, whitest,
Muslined from heel to head;

I have watched her walking, riding,
Shade-flecked by a leafy tree,
Or in fixed thought abiding
By the foam-fingered sea.

In woodlands I have known her,
When boughs were mourning loud,
In the rain-reek she has shown her
Wild-haired and watery-browed.
And once or twice she has cast me
As she pomped along the street
Court-clad, ere quite she had passed me,
A glance from her chariot-seat.

But in my memoried passion
For evermore stands she
In the gown of fading fashion
She wore that night when we,
Doomed long to part, assembled
In the snug small room; yea, when
She sang with lips that trembled,
'Shall I see his face again?'

A NIGHT IN NOVEMBER

I marked when the weather changed,
And the panes began to quake,
And the winds rose up and ranged,
That night, lying half-awake.

Dead leaves blew into my room,
And alighted upon my bed,
And a tree declared to the gloom
Its sorrow that they were shed.

THE OLD GOWN. 11 rain-reek] ⟨rain-smite⟩ *Hol.* 15 Court-clad,] ⟨Town-clad,⟩ *Hol.*

A NIGHT IN NOVEMBER. 4 night, lying] night I lay *Hol.*

One leaf of them touched my hand,
And I thought that it was you
There stood as you used to stand,
And saying at last you knew!

(?) 1913.

A DUETTIST TO HER PIANOFORTE*

Song of Silence

(E. L. H.—H. C. H.)

Since every sound moves memories,
        How can I play you
Just as I might if you raised no scene,
By your ivory rows, of a form between
My vision and your time-worn sheen,
        As when each day you
Answered our fingers with ecstasy?
So it's hushed, hushed, hushed, you are for me!

And as I am doomed to counterchord
        Her notes no more
In those old things I used to know,
In a fashion, when we practised so,
'Good-night!—Good-bye!' to your pleated show
        Of silk, now hoar,
Each nodding hammer, and pedal and key,
For dead, dead, dead, you are to me!

I fain would second her, strike to her stroke,
        As when she was by,
Aye, even from the ancient clamorous 'Fall
Of Paris', or 'Battle of Prague' withal,

A DUETTIST TO HER PIANOFORTE. *Title* A] ⟨The⟩ *Hol.* *Subtitle* ⟨A Song of Silence⟩ *Hol.*
7 our] ⟨her⟩ *Hol.* 15 And nodding hammers, and pedal, and key, *Hol.*
16 dead, you] ~ ~ *Hol.*

To the 'Roving Minstrels', or 'Elfin Call'
Sung soft as a sigh:
But upping ghosts press achefully,
And mute, mute, mute, you are for me!

Should I fling your polyphones, plaints, and quavers
Afresh on the air,
Too quick would the small white shapes be here
Of the fellow twain of hands so dear;
And a black-tressed profile, and pale smooth ear;
—Then how shall I bear
Such heavily-haunted harmony?
Nay: hushed, hushed, hushed you are for me!

'WHERE THREE ROADS JOINED'*

Where three roads joined it was green and fair,
And over a gate was the sun-glazed sea,
And life laughed sweet when I halted there;
Yet there I never again would be.

I am sure those branchways are brooding now,
With a wistful blankness upon their face,
While the few mute passengers notice how
Spectre-beridden is the place;

Which nightly sighs like a laden soul,
And grieves that a pair, in bliss for a spell
Not far from thence, should have let it roll
Away from them down a plumbless well

23 ⟨But upping ghosts too ?painfully,?⟩ ⟨But pasts would press too achefully,⟩ *Hol.*
24 mute, you] ~ ~*Hol.* 31 heavily-haunted] ⟨sorely-haunted⟩ *Hol.*

'WHERE THREE ROADS JOINED'. *Title* Joined'] ⟨Met"⟩ *Hol.* *Headnote*: ⟨(Near Tresparret Posts, Cornwall)⟩ *Hol.*

1 joined] ⟨met⟩ *Hol.* 2 was] ⟨gleamed⟩ *Hol.* sun-glazed] sun-stroked *Hol.* 12 down] ⟨into⟩ *Hol.* well] ~; *Hol.*

While the phasm of him who fared starts up,
And of her who was waiting him sobs from near,
As they haunt there and drink the wormwood cup
They filled for themselves when their sky was clear.

Yes, I see those roads—now rutted and bare,
While over the gate is no sun-glazed sea;
And though life laughed when I halted there,
It is where I never again would be.

'AND THERE WAS A GREAT CALM'*

(On the Signing of the Armistice, Nov. 11, 1918)

I

There had been years of Passion—scorching, cold,
And much Despair, and Anger heaving high,
Care whitely watching, Sorrows manifold,
Among the young, among the weak and old,
And the pensive Spirit of Pity whispered, 'Why?'

II

Men had not paused to answer. Foes distraught
Pierced the thinned peoples in a brute-like blindness,
Philosophies that sages long had taught,
And Selflessness, were as an unknown thought,
And 'Hell!' and 'Shell!' were yapped at Lovingkindness.

III

The feeble folk at home had grown full-used
To 'dug-outs', 'snipers', 'Huns', from the war-adept

13 phasm] ⟨fetch⟩ *Hol.* fared] ⟨paused⟩ *Hol.* 15 wormwood] ⟨bitter⟩ *Hol.* 18 is] ⟨shines⟩ *Hol.* sun-glazed] sun-stroked *Hol.*

'AND THERE WAS A GREAT CALM'. *Times*, 11 Nov. 1920; *FEH* (1920). *MS1* HRC; *TS*, *P1* (*FEH*) Yale

Headnote date only T, FEH, Hol., MS1

1 scorching,] caustic, *T*; ⟨caustic,⟩ *Hol., MS1* cold,] ~— *TS–FEH* 4 old,] ~ ⟨,—⟩ *TS*; ~; *FEH* 5 pensive Spirit of Pity] Spirit of Compassion *T*; ⟨Spirit of Compassion⟩ *TS, Hol., MS1*

In the mornings heard, and at evetides perused;
To day-dreamt men in millions, when they mused—
To nightmare-men in millions when they slept.

IV

Waking to wish existence timeless, null,
Sirius they watched above where armies fell;
He seemed to check his flapping when, in the lull
Of night a boom came thencewise, like the dull
Plunge of a stone dropped into some deep well.

V

So, when old hopes that earth was bettering slowly
Were dead and damned, there sounded 'War is done!'
One morrow. Said the bereft, and meek, and lowly,
'Will men some day be given to grace? yea, wholly,
And in good sooth, as our dreams used to run?'

VI

Breathless they paused. Out there men raised their glance
To where had stood those poplars lank and lopped,
As they had raised it through the four years' dance
Of Death in the now familiar flats of France;
And murmured, 'Strange, this! How? All firing stopped?'

VII

Aye; all was hushed. The about-to-fire fired not,
The aimed-at moved away in trance-lipped song.
One checkless regiment slung a clinching shot
And turned. The Spirit of Irony smirked out, 'What?
Spoil peradventures woven of Rage and Wrong?'

13 perused;] ~. *TS*; ~⟨.⟩; *P1* 15 millions] ~, *TS–FEH*, *MS1* 17 ⟨Sirius would glitter over the eastern dell;⟩ *Hol.*, *MS1* fell;] ~: *TS–FEH* 19 thencewise,] ⟨seaways,⟩ *Hol.*, *MS1* 20 Plunge] Echo *T*; ⟨Echo⟩ *TS*, *Hol.*, *MS1* 22 sounded] ~, *TS–FEH* 23 morrow.] ~.— *TS–FEH*, *Hol.*, *MS1* 29 Death] ~, *TS–FEH* flats] mud *T*; ⟨mud⟩ *TS*, *Hol.*, *MS1* 31 not,] ~. *T*, *TS–FEH* 34 smirked out,] smirked *T*, *TS–FEH*; smirked, *Hol.*, *MS1* 'What?] ~?— *TS–FEH*

VIII

Thenceforth no flying fires inflamed the gray,
No hurtlings shook the dewdrop from the thorn,
No moan perplexed the mute bird on the spray;
Worn horses mused: 'We are not whipped to-day';
No weft-winged engines blurred the moon's thin horn.

IX

Calm fell. From Heaven distilled a clemency;
There was peace on earth, and silence in the sky;
Some could, some could not, shake off misery:
The Sinister Spirit sneered: 'It had to be!'
And again the Spirit of Pity whispered, 'Why?'

HAUNTING FINGERS*

A Phantasy in a Museum of Musical Instruments

'Are you awake,
Comrades, this silent night?
Well 'twere if all of our glossy gluey make
Lay in the damp without, and fell to fragments quite!'

'O viol, my friend,
I watch, though Phosphor nears,
And I fain would drowse away to its utter end
This dumb dark stowage after our loud melodious years!'

And they felt past handlers clutch them,
Though none was in the room,
Old players' dead fingers touch them,
Shrunk in the tomb.

36 gray,] ⟨sky,⟩ *Hol.* 42 peace . . . silence] *caps. TS–FEH* sky;] ~: *TS–FEH* 45 ⟨And the Spirit of Compassion whispered "Why?"⟩ *Hol.* whispered,] ~ *TS–FEH, MS1*

HAUNTING FINGERS. *New Republic*, 21 Dec. 1921; *FEH* (1922). *MS1* DCM; *TS, P1, P2* (*FEH*) Fales

Title ⟨The Dead Fingers⟩ *MS1*; The Haunting Fingers *NR*

6 I sleep not, though dawn nears, *NR*; *variant line del. MS1, Hol.* 9–12 *ital., del. MS1* 11 them,] ~ *Hol.*

"'Cello, good mate,
You speak my mind as yours:
Doomed to this voiceless, crippled, corpselike state,
Who, dear to famed Amphion, trapped here, long endures?

'Once I could thrill
The populace through and through,
Wake them to passioned pulsings past their will.'. . .
(A contra-basso spake so, and the rest sighed anew.)

And they felt old muscles travel
Over their tense contours,
And with long skill unravel
Cunningest scores.

'The tender pat
Of her aery finger-tips
Upon me daily—I rejoiced thereat!'
(Thuswise a harpsichord, as 'twere from dampered lips.)

'My keys' white shine,
Now sallow, met a hand
Even whiter. . . . Tones of hers fell forth with mine
In sowings of sound so sweet no lover could withstand!'

And its clavier was filmed with fingers
Like tapering flames—wan, cold—
Or the nebulous light that lingers
In charnel mould.

16 What vibrant frame so trapped and taken long endures?" *NR*; *variant line del. MS1*, *Hol.*; Who here, of Ariel-lineage, trapped so, long endures?" *MS1*, *Hol.*; Who here of Ariel-lineage trapped so long endures?" *TS–FEH* 20 spake] spake *NR*, *Hol.*; ⟨spoke⟩ *MS1*, *TS* 21–4 *ital.*, *del. MS1* 21 old muscles] dead touches *NR*; ⟨dead fingers⟩ ⟨old touches⟩ *MS1* 23 long] old *NR*; ⟨old⟩ *MS1* 28 (Thuswise] ⟨—⟩ (~*MS1*, *Hol.* as 'twere from] as from *NR*, *MS1*, *TS–FEH*, *LL*; ⟨as from⟩ *Hol.* 32 sweet] ~, *TS–FEH* 33–6 *ital. MS1* 33 ⟨And its ledge was freaked with fingers⟩ *MS1* 34 Like weak wan flames in the air, *NR*; *variant line del. MS1*, *Hol.* 35 the nebulous light] a phosphorous gleam *NR*; ⟨a phosphorous ⟨⟨gleam⟩⟩ light⟩ *MS1*; ⟨a phosphorous gleam⟩ *Hol.* 36 In mould laid bare. *NR*; *variant line del. MS1*, *Hol.*

'Gayer than most
Was I,' reverbed a drum;
'The regiments, marchings, throngs, hurrahs! What a host
I stirred—even when crape mufflings gagged me well-nigh dumb!'

Trilled an aged viol:
'Much tune have I set free
To spur the dance, since my first timid trial
Where I had birth—far hence, in sun-swept Italy!'

And he feels apt touches on him
From those that pressed him then;
Who seem with their glance to con him,
Saying, 'Not again!'

'A holy calm,'
Mourned a shawm's voice subdued,
'Steeped my Cecilian rhythms when hymn and psalm
Poured from devout souls met in Sabbath sanctitude.'

'I faced the sock
Nightly,' twanged a sick lyre,
'Over ranked lights! O charm of life in mock,
O scenes that fed love, hope, wit, rapture, mirth, desire!'

Thus they, till each past player
Stroked thinner and more thin,
And the morning sky grew grayer,
And day crawled in.

39 throngs, hurrahs!] ⟨throngs!⟩ *MS1* 41 Trilled] Thrilled *NR* 45–8 *ital., del. MS1* 45 apt touches] the dead fingers *NR*; ⟨the dead fingers⟩ *MS1*; the apt touches *MS1*, *Hol.*, *TS–FEH* 46 From those that] Of those who *NR*, *MS1*, *TS–FEH*; Of those ⟨who⟩ that *Hol.* 47 Who] ⟨They⟩ *MS1* 51 "Would steep my rhythms when Sabbath hymn and psalm *NR*; *variant line del. MS1*, *Hol.* 52 Sabbath] weekly *NR*; ⟨weekly⟩ *MS1*, *Hol.* 54 twanged a sick lyre,] *in parentheses NR*, *MS1*, *Hol.*, *TS–FEH* 57–60 *ital. MS1* 57 past] dead *NR*; ⟨dead⟩ *MS1* 59 grayer, *MS1*, *Hol.*, *TS–FEH*, WE] ~ *LL*, *CP* 60 crawled] looked *NR*; ⟨looked⟩ *MS1*, *Hol.*

THE WOMAN I MET*

A stranger, I threaded sunken-hearted
A lamp-lit crowd;
And anon there passed me a soul departed,
Who mutely bowed.
In my far-off youthful years I had met her,
Full-pulsed; but now, no more life's debtor,
Onward she slid
In a shroud that furs half-hid.

'Why do you trouble me, dead woman,
Trouble me;
You whom I knew when warm and human?
—How it be
That you quitted earth and are yet upon it
Is, to any who ponder on it,
Past being read!'
'Still, it is so,' she said.

'These were my haunts in my olden sprightly
Hours of breath;
Here I went tempting frail youth nightly
To their death;
But you deemed me chaste—me, a tinselled sinner!
How thought you one with pureness in her
Could pace this street
Eyeing some man to greet?

'Well; your very simplicity made me love you
Mid such town dross,
Till I set not Heaven itself above you,
Who grew my Cross;
For you'd only nod, despite how I sighed for you;
So you tortured me, who fain would have died for you!
—What I suffered then
Would have paid for the sins of ten!

THE WOMAN I MET. *London Mercury*, Apr. 1921. *TS* (*LM*) Berg
6 Full-pulsed;] ⟨Flesh-clad;⟩ *Hol.* 27 you,] ~; *TS* 28 But you were my Cross, *TS*; *variant line del. Hol.* 30 So you] Yea, *TS*, *LM*; ⟨So you⟩ ⟨And⟩ *Hol.*

'Thus went the days. I feared you despised me
To fling me a nod
Each time, no more: till love chastised me
As with a rod
That a fresh bland boy of no assurance
Should fire me with passion beyond endurance,
While others all
I hated, and loathed their call.

'I said: "It is his mother's spirit
Hovering around
To shield him, maybe!" I used to fear it,
As still I found
My beauty left no least impression,
And remnants of pride withheld confession
Of my true trade
By speaking; so I delayed.

'I said: "Perhaps with a costly flower
He'll be beguiled."
I held it, in passing you one late hour,
To your face: you smiled,
Keeping step with the throng; though you did not see there
A single one that rivalled me there! . . .
Well: it's all past.
I died in the Lock at last.'

So walked the dead and I together
The quick among,
Elbowing our kind of every feather
Slowly and long;
Yea, long and slowly. That a phantom should stalk there
With me seemed nothing strange, and talk there
That winter night
By flaming jets of light.

37 boy] ⟨youth⟩ *Hol.*
41 ⟨Whether it was your mother's spirit⟩ *Hol.*
42 Hovering] ⟨Hovered⟩ *Hol.*
43 him, maybe!"] ⟨you, I knew not.⟩ *Hol.*

She showed me Juans who feared their call-time,
Guessing their lot;
She showed me her sort that cursed their fall-time,
And that did not.
Till suddenly murmured she: 'Now, tell me,
Why asked you never, ere death befell me,
To have my love,
Much as I dreamt thereof?'

I could not answer. And she, well weeting
All in my heart,
Said: 'God your guardian kept our fleeting
Flesh apart!'
Sighing and drawing her furs around her
Over the shroud that tightly bound her,
With wafts as from clay
She turned and thinned away.

London, 1918.

'IF IT'S EVER SPRING AGAIN'*

(Song)

If it's ever spring again,
Spring again,
I shall go where went I when
Down the moor-cock splashed, and hen,
Seeing me not, amid their flounder,
Standing with my arm around her;
If it's ever spring again,
Spring again,
I shall go where went I then.

65 ⟨She showed me who were to cease next fall-time,⟩ *Hol.* Juans] ⟨rakes⟩ *TS*, *Hol.* 66 Guessing] ⟨Wailing⟩ *Hol.* 67 ⟨She showed me those that knew their call-time,⟩ *Hol.* sort] kind *TS*; ⟨kind⟩ *Hol.* 69 Now,] ~ *TS* 76 Flesh *DCM3*] Forms *all other texts* 79 as from] ⟨cold as⟩ *Hol.* *Place/date* London: ⟨about⟩ 1918. *Hol.*

'IF IT'S EVER SPRING AGAIN'. 4 ⟨Dipt the moor-cock, and his hen,⟩ *Hol.*

If it's ever summer-time,
Summer-time,
With the hay crop at the prime,
And the cuckoos—two—in rhyme,
As they used to be, or seemed to,
We shall do as long we've dreamed to,
If it's ever summer-time,
Summer-time,
With the hay, and bees achime.

THE TWO HOUSES

In the heart of night,
When farers were not near,
The left house said to the house on the right,
'I have marked your rise, O smart newcomer here.'

Said the right, cold-eyed:
'Newcomer here I am,
Hence haler than you with your cracked old hide,
Loose casements, wormy beams, and doors that jam.

'Modern my wood,
My hangings fair of hue;
While my windows open as they should,
And water-pipes thread all my chambers through.

'Your gear is gray,
Your face wears furrows untold.'
'—Yours might,' mourned the other, 'if you held, brother,
The Presences from aforetime that I hold.

13 ⟨And two cuckoo notes in rhyme,⟩ *Hol.*

THE TWO HOUSES. *Dial* (New York), Aug. 1921
5 The other replied, *D*; *variant line del. Hol.* cold-eyed:] ⟨?-eyed⟩ *Hol.*
7 haler] stronger *D*; ⟨stronger⟩ *Hol.* 15 mourned] said *D*; ⟨said⟩ *Hol.*

'You have not known
Men's lives, deaths, toils, and teens;
You are but a heap of stick and stone:
A new house has no sense of the have-beens.

'Void as a drum
You stand: I am packed with these,
Though, strangely, living dwellers who come
See not the phantoms all my substance sees!

'Visible in the morning
Stand they, when dawn drags in;
Visible at night; yet hint or warning
Of these thin elbowers few of the inmates win.

'Babes new-brought-forth
Obsess my rooms; straight-stretched
Lank corpses, ere outborne to earth;
Yea, throng they as when first from the 'Byss upfetched.

'Dancers and singers
Throb in me now as once;
Rich-noted throats and gossamered flingers
Of heels; the learned in love-lore and the dunce.

'Note here within
The bridegroom and the bride,
Who smile and greet their friends and kin,
And down my stairs depart for tracks untried.

'Where such inbe,
A dwelling's character
Takes theirs, and a vague semblancy
To them in all its limbs, and light, and atmosphere.

26 drags] crawls *D*; ⟨crawls⟩ *Hol.* 32 'Byss] void *D*, *Hol.* 44 limbs,] ~ *Hol.* light,] ~ *Hol.*

'Yet the blind folk
My tenants, who come and go
In the flesh mid these, with souls unwoke,
Of such sylph-like surrounders do not know.'

'—Will the day come',
Said the new one, awestruck, faint,
'When I shall lodge shades dim and dumb—
And with such spectral guests become acquaint?'

'—That will it, boy;
Such shades will people thee,
Each in his misery, irk, or joy,
And print on thee their presences as on me.'

ON STINSFORD HILL AT MIDNIGHT*

I glimpsed a woman's muslined form
Sing-songing airily
Against the moon; and still she sang,
And took no heed of me.

Another trice, and I beheld
What first I had not scanned,
That now and then she tapped and shook
A timbrel in her hand.

So late the hour, so white her drape,
So strange the look it lent
To that blank hill, I could not guess
What phantastry it meant.

50 new one,] new-built, *D*; ⟨Said the new-built, awestruck, faint,⟩ ⟨Said the new one who had half-⟩ From the new one, awestruck, faint, *Hol.* 54 ⟨Yea. Thrust like shades on thee,⟩ *Hol.* 56 ⟨And print in thee their histories as in me."⟩ *Hol.*

ON STINSFORD HILL. 6 ⟨What I had not first scanned,⟩ *Hol.* 11 blank] ⟨lone⟩ *Hol.* 12 ⟨What her appearance meant.⟩ ⟨What her fantastry meant.⟩ *Hol.*

Then burst I forth: 'Why such from you?
  Are you so happy now?'
Her voice swam on; nor did she show
  Thought of me anyhow.

I called again: 'Come nearer; much
  That kind of note I need!'
The song kept softening, loudening on,
  In placid calm unheed.

'What home is yours now?' then I said;
  'You seem to have no care.'
But the wild wavering tune went forth
  As if I had not been there.

'This world is dark, and where you are',
  I said, 'I cannot be!'
But still the happy one sang on,
  And had no need of me.

THE FALLOW DEER AT THE LONELY HOUSE

One without looks in to-night
    Through the curtain-chink
From the sheet of glistening white;
One without looks in to-night
    As we sit and think
    By the fender-brink.

We do not discern those eyes
    Watching in the snow;
Lit by lamps of rosy dyes
We do not discern those eyes
    Wondering, aglow,
    Fourfooted, tiptoe.

15 swam] ⟨went⟩ *Hol.*

THE FALLOW DEER. *MS1* Cheltenham College Library

THE SELFSAME SONG*

A bird sings the selfsame song,
With never a fault in its flow,
That we listened to here those long
 Long years ago.

A pleasing marvel is how
A strain of such rapturous rote
Should have gone on thus till now
 Unchanged in a note!

—But it's not the selfsame bird.—
No: perished to dust is he. . . .
As also are those who heard
 That song with me.

THE WANDERER*

There is nobody on the road
 But I,
And no beseeming abode
 I can try
For shelter, so abroad
 I must lie.

The stars feel not far up,
 And to be
The lights by which I sup
 Glimmeringly,
Set out in a hollow cup
 Over me.

THE SELFSAME SONG. 1 sings] ⟨sings⟩*Hol.*; bills *Hol.*, *LL22a*, *22b* 3 those] ⟨so⟩ *Hol.* 4 Long] ⟨Those⟩ *Hol.* 11 are those] ⟨is she⟩ *Hol.*

THE WANDERER. 3 beseeming] ⟨snug near⟩ *Hol.* 7 feel] ⟨seem⟩ *Hol.*

They wag as though they were
    Panting for joy
Where they shine, above all care,
    And annoy,
And demons of despair—
    Life's alloy.

Sometimes outside the fence
    Feet swing past,
Clock-like, and then go hence,
    Till at last
There is a silence, dense,
    Deep, and vast.

A wanderer, witch-drawn
    To and fro,
To-morrow, at the dawn,
    On I go,
And where I rest anon
    Do not know!

Yet it's meet—this bed of hay
    And roofless plight;
For there's a house of clay,
    My own, quite,
To roof me soon, all day
    And all night.

A WIFE COMES BACK*

This is the story a man told me
Of his life's one day of dreamery.

13 wag] ⟨look⟩ *Hol.* 17 demons] ⟨demons⟩ ⟨drenchings⟩ *Hol.* 20 ⟨Steps pad past,⟩ *Hol.* 21 Clock-like,] ⟨Draw hither,⟩ *Hol.* 31 Yet it's meet—] ⟨Still, it's well—⟩ *Hol.*

A woman came into his room
Between the dawn and the creeping day:
She was the years-wed wife from whom
He had parted, and who lived far away,
As if strangers they.

He wondered, and as she stood
She put on youth in her look and air,
And more was he wonderstruck as he viewed
Her form and flesh bloom yet more fair
While he watched her there;

Till she freshed to the pink and brown
That were hers on the night when first they met,
When she was the charm of the idle town,
And he the pick of the club-fire set. . . .
His eyes grew wet,

And he stretched his arms: 'Stay—rest!—'
He cried. 'Abide with me so, my own!'
But his arms closed in on his hard bare breast;
She had vanished with all he had looked upon
Of her beauty: gone.

He drest, and drew downstairs,
But she was not in the house, he found;
And he passed out under the leafy pairs
Of the avenue elms, and searched around
To the park-pale bound.

He mounted, and rode till night
To the city to which she had long withdrawn,
The vision he bore all day in his sight
Being her young self as pondered on
In the dim of dawn.

A WIFE COMES BACK. 5 years-wed] years'-wed *Hol.* 6 and who lived] ⟨who had gone⟩ *Hol.* away,] ~ *Hol.* 7 ⟨She was furrowed gray.⟩ ⟨Long since, for aye.⟩ *Hol.* 16 club-fire] ⟨dancing⟩ *Hol.* 21 ⟨And utterly she had vanished, gone⟩ *Hol.* 22 ⟨From the twilight wan.⟩ *Hol.* 23 drest, *DCM3*] clothed, *all other texts* 31 pondered on] ⟨gazed upon⟩ *Hol.*

'—The lady here long ago—
Is she now here?—young—or such age as she is?'
'—She is still here.'—'Thank God. Let her know;
She'll pardon a comer so late as this
Whom she'd fain not miss.'

She received him—an ancient dame,
Who hemmed, with features frozen and numb,
'How strange!—I'd almost forgotten your name!—
A call just now—is troublesome;
Why did you come?'

A YOUNG MAN'S EXHORTATION

Call off your eyes from care
By some determined deftness; put forth joys
Dear as excess without the core that cloys,
And charm Life's lourings fair.

Exalt and crown the hour
That girdles us, and fill it full with glee,
Blind glee, excelling aught could ever be
Were heedfulness in power.

Send up such touching strains
That limitless recruits from Fancy's pack
Shall rush upon your tongue, and tender back
All that your soul contains.

For what do we know best?
That a fresh love-leaf crumpled soon will dry,
And that men moment after moment die,
Of all scope dispossest.

34 ⟨Lives she now here?—young—I mean, as she is?"⟩ *Hol.* 38 received him—] entered— *Hol.* ancient] ⟨aged⟩ *Hol.* 39 hemmed,] ⟨said,⟩ *Hol.* 40 strange!—] ⟨strange!—⟩ queer!— *Hol.*

A YOUNG MAN'S EXHORTATION. *Title* ⟨An Exhortation⟩ *Hol.* 14 soon] ⟨long⟩ *Hol.*

If I have seen one thing
It is the passing preciousness of dreams;
That aspects are within us; and who seems
Most kingly is the King.

1867: Westbourne Park Villas.

AT LULWORTH COVE A CENTURY BACK*

Had I but lived a hundred years ago
I might have gone, as I have gone this year,
By Warmwell Cross on to a Cove I know,
And Time have placed his finger on me there:

'*You see that man?*'—I might have looked, and said,
'O yes: I see him. One that boat has brought
Which dropped down Channel round Saint Alban's Head.
So commonplace a youth calls not my thought.'

'*You see that man?*'—'Why yes; I told you; yes:
Of an idling town-sort; thin; hair brown in hue;
And as the evening light scants less and less
He looks up at a star, as many do.'

'*You see that man?*'—'Nay, leave me!' then I plead,
'I have fifteen miles to vamp across the lea,
And it grows dark, and I am weary-kneed:
I have said the third time; yes, that man I see!'

'Good. That man goes to Rome—to death, despair;
And no one notes him now but you and I:
A hundred years, and the world will follow him there,
And bend with reverence where his ashes lie.'

September 1920.

19 aspects] ⟨seasons⟩ *Hol.*
Date/place 1867:] ⟨(recopied.)⟩ *Hol.*

AT LULWORTH COVE. 7 round] ⟨from⟩ *Hol.* 9 I told you; yes:] ⟨I told you so⟩ *Hol.* 11 scants] wanes *Hol.* 14 fifteen] ⟨twenty⟩ *Hol.* vamp] ⟨go⟩ *Hol.* 19 A hundred years hence folk will follow him there, *Hol.*

A BYGONE OCCASION

(Song)

That night, that night,
That song, that song!
Will such again be evened quite
Through lifetimes long?

No mirth was shown
To outer seers,
But mood to match has not been known
In modern years.

O eyes that smiled,
O lips that lured;
That such would last was one beguiled
To think ensured!

That night, that night,
That song, that song;
O drink to its recalled delight,
Though tears may throng!

TWO SERENADES*

I

On Christmas Eve

Late on Christmas Eve, in the street alone,
Outside a house, on the pavement-stone,
I sang to her, as we'd sung together
On former eves ere I felt her tether.—

A BYGONE OCCASION. 16 ⟨Its praise prolong!⟩ *Hol.*

Above the door of green by me
Was she, her casement seen by me;
But she would not heed
What I melodied
In my soul's sore need—
She would not heed.

Cassiopeia overhead,
And the Seven of the Wain, heard what I said
As I bent me there, and voiced, and fingered
Upon the strings. . . . Long, long I lingered:
Only the curtains hid from her
One whom caprice had bid from her;
But she did not come,
And my heart grew numb
And dull my strum;
She did not come.

II

A Year Later

I skimmed the strings; I sang quite low;
I hoped she would not come or know
That the house next door was the one now dittied,
Not hers, as when I had played unpitied;
—Next door, where dwelt a heart fresh stirred,
My new Love, of good will to me,
Unlike my old Love chill to me,
Who had not cared for my notes when heard:
Yet that old Love came
To the other's name
As hers were the claim;
Yea, the old Love came.

TWO SERENADES. 5 Above] ⟨Within⟩ *Hol.* 8 melodied] ~⟨;⟩ *Hol.* 12 Seven] *l.c. Hol.* 13 voiced,] ~ *Hol.* 18 numb] ~⟨;⟩, *Hol.* 30 name] ~⟨,⟩ *Hol.* 31 hers] ⟨she⟩ *Hol.*

My viol sank mute, my tongue stood still,
I tried to sing on, but vain my will:
I prayed she would guess of the later, and leave me;
She stayed, as though, were she slain by the smart,
She would bear love's burn for a newer heart.
The tense-drawn moment wrought to bereave me
Of voice, and I turned in a dumb despair
At her finding I'd come to another there.
Sick I withdrew
At love's grim hue
Ere my last Love knew;
Sick I withdrew.

From an old copy.

THE WEDDING MORNING

Tabitha dressed for her wedding:—
'Tabby, why look so sad?'
'—O I feel a great gloominess spreading, spreading,
Instead of supremely glad! . . .

'I called on Carry last night,
And he came whilst I was there,
Not knowing I'd called. So I kept out of sight,
And I heard what he said to her:

'"—Ah, I'd far liefer marry
You, Dear, to-morrow!" he said,
"But that cannot be."—O I'd give him to Carry,
And willingly see them wed,

'But how can I do it when
His baby will soon be born?
After that I hope I may die. And then
She can have him. I shall not mourn!'

35 prayed] ⟨hop[ed]⟩ *Hol.* 40 ⟨At her seeing I'd come to a warmer there.⟩ *Hol.*

THE WEDDING MORNING. 10 Dear,] *l.c. Hol.*

END OF THE YEAR 1912*

You were here at his young beginning,
  You are not here at his agèd end;
Off he coaxed you from Life's mad spinning,
  Lest you should see his form extend
    Shivering, sighing,
    Slowly dying,
  And a tear on him expend.

So it comes that we stand lonely
  In the star-lit avenue,
Dropping broken lipwords only,
  For we hear no songs from you,
    Such as flew here
    For the new year
  Once, while six bells swung thereto.

THE CHIMES PLAY 'LIFE'S A BUMPER!'

'Awake! I'm off to cities far away,'
I said; and rose, on peradventures bent.
The chimes played 'Life's a Bumper!' long that day
To the measure of my walking as I went:
Their sweetness frisked and floated on the lea,
As they played out 'Life's a Bumper!' there to me.

'Awake!' I said. 'I go to take a bride!'
—The sun arose behind me ruby-red
As I journeyed townwards from the countryside,
The chiming bells saluting near ahead.
Their sweetness swelled in tripping tings of glee
As they played out 'Life's a Bumper!' there to me.

END OF THE YEAR 1912. *Title* ⟨End of the Old Year⟩ *Hol.* 2 agèd] aged *Hol.* 3 coaxed] ⟨sent⟩ *Hol.* mad] ⟨mad⟩ ⟨dazed⟩ *Hol.*

THE CHIMES PLAY. 3 Bumper!'] ~" *Hol.* long] on *LL22a, 22b* 6 Bumper!'] ~" *Hol.* 11 tings] ⟨notes⟩ *Hol.* 12 Bumper!'] ~" *Hol.*

'Again arise.' I seek a turfy slope,
And go forth slowly on an autumn noon,
And there I lay her who has been my hope,
And think, 'O may I follow hither soon!'
While on the wind the chimes come cheerily,
Playing out 'Life's a Bumper!' there to me.

1913.

'I WORKED NO WILE TO MEET YOU'*

(Song)

I worked no wile to meet you,
  My sight was set elsewhere,
I sheered about to shun you,
  And lent your life no care.
I was unprimed to greet you
  At such a date and place,
Constraint alone had won you
  Vision of my strange face!

You did not seek to see me
  Then or at all, you said,
—Meant passing when you neared me,
  But stumblingblocks forbade.
You even had thought to flee me,
  By other mindings moved;
No influent star endeared me,
  Unknown, unrecked, unproved!

What, then, was there to tell us
  The flux of flustering hours
Of their own tide would bring us
  By no device of ours

13 arise.'] ~!" *Hol.* 17 While on the wind] ⟨And from afar⟩ *Hol.*
18 Bumper!'] ~" *Hol.*

'I WORKED NO WILE'. 12 ⟨Till lets inhibited.⟩ *Hol.*

To where the daysprings well us
   Heart-hydromels that cheer,
Till Time enearth and swing us
   Round with the turning sphere.

AT THE RAILWAY STATION, UPWAY

'There is not much that I can do,
For I've no money that's quite my own!'
   Spoke up the pitying child—
A little boy with a violin
At the station before the train came in,—
'But I can play my fiddle to you,
And a nice one 'tis, and good in tone!'

   The man in the handcuffs smiled;
The constable looked, and he smiled, too,
   As the fiddle began to twang;
And the man in the handcuffs suddenly sang
         With grimful glee:
         'This life so free
         Is the thing for me!'
And the constable smiled, and said no word,
As if unconscious of what he heard;
And so they went on till the train came in—
The convict, and boy with the violin.

SIDE BY SIDE

So there sat they,
The estranged two,
Thrust in one pew
By chance that day;
Placed so, breath-nigh,
Each comer unwitting
Who was to be sitting
In touch close by.

AT THE RAILWAY STATION. 12 Uproariously: *LL*

Thus side by side
Blindly alighted,
They seemed united
As groom and bride,
Who'd not communed
For many years—
Lives from twain spheres
With hearts distuned.

Her fringes brushed
His garment's hem
As the harmonies rushed
Through each of them:
Her lips could be heard
In the creed and psalms,
And their fingers neared
At the giving of alms.

And women and men,
The matins ended,
By looks commended
Them, joined again.
Quickly said she,
'Don't undeceive them—
Better thus leave them:'
'Quite so,' said he.

Slight words!—the last
Between them said,
Those two, once wed,
Who had not stood fast.
Diverse their ways
From the western door,
To meet no more
In their span of days.

SIDE BY SIDE. 16 distuned.] ⟨untuned.⟩ *Hol.* 17 fringes] ⟨fingers⟩ *Hol.* 25 ⟨And friends smiled when⟩ ⟨People smiled when⟩ *Hol.* 27 By looks] ⟨And much⟩ *Hol.*

DREAM OF THE CITY SHOPWOMAN

'Twere sweet to have a comrade here,
Who'd vow to love this garreteer,
By city people's snap and sneer
Tried oft and hard!

We'd rove a truant cock and hen
To some snug solitary glen,
And never be seen to haunt again
This teeming yard.

Within a cot of thatch and clay
We'd list the flitting pipers play,
Our lives a twine of good and gay
Enwreathed discreetly;

Our blithest deeds so neighbouring wise
That doves should coo in soft surprise,
'These must belong to Paradise
Who live so sweetly.'

Our clock should be the closing flowers,
Our sprinkle-bath the passing showers,
Our church the alleyed willow bowers,
The truth our theme;

And infant shapes might soon abound:
Their shining heads would dot us round
Like mushroom balls on grassy ground. . . .
—But all is dream!

O God, that creatures framed to feel
A yearning nature's strong appeal
Should writhe on this eternal wheel
In rayless grime;

DREAM OF THE CITY SHOPWOMAN. 3 people's] peoples' *Hol.* 5 cock and] ⟨cock and⟩ ⟨couple⟩ *Hol.*

And vainly note, with wan regret,
Each star of early promise set;
Till Death relieves, and they forget
Their one Life's time!

Westbourne Park Villas, 1866.

A MAIDEN'S PLEDGE

(Song)

I do not wish to win your vow
To take me soon or late as bride,
And lift me from the nook where now
I tarry your farings to my side.
I am blissful ever to abide
In this green labyrinth—let all be,
If but, whatever may betide,
You do not leave off loving me!

Your comet-comings I will wait
With patience time shall not wear through;
The yellowing years will not abate
My largened love and truth to you,
Nor drive me to complaint undue
Of absence, much as I may pine,
If never another 'twixt us two
Shall come, and you stand wholly mine.

THE CHILD AND THE SAGE

You say, O Sage, when weather-checked,
'I have been favoured so
With cloudless skies, I must expect
This dash of rain or snow.'

Place/date ⟨(From old MS.)⟩ *Hol.*

A MAIDEN'S PLEDGE. 4 ⟨I count your comings to my side.⟩ *Hol.* 12 ⟨My large and deathless love for you,⟩ ⟨My largening love and temper true,⟩ My largening love and truth ⟨in⟩ to you, *Hol.* 16 stand] keep *Hol.*

'Since health has been my lot,' you say,
'So many months of late,
I must not chafe that one short day
Of sickness mars my state.'

You say, 'Such bliss has been my share
From Love's unbroken smile,
It is but reason I should bear
A cross therein awhile.'

And thus you do not count upon
Continuance of joy;
But, when at ease, expect anon
A burden of annoy.

But, Sage—this Earth—why not a place
Where no reprisals reign,
Where never a spell of pleasantness
Makes reasonable a pain?

December 21, 1908.

MISMET

I

He was leaning by a face,
He was looking into eyes,
And he knew a trysting-place,
And he heard seductive sighs;
But the face,
And the eyes,
And the place,
And the sighs,
Were not, alas, the right ones—the ones meet for him—
Though fine and sweet the features, and the feelings all abrim.

THE CHILD AND THE SAGE. 11 It is] ⟨But⟩ *Hol.*
Date Dec. 21. 1908./⟨(recopied)⟩ *Hol.*

MISMET. 10 fine] soft *Hol.* feelings all abrim.] ⟨promise not dim.⟩ *Hol.*

II

She was looking at a form,
She was listening for a tread,
She could feel a waft of charm
When a certain name was said;
    But the form,
    And the tread,
    And the charm,
    And name said,
Were the wrong ones for her, and ever would be so,
While the heritor of the right it would have saved her soul to know!

AN AUTUMN RAIN-SCENE*

There trudges one to a merrymaking
    With a sturdy swing,
  On whom the rain comes down.

To fetch the saving medicament
    Is another bent,
  On whom the rain comes down.

One slowly drives his herd to the stall
    Ere ill befall,
  On whom the rain comes down.

This bears his missives of life and death
    With quickening breath,
  On whom the rain comes down.

One watches for signals of wreck or war
    From the hill afar,
  On whom the rain comes down.

17 charm,] ~ *Hol.*, *LL*   18 And] ⟨And⟩ Of the *Hol.*; Of *LL22a*, *22b*

AN AUTUMN RAIN-SCENE. *Fortnightly Review*, 1 Dec. 1921. *P1* (*FR*) DCM
Title A December Rain-scene *FR*

Careless to gain a shelter or none,
Unhired moves one,
On whom the rain comes down.

And another knows nought of its chilling fall
Upon him at all,
On whom the rain comes down.

October 1904.

MEDITATIONS ON A HOLIDAY

(A New Theme to an Old Folk-Measure)

'Tis a May morning,
All-adorning,
No cloud warning
Of rain to-day.
Where shall I go to,
Go to, go to?—
Can I say No to
Lyonnesse-way?

Well—what reason
Now at this season
Is there for treason
To other shrines?
Tristram is not there,
Isolt forgot there,
New eras blot there
Sought-for signs!

16 Careless to *DCM3*] No care if he *all other texts* 17 ⟨Unhired moves one,⟩ Unhired, moves one *P1*
Date om. FR

MEDITATIONS ON A HOLIDAY. *Title* ⟨A Meditation on a Holiday⟩ *Hol.* *Headnote* ⟨To an old folk-metre⟩ ⟨(A chime to an old folk-metre)⟩ (A new chime to an old folk-metre) *Hol.*; (A new theme to an old folk-jingle) *LL*
2 ⟨Dull skies scorning,⟩ All things adorning, *Hol.*

Stratford-on-Avon—
Poesy-paven—
I'll find a haven
    There, somehow!—
Nay—I'm but caught of
Dreams long thought of,
The Swan knows nought of
    His Avon now!

What shall it be, then,
I go to see, then,
Under the plea, then,
    Of votary?
I'll go to Lakeland,
Lakeland, Lakeland,
Certainly Lakeland
    Let it be.

But—why to that place,
That place, that place,
Such a hard come-at place
    Need I fare?
When its bard cheers no more,
Loves no more, fears no more,
Sees no more, hears no more
    Anything there!

Ah, there is Scotland,
Burns's Scotland,
And Waverley's. To what land
    Better can I hie?—
Yet—if no whit now
Feel those of it now—
Care not a bit now
    For it—why I?

28 votary?] poesy? *Hol.* 35 That nigh-forgot place *Hol.* 37 more,] ~ *Hol.* 43 And Waverley's.] Scott's too. *Hol.*

I'll seek a town street,
Aye, a brick-brown street,
Quite a tumbledown street,
    Drawing no eyes.
For a Mary dwelt there,
And a Percy felt there
Heart of him melt there,
    A Claire likewise.

Why incline to *that* city,
Such a city, *that* city,
Now a mud-bespat city!—
    Care the lovers who
Now live and walk there,
Sit there and talk there,
Buy there, or hawk there,
    Or wed, or woo?

Laughters in a volley
Greet so fond a folly
As nursing melancholy
    In this and that spot,
Which, with most endeavour,
Those can visit never,
But for ever and ever
    Will now know not!

If, on lawns Elysian,
With a broadened vision
And a faint derision
    Conscious be they,
How they might reprove me
That these fancies move me,
Think they ill behoove me,
    Smile, and say:

58 *That* city, *that* city, *Hol.* 60 Care those who *Hol.* 63 ⟨Or recklessly stalk there,⟩ *Hol.* Buy there,] ~ *Hol.* 65 Laughters] Curses *Hol.* 68 spot,] ~ *Hol.* 70 visit] call up *Hol.* 72 Will now] ⟨Now will⟩ *Hol.* 73 on lawns] ⟨in fields⟩ *Hol.*

'What!—our hoar old houses,
Where the bygone drowses,
Nor a child nor spouse is
Of our name at all?
Such abodes to care for,
Inquire about and bear for,
And suffer wear and tear for—
How weak of you and small!'

May 1921.

AN EXPERIENCE

Wit, weight, or wealth there was not
In anything that was said,
In anything that was done;
All was of scope to cause not
A triumph, dazzle, or dread
To even the subtlest one,
My friend,
To even the subtlest one.

But there was a new afflation—
An aura zephyring round,
That care infected not:
It came as a salutation,
And, in my sweet astound,
I scarcely witted what
Might pend,
I scarcely witted what.

81 hoar] gray *Hol.* 82 *WE, DCM3*] ⟨Where all life now drowses,⟩ Where the past now drowses, *Hol.*; Where the past dead-drowses, *LL, CP* 85 abodes] ⟨spots⟩ *Hol.* 88 How] ⟨Is⟩ *Hol.*
Date ⟨April 21, 1921⟩ *Hol.*

AN EXPERIENCE. 2 In any speech that was sped, *Hol.* 3 anything] any deed *Hol.* 4 scope] ⟨compass⟩ *Hol.* 6 subtlest] ⟨gentlest⟩ *Hol.* 8 subtlest] ⟨gentlest⟩ *Hol.* 9 a new afflation—] an exhalation *Hol.* 10 ⟨Of some new thing round,⟩ Of some new aura round, *Hol.*

The hills in samewise to me
  Spoke, as they grayly gazed,
  —First hills to speak so yet!
The thin-edged breezes blew me
  What I, though cobwebbed, crazed,
  Was never to forget,
          My friend,
  Was never to forget!

THE BEAUTY*

O do not praise my beauty more,
  In such word-wild degree,
And say I am one all eyes adore;
  For these things harass me!

But do for ever softly say:
  'From now unto the end
Come weal, come wanzing, come what may,
  Dear, I will be your friend.'

I hate my beauty in the glass:
  My beauty is not I:
I wear it: none cares whether, alas,
  Its wearer live or die!

The inner I O care for, then,
  Yea, me and what I am,
And shall be at the gray hour when
  My cheek begins to clam.

THE BEAUTY. 5 softly] ⟨gently⟩ *Hol.*   15 the] that *Hol.*

THE COLLECTOR CLEANS HIS PICTURE*

Fili hominis, ecce ego tollo a te desiderabile oculorum tuorum in plaga.
—Ezech. xxiv. 16.

How I remember cleaning that strange picture! . . .
I had been deep in duty for my sick neighbour—
His besides my own—over several Sundays,
Often, too, in the week; so with parish pressures,
Baptisms, burials, doctorings, conjugal counsel—
All the whatnots asked of a rural parson—
Faith, I was well-nigh broken, should have been fully
Saving for one small secret relaxation,
One that in mounting manhood had grown my hobby.

This was to delve at whiles for easel-lumber,
Stowed in the backmost slums of a soon-reached city,
Merely on chance to uncloak some worthy canvas,
Panel, or plaque, blacked blind by uncouth adventure,
Yet under all concealing a precious art-feat.
Such I had found not yet. My latest capture
Came from the rooms of a trader in ancient house-gear
Who had no scent of beauty or soul for brushcraft.
Only a tittle cost it—murked with grime-films,
Gatherings of slow years, thick-varnished over,
Never a feature manifest of man's painting.

So, one Saturday, time ticking hard on midnight
Ere an hour subserved, I set me upon it.
Long with coiled-up sleeves I cleaned and yet cleaned,
Till a first fresh spot, a high light, looked forth,
Then another, like fair flesh, and another;
Then a curve, a nostril, and next a finger,

THE COLLECTOR CLEANS HIS PICTURE. 2 deep in] ⟨doing⟩ *Hol.* 5 Baptisms,] ⟨Christenings,⟩ *Hol.* conjugal] ⟨marital⟩ *Hol.* 6 rural] ⟨country⟩ *Hol.* 8 Saving] Save *Hol.* 9 mounting] ⟨early⟩ *Hol.* 19 slow] ⟨long⟩ *Hol.* 20 manifest of man's] ⟨showing of any⟩ *Hol.* 23 coiled-up] rolled up *Hol.* 24 fresh] ⟨bright⟩ *Hol.* looked] ⟨peeped⟩ *Hol.* 25 fair] ⟨fair⟩ ⟨smooth⟩ *Hol.* 26 nostril,] ⟨nose-tip,⟩ *Hol.*

Tapering, shapely, significantly pointing slantwise.
'Flemish?' I said. 'Nay, Spanish. . . . But, nay, Italian!'
—Then meseemed it the guise of the ranker Venus,
Named of some Astarte, of some Cotytto.
Down I knelt before it and kissed the panel,
Drunk with the lure of love's inhibited dreamings.

Till the dawn I rubbed, when there leered up at me
A hag, that had slowly emerged from under my hands there,
Pointing the slanted finger towards a bosom
Eaten away of a rot from the lusts of a lifetime. . . .
—I could have ended myself at the lashing lesson!
Stunned I sat till roused by a clear-voiced bell-chime,
Fresh and sweet as the dew-fleece under my luthern.
It was the matin service calling to me
From the adjacent steeple.

THE WOOD FIRE

(A Fragment)

'This is a brightsome blaze you've lit, good friend, to-night!'
'—Aye, it has been the bleakest spring I have felt for years,
And nought compares with cloven logs to keep alight:
I buy them bargain-cheap of the executioners,
As I dwell near; and they wanted the crosses out of sight
By Passover, not to affront the eyes of visitors.

27 ⟨Tapering, shapely, and delicately pointing slantwise.⟩ ⟨Fair, but mature, significantly pointing slantwise.⟩ *Hol.* 29 guise] ⟨form⟩ ⟨shape⟩ *Hol.* ranker] warmer *Hol.* 33 leered] gazed *LL22a*, *22b* 34 that had slowly] ⟨that slow⟩ *Hol.* 35 ⟨Grinning, the finger pointed towards a bosom⟩ The significant finger pointed towards a bosom *Hol.* 37 —I] I *Hol.* at the lashing lesson!] in heart-shook horror. *LL22a*, *22b*

THE WOOD FIRE. 5 dwell] ⟨live⟩ *Hol.*

'Yes, they're from the crucifixions last week-ending
At Kranion. We can sometimes use the poles again,
But they get split by the nails, and 'tis quicker work than mending
To knock together new; though the uprights now and then
Serve twice when they're let stand. But if a feast's impending,
As lately, you've to tidy up for the comers' ken.

'Though only three were impaled, you may know it didn't pass off
So quietly as was wont? That Galilee carpenter's son
Who boasted he was king, incensed the rabble to scoff:
I heard the noise from my garden. This piece is the one he was on. . . .
Yes, it blazes up well if lit with a few dry chips and shroff;
And it's worthless for much else, what with cuts and stains thereon.'

SAYING GOOD-BYE

(Song)

We are always saying
'Good-bye, good-bye!'
In work, in playing,
In gloom, in gaying:
At many a stage
Of pilgrimage
From youth to age
We say, 'Good-bye,
Good-bye!'

We are undiscerning
Which go to sigh,
Which will be yearning
For soon returning;

SAYING GOOD-BYE. 11 go] ⟨part⟩ *Hol.*

And which no more
Will dark our door,
Or tread our shore,
But go to die,
    To die.

Some come from roaming
    With joy again;
Some, who come homing
By stealth at gloaming,
    Had better have stopped
    Till death, and dropped
    By strange hands propped,
    Than come so fain,
        So fain.

So, with this saying,
    'Good-bye, good-bye,'
We speed their waying
Without betraying
    Our grief, our fear
    No more to hear
    From them, close, clear,
    Again: 'Good-bye,
        Good-bye!'

ON THE TUNE CALLED THE OLD-HUNDRED-AND-FOURTH*

We never sang together
  Ravenscroft's terse old tune
On Sundays or on weekdays,
In sharp or summer weather,
  At night-time or at noon.

15 our] ⟨the⟩ *Hol.* 16 our] ⟨the⟩ *Hol.* 22 at] ⟨in the⟩ *Hol.* 24 Till death,] ⟨Afar,⟩ *Hol.* 25 ⟨To death unpropped,⟩ *Hol.* 28 saying,] ~ *Hol.* 34 ⟨From them, so dear,⟩ *Hol.* 35 ⟨"Good-bye, good-bye,⟩ *Hol.*

ON THE TUNE. *Title* ⟨On a Tune by Dr. Gauntlett⟩ ⟨On a Tune by Ravenscroft⟩ *Hol.*

2 ⟨Old Dr. Gauntlett's tune⟩ ⟨Tom Ravenscroft's terse tune⟩ Old Ravenscroft's terse tune *Hol.* 3 ⟨On Sundays⟩ *Hol.*

Why did we never sing it,
  Why never so incline
On Sundays or on weekdays,
Even when soft wafts would wing it
  From your far floor to mine?

Shall we that tune, then, never
  Stand voicing side by side
On Sundays or on weekdays? . . .
Or shall we, when for ever
  In Sheol we abide,

Sing it in desolation,
  As we might long have done
On Sundays or on weekdays
With love and exultation
  Before our sands had run?

THE OPPORTUNITY*

(For H. P.)

Forty springs back, I recall,
  We met at this phase of the Maytime:
We might have clung close through all,
  But we parted when died that daytime.

We parted with smallest regret;
  Perhaps should have cared but slightly,
Just then, if we never had met:
  Strange, strange that we lived so lightly!

8 ⟨On Sundays⟩ *Hol.* 13 ⟨On Sundays?⟩ *Hol.* weekdays? . . .] ~ ? *Hol.* 15 Sheol] ⟨Tophet⟩ ⟨Haides⟩ *Hol.* 18 ⟨On Sundays⟩ *Hol.* 20 run?] ~ ! *Hol.*

THE OPPORTUNITY. 1–4
⟨Forty springs back, to a breath,
  We met at this stroke of the daytime:
We might have clung close till death,
  But we parted when passed that Maytime.⟩ *Hol.*
4 died] passed *Hol.*

Had we mused a little space
  At that critical date in the Maytime,
One life had been ours, one place,
  Perhaps, till our long cold claytime.

—This is a bitter thing
  For thee, O man: what ails it?
The tide of chance may bring
  Its offer; but nought avails it!

EVELYN G. OF CHRISTMINSTER*

I can see the towers
In mind quite clear
Not many hours'
Faring from here;
But how up and go,
And briskly bear
Thither, and know
That you are not there?

Though the birds sing small,
And apple and pear
On your trees by the wall
Are ripe and rare,
Though none excel them,
I have no care
To taste them or smell them
And you not there.

Though the College stones
Are stroked with the sun,

10 ⟨At that critical stroke of the daytime,⟩ *Hol.* 13 —This] This *Hol.*

EVELYN G. OF CHRISTMINSTER. *Title* ⟨To Evelyn of Christminster⟩ *Hol.* 3 hours'] hours *Hol.* 4 Faring] ⟨By road⟩ ⟨Wayfaring⟩ *Hol.* 6 bear] ⟨fare⟩ *Hol.* 9 birds sing] ⟨brook purls⟩ *Hol.* 12 ⟨?Are ripe to bear,?⟩ ⟨Are ripe-brink and rare⟩ *Hol.* 18 ⟨Still meet the sun,⟩ *Hol.* stroked] smit *LL*

And the gownsmen and Dons
Who held you as one
Of brightest brow
Still think as they did,
Why haunt with them now
Your candle is hid?

Towards the river
A pealing swells:
They cost me a quiver—
Those prayerful bells!
How go to God,
Who can reprove
With so heavy a rod
As your swift remove!

The chorded keys
Wait all in a row,
And the bellows wheeze
As long ago.
And the psalter lingers,
And organist's chair;
But where are your fingers
That once wagged there?

Shall I then seek
That desert place
This or next week,
And those tracks trace
That fill me with cark
And cloy; nowhere
Being movement or mark
Of you now there!

19 gownsmen] ⟨wardens⟩ Wardens *Hol.*; graduates *LL22a, 22b* Dons] ⟨*l.c.*⟩ *Hol.* 22 Still think] ⟨Think⟩ *Hol.* 23 haunt with] ⟨visit⟩ *Hol.* 24 candle] ⟨face⟩ *Hol.* 25 Towards] ⟨The orga[n]⟩ *Hol.* 27 ⟨They make me quiver—⟩ *Hol.* 29 ⟨How think of God,⟩ *Hol.* 31 ⟨With this hard rod⟩ *Hol.* 32 ⟨Of your quick remove!⟩ *Hol.* 33 chorded] ⟨organ⟩ *Hol.* 38 And] ⟨And the⟩ *Hol.* 40 wagged] ⟨played⟩ *Hol.* 46 ⟨Of soul; nowhere⟩ *Hol.* 48 there!] ~⟨?⟩! *Hol.*

THE RIFT

(Song: Minor Mode)

'Twas just at gnat and cobweb-time,
When yellow begins to show in the leaf,
That your old gamut changed its chime
From those true tones—of span so brief!—
That met my beats of joy, of grief,
As rhyme meets rhyme.

So sank I from my high sublime!
We faced but chancewise after that,
And never I knew or guessed my crime. . . .
Yes; 'twas the date—or nigh thereat—
Of the yellowing leaf; at moth and gnat
And cobweb-time.

VOICES FROM THINGS GROWING IN A CHURCHYARD*

These flowers are I, poor Fanny Hurd,
Sir or Madam,
A little girl here sepultured.
Once I flit-fluttered like a bird
Above the grass, as now I wave
In daisy shapes above my grave,
All day cheerily,
All night eerily!

THE RIFT. *Headnote* Mode] ⟨Key⟩ *Hol.*
4 span] ⟨life⟩ *Hol.* 7 high] ⟨soar⟩ *Hol.*

VOICES FROM THINGS GROWING. *London Mercury*, Dec. 1921; *FEH* (1922). *TS*, *P1*, *P2* (*FEH*) *Fales*
Title Voices from Things Growing *LM*, *TS–FEH*
1 flowers] ⟨leaves⟩ *Hol.* 2 Madam,] ⟨Madame,⟩ *TS* [*thus also in lines 10 and 18*] 5 grass,] bents, *LM*, *TS–FEH*, *Hol.* 8 eerily!] ~. *TS–FEH*

—I am one Bachelor Bowring, 'Gent',
Sir or Madam;
In shingled oak my bones were pent;
Hence more than a hundred years I spent
In my feat of change from a coffin-thrall
To a dancer in green as leaves on a wall,
All day cheerily,
All night eerily!

—I, these berries of juice and gloss,
Sir or Madam,
Am clean forgotten as Thomas Voss;
Thin-urned, I have burrowed away from the moss
That covers my sod, and have entered this yew,
And turned to clusters ruddy of view,
All day cheerily,
All night eerily!

—The Lady Gertrude, proud, high-bred,
Sir or Madam,
Am I—this laurel that shades your head;
Into its veins I have stilly sped,
And made them of me; and my leaves now shine,
As did my satins superfine,
All day cheerily,
All night eerily!

—I, who as innocent withwind climb,
Sir or Madam,
Am one Eve Greensleeves, in olden time
Kissed by men from many a clime,
Beneath sun, stars, in blaze, in breeze,
As now by glowworms and by bees,
All day cheerily,
All night eerily!

13 feat] growth *LM*, *TS–FEH*; ⟨growth⟩ *Hol.* 16 eerily!] ~. *TS–FEH*, *Hol.* [*thus also in lines 24, 32, 40, 48, and 56*] 19 ⟨Am he who was known as Thomas Voss;⟩ *Hol.* 27 ⟨This laurel is that shades your head;⟩ *Hol.* 29 them] ⟨it⟩ *Hol.* 31 cheerily,] ~ *TS* 33 ⟨—I, this innocent flower that climbs,⟩ *Hol.* 35 Eve] Bet *LM*, *TS–FEH*, *Hol.* time] ⟨times⟩ *Hol.* 36 many a clime,] ⟨many climes⟩ *Hol.* 39 cheerily,] ~ *TS*

—I'm old Squire Audeley Grey, who grew,
Sir or Madam,
Aweary of life, and in scorn withdrew;
Till anon I clambered up anew
As ivy-green, when my ache was stayed,
And in that attire I have longtime gayed
All day cheerily,
All night eerily!

—And so these maskers breathe to each
Sir or Madam
Who lingers there, and their lively speech
Affords an interpreter much to teach,
As their murmurous accents seem to come
Thence hitheraround in a radiant hum,
All day cheerily,
All night eerily!

ON THE WAY

The trees fret fitfully and twist,
Shutters rattle and carpets heave,
Slime is the dust of yestereve,
And in the streaming mist
Fishes might seem to fin a passage if they list.

But to his feet,
Drawing nigh and nigher
A hidden seat,
The fog is sweet
And the wind a lyre.

43 in scorn withdrew;] ⟨its senseless hue;⟩ *Hol.* 46 longtime] long time *LM*, *TS–FEH* 47 cheerily,] ~ *TS* 49 —And so they breathe, these growths, to each *LM*, *TS–FEH*; And so they breathe, these masks, to each *LL22a*, *22b*

ON THE WAY. 1 fret] writhe *Hol.* 9 fog] ⟨sun⟩ *Hol.*

A vacant sameness grays the sky,
A moisture gathers on each knop
Of the bramble, rounding to a drop,
That greets the goer-by
With the cold listless lustre of a dead man's eye.

But to her sight,
Drawing nigh and nigher
Its deep delight,
The fog is bright
And the wind a lyre.

'SHE DID NOT TURN'

She did not turn,
But passed foot-faint with averted head
In her gown of green, by the bobbing fern,
Though I leaned over the gate that led
From where we waited with table spread;
But she did not turn:
Why was she near there if love had fled?

She did not turn,
Though the gate was whence I had often sped
In the mists of morning to meet her, and learn
Her heart, when its moving moods I read
As a book—she mine, as she sometimes said;
But she did not turn,
And passed foot-faint with averted head.

GROWTH IN MAY

I enter a daisy-and-buttercup land,
And thence thread a jungle of grass:

15 listless lustre] ⟨lustre listless⟩ *Hol.* 16 sight,] ⟨sprite,⟩ *Hol.* 19 fog] ⟨sky⟩ *Hol.*

'SHE DID NOT TURN'. 2 passed foot-faint] ⟨ ? past⟩ *Hol.* 7 near] ⟨found⟩ *Hol.* 14 passed foot-faint] ⟨ ? past⟩ *Hol.*

Hurdles and stiles scarce visible stand
  Above the lush stems as I pass.

Hedges peer over, and try to be seen,
  And seem to reveal a dim sense
That amid such ambitious and elbow-high green
  They make a mean show as a fence.

Elsewhere the mead is possessed of the neats,
  That range not greatly above
The rich rank thicket which brushes their teats,
  And *her* gown, as she waits for her Love.

Near Chard.

THE CHILDREN AND SIR NAMELESS*

Sir Nameless, once of Athelhall, declared:
'These wretched children romping in my park
Trample the herbage till the soil is bared,
And yap and yell from early morn till dark!
Go keep them harnessed to their set routines:
Thank God I've none to hasten my decay;
For green remembrance there are better means
Than offspring, who but wish their sires away.'

Sir Nameless of that mansion said anon:
'To be perpetuate for my mightiness
Sculpture must image me when I am gone.'
—He forthwith summoned carvers there express

GROWTH IN MAY. 3 scarce] ⟨scarcely⟩ *Hol.* 4 stems as] ⟨growth as⟩ growths *Hol.* 5 try] ⟨strain⟩ *Hol.* 6 ⟨Though as if they reveal a dim sense⟩ *Hol.* 8 a mean] ⟨but poor⟩ *Hol.* 10 ⟨That lift them but little above⟩ *Hol.* 11 rich rank] ⟨rank-rising⟩ *Hol.* 12 Love] ⟨*l.c.*⟩ *Hol.*

THE CHILDREN AND SIR NAMELESS. *Salisbury Times and South Wilts Gazette*, 21 Apr. 1922; *Nash's and Pall Mall Magazine*, May 1922

Title ⟨The Children versus Sir Nameless⟩ *Hol.*

1 ⟨Sir Nicholas, of Athelhall, declared:⟩ *Hol.* 6 I've] I have *ST*, *NPM* 9 Nameless] ⟨Nicholas⟩ *Hol.* 12 —He forthwith called an architect express *Hol.*

To shape a figure stretching seven-odd feet
(For he was tall) in alabaster stone,
With shield, and crest, and casque, and sword complete:
When done a statelier work was never known.

Three hundred years hied; Church-restorers came,
And, no one of his lineage being traced,
They thought an effigy so large in frame
Best fitted for the floor. There it was placed,
Under the seats for schoolchildren. And they
Kicked out his name, and hobnailed off his nose;
And, as they yawn through sermon-time, they say,
'Who was this old stone man beneath our toes?'

AT THE ROYAL ACADEMY*

These summer landscapes—clump, and copse, and croft—
Woodland and meadowland—here hung aloft,
Gay with limp grass and leafery new and soft,

Seem caught from the immediate season's yield
I saw last noonday shining over the field,
By rapid snatch, while still are uncongealed

The saps that in their live originals climb;
Yester's quick greenage here set forth in mime
Just as it stands, now, at our breathing-time.

But these young foils so fresh upon each tree,
Soft verdures spread in sprouting novelty,
Are not this summer's, though they feign to be.

13 shape] limn *Hol.* 15 casque,] ruff, *Hol.* 16 statelier] nobler *Hol.* 17 Three] Two *Hol.* Church-restorers] ⟨Churchwardens⟩ ⟨till Church-restorers⟩ *Hol.* 19 thought] ⟨felt⟩ *Hol.* 21 Under] ⟨Beneath⟩ *Hol.*

AT THE ROYAL ACADEMY. 6 snatch,] touch, *Hol.* 9 stands, now, at] ⟨stands at this⟩ stands now at *Hol.* 10 fresh] ⟨green⟩ *Hol.* 11 ⟨These verdures spread in freshest novelty,⟩ *Hol.* verdures] ⟨verdures⟩ ⟨carpets⟩ *Hol.*

Last year their May to Michaelmas term was run,
Last autumn browned and buried every one,
And no more know they sight of any sun.

HER TEMPLE*

Dear, think not that they will forget you:
—If craftsmanly art should be mine
I will build up a temple, and set you
Therein as its shrine.

They may say: 'Why a woman such honour?'
—Be told, 'O, so sweet was her fame,
That a man heaped this splendour upon her;
None now knows his name.'

A TWO-YEARS' IDYLL*

Yes; such it was;
Just those two seasons unsought,
Sweeping like summertide wind on our ways;
Moving, as straws,
Hearts quick as ours in those days;
Going like wind, too, and rated as nought
Save as the prelude to plays
Soon to come—larger, life-fraught:
Yes; such it was.

'Nought' it was called,
Even by ourselves—that which springs
Out of the years for all flesh, first or last,
Commonplace, scrawled
Dully on days that go past.
Yet, all the while, it upbore us like wings
Even in hours overcast:
Aye, though this best thing of things,
'Nought' it was called!

HER TEMPLE. 4 ⟨Therein as its centremost shrine.⟩ *Hol.* 6 —Be told,] ⟨And be told,⟩ *Hol.* 8 ⟨I do not remember his name."⟩ *Hol.*

What seems it now?
Lost: such beginning was all;
Nothing came after: romance straight forsook
Quickly somehow
Life when we sped from our nook,
Primed for new scenes with designs smart and tall. . . .
—A preface without any book,
A trumpet uplipped, but no call;
That seems it now.

BY HENSTRIDGE CROSS AT THE YEAR'S END*

(From this centuries-old cross-road the highway leads east to London, north to Bristol and Bath, west to Exeter and the Land's End, and south to the Channel coast.)

Why go the east road now? . . .
That way a youth went on a morrow
After mirth, and he brought back sorrow
Painted upon his brow:
Why go the east road now?

Why go the north road now?
Torn, leaf-strewn, as if scoured by foemen,
Once edging fiefs of my forefolk yeomen,
Fallows fat to the plough:
Why go the north road now?

Why go the west road now?
Thence to us came she, bosom-burning,
Welcome with joyousness returning. . . .
She sleeps under the bough:
Why go the west road now?

BY HENSTRIDGE CROSS. *Fortnightly Review*, 1 Dec. 1919. *TS* Stourhead House, Wilts. *Title* By Mellstock Cross at the Year's End *TS*, *FR* *Headnote om.* *TS*, *FR* 2 That way went one on a morrow *TS* 4 Painted] Graven *TS* 7 Torn,] Scarred *TS* foemen,] ~— *TS* 8 forefolk-yeomen— *TS* 9 Stalwart peers of the plough; *TS*, *FR*; *variant line del. Hol.* 13 Welcome] Welcomes *TS*

Why go the south road now?
That way marched they some are forgetting,
Stark to the moon left, past regretting
Loves who have falsed their vow. . . .
Why go the south road now?

Why go any road now?
White stands the handpost for brisk onbearers,
'Halt!' is the word for wan-cheeked farers
Musing on Whither, and How. . . .
Why go any road now?

'Yea: we want new feet now,'
Answer the stones. 'Want chit-chat, laughter:
Plenty of such to go hereafter
By our tracks, we trow!
We are for new feet now.'

During the War.

PENANCE

'Why do you sit, O pale thin man,
At the end of the room
By that harpsichord, built on the quaint old plan?
—It is cold as a tomb,
And there's not a spark within the grate;
And the jingling wires
Are as vain desires
That have lagged too late.'

18 Stark in a trench left, *TS* 22 onbearers,] blithe farers, *TS* 23 farers] carers *TS* 24 Whither,] ~ *TS* 26 Roads are for others now; *TS*; Such are for new feet now; *FR* now' *Hol.*] ~" *all printed texts* 27 Hark there to chit-chat, kisses, laughter; *TS*, *FR*; ⟨Echo these: Hearken to chit-chat, laughter:⟩ ⟨Echo these stones. "List to chit-chat, laughter:⟩ *Hol.* Answer the] Echo these *Hol.* 28 Yea, there be plenty to go hereafter *TS*, *FR* 29 our tracks,] these ways, *TS*, *FR*; ⟨our tracks,⟩ each track, *Hol.* we trow!] I trow; . . . *TS*; I trow! . . . *FR* 30 Roads are for others now. *TS*; They are for new feet now. *FR*

PENANCE. 1 pale thin] thin pale *Hol.* 3 quaint] flat *Hol.* 8 ⟨That lag too late."⟩ *Hol.*

'Why do I? Alas, far times ago
A woman lyred here
In the evenfall; one who fain did so
From year to year;
And, in loneliness bending wistfully,
Would wake each note
In sick sad rote,
None to listen or see!

'I would not join. I would not stay,
But drew away,
Though the winter fire beamed brightly. . . . Aye!
I do to-day
What I would not then; and the chill old keys,
Like a skull's brown teeth
Loose in their sheath,
Freeze my touch; yes, freeze.'

'I LOOK IN HER FACE'

(Song: Minor)

I look in her face and say,
'Sing as you used to sing
About Love's blossoming';
But she hints not Yea or Nay.

'Sing, then, that Love's a pain,
If, Dear, you think it so,
Whether it be or no';
But dumb her lips remain.

9 far times] ⟨years, years⟩ *Hol.* 10 ⟨There was one sat here⟩ *Hol.* lyred] played *Hol.* 13 loneliness] ⟨loneliness⟩ ⟨lonesomeness⟩ loneness *Hol.* 14 wake] ⟨touch⟩ *Hol.* 16 listen] ⟨hear⟩ *Hol.* 19 beamed] ⟨smiled⟩ *Hol.* 21 old] ⟨bone⟩ *Hol.*

'I LOOK IN HER FACE'. 5–8 *om. Hol.*

I go to a far-off room,
A faint song ghosts my ear;
Which song I cannot hear,
But it seems to come from a tomb.

AFTER THE WAR

Last Post sounded
Across the mead
To where he loitered
With absent heed.
Five years before
In the evening there
Had flown that call
To him and his Dear.
'You'll never come back;
Good-bye!' she had said;
'Here I'll be living,
And my Love dead!'

Those closing minims
Had been as shafts darting
Through him and her pressed
In that last parting;
They thrilled him not now,
In the selfsame place
With the selfsame sun
On his war-seamed face.
'Lurks a god's laughter
In this?' he said,
'That I am the living
And she the dead!'

9–12 I hasten out of the room,
And then from my far retreat
I hear her singing sweet,
And it seems to come from a tomb. *Hol.*

AFTER THE WAR. 6 ⟨To his Dear and him there⟩ *Hol.* 8 ⟨On the evening air.⟩ *Hol.* 11 I'll] ⟨I shall⟩ *Hol.* 15 ⟨On him, with her pressed⟩ ⟨On him, to her pressed⟩ *Hol.* 17 They] ⟨But they⟩ *Hol.*

'IF YOU HAD KNOWN'

If you had known
When listening with her to the far-down moan
Of the white-selvaged and empurpled sea,
And rain came on that did not hinder talk,
Or damp your flashing facile gaiety
In turning home, despite the slow wet walk
By crooked ways, and over stiles of stone;
If you had known

You would lay roses,
Fifty years thence, on her monument, that discloses
Its graying shape upon the luxuriant green;
Fifty years thence to an hour, by chance led there,
What might have moved you?—yea, had you foreseen
That on the tomb of the selfsame one, gone where
The dawn of every day is as the close is,
You would lay roses!

1920.

THE CHAPEL-ORGANIST*

(A.D. 185–)

I've been thinking it through, as I play here to-night, to play never again,
By the light of that lowering sun peering in at the window-pane,
And over the back-street roofs, throwing shades from the boys of the chore
In the gallery, right upon me, sitting up to these keys once more. . . .

'IF YOU HAD KNOWN'. *Title* ⟨"If I had known"⟩ *Hol.*
1 you] ⟨I⟩ *Hol.* 2 listening with her] ⟨we two listened⟩ ⟨you two listened⟩ *Hol.* 8 you] ⟨I⟩ *Hol.* 9 ⟨I should lay roses,⟩ *Hol.* 13 you?—] ⟨me?—⟩ *Hol.* yea,] ⟨yea,⟩ ⟨what!—⟩ *Hol.* you] I *Hol.* 14 gone] ⟨passed⟩ *Hol.* 16 ⟨I should lay roses!⟩ *Hol.*

THE CHAPEL-ORGANIST. 1 I've been thinking and thinking it ⟨over⟩ through, as I play here to-night again, *Hol.* 2 By] In *Hol.* peering] ⟨coming⟩ *Hol.* 4 up to] ⟨over⟩ *Hol.*

How I used to hear tongues ask, as I sat here when I was new:
'Who is she playing the organ? She touches it mightily true!'
'She travels from Havenpool Town,' the deacon would softly speak,
'The stipend can hardly cover her fare hither twice in the week.'
(It fell far short of doing, indeed; but I never told,
For I have craved minstrelsy more than lovers, or beauty, or gold.)

'Twas so he answered at first, but the story grew different later:
'It cannot go on much longer, from what we hear of her now!'
At the meaning wheeze in the words the inquirer would shift his place
Till he could see round the curtain that screened me from people below.
'A handsome girl,' he would murmur, upstaring, (and so I am).
'But—too much sex in her build; fine eyes, but eyelids too heavy;
A bosom too full for her age; in her lips too voluptuous a dye.'
(It may be. But who put it there? Assuredly it was not I.)

I went on playing and singing when this I had heard, and more,
Though tears half-blinded me; yes, I remained going on and on,
Just as I used me to chord and to sing at the selfsame time! . . .

[*no stanza break*]

6 touches] plays *Hol.* 7 travels] ⟨comes all the way⟩ *Hol.* 9 doing, indeed;] ⟨doing as much, indeed;⟩ *Hol.* 10 minstrelsy] music *Hol.* 13 wheeze] ⟨tone⟩ *Hol.* 17 lips] face *Hol.* dye.'] look." *LL* 21 chord] play *Hol.*

For it's a contralto—my voice is; they'll hear it again here to-night
In the psalmody notes that I love far beyond every lower delight.

Well, the deacon, in fact, that day had learnt new tidings about me;
They troubled his mind not a little, for he was a worthy man.
(He trades as a chemist in High Street, and during the week he had sought
His fellow-deacon, who throve as a bookbinder over the way.)
'These are strange rumours,' he said. 'We must guard the good name of the chapel.
If, sooth, she's of evil report, what else can we do but dismiss her?'
'—But get such another to play here we cannot for double the price!'
It settled the point for the time, and I triumphed awhile in their strait,
And my much-beloved grand semibreves went living on, pending my fate.

At length in the congregation more headshakes and murmurs were rife,
And my dismissal was ruled, though I was not warned of it then.
But a day came when they declared it. The news entered me as a sword;
I was broken; so pallid of face that they thought I should faint, they said.
I rallied. 'O, rather than go, I will play you for nothing!' said I.

[*no stanza break*]

22 For it's] ⟨It's⟩ *Hol.* 23 far . . . delight.] ⟨more than life or than world or than flesh.⟩ *Hol.*; more than world or than flesh or than life. *Hol.*, *LL* 24 learnt] ⟨heard⟩ *Hol.* 29 If, sooth,] ⟨If, really her sooth,⟩ *Hol.* 32 grand] ⟨sweet⟩ *Hol.* on, pending my fate.] on under my fingers. *LL* 38 spoke] ⟨said⟩ *Hol.* forfeit] ⟨let go⟩ *Hol.*

'Twas in much desperation I spoke it, for bring me to forfeit I could not
Those melodies chorded so richly for which I had laboured and lived.
They paused. And for nothing I played at the chapel through Sundays again,
Upheld by that art which I loved more than blandishments lavished of men.

But it fell that murmurs anew from the flock broke the pastor's peace.
Some member had seen me at Havenpool, comrading close a sea-captain.
(O yes; I was thereto constrained, lacking means for the fare to and fro.)
Yet God knows, if aught He knows ever, I loved the Old-Hundredth, Saint Stephen's,
Mount Zion, New Sabbath, Miles-Lane, Holy Rest, and Arabia, and Eaton,
Above all embraces of body by wooers who sought me and won! . . .
Next week 'twas declared I was seen coming home with a swain ere the sun.
The deacons insisted then, strong; and forgiveness I did not implore.
I saw all was lost for me, quite, but I made a last bid in my throbs.
My bent, finding victual in lust, men's senses had libelled my soul,

[*no stanza break*]

40 again,] ⟨on,⟩ anon, *Hol.*; anon, *LL22a*, *22b* 42 But it fell that] ⟨But a time was when⟩ *Hol.* anew] again *LL22a*, *22b* 43 ⟨Some member saw me at Havenpool, closely consorting with sailors.⟩ *Hol.* 44 O yes;] Yes; *LL22a*, *22b* I was thereto] ⟨thereto had I been⟩ *Hol.* 45 He] *l.c.* *Hol.* 46 ⟨The Hundred-and Thirteenth, Barthélémon, Irish, Arabia, and Eaton,⟩ The Hundred-and Thirteenth, New Sabbath, Mount Ephraim, Arabia, and Eaton, *Hol.* 48 swain ere the sun.] lover at dawn. *LL* 49 ⟨and I did not implore them forgiveness.⟩ *Hol.* 50 throbs.] ⟨smart⟩ *Hol.* 51 High love had been beaten by lust; and the senses had conquered the soul, *LL22a*, *22b*; High love finding victual in lust men's senses had libelled my soul, *LL22c* senses] ⟨body⟩ *Hol.*

But the soul should die game, if I knew it! I turned to my masters and said:
'I yield, Gentlemen, without parlance. But—let me just hymn you *once* more!
It's a little thing, Sirs, that I ask; and a passion is music with me!'
They saw that consent would cost nothing, and show as good grace, as knew I,
Though tremble I did, and feel sick, as I paused thereat, dumb for their words.
They gloomily nodded assent, saying, 'Yes, if you care to. Once more,
And only once more, understand.' To that with a bend I agreed.
—'You've a fixed and a far-reaching look,' spoke one who had eyed me awhile.
'I've a fixed and a far-reaching plan, and my look only showed it,' I smile.

This evening of Sunday is come—the last of my functioning here.
'She plays as if she were possessed!' they exclaim, glancing upward and round.
'Such harmonies I never dreamt the old instrument capable of!'
Meantime the sun lowers and goes; shades deepen; the lights are turned up,
And the people voice out the last singing: tune Tallis: the Evening Hymn.
(I wonder Dissenters sing Ken: it shows them more liberal in spirit
At this little chapel down here than at certain new others I know.)
I sing as I play. Murmurs some one: 'No woman's throat richer than hers!'

[*no stanza break*]

53 just hymn] ⟨play to⟩ *Hol.* 56 thereat,] ⟨there,⟩ *Hol.* 59 spoke] ⟨observed⟩ *Hol.* awhile.] ⟨there.⟩ *Hol.* 60 and a] ⟨and⟩ *Hol.* I smile.] said I. *LL22a, 22b* 65 tune] ⟨'twas⟩ *Hol.* 68 some one:] ⟨one:⟩ *Hol.* throat] ⟨voi⟩ *Hol.*

'True: in these parts,' think I. 'But, my man, never
more will its richness outspread.'
And I sing with them onward: 'The grave dread as little
do I as my bed.'

I lift up my feet from the pedals; and then, while my
eyes are still wet
From the symphonies born of my fingers, I do that
whereon I am set,
And draw from my 'full round bosom', (their words;
how can *I* help its heave?)
A bottle blue-coloured and fluted—a vinaigrette, they
may conceive—
And before the choir measures my meaning, reads aught in
my moves to and fro,
I drink from the phial at a draught, and they think it a
pick-me-up; so.
Then I gather my books as to leave, bend over the keys
as to pray.
When they come to me motionless, stooping, quick death
will have whisked me away.

'Sure, nobody meant her to poison herself in her haste,
after all!'
The deacons will say as they carry me down and the
night shadows fall,
'Though the charges were true,' they will add. 'It's a
case red as scarlet withal!'
I have never once minced it. Lived chaste I have not.
Heaven knows it above! . . .

[*no stanza break*]

69 ⟨"Yes:⟩ "True: in these parts, at least," ponder I. "But my man, you will hear it no more." *Hol.*; "True: in these parts, at least," ponder I. "But, my man, you will hear it no more." *LL* 70 ⟨"The grave as little dread I as my bed."⟩ *Hol.* 71 lift up] ⟨lift⟩ *Hol.* 72 ⟨I do the last deed of farewell.⟩ *Hol.* 73 heave?)] ⟨shape?)⟩ *Hol.* 74 conceive—] ⟨suppose—⟩ *Hol.* 75 reads . . . fro,] ⟨or sees an intent in my moves,⟩ *Hol.* 76 pick-me-up;] ~ : *Hol.* 77 as . . . pray.] ⟨as to go, and ⟨⟨I⟩⟩ bend on the keys as in prayer.⟩ *Hol.* 80 night shadows] ⟨shadows⟩ *Hol.* 81 'It's a] ⟨"A⟩ *Hol.* 82 I have never once minced it.] ⟨True they were⟩ I have never denied it. *Hol.*

But past all the heavings of passion—it's music has been my life-love! . . .
That tune did go well—this last playing! . . . I reckon they'll bury me here. . . .
Not a soul from the seaport my birthplace—will come, or bestow me . . . a tear.

FETCHING HER

An hour before the dawn,
My friend,
You lit your waiting bedside-lamp,
Your breakfast-fire anon,
And outing into the dark and damp
You saddled, and set on.

Thuswise, before the day,
My friend,
You sought her on her surfy shore,
To fetch her thence away
Unto your own new-builded door
For a staunch lifelong stay.

You said: 'It seems to be,
My friend,
That I were bringing to my place
The pure brine breeze, the sea,
The mews—all her old sky and space,
In bringing her with me!'

—But time is prompt to expugn,
My friend,
Such magic-minted conjurings:
The brought breeze fainted soon,
And then the sense of seamews' wings,
And the shore's sibilant tune.

84 reckon] ⟨suppose⟩ *Hol.* 85 ⟨Not a soul from my—native seaport—will come, or drop me a tear.⟩ *Hol.* me . . .] ~— *Hol.*

FETCHING HER. 19 time] *cap. Hol.* 24 sibilant] ⟨murmuring⟩ *Hol.*

So, it had been more due,
My friend,
Perhaps, had you not pulled this flower
From the craggy nook it knew,
And set it in an alien bower;
But left it where it grew!

'COULD I BUT WILL'

(Song: Verses 1, 3, key major; verse 2, key minor)

Could I but will,
Will to my bent,
I'd have afar ones near me still,
And music of rare ravishment,
In strains that move the toes and heels!
And when the sweethearts sat for rest
The unbetrothed should foot with zest
Ecstatic reels.

Could I be head,
Head-god, 'Come, now,
Dear girl,' I'd say, 'whose flame is fled,
Who liest with linen-banded brow,
Stirred but by shakes from Earth's deep core—'
I'd say to her: 'Unshroud and meet
That Love who kissed and called thee Sweet!—
Yea, come once more!'

Even half-god power
In spinning dooms
Had I, this frozen scene should flower,
And sand-swept plains and Arctic glooms

'COULD I BUT WILL'. 13 deep] ⟨molt⟩ *Hol.*
17–19 ⟨O had I power
Power to spin
I'd make this frozen scene to flower,⟩ *Hol.*
20 sand-swept] desert *Hol.*

Should green them gay with waving leaves,
Mid which old friends and I would walk
With weightless feet and magic talk
Uncounted eves.

SHE REVISITS ALONE THE CHURCH OF HER MARRIAGE

I have come to the church and chancel,
Where all's the same!
—Brighter and larger in my dreams
Truly it shaped than now, meseems,
Is its substantial frame.
But, anyhow, I made my vow,
Whether for praise or blame,
Here in this church and chancel
Where all's the same.

Where touched the check-floored chancel
My knees and his?
The step looks shyly at the sun,
And says, "'Twas here the thing was done,
For bale or else for bliss!'
Of all those there I least was ware
Would it be that or this
When touched the check-floored chancel
My knees and his!

Here in this fateful chancel
Where all's the same,
I thought the culminant crest of life
Was reached when I went forth the wife
I was not when I came.
Each commonplace one of my race,
Some say, has such an aim—
To go from a fateful chancel
As not the same.

SHE REVISITS ALONE. *Title* She] ⟨A Lady⟩ *Hol.*
19 fateful] ⟨chosen⟩ *Hol.* 26 fateful] ⟨chosen⟩ *Hol.*

Here, through this hoary chancel
Where all's the same,
A thrill, a gaiety even, ranged
That morning when it seemed I changed
My nature with my name.
Though now not fair, though gray my hair,
He loved me, past proclaim,
Here in this hoary chancel,
Where all's the same.

AT THE ENTERING OF THE NEW YEAR

I

(Old Style)

Our songs went up and out the chimney,
And roused the home-gone husbandmen;
Our allemands, our heys, poussettings,
Our hands-across and back again,
Sent rhythmic throbbings through the casements
On to the white highway,
Where nighted farers paused and muttered,
'Keep it up well, do they!'

The contrabasso's measured booming
Sped at each bar to the parish bounds,
To shepherds at their midnight lambings,
To stealthy poachers on their rounds;
And everybody caught full duly
The notes of our delight,
As Time unrobed the Youth of Promise
Hailed by our sanguine sight.

34 me,] ⟨once,⟩ *Hol.* 36 Who's not the same ⟨!⟩. *Hol.*

AT THE ENTERING. *Athenaeum*, 31 Dec. 1920. *P1–4* (*A*) Berg
1 (Old Style)] ⟨Old Times⟩ ⟨Old Time⟩ *P1* 2 husbandmen;] ~⟨,⟩; *P1* 8 well,] ~ *P1–A* 10 ⟨Sped at each bar to the parish bounds,⟩ Sped, as the old year touched its bounds, *P1*; ⟨its⟩ his *P2*; Sped, as the old year touched his bounds, *P3–4*, *A* 14 delight,] ~ *Hol.* 15 Except for our heedless headstoned neighbours, *P1*; *variant line del. P2, Hol.* Youth] *l.c. P2–3*; ⟨*l.c.*⟩ *P4* Promise] *l.c. P2–4*, *A*; ⟨*l.c.*⟩ *Hol.* 16 ⟨Still⟩ Mute in the moon's cold light. *P1*; *variant line del. P2, Hol.*

II

(New Style)

We stand in the dusk of a pine-tree limb,
As if to give ear to the muffled peal,
Brought or withheld at the breeze's whim;
But our truest heed is to words that steal
From the mantled ghost that looms in the gray,
And seems, so far as our sense can see,
To feature bereaved Humanity,
As it sighs to the imminent year its say:—

'O stay without, O stay without,
Calm comely Youth, untasked, untired;
Though stars irradiate thee about
Thy entrance here is undesired.
Open the gate not, mystic one;
Must we avow what we would close confine?
With thee, good friend, we would have converse none,
Albeit the fault may not be thine.'

December 31. *During the War.*

THEY WOULD NOT COME

I travelled to where in her lifetime
She'd knelt at morning prayer,
To call her up as if there;
But she paid no heed to my suing,
As though her old haunt could win not
A thought from her spirit, or care.

II (New Style)] ⟨New Times⟩ ⟨New Time⟩ *P1* 21 ghost] form *P1–A*; ⟨form⟩ *Hol.* 23 bereaved] ⟨bereft⟩ *P1* Humanity,] *l.c. P1–A*; ⟨*l.c.*⟩ *Hol.* 24 say:—] ~: *P1–A* 26 comely] ⟨comely⟩ ⟨mystic⟩ *P2* Youth,] *l.c. P1–3*; ⟨*l.c.*⟩ *P4* 29 mystic] hopeful *P1*; ⟨hopeful⟩ *P2, Hol.* one;] ~⟨;⟩: *P2* 30 avow] unseal *P1*; ⟨unseal⟩ *P2, Hol.* 31 *rom. P1–A* *good*] my *P1*; ⟨my⟩ *P2, Hol.*
Date om. P1–A; ⟨Dec. 1917 or 1918⟩ *Hol.*

THEY WOULD NOT COME. 6 spirit,] ~ *Hol.*

I went where my friend had lectioned
  The prophets in high declaim,
  That my soul's ear the same
Full tones should catch as aforetime;
But silenced by gear of the Present
  Was the voice that once there came!

Where the ocean had sprayed our banquet
  I stood, to recall it as then:
  The same eluding again!
No vision. Shows contingent
Affrighted it further from me
  Even than from my home-den.

When I found them no responders,
  But fugitives prone to flee
  From where they had used to be,
It vouched I had been led hither
As by night wisps in bogland,
  And bruised the heart of me!

AFTER A ROMANTIC DAY*

  The railway bore him through
An earthen cutting out from a city:
  There was no scope for view,
Though the frail light shed by a slim young moon
  Fell like a friendly tune.

  Fell like a liquid ditty,
And the blank lack of any charm
  Of landscape did no harm.

[*no stanza break*]

10 aforetime;] ~: *Hol.* 11 Present] *l.c.* *Hol.* 15 ⟨The same same waking again!⟩ *Hol.*

AFTER A ROMANTIC DAY. *Epigraph* ⟨"Your young men shall see visions"⟩ *Hol.* 1 ⟨The railway-train moved through⟩ *Hol.* 2 out from] ⟨near⟩ *Hol.*

The bald steep cutting, rigid, rough,
And moon-lit, was enough
For poetry of place: its weathered face
Formed a convenient sheet whereon
The visions of his mind were drawn.

THE TWO WIVES*

(Smoker's Club-Story)

I waited at home all the while while they were boating together—
My wife and my near neighbour's wife:
Till there entered a woman I loved more than life,
And we sat and sat on, and beheld the uprising dark weather,
With a sense that some mischief was rife.

Tidings came that the boat had capsized, and that one of the ladies
Was drowned—which of them was unknown:
And I marvelled—my friend's wife?—or was it my own
Who had gone in such wise to the land where the sun as the shade is?
—We learnt it was *his* had so gone.

Then I cried in unrest: 'He is free! But no good is releasing
To him as it would be to me!'
'—But it is,' said the woman I loved, quietly.
'How?' I asked her. '—Because he has long loved me too without ceasing,
And it's just the same thing, don't you see.'

9 rigid,] ⟨rock-sided,⟩ inflexible, *Hol.*

THE TWO WIVES. *Headnote* Smoker's] ⟨Grim Smoker's⟩

'I KNEW A LADY'

(Club Song)

I knew a lady when the days
  Grew long, and evenings goldened;
  But I was not emboldened
By her prompt eyes and winning ways.

And when old Winter nipt the haws,
  'Another's wife I'll be,
  And then you'll care for me,'
She said, 'and think how sweet I was!'

And soon she shone as another's wife:
  As such I often met her,
  And sighed, 'How I regret her!
My folly cuts me like a knife!'

And then, to-day, her husband came,
  And moaned, 'Why did you flout her?
  Well could I do without her!
For both our burdens you are to blame!'

A HOUSE WITH A HISTORY

There is a house in a city street
  Some past ones made their own;
Its floors were criss-crossed by their feet,
    And their babblings beat
  From ceiling to white hearth-stone.

And who are peopling its parlours now?
  Who talk across its floor?
Mere freshlings are they, blank of brow,
    Who read not how
  Its prime had passed before

'I KNEW A LADY'. *Headnote* 〈(A Song by a 〈〈?〉〉 Gentleman)〉 *Hol.*

Their raw equipments, scenes, and says
  Afflicted its memoried face,
That had seen every larger phase
    Of human ways
  Before these filled the place.

To them that house's tale is theirs,
  No former voices call
Aloud therein. Its aspect bears
    Their joys and cares
  Alone, from wall to wall.

A PROCESSION OF DEAD DAYS*

I see the ghost of a perished day;
I know his face, and the feel of his dawn:
'Twas he who took me far away
  To a spot strange and gray:
Look at me, Day, and then pass on,
But come again: yes, come anon!

Enters another into view;
His features are not cold or white,
But rosy as a vein seen through:
  Too soon he smiles adieu.
Adieu, O ghost-day of delight;
But come and grace my dying sight.

Enters the day that brought the kiss:
He brought it in his foggy hand
To where the mumbling river is,
  And the high clematis;
It lent new colour to the land,
And all the boy within me manned.

A HOUSE WITH A HISTORY. 13 ⟨That had seen all its larger days⟩ *Hol.* 14 ⟨Of human plays⟩ *Hol.* 15 these] ⟨they⟩ *Hol.* 16 ⟨The story of that house is theirs,⟩ *Hol.* 18 Aloud] ⟨To them⟩ *Hol.*

A PROCESSION OF DEAD DAYS. 2 ⟨I know his face as he rises wan:⟩ *Hol.* 6 yes,] ⟨yea,⟩ *Hol.* 8 cold] ⟨wan⟩ *Hol.*

Ah, this one. Yes, I know his name,
He is the day that wrought a shine
Even on a precinct common and tame,
  As 'twere of purposed aim.
He shows him as a rainbow sign
Of promise made to me and mine.

The next stands forth in his morning clothes,
And yet, despite their misty blue,
They mark no sombre custom-growths
  That joyous living loathes,
But a meteor act, that left in its queue
A train of sparks my lifetime through.

I almost tremble at his nod—
This next in train—who looks at me
As I were slave, and he were god
  Wielding an iron rod.
I close my eyes; yet still is he
In front there, looking mastery.

In semblance of a face averse
The phantom of the next one comes:
I did not know what better or worse
  Chancings might bless or curse
When his original glossed the thrums
Of ivy, bringing that which numbs.

Yes; trees were turning in their sleep
Upon their windy pillows of gray
When he stole in. Silent his creep
  On the grassed eastern steep. . . .
I shall not soon forget that day,
And what his third hour took away!

23 sign] ⟨shin[e]⟩ *Hol.* 29 But a shaped act, that in its queue *Hol.* 30 Left a star-track my lifetime through. *Hol.* 37 In the similitude of a nurse *LL22a, 22b* 41 glossed] ⟨rayed⟩ *Hol.* 44 ⟨Upon their pillows of pallid wind⟩ *Hol.* 46 ⟨Down the gray eastern steep. . . .⟩ *Hol.* 47 I shall forget not soon that day, *Hol.*

HE FOLLOWS HIMSELF*

In a heavy time I dogged myself
Along a louring way,
Till my leading self to my following self
Said: 'Why do you hang on me
So harassingly?'

'I have watched you, Heart of mine,' I cried,
'So often going astray
And leaving me, that I have pursued,
Feeling such truancy
Ought not to be.'

He said no more, and I dogged him on
From noon to the dun of day
By prowling paths, until anew
He begged: 'Please turn and flee!—
What do you see?'

'Methinks I see a man', said I,
'Dimming his hours to gray.
I will not leave him while I know
Part of myself is he
Who dreams such dree!'

'I go to my old friend's house,' he urged,
'So do not watch me, pray!'
'Well, I will leave you in peace,' said I,
'Though of this poignancy
You should fight free:

'Your friend, O other me, is dead;
You know not what you say.'
—'That do I! And at his green-grassed door
By night's bright galaxy
I bend a knee.'

HE FOLLOWS HIMSELF. 6 mine,'] ⟨me,"⟩ *Hol.* 14 'Please] ⟨"Pray⟩ *Hol.* 20 dree!'] ~." *Hol.*

—The yew-plumes moved like mockers' beards,
Though only boughs were they,
And I seemed to go; yet still was there,
And am, and there haunt we
Thus bootlessly.

THE SINGING WOMAN

There was a singing woman
Came riding across the mead
At the time of the mild May weather,
Tameless, tireless;
This song she sung: 'I am fair, I am young!'
And many turned to heed.

And the same singing woman
Sat crooning in her need
At the time of the winter weather;
Friendless, fireless,
She sang this song: 'Life, thou'rt too long!'
And there was none to heed.

WITHOUT, NOT WITHIN HER

It was what you bore with you, Woman,
Not inly were,
That throned you from all else human,
However fair!

It was that strange freshness you carried
Into a soul
Whereon no thought of yours tarried
Two moments at all.

35 ⟨Thus restlessly.⟩ *Hol.*

WITHOUT, NOT WITHIN HER. 2 ⟨Not what you were,⟩ *Hol.* 4 fair!] ~. *Hol.* 8 ⟨That did it all.⟩ One moment at all. *Hol.*

And out from his spirit flew death,
And bale, and ban,
Like the corn-chaff under the breath
Of the winnowing-fan.

'O I WON'T LEAD A HOMELY LIFE'*

(To an old air)

'O I won't lead a homely life
As father's Jack and mother's Jill,
But I will be a fiddler's wife,
With music mine at will!
Just a little tune,
Another one soon,
As I merrily fling my fill!'

And she became a fiddler's Dear,
And merry all day she strove to be;
And he played and played afar and near,
But never at home played he
Any little tune
Or late or soon;
And sunk and sad was she!

IN THE SMALL HOURS

I lay in my bed and fiddled
With a dreamland viol and bow,
And the tunes flew back to my fingers
I had melodied years ago.

9 his] ⟨my⟩ *Hol.*

'O I WON'T LEAD'. *MS1* Adams [*see explanatory notes*]
Headnote ⟨To an old tune⟩ *Hol.*
5 ⟨Another little tune,⟩ *Hol.* 7 fling] ⟨have⟩ *Hol.* 8 she became] ⟨O she was⟩ *Hol.* Dear,] *l.c. Hol.* 9 strove] ⟨thought⟩ *Hol.* 14 sunk] ⟨sick⟩ *Hol.*

IN THE SMALL HOURS. 4 melodied] played far *Hol.*

It was two or three in the morning
When I fancy-fiddled so
Long reels and country-dances,
And hornpipes swift and slow.

And soon anon came crossing
The chamber in the gray
Figures of jigging fieldfolk—
Saviours of corn and hay—
To the air of 'Haste to the Wedding',
As after a wedding-day;
Yea, up and down the middle
In windless whirls went they!

There danced the bride and bridegroom,
And couples in a train,
Gay partners time and travail
Had longwhiles stilled amain! . . .
It seemed a thing for weeping
To find, at slumber's wane
And morning's sly increeping,
That Now, not Then, held reign.

THE LITTLE OLD TABLE

Creak, little wood thing, creak,
When I touch you with elbow or knee;
That is the way you speak
Of one who gave you to me!

You, little table, she brought—
Brought me with her own hand,
As she looked at me with a thought
That I did not understand.

—Whoever owns it anon,
And hears it, will never know
What a history hangs upon
This creak from long ago.

THE LITTLE OLD TABLE. 6 Brought me] ⟨Me hither⟩ ⟨Her to me⟩ *Hol.*

VAGG HOLLOW*

Vagg Hollow is a marshy spot on the old Roman Road near Ilchester, where 'things' are seen. Merchandise was formerly fetched inland from the canal-boats at Load-Bridge by waggons this way.

'What do you see in Vagg Hollow,
Little boy, when you go
In the morning at five on your lonely drive?'
'—I see men's souls, who follow
Till we've passed where the road lies low,
When they vanish at our creaking!

'They are like white faces speaking
Beside and behind the waggon—
One just as father's was when here.
The waggoner drinks from his flagon,
(Or he'd flinch when the Hollow is near)
But he does not give me any.

'Sometimes the faces are many;
But I walk along by the horses,
He asleep on the straw as we jog;
And I hear the loud water-courses,
And the drops from the trees in the fog,
And watch till the day is breaking,

'And the wind out by Tintinhull waking;
I hear in it father's call
As he called when I saw him dying,
And he sat by the fire last Fall,
And mother stood by sighing;
But I'm not afraid at all!'

VAGG HOLLOW. *Headnote first sentence only Hol.*
8 Beside] Before *Hol.* 9 One just as] One as *Hol.* 11 Hollow] *l.c. Hol.* 16 hear the loud] ⟨hark at the⟩ *Hol.*

THE DREAM IS—WHICH?

I am laughing by the brook with her,
  Splashed in its tumbling stir;
And then it is a blankness looms
  As if I walked not there,
Nor she, but found me in haggard rooms,
  And treading a lonely stair.

With radiant cheeks and rapid eyes
  We sit where none espies;
Till a harsh change comes edging in
  As no such scene were there,
But winter, and I were bent and thin,
  And cinder-gray my hair.

We dance in heys around the hall,
  Weightless as thistleball;
And then a curtain drops between,
  As if I danced not there,
But wandered through a mounded green
  To find her, I knew where.

March 1913.

THE COUNTRY WEDDING*

(A Fiddler's Story)

Little fogs were gathered in every hollow,
But the purple hillocks enjoyed fine weather
As we marched with our fiddles over the heather
—How it comes back!—to their wedding that day.

THE DREAM IS—WHICH?. *Title* ⟨As if not there⟩ *Hol.*
1 ⟨We laughingly go up the glades,⟩ *Hol.* 2 ⟨Ethereal as two shades;⟩ *Hol.* 5 haggard] ⟨vacant⟩ *Hol.* 17 wandered] tottered *Hol.*

THE COUNTRY WEDDING. *FEH* (1917). *TS*, *P1* (*FEH*) RLP
Title The Fiddler's Story *TS–FEH*

Our getting there brought our neighbours and all, O!
Till, two and two, the couples stood ready.
And her father said: 'Souls, for God's sake, be steady!'
And we strung up our fiddles, and sounded out 'A'.

The groomsman he stared, and said, 'You must follow!'
But we'd gone to fiddle in front of the party,
(Our feelings as friends being true and hearty)
And fiddle in front we did—all the way.

Yes, from their door by Mill-tail-Shallow,
And up Styles-Lane, and by Front-Street houses,
Where stood maids, bachelors, and spouses,
Who cheered the songs that we knew how to play.

I bowed the treble before her father,
Michael the tenor in front of the lady,
The bass-viol Reub—and right well played he!—
The serpent Jim; ay, to church and back.

I thought the bridegroom was flurried rather,
As we kept up the tune outside the chancel,
While they were swearing things none can cancel
Inside the walls to our drumstick's whack.

'Too gay!' she pleaded. 'Clouds may gather,
And sorrow come.' But she gave in, laughing,
And by supper-time when we'd got to the quaffing
Her fears were forgot, and her smiles weren't slack.

A grand wedding 'twas! And what would follow
We never thought. Or that we should have buried her
On the same day with the man that married her,
A day like the first, half hazy, half clear.

5–8 *om. TS–FEH* 5 our] ⟨out⟩ *Hol.* and all,] ⟨—all⟩ ⟨aye, all⟩ and all *Hol.* 7 And her] ⟨Her⟩ *Hol.* sake,] ~ *Hol.* 8 sounded out] ⟨all sounded⟩ then sounded *Hol.* 9 The groomsman stared, *TS–FEH* said,] ~ *TS–FEH* 16 we knew to play. *TS–FEH* 21 rather,] ~ *TS–FEH, Hol.* 22 chancel,] ~ *TS–FEH, Hol.* 24 Inside] ⟨Inside⟩ Within *P1*; Within *FEH* 27 quaffing] ~, *TS–FEH* 28 forgot,] ~ *Hol.* 32 hazy,] hazed *TS–FEH*

Yes: little fogs were in every hollow,
Though the purple hillocks enjoyed fine weather,
When we went to play 'em to church together,
And carried 'em there in an after year.

FIRST OR LAST

(Song)

If grief come early
Joy comes late,
If joy come early
Grief will wait;
Aye, my dear and tender!

Wise ones joy them early
While the cheeks are red,
Banish grief till surly
Time has dulled their dread.

And joy being ours
Ere youth has flown,
The later hours
May find us gone;
Aye, my dear and tender!

LONELY DAYS*

Lonely her fate was,
Environed from sight
In the house where the gate was
Past finding at night.

[*no stanza break*]

36 And went to carry them there next year. *TS–FEH*; *variant line del. Hol.* 'em] them *Hol.*

LONELY DAYS. 2 Environed] Screened *Hol.* 4 ⟨Locked at night.⟩ ⟨Unfindable quite.⟩ *Hol.*

None there to share it,
No one to tell:
Long she'd to bear it,
And bore it well.

Elsewhere just so she
Spent many a day;
Wishing to go she
Continued to stay.
And people without
Basked warm in the air,
But none sought her out,
Or knew she was there.
Even birthdays were passed so,
Sunny and shady:
Years did it last so
For this sad lady.
Never declaring it,
No one to tell,
Still she kept bearing it—
Bore it well.

The days grew chillier,
And then she went
To a city, familiar
In years forespent,
When she walked gaily
Far to and fro,
But now, moving frailly,
Could nowhere go.
The cheerful colour
Of houses she'd known
Had died to a duller
And dingier tone.

[*no stanza break*]

9 ⟨Elsewhere so she⟩ *Hol.* 14 warm in the] ⟨in the warm⟩ *Hol.* 23 Still she kept] ⟨She went on⟩ Still she went *Hol.* 24 Bore] ⟨And bore⟩ *Hol.* 30 ⟨One of a row,⟩ *Hol.* 35 died to] ⟨turned to⟩ donned them *Hol.* 37 were now] ⟨were⟩ *Hol.*

Streets were now noisy
Where once had rolled
A few quiet coaches,
Or citizens strolled.
Through the party-wall
Of the memoried spot
They danced at a ball
Who recalled her not.
Tramlines lay crossing
Once gravelled slopes,
Metal rods clanked,
And electric ropes.
So she endured it all,
Thin, thinner wrought,
Until time cured it all,
And she knew nought.

Versified from a Diary.

'WHAT DID IT MEAN?'

What did it mean that noontide, when
  You bade me pluck the flower
Within the other woman's bower,
  Whom I knew nought of then?

I thought the flower blushed deeplier—aye,
And as I drew its stalk to me
It seemed to breathe: 'I am, I see,
Made use of in a human play.'

And while I plucked, upstarted sheer
As phantom from the pane thereby
A corpse-like countenance, with eye
That iced me by its baleful peer—
  Silent, as from a bier. . . .

44 recalled] ⟨knew⟩ *Hol.* 47 ⟨And metal clanked,⟩ *Hol.* 49 endured] ⟨could bear⟩ *Hol.* 50 Thin,] ⟨Spinning⟩ *Hol.* 51 ⟨And had to bear it all,⟩ *Hol.* time] *cap. Hol.*

'WHAT DID IT MEAN?'. 9 And] ⟨Whe⟩ *Hol.* 10 pane] shade *Hol.* 12 iced] ⟨blasted⟩ ⟨froze⟩ *Hol.*

When I came back your face had changed,
It was no face for me;
O did it speak of hearts estranged,
And deadly rivalry
In times before
I darked your door,
To seise me of
Mere second love,
Which still the haunting first deranged?

AT THE DINNER-TABLE

I sat at dinner in my prime,
And glimpsed my face in the sideboard-glass,
And started as if I had seen a crime,
And prayed the ghastly show might pass.

Wrenched wrinkled features met my sight,
Grinning back to me as my own;
I well-nigh fainted with affright
At finding me a haggard crone.

My husband laughed. He had slily set
A warping mirror there, in whim
To startle me. My eyes grew wet;
I spoke not all the eve to him.

He was sorry, he said, for what he had done,
And took away the distorting glass,
Uncovering the accustomed one;
And so it ended? No, alas,

AT THE DINNER-TABLE. 4 show] ⟨sight⟩ *Hol.* 5 ⟨An aged woman's face was there,⟩ ⟨An old crone's features met my sight,⟩ *Hol.* 7 with affright] ⟨at the scare⟩ ⟨at the fright⟩ *Hol.* 8 ⟨Of finding me so haggard grown.⟩ *Hol.* 11 startle] ⟨frighten⟩ *Hol.* 12 eve] ⟨day⟩ *Hol.* 15 Uncovering] And put there *Hol.*

Fifty years later, when he died,
I sat me in the selfsame chair,
Thinking of him. Till, weary-eyed,
I saw the sideboard facing there;

And from its mirror looked the lean
Thing I'd become, each wrinkle and score
The image of me that I had seen
In jest there fifty years before.

THE MARBLE TABLET*

There it stands, though alas, what a little of her
  Shows in its cold white look!
Not her glance, glide, or smile; not a tittle of her
  Voice like the purl of a brook;
  Not her thoughts, that you read like a book.

It may stand for her once in November
  When first she breathed, witless of all;
Or in heavy years she would remember
  When circumstance held her in thrall;
  Or at last, when she answered her call!

Nothing more. The still marble, date-graven,
  Gives all that it can, tersely lined;
That one has at length found the haven
  Which every one other will find;
  With silence on what shone behind.

St. Juliot: *September* 8, 1916.

20 there;] ~, *Hol.* 21 looked] ⟨grinned⟩ *Hol.* 22 I'd] ⟨I had⟩ *Hol.*

THE MARBLE TABLET. *Title* The Marble Monument *Hol.* *Headnote* (At St. Juliot) *Hol.*
Place/date September, 1916 *Hol.*

THE MASTER AND THE LEAVES*

I

We are budding, Master, budding,
  We of your favourite tree;
March drought and April flooding
  Arouse us merrily,
Our stemlets newly studding;
  And yet you do not see!

II

We are fully woven for summer
  In stuff of limpest green,
The twitterer and the hummer
  Here rest of nights, unseen,
While like a long-roll drummer
  The nightjar thrills the treen.

III

We are turning yellow, Master,
  And next we are turning red,
And faster then and faster
  Shall seek our rooty bed,
All wasted in disaster!
  But you lift not your head.

IV

—'I mark your early going,
  And that you'll soon be clay,

THE MASTER AND THE LEAVES. *The Owl*, May 1919; *FEH* (1919). *TS*, *P1* (*FEH*) Buffalo

1 Master,] *l.c. O*, *TS–FEH*, *Hol.* 5 The stemlets brightly studding; *O*, *TS–FEH* newly] ⟨brightly⟩ *Hol.* 6 see!] ~. *O*, *TS–FEH* 8 stuff] modes *O*, *TS–FEH* 10 Here rest their rounds between, *O*, *TS–FEH*; *variant line del. Hol.* 11 long-roll] "long-roll" *O*, *TS–FEH* 12 nightjar] night-hawk *O*, *TS–FEH*, *Hol.* 13 Master,] *l.c. O*, *TS–FEH*, *Hol.* 16 bed,] ~— *O*, *TS–FEH*; ~⟨—⟩, *Hol.* 17 disaster!] ~ *O*, *TS–FEH* 18 The magic show we spread! *O*, *TS–FEH*; *variant line del. Hol.* 19 —'I] "I *O*, *TS–FEH*

I have seen your summer showing
As in my youthful day;
But why I seem unknowing
Is too sunk in to say!'

1917.

LAST WORDS TO A DUMB FRIEND*

Pet was never mourned as you,
Purrer of the spotless hue,
Plumy tail, and wistful gaze
While you humoured our queer ways,
Or outshrilled your morning call
Up the stairs and through the hall—
Foot suspended in its fall—
While, expectant, you would stand
Arched, to meet the stroking hand;
Till your way you chose to wend
Yonder, to your tragic end.

Never another pet for me!
Let your place all vacant be;
Better blankness day by day
Than companion torn away.
Better bid his memory fade,
Better blot each mark he made,
Selfishly escape distress
By contrived forgetfulness,
Than preserve his prints to make
Every morn and eve an ache.

From the chair whereon he sat
Sweep his fur, not wince thereat;
Rake his little pathways out
Mid the bushes roundabout;

23 But why] But—why *TS–FEH* 24 sunk in] deep down *O*; ⟨deep⟩ far down *TS*; ⟨far⟩ deep down *P1*; ⟨deep down⟩ *Hol.*
Date om. TS–FEH

Smooth away his talons' mark
From the claw-worn pine-tree bark,
Where he climbed as dusk embrowned,
Waiting us who loitered round.

Strange it is this speechless thing,
Subject to our mastering,
Subject for his life and food
To our gift, and time, and mood;
Timid pensioner of us Powers,
His existence ruled by ours,
Should—by crossing at a breath
Into safe and shielded death,
By the merely taking hence
Of his insignificance—
Loom as largened to the sense,
Shape as part, above man's will,
Of the Imperturbable.

As a prisoner, flight debarred,
Exercising in a yard,
Still retain I, troubled, shaken,
Mean estate, by him forsaken;
And this home, which scarcely took
Impress from his little look,
By his faring to the Dim
Grows all eloquent of him.

Housemate, I can think you still
Bounding to the window-sill,
Over which I vaguely see
Your small mound beneath the tree,
Showing in the autumn shade
That you moulder where you played.

October 2, 1904.

LAST WORDS. 33 mood;] ~, *Hol.* 40 as largened] ⟨majestic⟩ *Hol.* 54 Your small] ⟨Smallest⟩ *Hol.*

A DRIZZLING EASTER MORNING

And he is risen? Well, be it so. . . .
And still the pensive lands complain,
And dead men wait as long ago,
As if, much doubting, they would know
What they are ransomed from, before
They pass again their sheltering door.

I stand amid them in the rain,
While blusters vex the yew and vane;
And on the road the weary wain
Plods forward, laden heavily;
And toilers with their aches are fain
For endless rest—though risen is he.

ON ONE WHO LIVED AND DIED WHERE HE WAS BORN*

When a night in November
  Blew forth its bleared airs
An infant descended
  His birth-chamber stairs
  For the very first time,
  At the still, midnight chime;
All unapprehended
  His mission, his aim.—
Thus, first, one November,
An infant descended
    The stairs.

On a night in November
  Of weariful cares,

A DRIZZLING EASTER MORNING. *Title* Drizzling] ⟨Wet⟩ *Hol.* 2 pensive] ⟨peopled⟩ *Hol.*

ON ONE WHO LIVED. 1 a night] an eve *Hol.* 2 bleared] ⟨dull⟩ moist *Hol.* 12 a night] an eve *Hol.*

A frail aged figure
Ascended those stairs
For the very last time:
All gone his life's prime,
All vanished his vigour,
And fine, forceful frame:
Thus, last, one November
Ascended that figure
Upstairs.

On those nights in November—
Apart eighty years—
The babe and the bent one
Who traversed those stairs
From the early first time
To the last feeble climb—
That fresh and that spent one—
Were even the same:
Yea, who passed in November
As infant, as bent one,
Those stairs.

Wise child of November!
From birth to blanched hairs
Descending, ascending,
Wealth-wantless, those stairs;
Who saw quick in time
As a vain pantomime
Life's tending, its ending,
The worth of its fame.
Wise child of November,
Descending, ascending
Those stairs!

22 ⟨The stairs.⟩ *Hol.* 23 nights] eves *Hol.* 32 as] ⟨as⟩ ⟨and⟩ *Hol.* 37 Wealth-] ⟨World-⟩ *Hol.* stairs;] ~. *Hol.*

THE SECOND NIGHT

(Ballad)

I missed one night, but the next I went;
    It was gusty above, and clear;
She was there, with the look of one ill-content,
    And said: 'Do not come near!'

—'I am sorry last night to have failed you here,
    And now I have travelled all day;
And it's long rowing back to the West-Hoe Pier,
    So brief must be my stay.'

—'O man of mystery, why not say
    Out plain to me all you mean?
Why you missed last night, and must now away
    Is—another has come between!'

—'O woman so mocking in mood and mien,
    So be it!' I replied:
'And if I am due at a differing scene
    Before the dark has died,

''Tis that, unresting, to wander wide
    Has ever been my plight,
And at least I have met you at Cremyll side
    If not last eve, to-night.'

—'You get small rest—that read I quite;
    And so do I, maybe;
Though there's a rest hid safe from sight
    Elsewhere awaiting me!'

A mad star crossed the sky to the sea,
    Wasting in sparks as it streamed,
And when I looked back at her wistfully
    She had changed, much changed, it seemed:

THE SECOND NIGHT. 16 dark] night *Hol.* 17 ''Tis] ⟨"It is⟩ *Hol.*
27 And when I looked to where stood she *LL22a*, *22b*

The sparks of the star in her pupils gleamed,
 She was vague as a vapour now,
And ere of its meaning I had dreamed
 She'd vanished—I knew not how.

I stood on, long; each cliff-top bough,
 Like a cynic nodding there,
Moved up and down, though no man's brow
 But mine met the wayward air.

Still stood I, wholly unaware
 Of what had come to pass,
Or had brought the secret of my new Fair
 To my old Love, alas!

I went down then by crag and grass
 To the boat wherein I had come.
Said the man with the oars: 'This news of the lass
 Of Edgcumbe, is sharp for some!

'Yes: found this daybreak, stiff and numb
 On the shore here, whither she'd sped
To meet her lover last night in the glum,
 And he came not, 'tis said.

'And she leapt down, heart-hit. Pity she's dead:
 So much for the faithful-bent!' . . .
I looked, and again a star overhead
 Shot through the firmament.

SHE WHO SAW NOT

 'Did you see something within the house
That made me call you before the red sunsetting?
Something that all this common scene endows
With a richened impress there can be no forgetting?'

30 ⟨She was large as a goddess now,⟩ *Hol.* 44 sharp] ⟨sad⟩ *Hol.* some!] ~. *Hol.* 45 daybreak,] ⟨morning,⟩ *Hol.* 49 ⟨"And she leapt down, heart-hit: they found her dead:⟩ *Hol.* 51 ⟨I looked back, and ⟨⟨a star⟩⟩ a new star overhead⟩ *Hol.* looked,] ~ *Hol.*

'—I have found nothing to see therein,
O Sage, that should have made you urge me to enter,
Nothing to fire the soul, or the sense to win:
I rate you as a rare misrepresenter!'

'—Go anew, Lady,—in by the right. . . .
Well: why does your face not shine like the face of
Moses?'
'—I found no moving thing there save the light
And shadow flung on the wall by the outside roses.'

'—Go yet once more, pray. Look on a seat.'
'—I go. . . . O Sage, it's only a man that sits there
With eyes on the sun. Mute,—average head to feet.'
'—No more?'—'No more. Just one the place befits there,

'As the rays reach in through the open door,
And he looks at his hand, and the sun glows through his
fingers,
While he's thinking thoughts whose tenour is no more
To me than the swaying rose-tree shade that lingers.'

No more. And years drew on and on
Till no sun came, dank fogs the house enfolding;
And she saw inside, when the form in the flesh had gone,
As a vision what she had missed when the real beholding.

THE OLD WORKMAN

'Why are you so bent down before your time,
Old mason? Many have not left their prime
So far behind at your age, and can still
Stand full upright at will.'

SHE WHO SAW NOT. 15 average] ⟨average⟩ ⟨common⟩ *Hol.* 16 there,] ~ *Hol.*

THE OLD WORKMAN. *Title* ⟨The Old Mason⟩ *Hol.*
1 time,] ~ *Hol.* 3 So] ⟨O'er⟩ *Hol.*

He pointed to the mansion-front hard by,
And to the stones of the quoin against the sky;
'Those upper blocks', he said, 'that there you see,
It was that ruined me.'

There stood in the air up to the parapet
Crowning the corner height, the stones as set
By him—ashlar whereon the gales might drum
For centuries to come.

'I carried them up', he said, 'by a ladder there;
The last was as big a load as I could bear;
But on I heaved; and something in my back
Moved, as 'twere with a crack.

'So I got crookt. I never lost that sprain;
And those who live there, walled from wind and rain
By freestone that I lifted, do not know
That my life's ache came so.

'They don't know me, or even know my name,
But good I think it, somehow, all the same
To have kept 'em safe from harm, and right and tight,
Though it has broke me quite.

'Yes; that I fixed it firm up there I am proud,
Facing the hail and snow and sun and cloud,
And to stand storms for ages, beating round
When I lie underground.'

THE SAILOR'S MOTHER*

'O whence do you come,
Figure in the night-fog that chills me numb?'

7 see,] ~ *Hol.* 11 ashlar] ⟨a face⟩ *Hol.* 14 The last] ⟨And⟩ *Hol.* 16 'twere] ⟨it were⟩ *Hol.* 19 freestone] ⟨ashlar⟩ *Hol.*

THE SAILOR'S MOTHER. *Anglo-Italian Review*, Sept. 1918

'I come to you across from my house up there,
And I don't mind the brine-mist clinging to me
That blows from the quay,
For I heard him in my chamber, and thought you unaware.'

'But what did you hear,
That brought you blindly knocking in this middle-watch so drear?'

'My sailor son's voice as 'twere calling at your door,
And I don't mind my bare feet clammy on the stones,
And the blight to my bones,
For he only knows of *this* house I lived in before.'

'Nobody's nigh,
Woman like a skeleton, with socket-sunk eye.'

'Ah—nobody's nigh! And my life is drearisome,
And this is the old home we loved in many a day
Before he went away;
And the salt fog mops me. And nobody's come!'

From 'To Please his Wife.'

OUTSIDE THE CASEMENT*

(A Reminiscence of the War)

We sat in the room
And praised her whom
We saw in the portico-shade outside:
She could not hear
What was said of her,
But smiled, for its purport we did not hide.

4 brine-mist] ⟨salt mist⟩ *Hol.* 6 unaware.'] ⟨not aware."⟩ *Hol.* 7 'But] ⟨"O⟩ *Hol.* 8 ⟨That brought you knocking in the middle-watch drear?"⟩ *Hol.* blindly] ⟨quick⟩ *Hol.* so drear?'] drear?" *AIR* 10 clammy] ⟨here⟩ *Hol.* 11 blight] ⟨chill⟩ *Hol.* 12 of *this* house] ⟨the house that⟩ *Hol.* 13 ⟨"O nobody's nigh,⟩ *Hol.* 14 socket-sunk] ⟨sunken⟩ *Hol.* 16 ⟨And this is the old house in which we used to stay⟩ *Hol.* 18 mops] smears *AIR*; ⟨mops⟩ ⟨smears⟩ *Hol.*
Tailnote om. AIR

Then in was brought
That message, fraught
With evil fortune for her out there,
Whom we loved that day
More than any could say,
And would fain have fenced from a waft of care.

And the question pressed
Like lead on each breast,
Should we cloak the tidings, or call her and tell?
It was too intense
A choice for our sense,
As we pondered and watched her we loved so well.

Yea, spirit failed us
At what assailed us;
How long, while seeing what soon must come,
Should we counterfeit
No knowledge of it,
And stay the stroke that would blanch and numb?

And thus, before
For evermore
Joy left her, we practised to beguile
Her innocence when
She now and again
Looked in, and smiled us another smile.

THE PASSER-BY*

(L. H. Recalls her Romance)

He used to pass, well-trimmed and brushed,
My window every day,

OUTSIDE THE CASEMENT. 7 in] ⟨to us⟩ *Hol.* 8 ⟨Battle news, fraught⟩ *Hol.* 15 cloak] ⟨hide⟩ *Hol.* 17 choice] ⟨point⟩ *Hol.* 18 As we pondered and] ⟨To weigh as we⟩ *Hol.* 19 Yea,] ⟨Yes,⟩ *Hol.*

THE PASSER-BY. *Headnote* ⟨(⟩ In Memoriam L____ H____. ⟨)⟩/(*She speaks*) *Hol.*

And when I smiled on him he blushed,
That youth, quite as a girl might; aye,
In the shyest way.

Thus often did he pass hereby,
That youth of bounding gait,
Until the one who blushed was I,
And he became, as here I sate,
My joy, my fate.

And now he passes by no more,
That youth I loved too true!
I grieve should he, as here of yore,
Pass elsewhere, seated in his view,
Some maiden new!

If such should be, alas for her!
He'll make her feel him dear,
Become her daily comforter,
Then tire him of her beauteous gear,
And disappear!

'I WAS THE MIDMOST'

I was the midmost of my world
When first I frisked me free,
For though within its circuit gleamed
But a small company,
And I was immature, they seemed
To bend their looks on me.

She was the midmost of my world
When I went further forth,
And hence it was that, whether I turned
To south, east, west, or north,
Beams of an all-day Polestar burned
From that new axe of earth.

4 aye,] ~ *Hol.* 5 way.] ~! *Hol.* 11 by] here *Hol.*
14 seated] ⟨windowed⟩ *Hol.* 18 comforter,] ⟨harbinger,⟩ *Hol.*

Where now is midmost in my world?
  I trace it not at all:
No midmost shows it here, or there,
  When wistful voices call
'We are fain! We are fain!' from everywhere
  On Earth's bewildering ball!

A SOUND IN THE NIGHT

(Woodsford Castle: 17—)

'What do I catch upon the night-wind, husband?—
What is it sounds in this house so eerily?
It seems to be a woman's voice: each little while I hear it,
    And it much troubles me!'

''Tis but the eaves dripping down upon the plinth-slopes:
Letting fancies worry thee!—sure 'tis a foolish thing,
When we were on'y coupled half-an-hour before the noontide,
    And now it's but evening.'

'Yet seems it still a woman's voice outside the castle, husband,
And 'tis cold to-night, and rain beats, and this is a lonely place.
Didst thou fathom much of womankind in travel or adventure
    Ere ever thou sawest my face?'

'It may be a tree, bride, that rubs his arms acrosswise,
If it is not the eaves-drip upon the lower slopes,

'I WAS THE MIDMOST'. 15 here, or there,] ⟨anywhere,⟩ *Hol.* 16 wistful] ⟨vibrant⟩ *Hol.*

A SOUND IN THE NIGHT. 6 sure 'tis] ⟨it is⟩ *Hol.* 7 on'y coupled half-an-hour] ⟨only married about an hour⟩ *Hol.* 8 now it's but] ⟨it's only now⟩ *Hol.* 10 'tis] ⟨it's⟩ *Hol.*

Or the river at the bend, where it whirls about the hatches
Like a creature that sighs and mopes.'

'Yet it still seems to me like the crying of a woman,
And it saddens me much that so piteous a sound
On this my bridal night when I would get agone from sorrow
Should so ghost-like wander round!'

'To satisfy thee, Love, I will strike the flint-and-steel, then,
And set the rush-candle up, and undo the door,
And take the new horn-lantern that we bought upon our journey,
And throw the light over the moor.'

He struck a light, and breeched and booted in the further chamber,
And lit the new horn-lantern and went from her sight,
And vanished down the turret; and she heard him pass the postern,
And go out into the night.

She listened as she lay, till she heard his step returning,
And his voice as he unclothed him: ''Twas nothing, as I said,
But the nor'-west wind a-blowing from the moor ath'art the river,
And the tree that taps the gurgoyle-head.'

'Nay, husband, you perplex me; for if the noise I heard here,
Awaking me from sleep so, were but as you avow,
The rain-fall, and the wind, and the tree-bough, and the river,
Why is it silent now?

14 lower] ⟨plinth⟩ *Hol.* 19 I would] ⟨I'd⟩ *Hol.* 23 bought] ⟨brought⟩ *Hol.* 26 horn-lantern] ~, *Hol.* 31 ath'art] ⟨across⟩ *Hol.* 32 taps] ⟨beats⟩ *Hol.* 35 rain-fall,] ⟨rain-storm,⟩ rain-fall *Hol.*

'And why is thy hand and thy clasping arm so shaking,
And thy sleeve and tags of hair so muddy and so wet,
And why feel I thy heart a-thumping every time thou kissest me,
    And thy breath as if hard to get?'

He lay there in silence for a while, still quickly breathing,
Then started up and walked about the room resentfully:
'O woman, witch, whom I, in sooth, against my will have wedded,
    Why castedst thou thy spells on me?

'There was one I loved once: the cry you heard was her cry:
She came to me to-night, and her plight was passing sore,
As no woman. . . . Yea, and it was e'en the cry you heard wife,
    But she will cry no more!

'And now I can't abide thee: this place, it hath a curse on't.
This farmstead once a castle: I'll get me straight away!'
He dressed this time in darkness, unspeaking, as she listened,
    And went ere the dawn turned day.

They found a woman's body at a spot called Rocky Shallow,
Where the Froom stream curves amid the moorland, washed aground,
And they searched about for him, the yeoman, who had darkly known her,
    But he could not be found.

39 a-thumping] thumping *Hol.* 47 As] Such as *Hol.* it was e'en] ⟨that was⟩ *Hol.* 50 farmstead] homestead *Hol.* me straight] from it *Hol.* 55 him,] ~ *Hol.*

And the bride left for good-and-all the farmstead once a castle,
And in a county far away lives, mourns, and sleeps alone,
And thinks in windy weather that she hears a woman crying,
And sometimes an infant's moan.

ON A DISCOVERED CURL OF HAIR*

When your soft welcomings were said,
This curl was waving on your head,
And when we walked where breakers dinned
It sported in the sun and wind,
And when I had won your words of grace
It brushed and clung about my face.
Then, to abate the misery
Of absentness, you gave it me.

Where are its fellows now? Ah, they
For brightest brown have donned a gray,
And gone into a caverned ark,
Ever unopened, always dark!

Yet this one curl, untouched of time,
Beams with live brown as in its prime,
So that it seems I even could now
Restore it to the living brow
By bearing down the western road
Till I had reached your old abode.

February 1913.

57 farmstead] homestead *Hol.*

ON A DISCOVERED CURL OF HAIR. 13 of] ⟨by⟩ *Hol.*

AN OLD LIKENESS*

(Recalling R. T.)

Who would have thought
That, not having missed her
Talks, tears, laughter
In absence, or sought
To recall for so long
Her gamut of song;
Or ever to waft her
Signal of aught
That she, fancy-fanned,
Would well understand,
I should have kissed her
Picture when scanned
Yawning years after!

Yet, seeing her poor
Dim-outlined form
Chancewise at night-time,
Some old allure
Came on me, warm,
Fresh, pleadful, pure,
As in that bright time
At a far season
Of love and unreason,
And took me by storm
Here in this blight-time!

And thus it arose
That, yawning years after
Our early flows
Of wit and laughter,

AN OLD LIKENESS. *Title* ⟨The Old Portrait⟩ *Hol.*
3 Talks,] ⟨Words,⟩ *Hol.* 5 recall] read *Hol.* 6 gamut] volume *Hol.* 7 Or ever] ⟨Ever⟩ *Hol.* 9 Happening at hand *Hol.* 10 In her own land, *Hol.* 13 Yawning] ⟨Forty⟩ Thirty *Hol.* 16 Chancewise] By chance *Hol.* 17 Some] The *Hol.* 19 ⟨New,⟩ Fresh, sweet, and pure, *Hol.* 21 far] far-off *Hol.* 24 this] ⟨my⟩ *Hol.* 26 yawning] ⟨forty⟩ thirty *Hol.*

And framing of rhymes
At idle times,
At sight of her painting,
Though she lies cold
In churchyard mould,
I took its feinting
As real, and kissed it,
As if I had wist it
Herself of old.

HER APOTHEOSIS*

'Secretum meum mihi'

(Faded Woman's Song)

There were years vague of measure,
  Needless the asking when;
No honours, praises, pleasure
  Reached common maids from men.

And hence no lures bewitched them,
  No hand was stretched to raise,
No gracious gifts enriched them,
  No voices sang their praise.

29 of rhymes] ⟨rhymes⟩ *Hol.* 31 painting,] ~ ; *Hol.* 32 lies] ⟨was⟩ *Hol.* 36 had wist] ⟨wist⟩ *Hol.*

HER APOTHEOSIS. *Epigraph om. Hol.* *Headnote* (Woman's Song) *Hol.*
Hol. reads:

There was a certain summer,
  No record vouches when;
With ailments, wars, and tumults
  As usual among men.

No people did me honour,
  No hand was stretched to raise,
No enterprize enriched me,
  No voices sang my praise.

Yet an iris at that season
  Amid the accustomed slight
From denseness, dull unreason,
  Ringed me with living light.

'SACRED TO THE MEMORY'*

(Mary H.)

That 'Sacred to the Memory'
Is clearly carven there I own,
And all may think that on the stone
The words have been inscribed by me
In bare conventionality.

But ⟨a halo⟩ an aureole at that season
  Amid the accustomed blight
Of scorn, offence, unreason,
  Ringed me with living light.

LL22a, *22b* read:

There was a spell of leisure,
  No record vouches when;
With honours, praises, pleasure
  To womankind from men.

But no such lures bewitched me,
  No hand was stretched to raise,
No gracious gifts enriched me,
  No voices sang my praise.
(ll. 9–12 *as in established text*)

LL22c reads:

There were blank years of leisure,
  No record vouches when;
No honours, praises, pleasure
  Reached common maids from men.

And hence no lures bewitched me,
  No hand was stretched to raise,
No gracious gifts enriched me,
  No voices sang my praise.
(ll. 9–12 *as in established text*)

'SACRED TO THE MEMORY'. *Dedication* (M.H.) *Hol.*
5 bare] mere *Hol.*

They know not and will never know
That my full script is not confined
To that stone space, but stands deep lined
Upon the landscape high and low
Wherein she made such worthy show.

TO A WELL-NAMED DWELLING

Glad old house of lichened stonework,
What I owed you in my lone work,
Noon and night!
Whensoever faint or ailing,
Letting go my grasp and failing,
You lent light.

How by that fair title came you?
Did some forward eye so name you
Knowing that one,
Stumbling down his century blindly,
Would remark your sound, so kindly,
And be won?

Smile in sunlight, sleep in moonlight,
Bask in April, May, and June-light,
Zephyr-fanned;
Let your chambers show no sorrow,
Blanching day, or stuporing morrow,
While they stand.

THE WHIPPER-IN

'My father was the whipper-in,—
Is still—if I'm not misled?

7 my] the *Hol.* confined] ⟨contained⟩ *Hol.* 8 ⟨In that dried phrase, but stands ingrained⟩ *Hol.* 9 Upon] ⟨Throughout⟩ *Hol.* 10 such worthy] so fair a *Hol.*

TO A WELL-NAMED DWELLING. *Title* Well-Named] ⟨Well-Called⟩ *Hol.* 2 my] ⟨my⟩ ⟨the⟩ *Hol.* 3 Noon and] ⟨Of my⟩ *Hol.* 6 lent] ⟨held⟩ shed *Hol.* 10 Stumbling] Sauntering *LL* 16 show] hold *Hol.*

And now I see, where the hedge is thin,
  A little spot of red;
  Surely it is my father
  Going to the kennel-shed!

'I cursed and fought my father—aye,
  And sailed to a foreign land;
And feeling sorry, I'm back, to stay,
  Please God, as his helping hand.
  Surely it is my father
  Near where the kennels stand?'

'—True. Whipper-in he used to be
  For twenty years or more;
And you did go away to sea
  As youths have done before.
  Yes, oddly enough that red there
  Is the very coat he wore.

'But he—he's dead; was thrown somehow,
  And gave his back a crick,
And though that is his coat, 'tis now
  The scarecrow of a rick;
  You'll see when you get nearer—
  'Tis spread out on a stick.

'You see, when all had settled down
  Your mother's things were sold,
And she went back to her own town,
  And the coat, ate out with mould,
  Is now used by the farmer
  For scaring, as 'tis old.'

THE WHIPPER-IN. 7 cursed and fought] ⟨quarrelled with⟩ *Hol.* 9 ⟨And now I'm back again to stay,⟩ *Hol.* sorry,] ~ *Hol.* 10 Please God, as] ⟨And be⟩ *Hol.*

A MILITARY APPOINTMENT*

(Scherzando)

'So back you have come from the town, Nan, dear!
And have you seen him there, or near—
That soldier of mine—
Who long since promised to meet me here?'

'—O yes, Nell: from the town I come,
And have seen your lover on sick-leave home—
That soldier of yours—
Who swore to meet you, or Strike-him-dumb;

'But has kept himself of late away;
Yet,—in short, he's coming, I heard him say—
That lover of yours—
To this very spot on this very day.'

'—Then I'll wait, I'll wait, through wet or dry!
I'll give him a goblet brimming high—
This lover of mine—
And not of complaint one word or sigh!'

'—Nell, him I have chanced so much to see,
That—he has grown the lover of me!—
That lover of yours—
And it's here our meeting is planned to be.'

THE MILESTONE BY THE RABBIT-BURROW

(On Yell'ham Hill)

In my loamy nook
As I dig my hole
I observe men look

A MILITARY APPOINTMENT. *Headnote* (Scherzo) *Hol.*
1 Nan, dear!] ⟨my dear!⟩ Ann dear! *Hol.* 5 ⟨"—O yes: from the town indeed I come,⟩ *Hol.* 9 ⟨"Who has kept himself too long away;⟩ *Hol.* 10 Yet,—] ⟨And,⟩ *Hol.* 17 ⟨"—But him I have lately chanced to see,⟩ *Hol.* '—Nell,] "—But *Hol.* 18 ⟨Until—he grew the lover of me!—⟩ *Hol.* 20 meeting] ⟨tryst⟩ *Hol.*

At a stone, and sigh
As they pass it by
To some far goal.

Something it says
To their glancing eyes
That must distress
The frail and lame,
And the strong of frame
Gladden or surprise.

Do signs on its face
Declare how far
Feet have to trace
Before they gain
Some blest champaign
Where no gins are?

THE LAMENT OF THE LOOKING-GLASS*

Words from the mirror softly pass
  To the curtains with a sigh:
'Why should I trouble again to glass
  These smileless things hard by,
Since she I pleasured once, alas,
  Is now no longer nigh!

'I've imaged shadows of coursing cloud,
  And of the plying limb
On the pensive pine when the air is loud
  With its aerial hymn;
But never do they make me proud
  To catch them within my rim!

THE LAMENT OF THE LOOKING-GLASS. 4 smileless] 〈?moveless?〉 *Hol.* 7 coursing] dark *Hol.* 8 plying] swaying *Hol.* 9 On] Of *Hol.* pensive pine] 〈sycamore〉 *Hol.* 12 within] 〈in〉 *Hol.*

'I flash back phantoms of the night
 That sometimes flit by me,
I echo roses red and white—
 The loveliest blooms that be—
But now I never hold to sight
 So sweet a flower as she.'

CROSS-CURRENTS

They parted—a pallid, trembling pair,
 And rushing down the lane
He left her lonely near me there;
 —I asked her of their pain.

'It is for ever,' at length she said,
 'His friends have schemed it so,
That the long-purposed day to wed
 Never shall we two know.'

'In such a cruel case,' said I,
 'Love will contrive a course?'
'—Well, no . . . A thing may underlie,
 Which robs that of its force;

'A thing I could not tell him of,
 Though all the year I have tried;
This: never could I have given him love,
 Even had I been his bride.

'So, when his kinsfolk stop the way
 Point-blank, there could not be
A happening in the world to-day
 More opportune for me!

16 blooms] ⟨buds⟩ *Hol.* 18 flower] ⟨bud⟩ *Hol.*

CROSS-CURRENTS. 1 pallid, trembling] ⟨tearful, trembling⟩ ⟨silent, sombre⟩ pensive, trembling *Hol.* 11 no . . .] ~⟨!⟩ . . . *Hol.* 15 This:] ⟨That⟩ *Hol.*

'Yet hear—no doubt to your surprise—
I am grieving, for his sake,
That I have escaped the sacrifice
I was distressed to make!'

THE OLD NEIGHBOUR AND THE NEW

'Twas to greet the new rector I called here,
But in the arm-chair I see
My old friend, for long years installed here,
Who palely nods to me.

The new man explains what he's planning
In a smart and cheerful tone,
And I listen, the while that I'm scanning
The figure behind his own.

The newcomer urges things on me;
I return a vague smile thereto,
The olden face gazing upon me
Just as it used to do!

And on leaving I scarcely remember
Which neighbour to-day I have seen,
The one carried out in September,
Or him who but entered yestreen.

THE CHOSEN*

Ατινά ἐστιν ἀλληγορούμενα

'A woman for whom great gods might strive!'
I said, and kissed her there:

22 grieving,] sorry, *LL* 23 have escaped] ⟨escape⟩ *Hol.* 24 distressed] prepared *LL22a*, *22b*

THE OLD NEIGHBOUR AND THE NEW. 1 rector] ⟨tenant⟩ *Hol.* 9 things] ⟨facts⟩ *Hol.* 11 olden face] old dweller *Hol.* 12 it] he *Hol.*

THE CHOSEN. *Epigraph* ἀλληγορούμενα] ~ ⟨Gal. IV.14⟩ *Hol.*

And then I thought of the other five,
    And of how charms outwear.

I thought of the first with her eating eyes,
And I thought of the second with hers, green-gray,
And I thought of the third, experienced, wise,
And I thought of the fourth who sang all day.

And I thought of the fifth, whom I'd called a jade,
    And I thought of them all, tear-fraught;
And that each had shown her a passable maid,
    Yet not of the favour sought.

So I traced these words on the bark of a beech,
Just at the falling of the mast:
'After scanning five; yes, each and each,
I've found the woman desired—at last!'

'—I feel a strange benumbing spell,
    As one ill-wished!' said she.
And soon it seemed that something fell
    Was starving her love for me.

'I feel some curse. O, *five* were there?'
And wanly she swerved, and went away.
I followed sick: night numbed the air,
And dark the mournful moorland lay.

I cried: 'O darling, turn your head!'
    But never her face I viewed;
'O turn, O turn!' again I said,
    And miserably pursued.

At length I came to a Christ-cross stone
Which she had passed without discern;
And I knelt upon the leaves there strown,
And prayed aloud that she might turn.

3 thought of] ⟨mused on⟩ *Hol.* 11 that] ⟨I felt⟩ *Hol.* 12 Yet] ⟨But⟩ *Hol.* 13 traced] cut *Hol.* 22 swerved,] turned, *Hol.* 23 numbed] chilled *Hol.*

I rose, and looked; and turn she did;
    I cried, 'My heart revives!'
'Look more,' she said. I looked as bid;
    Her face was all the five's.

All the five women, clear come back,
I saw in her—with her made one,
The while she drooped upon the track,
And her frail term seemed well-nigh run.

She'd half forgot me in her change;
    'Who are you? Won't you say
Who you may be, you man so strange,
    Following since yesterday?'

I took the composite form she was,
And carried her to an arbour small,
Not passion-moved, but even because
In one I could atone to all.

And there she lies, and there I tend,
    Till my life's threads unwind,
A various womanhood in blend—
    Not one, but all combined.

THE INSCRIPTION*

(A Tale)

Sir John was entombed, and the crypt was closed, and she,
Like a soul that could meet no more the sight of the sun,
Inclined her in weepings and prayings continually,
    As his widowed one.

41 in her change;] ⟨—weary, wan;⟩ *Hol.* 42 say] ~⟨?⟩ *Hol.* 43 man so strange,] ⟨piteous man,⟩ *Hol.* 47 passion-moved,] ⟨passioned now,⟩ ⟨for love,⟩ *Hol.* 51 A various] ⟨The form of⟩ *Hol.* blend—] ~⟨,⟩ *Hol.* 52 ⟨Not one, but all combined.⟩ ⟨As one, the sex combined.⟩ *Hol.*

THE INSCRIPTION. *Title* ⟨The Words on the Brass⟩ *Hol.*

And to pleasure her in her sorrow, and fix his name
As a memory Time's fierce frost should never kill,
She caused to be richly chased a brass to his fame,
Which should link them still;

For she bonded her name with his own on the brazen page,
As if dead and interred there with him, and cold, and numb,
(Omitting the day of her dying and year of her age
Till her end should come;)

And implored good people to pray **'Of their Charytie
For these twaine Soules'**,—yea, she who did last remain
Forgoing Heaven's bliss if ever with spouse should she
Again have lain.

Even there, as it first was set, you may see it now,
Writ in quaint Church-text, with the date of her death left bare,
In the aged Estminster aisle, where the folk yet bow
Themselves in prayer.

Thereafter some years slid, till there came a day
When it slowly began to be marked of the standers-by
That she would regard the brass, and would bend away
With a drooping sigh.

Now the lady was fair as any the eye might scan
Through a summer day of roving—a type at whose lip
Despite her maturing seasons, no meet man
Would be loth to sip.

And her heart was stirred with a lightning love to its pith
For a newcomer who, while less in years, was one
Full eager and able to make her his own forthwith,
Restrained of none.

14 —yea, she] ⟨—she⟩ *Hol.* 19 aged] well-known *Hol.* 21 slid,] ⟨slipt,⟩ *Hol.* 23 brass,] script, *Hol.* 28 sip.] ~; *Hol.* 30 newcomer who, while] ⟨man who, albeit⟩ *Hol.*

But she answered Nay, death-white; and still as he urged
She adversely spake, overmuch as she loved the while,
Till he pressed for why, and she led with the face of one
scourged
To the neighbouring aisle,

And showed him the words, ever gleaming upon her pew,
Memorizing her there as the knight's eternal wife,
Or falsing such, debarred inheritance due
Of celestial life.

He blenched, and reproached her that one yet undeceased
Should bury her future—that future which none can spell;
And she wept, and purposed anon to inquire of the priest
If the price were hell

Of her wedding in face of the record. Her lover agreed,
And they parted before the brass with a shudderful kiss,
For it seemed to flash out on their impulse of passionate
need,
'Mock ye not this!'

Well, the priest, whom more perceptions moved than one,
Said she erred at the first to have written as if she were
dead
Her name and adjuration; but since it was done
Nought could be said

Save that she must abide by the pledge, for the peace of
her soul,
And so, by her life, maintain the apostrophe good,
If she wished anon to reach the coveted goal
Of beatitude.

33 death-white;] ~, *Hol.* still as] ⟨as still⟩ *Hol.* urged] ~⟨,⟩ *Hol.*
49 Well, the priest whom, haply, more motives ⟨moved⟩ had moved than one, *Hol.*
50 written] ⟨writ⟩ *Hol.*

To erase from the consecrate text her prayer as there prayed
Would aver that the joys of the earth had so wound her about,
That prayers for her joy above by Jesu's aid
Could be done without.

Moreover she thought of the laughter, the shrug, the jibe
That would rise at her back in the nave when she should pass
As another's avowed by the words she had chosen to inscribe
On the changeless brass.

And so for months she replied to her Love: 'No, no';
While sorrow was gnawing her beauties ever and more,
Till he, long-suffering and weary, grew to show
Less warmth than before.

And, after an absence, wrote words absolute:
That he gave her till Midsummer morn to make her mind clear;
And that if, by then, she had not said Yea to his suit,
He should wed elsewhere.

Thence on, at unwonted times through the lengthening days
She was seen in the church—at dawn, or when the sun dipt
And the moon rose, standing with hands joined, blank of gaze,
Before the script.

58 *DCM3*] Would aver that, since earth's joys drew her most, past doubt, *Hol.*; Would aver that, since earth's joys most drew her, past doubt, *all other texts* 59 That *DCM3*] ⟨Their⟩ Friends' *Hol.*; Friends' *all other texts* above] ~⟨,⟩ *Hol.* aid] ~, *Hol.* 66 was gnawing] ⟨gnawed at⟩ *Hol.* 67 long-suffering and weary,] ⟨longsuffering, weary,⟩ *Hol.* 68 before.] ~, *Hol.*

She thinned as he came not; shrank like a creature that cowers
As summer drew nearer; but yet had not promised to wed,
When, just at the zenith of June, in the still night hours,
She was missed from her bed.

'The church!' they whispered with qualms; 'where often she sits.'
They found her: facing the brass there, else seeing none,
But feeling the words with her finger, gibbering in fits;
And she knew them not one.

And so she remained, in her handmaids' charge; late, soon,
Tracing words in the air with her finger, as seen that night—
Those incised on the brass—till at length unwatched one noon,
She vanished from sight.

And, as talebearers tell, thence on to her last-taken breath
Was unseen, save as wraith that in front of the brass made moan;
So that ever the way of her life and the time of her death
Remained unknown.

And hence, as indited above, you may read even now
The quaint Church-text, with the date of her death left bare,
In the aged Estminster aisle, where folk yet bow
Themselves in prayer.

October 30, 1907.

78 yet] still *LL* 79 zenith] ⟨entry⟩ *Hol.* 82 They found her there: she faced the brass, seeing none, *Hol.* 83 But feeling] ⟨And followed⟩ And was feeling *Hol.* fits;] ~, *Hol.* 84 And knew them not one. *Hol.* 87 length] ~, *Hol.* 94 Church-text,] ⟨church-script,⟩ *Hol.* 95 aged] well-known *Hol.*

THE MARBLE-STREETED TOWN*

I reach the marble-streeted town,
Whose 'Sound' outbreathes its air
Of sharp sea-salts;
I see the movement up and down
As when she was there.
Ships of all countries come and go,
The bandsmen boom in the sun
A throbbing waltz;
The schoolgirls laugh along the Hoe
As when she was one.

I move away as the music rolls:
The place seems not to mind
That she—of old
The brightest of its native souls—
Left it behind!
Over this green aforedays she
On light treads went and came,
Yea, times untold;
Yet none here knows her history—
Has heard her name.

Plymouth (1914?).

A WOMAN DRIVING

How she held up the horses' heads,
Firm-lipped, with steady rein,
Down that grim steep the coastguard treads,
Till all was safe again!

THE MARBLE-STREETED TOWN. 2 air] ⟨clear⟩ *Hol.* 3 ⟨Scent of sea-salts;⟩ *Hol.* 5 ⟨As she were there.⟩ *Hol.* 7 boom] play *Hol.* 10 ⟨As she were one.⟩ *Hol.*
Place/date Plymouth (1913?). *Hol.*

With form erect and keen contour
She passed against the sea,
And, dipping into the chine's obscure,
Was seen no more by me.

To others she appeared anew
At times of dusky light,
But always, so they told, withdrew
From close and curious sight.

Some said her silent wheels would roll
Rutless on softest loam,
And even that her steeds' footfall
Sank not upon the foam.

Where drives she now? It may be where
No mortal horses are,
But in a chariot of the air
Towards some radiant star.

A WOMAN'S TRUST

If he should live a thousand years
He'd find it not again
That scorn of him by men
Could less disturb a woman's trust
In him as a steadfast star which must
Rise scathless from the nether spheres:
If he should live a thousand years
He'd find it not again.

A WOMAN DRIVING. 7 obscure,] ~ *Hol.* 11 always,] slowly, *Hol.* 12 Until she vanished quite. *Hol.*

A WOMAN'S TRUST. 2 It could not ⟨chance⟩ happen again *Hol.* 3 That] ⟨Such⟩ *Hol.* 4 Could less] ⟨Should not⟩ Should less *Hol.* 5 ⟨That, in time's turns he would and must⟩ In him as a star which would and must *Hol.* 8 It could not ⟨chance⟩ happen again. *Hol.*

She waited like a little child,
Unchilled by damps of doubt,
While from her eyes looked out
A confidence sublime as Spring's
When stressed by Winter's loiterings.
Thus, howsoever the wicked wiled,
She waited like a little child
Unchilled by damps of doubt.

Through cruel years and crueller
Thus she believed in him
And his aurore, so dim;
That, after fenweeds, flowers would blow;
And above all things did she show
Her faith in his good faith with her;
Through cruel years and crueller
Thus she believed in him!

BEST TIMES

We went a day's excursion to the stream,
Basked by the bank, and bent to the ripple-gleam,
And I did not know
That life would show,
However it might flower, no finer glow.

I walked in the Sunday sunshine by the road
That wound towards the wicket of your abode,
And I did not think
That life would shrink
To nothing ere it shed a rosier pink.

12 Spring's] *l.c. Hol.* 13 ⟨In stress of winter's loiterings.⟩ *Hol.*

BEST TIMES. *Title* ⟨Best Times Not Again⟩ *Hol.*
2 And climbed the bank, and looked at the rippled gleam, *Hol.* 5 flower,] bloom, *Hol.* 7 wicket] gate *Hol.*

Unlooked for I arrived on a rainy night,
And you hailed me at the door by the swaying light,
And I full forgot
That life might not
Again be touching that ecstatic height.

And that calm eve when you walked up the stair,
After a gaiety prolonged and rare,
No thought soever
That you might never
Walk down again, struck me as I stood there.

Rewritten from an old draft.

THE CASUAL ACQUAINTANCE

While he was here with breath and bone,
To speak to and to see,
Would I had known—more clearly known—
What that man did for me

When the wind scraped a minor lay,
And the spent west from white
To gray turned tiredly, and from gray
To broadest bands of night!

But I saw not, and he saw not
What shining life-tides flowed
To me-ward from his casual jot
Of service on that road.

He would have said: ''Twas nothing new;
We all do what we can;
'Twas only what one man would do
For any other man.'

13 full] quite *Hol.* 16 eve] evening *Hol.* walked up] climbed *Hol.*
17 ⟨After a languid rising from your chair,⟩ *Hol.*

THE CASUAL ACQUAINTANCE. 1 with] in *LL22a, 22b* breath] ⟨flesh⟩ *Hol.*
8 bands] ⟨black⟩ *Hol.*

Now that I gauge his goodliness
He's slipped from human eyes;
And when he passed there's none can guess,
Or point out where he lies.

INTRA SEPULCHRUM

What curious things we said,
What curious things we did
Up there in the world we walked till dead
Our kith and kin amid!

How we played at love,
And its wildness, weakness, woe;
Yes, played thereat far more than enough
As it turned out, I trow!

Played at believing in gods
And observing the ordinances,
I for your sake in impossible codes
Right ready to acquiesce.

Thinking our lives unique,
Quite quainter than usual kinds,
We held that we could not abide a week
The tether of typic minds.

—Yet people who day by day
Pass by and look at us
From over the wall in a casual way
Are of this unconscious.

17 ⟨Now that I see his value well⟩ *Hol.* 18 slipped] ⟨gone⟩ *Hol.* 19 can guess,] ⟨to tell,⟩ *Hol.*

INTRA SEPULCHRUM. *Title* ⟨Epitaph on two of the⟩ *Hol.* 12 ready] willing *Hol.* 14 kinds,] lives, *Hol.* 16 Like other men and their wives. *Hol.* 19 casual] musing *Hol.*

And feel, if anything,
That none can be buried here
Removed from commonest fashioning,
Or lending note to a bier:

No twain who in heart-heaves proved
Themselves at all adept,
Who more than many laughed and loved,
Who more than many wept,

Or were as sprites or elves
Into blind matter hurled,
Or ever could have been to themselves
The centre of the world.

THE WHITEWASHED WALL*

Why does she turn in that shy soft way
Whenever she stirs the fire,
And kiss to the chimney-corner wall,
As if entranced to admire
Its whitewashed bareness more than the sight
Of a rose in richest green?
I have known her long, but this raptured rite
I never before have seen.

—Well, once when her son cast his shadow there,
A friend took a pencil and drew him
Upon that flame-lit wall. And the lines
Had a lifelike semblance to him.

22 ⟨That nothing is buried here⟩ *Hol.* 24 ⟨Or signalizing its bier:⟩ *Hol.* 25 heart-heaves] ⟨heart-heave⟩ *Hol.* 31 Or ever] ⟨Or that they were⟩ *Hol.* have been] ⟨be⟩ *Hol.*

THE WHITEWASHED WALL. *Reveille*, Nov. 1918
6 richest] a garden *R*; ⟨a garden⟩ *Hol.* 9 —Well, her soldier-son cast his shadow there, *R* 10 A] And a *R* drew] ⟨shaped⟩ *Hol.*

And there long stayed his familiar look;
But one day, ere she knew,
The whitener came to cleanse the nook,
And covered the face from view.

'Yes,' he said: 'My brush goes on with a rush,
And the draught is buried under;
When you have to whiten old cots and brighten,
What else can you do, I wonder?'
But she knows he's there. And when she yearns
For him, deep in the labouring night,
She sees him as close at hand, and turns
To him under his sheet of white.

JUST THE SAME

I sat. It all was past;
Hope never would hail again;
Fair days had ceased at a blast,
The world was a darkened den.

The beauty and dream were gone,
And the halo in which I had hied
So gaily gallantly on
Had suffered blot and died!

I went forth, heedless whither,
In a cloud too black for name:
—People frisked hither and thither;
The world was just the same.

15 nook,] ~ *Hol.* 22 For him, lone in the moaning night, *R* labouring] ⟨loud long⟩ *Hol.* 23 turns] ~⟨,⟩ *Hol.* 24 And kisses him under the white. *R*

JUST THE SAME. 4 The world] ⟨And life⟩ *Hol.* 11 frisked] ⟨plied⟩ *Hol.*

THE LAST TIME

The kiss had been given and taken,
And gathered to many past:
It never could reawaken;
But I heard none say: 'It's the last!'

The clock showed the hour and the minute,
But I did not turn and look:
I read no finis in it,
As at closing of a book.

But I read it all too rightly
When, at a time anon,
A figure lay stretched out whitely,
And I stood looking thereon.

THE SEVEN TIMES*

The dark was thick. A boy he seemed at that time
Who trotted by me with uncertain air;
'I'll tell my tale,' he murmured, 'for I fancy
A friend goes there? . . .'

Then thus he told. 'I reached—'twas for the first time—
A dwelling. Life was clogged in me with care;
I thought not I should meet an eyesome maiden,
But found one there.

'I entered on the precincts for the second time—
'Twas an adventure fit and fresh and fair—
I slackened in my footsteps at the porchway,
And found her there.

THE LAST TIME. 4 I] you *LL22a, 22b* [*also in lines 6, 9, and 12*] 5 showed] ⟨told⟩ *Hol.* 7 I] You *LL22a, 22b*

THE SEVEN TIMES. 3 tale,'] ~" *Hol.* 7 I thought not of a meeting with a maiden, *Hol.* 10 an adventure] ⟨a peradventure⟩ *Hol.* fair—] ~⟨,⟩— *Hol.*

'I rose and travelled thither for the third time,
  The hope-hues growing gayer and yet gayer
As I hastened round the boscage of the outskirts,
      And found her there.

'I journeyed to the place again the fourth time
  (The best and rarest visit of the rare,
As it seemed to me, engrossed about these goings),
      And found her there.

'When I bent me to my pilgrimage the fifth time
  (Soft-thinking as I journeyed I would dare
A certain word at token of good auspice),
      I found her there.

'That landscape did I traverse for the sixth time,
  And dreamed on what we purposed to prepare;
I reached a tryst before my journey's end came,
      And found her there.

'I went again—long after—aye, the seventh time;
  The look of things was sinister and bare
As I caught no customed signal, heard no voice call,
      Nor found her there.

'And now I gad the globe—day, night, and any time,
  To light upon her hiding unaware,
And, maybe, I shall nigh me to some nymph-niche,
      And find her there!'

'But how', said I, 'has your so little lifetime
  Given roomage for such loving, loss, despair?
A boy so young!' Forthwith I turned my lantern
      Upon him there.

17 time] ~, *Hol.* 19 engrossed about] embarked upon *Hol.* goings),] ~) *Hol.* 21 time] ~, *Hol.* 22 (Soft-thinking] ⟨(Thinking gently⟩ *Hol.*

His head was white. His small form, fine aforetime,
  Was shrunken with old age and battering wear,
An eighty-years long plodder saw I pacing
    Beside me there.

THE SUN'S LAST LOOK ON THE COUNTRY GIRL*

(M. H.)

The sun threw down a radiant spot
  On the face in the winding-sheet—
The face it had lit when a babe's in its cot;
And the sun knew not, and the face knew not
  That soon they would no more meet.

Now that the grave has shut its door,
  And lets not in one ray,
Do they wonder that they meet no more—
That face and its beaming visitor—
  That met so many a day?

December 1915.

IN A LONDON FLAT

I

'You look like a widower,' she said
Through the folding-doors with a laugh from the bed,
As he sat by the fire in the outer room,
Reading late on a night of gloom,

41 small] ⟨slight⟩ *Hol.* fine] ⟨feat⟩ *Hol.* 43 an eighty-years] ⟨a ninety-years'⟩ an eighty-years' *Hol.* plodder] ⟨pil⟩ *Hol.*

THE SUN'S LAST LOOK. 1 down] in *Hol.*

IN A LONDON FLAT. *Title* ⟨In a London Lodging 1888⟩ *Hol.* 2 folding-doors] ~⟨,⟩ *Hol.*

And a cab-hack's wheeze, and the clap of its feet
In its breathless pace on the smooth wet street,
Were all that came to them now and then. . . .
'You really do!' she quizzed again.

II

And the Spirits behind the curtains heard,
And also laughed, amused at her word,
And at her light-hearted view of him.
'Let's get him made so—just for a whim!'
Said the Phantom Ironic. ''Twould serve her right
If we coaxed the Will to do it some night.'
'O pray not!' pleaded the younger one,
The Sprite of the Pities. 'She said it in fun!'

III

But so it befell, whatever the cause,
That what she had called him he next year was;
And on such a night, when she lay elsewhere,
He, watched by those Phantoms, again sat there,
And gazed, as if gazing on far faint shores,
At the empty bed through the folding-doors
As he remembered her words; and wept
That she had forgotten them where she slept.

DRAWING DETAILS IN AN OLD CHURCH

I hear the bell-rope sawing,
And the oil-less axle grind,
As I sit alone here drawing
What some Gothic brain designed;

5 And] ⟨When⟩ *Hol.* 6 smooth wet] ⟨stones of the⟩ *Hol.* 7 ⟨Was all that came up now and then. . . .⟩ *Hol.* 8 do!'] ~⟨,⟩" *Hol.* 9 curtains] ⟨wainscot⟩ *Hol.* 10 also] likewise *Hol.* 14 some night.'] ⟨to-night."⟩ *Hol.* 18 called him] ⟨said⟩ *Hol.* 21 on far faint] ⟨at shining⟩ *Hol.* 22 folding-doors] ~⟨;⟩ *Hol.* 23 As] ⟨Till⟩ *Hol.*

DRAWING DETAILS. 2 ⟨And the axle grind,⟩ *Hol.*

And I catch the toll that follows
From the lagging bell,
Ere it spreads to hills and hollows
Where people dwell.

I ask not whom it tolls for,
Incurious who he be;
So, some morrow, when those knolls for
One unguessed, sound out for me,
A stranger, loitering under
In nave or choir,
May think, too, 'Whose, I wonder?'
But not inquire.

RAKE-HELL MUSES

Yes; since she knows not need,
Nor walks in blindness,
I may without unkindness
This true thing tell:

Which would be truth, indeed,
Though worse in speaking,
Were her poor footsteps seeking
A pauper's cell.

I judge, then, better far
She now have sorrow,
Than gladness that to-morrow
Might know its knell.—

8 ⟨Where the folk dwell.⟩ *Hol.*; Where the parish people dwell. *Hol.*, *LL22a*, *22b*; Where the people dwell. *LL22c* 12 ⟨Him, are for me,⟩ *Hol.* 16 But care not to inquire. *LL22a*, *22b*

RAKE-HELL MUSES. *Title* ⟨The Seducer Muses⟩ *Hol.* 4 This] A *LL* 12 Might know] ⟨May hear⟩ *Hol.*

It may be men there are
Could make of union
A lifelong sweet communion—
Or passioned spell;

But *I*, to save her name.
And bring salvation
By altar-affirmation
And bridal bell;

I, by whose rash unshame
These tears come to her:—
My faith would more undo her
Than my farewell!

Chained to me, year by year
My moody madness
Would make her olden gladness
An intermell.

She'll take the ill that's near,
And bear the blaming.
'Twill pass. Full soon her shaming
They'll cease to yell.

Our unborn, first her moan,
Will grow her guerdon,
Until from blot and burden
A joyance swell;

In that therein she'll own
My good part wholly,
My evil staining solely
My own vile fell.

16 Or] A *LL* passioned] ⟨passionate⟩ *Hol.* 27 Would wither her old gladness *LL* 28 Like famine fell. *LL* 29 near,] ~ *Hol.* 35 Until from] ⟨And out the⟩ *Hol.* 40 fell.] vell. *LL*

Of the disgrace, may be
'He shunned to share it,
Being false,' they'll say. I'll bear it;
Time will dispel

The calumny, and prove
This much about me,
That she lives best without me
Who would live well.

That, this once, not self-love
But good intention
Pleads that against convention
We two rebel.

For, is one moonlight dance,
One midnight passion,
A rock whereon to fashion
Life's citadel?

Prove they their power to prance
Life's miles together
From upper slope to nether
Who trip an ell?

—Years hence, or now apace,
May tongues be calling
News of my further falling
Sinward pell-mell:

Then this great good will grace
Our lives' division,
She's saved from more misprision
Though I plumb hell.

189–.

53 For,] ⟨Yea,⟩ *Hol.*

THE COLOUR*

(The following lines are partly original, partly remembered from a Wessex folk-rhyme)

'What shall I bring you?
Please will white do
Best for your wearing
The long day through?'
'—White is for weddings,
Weddings, weddings,
White is for weddings,
And that won't do.'

'What shall I bring you?
Please will red do
Best for your wearing
The long day through?'
'—Red is for soldiers,
Soldiers, soldiers,
Red is for soldiers,
And that won't do.'

'What shall I bring you?
Please will blue do
Best for your wearing
The long day through?'
'—Blue is for sailors,
Sailors, sailors,
Blue is for sailors,
And that won't do.'

'What shall I bring you?
Please will green do
Best for your wearing
The long day through?'

THE COLOUR. *Headnote* (*The following lines are partly made up* 〈*from*〉 *of a Wessex folk-rhyme.*) *Hol.* *original,*] *made up, LL, CP*
7 weddings,] ~ *Hol.* 15 soldiers,] ~ *Hol.* 23 sailors,] ~ *Hol.*

'—Green is for mayings,
Mayings, mayings,
Green is for mayings,
    And that won't do.'

'What shall I bring you
Then? Will black do
Best for your wearing
    The long day through?'
'—Black is for mourning,
Mourning, mourning,
Black is for mourning,
    And black will do.'

MURMURS IN THE GLOOM*

(Nocturne)

I wayfared at the nadir of the sun
Where populations meet, though seen of none;
    And millions seemed to sigh around
    As though their haunts were nigh around,
    And unknown throngs to cry around
        Of things late done.

'O Seers, who well might high ensample show'
(Came throbbing past in plainsong small and slow),
    'Leaders who lead us aimlessly,
    Teachers who train us shamelessly,
    Why let ye smoulder flamelessly
        The truths ye trow?

'Ye scribes, that urge the old medicament,
Whose fusty vials have long dried impotent,
    Why prop ye meretricious things,
    Denounce the sane as vicious things,
    And call outworn factitious things
        Expedient?

MURMURS IN THE GLOOM. 16 the] ⟨these⟩ *Hol.*

'O Dynasties that sway and shake us so,
Why rank your magnanimities so low
That grace can smooth no waters yet,
But breathing threats and slaughters yet
Ye grieve Earth's sons and daughters yet
As long ago?

'Live there no heedful ones of searching sight,
Whose accents might be oracles that smite
To hinder those who frowardly
Conduct us, and untowardly;
To lead the nations vawardly
From gloom to light?'

September 22, 1899.

EPITAPH

I never cared for Life: Life cared for me,
And hence I owed it some fidelity.
It now says, 'Cease; at length thou hast learnt to grind
Sufficient toll for an unwilling mind,
And I dismiss thee—not without regard
That thou didst ask no ill-advised reward,
Nor sought in me much more than thou couldst find.'

AN ANCIENT TO ANCIENTS*

Where once we danced, where once we sang,
Gentlemen,
The floors are sunken, cobwebs hang,

22 slaughters] ~, *Hol.* 25 'Live] ⟨"Are⟩ *Hol.* searching] ⟨vivid⟩ *Hol.* *Date* (Copied.) Sept. 22. 1899. *Hol.*

EPITAPH. 3 says,] ~ *Hol.* 5 thee—] ~⟨,⟩— *Hol.* 7 couldst] ⟨didst⟩ *Hol.*

AN ANCIENT TO ANCIENTS. *Century Magazine*, May 1922. *P1* (*CM*) HRC
3 sunken,] ⟨sunk, the⟩ *Hol.*

And cracks creep; worms have fed upon
The doors. Yea, sprightlier times were then
Than now, with harps and tabrets gone,
Gentlemen!

Where once we rowed, where once we sailed,
Gentlemen,
And damsels took the tiller, veiled
Against too strong a stare (God wot
Their fancy, then or anywhen!)
Upon that shore we are clean forgot,
Gentlemen!

We have lost somewhat, afar and near,
Gentlemen,
The thinning of our ranks each year
Affords a hint we are nigh undone,
That we shall not be ever again
The marked of many, loved of one,
Gentlemen.

In dance the polka hit our wish,
Gentlemen,
The paced quadrille, the spry schottische,
'Sir Roger'.—And in opera spheres
The 'Girl' (the famed 'Bohemian'),
And 'Trovatore', held the ears,
Gentlemen.

This season's paintings do not please,
Gentlemen,
Like Etty, Mulready, Maclise;
Throbbing romance has waned and wanned;
No wizard wields the witching pen
Of Bulwer, Scott, Dumas, and Sand,
Gentlemen.

4 And] ⟨The⟩ *Hol.* 5 sprightlier] brighter *CM*; ⟨brighter⟩ *Hol.* 11 stare] ⟨glare⟩ *P1* 12 fancy,] ~ . . . *P1*, *CM* 22 hit] ⟨met⟩ *P1*; met *CM*; ⟨met⟩ *Hol.* 24 spry] ⟨high⟩ *Hol.* 26 ⟨That sweet "Girl", (the "Bohemian"),⟩ ⟨Balfe's "Girl", (the famed "Bohemian"),⟩ *Hol.*

The bower we shrined to Tennyson,
Gentlemen,
Is roof-wrecked; damps there drip upon
Sagged seats, the creeper-nails are rust,
The spider is sole denizen;
Even she who voiced those rhymes is dust,
Gentlemen!

We who met sunrise sanguine-souled,
Gentlemen,
Are wearing weary. We are old;
These younger press; we feel our rout
Is imminent to Aïdes' den,—
That evening shades are stretching out,
Gentlemen!

And yet, though ours be failing frames,
Gentlemen,
So were some others' history names,
Who trode their track light-limbed and fast
As these youth, and not alien
From enterprise, to their long last,
Gentlemen.

Sophocles, Plato, Socrates,
Gentlemen,
Pythagoras, Thucydides,
Herodotus, and Homer,—yea,
Clement, Augustin, Origen,
Burnt brightlier towards their setting-day,
Gentlemen.

36 The bower] ⟨In bowers⟩ *Hol.* 38 ⟨The roofs are wrecked; rain drips upon⟩ *Hol.* damps there] there damps *CM*; ⟨there damps⟩ *Hol.* 41 voiced] read *LL* those] ⟨his⟩ *Hol.* 45 wearing] getting *CM*, *Hol.* 47 Aïdes'] Haides' *Hol.*; ⟨Haides'⟩ *P1* 48 That evening] ⟨The evening⟩ *Hol.*; That evening's *LL* 50 failing] faltering *CM*; ⟨aged⟩ *Hol.* 53 Who trod their track, light-stepped and fast *CM*; Who trode ⟨the race⟩ their track light-stepped and fast *Hol.* 57 ⟨Pythagoras, Homer, Socrates,⟩ *Hol.* 59 ⟨With Aeschylus, Thucydides,⟩ ⟨With Sophocles, Thucydides,⟩ *Hol.* 60 ⟨And Sophocles, and Plato,—yea,⟩ *Hol.* 61 Origen,] ~,⟨—⟩ *Hol.* 62 brightlier] ⟨brightest⟩ brightliest *Hol.*

And ye, red-lipped and smooth-browed; list,
Gentlemen;
Much is there waits you we have missed;
Much lore we leave you worth the knowing,
Much, much has lain outside our ken:
Nay, rush not: time serves: we are going,
Gentlemen.

AFTER READING PSALMS XXXIX., XL., ETC.*

Simple was I and was young;
Kept no gallant tryst, I;
Even from good words held my tongue,
Quoniam Tu fecisti!

Through my youth I stirred me not,
High adventure missed I,
Left the shining shrines unsought;
Yet—*me deduxisti!*

At my start by Helicon
Love-lore little wist I,
Worldly less; but footed on;
Why? *Me suscepisti!*

When I failed at fervid rhymes,
'Shall', I said, 'persist I?'
'*Dies*' (I would add at times)
'*Meos posuisti!*'

So I have fared through many suns;
Sadly little grist I
Bring my mill, or any one's,
Domine, *Tu scisti!*

64 ye,] you, *CM*, *Hol.*

AFTER READING PSALMS. 1 ⟨I was simple and was young;⟩ *Hol.* 2 tryst,] ~ *Hol.* 3 Even] ⟨Even⟩ Ev'n *Hol.* 4 *Tu*] ⟨*l.c.*⟩ *Hol.* 5 ⟨Through the days I have stirred me not,⟩ *Hol.* 6 adventure] ⟨adventure⟩ ⟨assayed have⟩ *Hol.* 7 shrines] ⟨shows⟩ *Hol.* 20 *Tu*] ⟨*l.c.*⟩ *Hol.*

And at dead of night I call:
    'Though to prophets list I,
Which hath understood at all?
    Yea: *Quem elegisti?*'

187–.

SURVIEW*

'Cogitavi vias meas'

A cry from the green-grained sticks of the fire
    Made me gaze where it seemed to be:
'Twas my own voice talking therefrom to me
On how I had walked when my sun was higher—
    My heart in its arrogancy.

'*You held not to whatsoever was true*,'
    Said my own voice talking to me:
'*Whatsoever was just you were slack to see;*
Kept not things lovely and pure in view,'
    Said my own voice talking to me.

'*You slighted her that endureth all*,'
    Said my own voice talking to me;
'*Vaunteth not, trusteth hopefully;*
That suffereth long and is kind withal,'
    Said my own voice talking to me.

'*You taught not that which you set about*,'
    Said my own voice talking to me;
'*That the greatest of things is Charity*. . . .'
—And the sticks burnt low, and the fire went out,
    And my voice ceased talking to me.

Date 187–/⟨[recopied]⟩ *Hol.*

SURVIEW. 5 ⟨My heart where it seemed to be.⟩ My heart where it best could be. *Hol.* 7 me:] ~; *Hol.* 8 *were slack*] ⟨*would shun*⟩ *Hol.* 13 '*Vaunteth*] ⟨"*That vaunteth*⟩ *Hol.* 18 *Charity*. . . .'] ~⟨!⟩". . . . *Hol.* 20 ceased] stopped *Hol.*

EXPLANATORY NOTES

Satires of Circumstance

History of Composition and Publication

Satires of Circumstance consists almost entirely of recently written poems. Of those to which Hardy attached dates of composition (including the dates cancelled on manuscripts), only two are from the 1890s, and none is earlier; all of the others are from the years 1910–14, including the two principal groups, 'Satires of Circumstance' (dated 1910 in the manuscript), and 'Poems of 1912–13'. About a third of the poems had previously appeared in periodicals; one, 'The Schreckhorn', was first published in *The Life and Letters of Leslie Stephen* (London: 1906).

The volume had been taking form almost since the publication of the previous one. Hardy wrote to Macmillan some nine months after *Time's Laughingstocks* appeared that he was accumulating another volume of verse (22 September 1910: BL Add. MS 54923), and by August 1913 he had decided that enough poems to fill a volume were lying in his drawer, though he did not gather them together until a year later (letter to Macmillan, 6 August 1913: BL Add. MS 54924). He proposed the title *Satires of Circumstance, Lyrics and Reveries* in July 1914, and sent the holograph to the publisher in August. The book was published on 17 November 1914. Hardy characteristically sent a list of corrections to Macmillan almost immediately (his covering letter is dated 5 February 1915), and a second impression, revised, was issued. There was a further reprint, without further corrections, in 1919.

In the first edition the fifteen 'Satires' were placed near the beginning of the book, before 'Poems of 1912–13', but Hardy came to feel that the tone of the satires clashed with other poems that were more important to him, and in later editions he moved them to the end (see note to 'Satires of Circumstance' below, p. 493). He also moved three poems—'The Spell of the Rose', 'St. Launce's Revisited', and 'Where the Picnic Was'—from the 'Lyrics and Reveries' section to the end of the 'Poems of 1912–13'. In both cases I have followed his revised order.

Other significant editions of *Satires of Circumstance* are:

The Wessex Edition (with *Moments of Vision*), Verse Volume IV (1919): in the corrected order, and with numerous textual revisions.

The Mellstock Edition, volume XXXVI (1920): a resetting of the Wessex Edition text, with a few corrections.

Collected Poems (1919): prepared at almost the same time as the Wessex Edition, but not textually identical with it.

Collected Poems (1920): five poems are slightly revised.

Collected Poems (1923): minor revisions to another eighteen poems.

The holograph printer's copy of *Satires of Circumstance*, in the Dorset County Museum, shows signs of considerable authorial uncertainty. The arrangement of the poems was changed in several instances: 'Wessex Heights', which originally stood first, was moved to its present position and replaced by 'In Front of the Landscape' and 'Channel Firing'; 'On the Doorstep', one of the 'Satires of Circumstance' in the *Fortnightly Review* publication, was included and then cancelled; a number of titles were changed. There are also many interlinear pencil notes, some of them written over in ink as tentative revisions were determined on and made permanent, others erased.

Other manuscripts of nine individual poems exist, and are reported in the notes. A tenth, of 'Places', given by Hardy to the Plymouth Free Public Library, was destroyed by bombing during the Second World War.

Explanatory Notes

Channel Firing. In *LY* (p. 161) this poem is described as 'prophetic': it was published four months before the beginning of the First World War.

l. 31 Parson Thirdly is mentioned in *Far From the Madding Crowd* (Ch. XLII).

The Convergence of the Twain. Hardy's poem on the sinking of the *Titanic* was first printed in the souvenir programme of a charity performance in aid of the victims, given at the Royal Opera House, Covent Garden, on 14 May 1912. A revised version of the poem appeared shortly after, in the *Fortnightly Review* for 1 June. In July an American bibliophile, George Barr McCutcheon, arranged for a limited edition of ten copies to be printed by Macmillan; Hardy signed the receipt for a fee of five guineas on 30 July. A first proof of this edition, with corrections in Hardy's hand, is in the Beinecke Library, Yale University. Two sets of a second, revised proof, also corrected by Hardy, together with letters and other materials relating to the edition, are in the Berg Collection of the New York Public Library.

A separate manuscript, in the Bancroft Library of the University of California, Berkeley, has the following note, in Hardy's hand, at the top of the first page:

> (Written to be sold in aid of the "Titanic" disaster fund, and republished in the Fortnightly Review for June 1912.)
> [Replica of Original MS.]

The text of this manuscript does not correspond to any printed version.

l. 3 Pride of Life: see I John 2:16.

After the Visit. *MS1* was written as a gift for Florence Dugdale, who later became Hardy's second wife, and was originally inserted in her inscribed copy of *TL* (Purdy, p. 161).

'*When I set out for Lyonnesse*'. Hardy made his first visit to St. Juliot, near Boscastle, Cornwall, on 7 March 1870. He went as an architect's assistant, to take a plan of the parish church, which his employer, the Weymouth architect G. R. Crickmay, was to rebuild. There Hardy met the vicar's sister-in-law, Emma Gifford, whom he later married (see *EL*, pp. 85–7, 98–9). In a letter to Mrs Henniker dated 23 December 1914, Hardy wrote of this poem, that it was exactly what happened. (*ORFW*, p. 165.) Later he sent a copy to Sydney Cockerell, remarking that he fancied the lines 'showed something of the song-ecstasy that a lyric should have' (letter dated 15 January 1917: *SCC*, p. 285).

In *Hol.*, above ll. 2 and 6, Hardy wrote in pencil, and then erased:

While night was waiting day

l. 3 Above *The* he wrote and erased *And.*

l. 7 Above *bechance* he wrote and erased *befall.*

A Thunderstorm in Town. Purdy (p. 161) associates the poem with Mrs Henniker.

Beyond the Last Lamp. Hardy lived in Upper Tooting, in South London, from 1878 to 1881.

The Face at the Casement. l. 3 In the margin of his copy of *SP* (*DCM2*) Hardy wrote opposite this line, in pencil: *? It befel so.*

l. 63 Song of Solomon 8:6: 'jealousy is cruel as the grave'. Hardy also used this verse as the epigraph to Ch. XXXVIII of *A Pair of Blue Eyes.*

'*My spirit will not haunt the mound*'. In *DCM2* Hardy pencilled below the title, and later erased: *A Woman's Presence* [*?*].

Wessex Heights. In *Hol.* Hardy originally placed this poem first in the volume. Florence Hardy mentioned 'Wessex Heights' in two letters to her friend Lady Hoare. On 6 December 1914 she wrote: 'It was written in '96, before I knew him—but the four people mentioned are actual women. One was dead and three living when it was written—now only one is living.' Three days later she added: '"Wessex Heights" will *always* wring my heart, for I know when it was written, a little while after the publication of "Jude", when he was so cruelly treated.' (Both letters are in the Wiltshire County Record Office, Trowbridge.)

l. 6 I Corinthians 13:4: 'Charity suffereth long, and is kind . . .'. Hardy also quotes this passage in 'The Blinded Bird' (*MV*), and in 'Surview' (*LL*).

l. 19 The tall-spired town is Salisbury.

The Schreckhorn. Leslie Stephen was editor of the *Cornhill* from 1871 to 1882, and published *Far From the Madding Crowd* and *The Hand of Ethelberta* there. He was also a keen mountaineer, and the first man to climb the Schreckhorn in the Swiss Alps (in 1861). Hardy first saw the mountain while on a European tour with his wife in 1897 (*LY*, pp. 66–7). The sonnet, together with Hardy's recollections of Stephen, was published in F. W. Maitland's *Life and Letters of Leslie Stephen* (London: 1906). Stephen's daughter, Virginia Woolf, wrote to Hardy when the poem appeared in *Satires of Circumstance*: 'That poem, and the reminiscences you contributed to Professor Maitland's Life of him, remain in my mind as incomparably the truest and most imaginative portrait of him in existence . . .'. (*The Question of Things Happening*, Letters of Virginia Woolf, vol. II, ed. Nigel Nicolson (London: 1976), p. 58.)

A Singer Asleep. The exact date of composition is uncertain. Purdy (p. 162) dates the poem 23 March 1910, the date of Hardy's visit to Swinburne's grave at Bonchurch, on the evidence of Hardy's own account (*LY*, p. 141). But in a letter to Frederic Harrison dated 13 March 1910 (HRC) Hardy refers to 'a half finished monody on Swinburne', which he thinks of sending to Harrison's son, Austin, the editor of the *English Review* (where the poem was published in the April 1910 issue). Hardy wrote on the fair copy of the poem that he made in 1920 or later (BL Ashley MS 4467): 'Written at Max Gate, Dorchester 1909'; this date is obviously an error, if it means *completed*, though the poem may have been begun then (Swinburne died in April 1909).

In a number of places on *MS1* Hardy tried out pencilled variants, and then erased them. In the space to the right of the title he considered several alternative words: *Sleeper*, *Restingplace*, *Sleepingplace*, *Sepulchre*, *Grave*, *Tomb*, *Recess*, *Couch*. To the right of l. 8 he tried *in green verdure*, *without licence*, and *irresponsibly*. Above *sunshine* in l. 14 he wrote *morning*, above *kisses* in l. 18 *bitter* and *pourings*, and below *wind* in the cancelled version of l. 25 *sounds*.

God's Funeral. Hardy offered the editor of the *Fortnightly Review* an alternative title: 'The Funeral of Jahveh' (*LY*, p. 147).

In a letter to Gosse dated 18 July 1913, Hardy wrote: '"God's Funeral" would have been enough in itself to damn me for the Laureateship, even if I had tried for or thought of it, which of course I did not. Fancy Nonconformity on the one hand, and Oxford on the other, pouring out their vials on poor Mr. Asquith for such an enormity!' (Berg.)

A cancelled passage from a draft of *LY* reads: 'However what happened was that nobody seemed to read more of the poem than the title, the result of this and kindred . . . lines of his being that . . . the poet was grotesquely denounced as a blaspheming atheist by a "phrasemongering literary contortionist" (as Hardy used to call him), and rebuked by dogmatists, because he had turned into verse the view of the age.' The draft is in DCM; it is quoted in Richard H. Taylor, ed., *The Personal Notebooks of Thomas Hardy* (London: 1978), p. 259. The 'contortionist' was G. K. Chesterton (see Hardy's satiric epitaph on Chesterton below, Volume Three of this edition).

MS1 is marked *Original MS.* in Hardy's hand, but it was not the copy text for *FR*. A note at the end reads: *First published in the Fortnightly Review from a type-written copy.*

Collins (p. 24) records the following conversation with Hardy concerning this poem:

C.: In the last stanza but one, does each mourner shake his head to mean 'yes' or 'no'?

H.: 'No.'

C.: So there were three sets of people—those who thought God was dead; those who thought that a false God was dead, but that the true one still lived; and those who thought that a new and purer God was still to make himself known to man?

H.: Yes.

Self-Unconscious. Purdy (p. 165) suggests Hardy's trip to Cornwall in 1913 as a probable occasion for this poem.

Collins (p. 24) records the following discussion with Hardy about the poem:

C.: In the last stanza but two, why and how 'should he have been shown' as he was? What difference would it have made?

H.: If he had realized then, when young, what he was, he would have acted differently. That is the tragedy of youth: when we know, it's too late to alter things.

Before and after Summer. The *New Weekly* version carries this footnote to the title: 'Written in 1910. Now first published.'

Hardy wrote to Frederic Harrison of this poem and 'The Year's Awakening' (23 March 1914): 'Please don't look at the "New Weekly"—I mean my contribution to it. Scott-James [the editor] came here one day, and I found that poor pair of stanzas in a drawer and could find nothing else, so I let him have them at his earnest request. Also another little scrap like it, which I hope he won't print.' (HRC.)

The Year's Awakening. See note to 'Before and after Summer' above.

Under the Waterfall. In *Hol.*, Hardy wrote and erased an alternative title: *The Lost Glass*.

Poems of 1912–13. Epigraph: Virgil, *Aeneid*, IV, 23: 'The traces of an old fire'.

Hardy's first wife, Emma Gifford Hardy, died on 27 November 1912 (see *LY*, p. 154). In March 1913, Hardy revisited the scenes of their courtship—St. Juliot, Cornwall, and the surrounding district, including Boscastle, Pentargon Bay, and Beeny Cliff—returning by way of Plymouth, where his wife had spent her first eighteen years (see *SR*, pp. 1–21).

The two had been increasingly alienated from each other in the later years of their marriage, but her death revived Hardy's earlier feelings for her, and touched him with remorse, as many of his letters show. In a letter to Clodd, written two weeks after Emma's death, Hardy wrote: 'Yes: what you say is true. One forgets all the recent years and differences, and the mind goes back to the early times when each was much to the other—in her case and mine intensely much.' (BL Ashley MS B3354.) Two years later, as he prepared the poems for publication in *SC*, he wrote to Mrs Henniker: 'Some of them I rather shrink from printing—those I wrote just after Emma died, when I looked back at her as she had originally been, and when I felt miserable lest I had not treated her considerately in her latter life. However I shall publish them as the only amends I can make . . .' (*ORFW*, p. 163).

In the first edition the group ended with 'The Phantom Horsewoman'. Hardy later moved the three final poems from the 'Lyrics and Reveries' section of the volume to conclude the group.

'*I found her out there*'. For Mrs Hardy's account of her first meeting with her future husband, see *SR*, pp. 31–4. A slightly different text of the account is printed in *EL*, pp. 90–3.

l. 12 In *DCM2* Hardy underlined *beats*, and wrote in the margin *sways* and *chimes*. He then erased the two words.

The Haunter. Title: above *The* in *Hol.*, in pencil, erased: *His.*
l. 11 In *Hol.*, below *dreamiest* in the cancelled line Hardy wrote in pencil and then erased *vaguest.*

The Voice. Hardy recalls the reunion described in the second stanza in *EL*, p. 103.

A Dream or No. Above the title in *Hol.* Hardy wrote in pencil and erased *The Fancy.*
l. 4 In *DCM2* Hardy underlined *claims*, and wrote in the margin *owns.* He later erased the revision.
l. 8 In *CP23* the full point at the end of the line is broken off. When Hardy corrected his own copy (*DCM3*), he inserted a comma there.
l. 21 In *Hol.* Hardy wrote in pencil and erased:

Is Saint-Juliot a place anywhere in the world?

l. 22 Macmillan's printer, R. & R. Clark, queried the spelling of *Vallency*, noting that it is spelled with one *l* in 'A Death-day Recalled'. Hardy replied: 'No: the two spellings are because of two pronunciations, which the metres require. The river is called either way indifferently.' (Clark.)
l. 24 In *Hol.* Hardy wrote in pencil and erased, below the last three words:

flounce-flinging mist?
tides skyward hurled?

A Death-day recalled. l. 3 See note to 'A Dream or No', l. 22, above.

Beeny Cliff. EL, p. 99 quotes from Hardy's diary of his first visit to St. Juliot in March 1870: 'March 10. Went with E. L. G. to Beeny Cliff. She on horseback. . . . On the cliff. . . . "The tender grace of a day", etc. The run down to the edge. The coming home.' [The marks of elision are in the text.]
l. 9 *again*: in Cockerell's copy of *SP* this is cancelled and replaced by *afresh.* A note in Cockerell's hand on the inside cover of the book reads: 'The corrections . . . were given to me by the author at Max Gate May 25, 1918.' (Adams.)

The Cheval-Glass. l. 11 Above *came* in *Hol.* Hardy wrote and erased *fared.*

The Re-Enactment. ll. 79–85 In *Hol.* there are many erased variants in the margins and between the lines. Most are illegible, but the following can be read:
l. 33 The compositor of *SC* mistook the comma at the end of the preceding line for an apostrophe after *years*, and set *years-long* as *years'-long*; this punctuation was retained in *CP* and *WE.*
l. 80 Above *its strong*: ⟨*the old*⟩
l. 83 ⟨And yea; the chamber's⟩
l. 85 ⟨And ? past kept making our⟩

Her Secret. Title: In *Hol.*, in pencil, erased: *The jealous husband.*
l. 9 A note from Hardy to the printer regarding corrections to the proofs of

WE reads for this line, 'for "glum" read "numb"', which suggests that there was an intermediate line between the *SC* and *WE* versions, which read:

Wrought his look lurid and glum.

A Conversation at Dawn. In *Hol.*, ll. 149–52 have been added in the margin.

A King's Soliloquy. Edward VII died on 6 May 1910, and was buried on 20 May. For Hardy's recollections of these events see *LY*, p. 142.

The Coronation. King George V was crowned on 22 June 1911.

Aquae Sulis. The title is the Roman name for Bath: it means 'the waters of Sul'. Sul was the early Britons' goddess of the springs.

'*I rose up as my custom is*'. l. 40 Below the line in *Hol.* Hardy wrote and erased several alternative lines. A number are variant endings to the cancelled version of the line: *To where no dawnlight falls*, *dawnstreak falls*, *glimmer falls*, *daybreak falls*, *lightshine falls*; another is a complete line: *Within my earthen walls.*

The Obliterate Tomb. The poem may refer to the tombs of Emma Hardy's family, the Giffords, in a churchyard in Charles Street, Plymouth. Memorial stones were removed, and the tombs mutilated, during church restorations. See Evelyn Hardy, *Thomas Hardy's Notebooks* (London: 1955), p. 80.

In *Hol.*, to the right of the title, Hardy wrote in pencil and then erased:

Version ? ?
He is deluded
by a dream

followed by three illegible lines.

In *Hol.* Hardy also wrote in pencil and erased the following revisions:

l. 15 Above *-place*: *-cells.*

l. 18 Above the first three words: *By starts upon*; below the same words: *At intervals.*

l. 22 Above *enemy*: *adversary.*

l. 23 Above *dingied*: *shadowed.*

l. 31 Above *some liegeness*: *allegiance.*

The Recalcitrants. Purdy notes (p. 168) that Hardy had suggested this title as a possible one for the periodical version of *Jude the Obscure.*

The Moth-Signal. Hardy uses the same 'signal' in *The Return of the Native*, Ch. IV. 4.

The Death of Regret. In a letter to Lady Hoare, dated 9 December 1914, Florence Hardy wrote of this poem: 'As it stands . . . it is a lament for a friend—a man, "to forget *him*"—"*his* last departure," etc. The poem was, in the first place, written about a cat—a little cat who was strangled in a rabbit wire on the barrow in sight of this house, and she is buried by a sycamore in our garden here. My husband thought the poem too good for a cat, and so made it apply to a person.' The letter is in the Wiltshire County Record Office, Trowbridge.

The Roman Gravemounds. The cat was Hardy's own 'study cat'. See his letter to Mrs Henniker, 19 December 1910 (*ORFW*, p. 142).

The Sacrilege. l. 135 Above *woman* in *Hol.* Hardy wrote and erased *hussy.*
l. 136 Hardy tried two drafts of the line in the margin of *Hol.*: *?Brought one to join the dead!"?* and *Sent one to swing till dead!"* He then adopted the latter.

The Abbey Mason. In a letter to Cockerell (15 May 1912) Hardy wrote of the anonymity of medieval artists: 'They seem in those days to have had no personal ambition: and thinking of this last year I was led to write a poem bearing on it.' (*SCC*, p. 275.)

Exeunt Omnes. 2 June 1913 was Hardy's seventy-third birthday.

Satires of Circumstance. Hardy clearly felt ill at ease with these poems. At the time of periodical publication in the *Fortnightly Review* in 1911 he wrote to Mrs Henniker: 'You will remember, I am sure, that being *satires* they are rather brutal. I express no feeling or opinion myself at all. They are from notes I made some twenty years ago, and then found were more fit for verse than prose.' (*ORFW*, p. 146.) When the bound volume appeared in November 1914 he began almost at once to write to friends, regretting that the satires had been included. To Cockerell he wrote on 30 December 1914: 'if I could have had my wish I should have kept the Satires and those akin to them in a separate book, as I think they injured the others that I cared most about' (Taylor), and to A. C. Benson (30 December 1914): 'I did not like them—particularly in the same volume with those written at a later date when my thoughts had been set on quite another track by painful events.' (Bancroft.) Four years later, when Gosse sent him his essay on Hardy's poetry, Hardy replied (16 April 1918): 'The little group of what you call "searchlight" satires . . . cost me much sadness in having to reprint them in the volume in 1915 [*sic*]. The scales had not fallen from my eyes when I wrote them, and when I reprinted them they had.' (Adams.) See also *LY*, p. 164.
The *Fortnightly Review* version of the group included eleven of the poems included here: nos. I–VII, IX–XI, and XIV, plus one poem, 'On the Doorstep', which Hardy also included as no. X in the holograph of the bound volume, but then cancelled (it is printed among the uncollected poems in Volume Three of this edition). In *Hol.*, the order of the poems has been altered to allow room for a late addition, VIII, 'In the Study', and 'At the Draper's' follows 'On the Death-Bed'.

III. By her Aunt's Grave. l. 6 In *Hol.*, below the line, Hardy wrote in pencil and erased:

I've not yet set it up.

IV. In the Room of the Bride-Elect. Hardy planned, but never wrote, a short story on a similar theme. See Evelyn Hardy, 'Thomas Hardy: Plots for Five Unpublished Stories', *London Magazine* (November 1958), 36.

VI. In the Cemetery. In *Hol.*, Hardy began a new line below line 8 with the words *I'll tell*, which he then cancelled.

VIII. In the Study. l. 16 is an interlined addition to *Hol.*—probably inserted after publication of the first edition.

XIII. On the Death-Bed. In *Hol.*, there are no quotation marks except for faintly pencilled double ones around ll. 15–18.

Moments of Vision

History of Composition and Publication

Moments of Vision contains more poems than any other of Hardy's individual volumes. Almost all of them were recent: of those that carry a date of composition only two were written earlier than 1912 (both are from 1893). Ten of the poems are from 1912 or 1913, and continue the elegiac themes of the 'Poems of 1912–13' in *Satires of Circumstance*; others of later dates recall his courtship and the early years of his marriage. Hardy continued in these years to draw on his earlier work, but mainly from 'old notes' and unfinished drafts (as in 'Love the Monopolist', marked 'Begun 1871').

Except for the 'Poems of War and Patriotism', very few of the poems in *Moments of Vision* had previously been published: six had appeared in various journals, and Hardy had included nine in his *Selected Poems* in 1916. Of the seventeen war poems, all but three had appeared in newspapers or magazines, or in anthologies of war writing published for charitable causes. 'Men Who March Away', the earliest of these poems, was printed in *The Times* on 9 September 1914, and was included as a postscript in *Satires of Circumstance*, published in November; Hardy moved it to its present position at the head of the war poems when he prepared copy for the Wessex Edition volume of *Satires of Circumstance* and *Moments of Vision* in May 1919. That order was also adopted in *Collected Poems*, and is followed here.

A few of the *Moments of Vision* poems were also published separately in Mrs Hardy's privately printed pamphlets, which began to appear during the war years. The first, 'To Shakespeare after Three Hundred Years', was issued in August 1916; it was followed by three other pamphlets containing poems from *Moments of Vision*: 'When I Weekly Knew' ('Quid Hic Agis?') in October 1916, a group of four war poems ('England to Germany', 'The Pity of It', 'I Met a Man', and 'A New Year's Eve in War Time') in March 1917, and three more war poems ('A Call to National Service', 'An Appeal to America', and 'Cry of the Homeless') in May 1917 (see Purdy, pp. 349–50 for further details). The pamphlets contain a few significant variations, and I have cited them in textual notes.

Hardy sent the text of *Moments of Vision* to Macmillan in August 1917, and the book was published on 30 November. At the time of publication he wrote in his journal: 'I do not expect much notice will be taken of these poems: they mortify the human sense of self-importance by showing, or suggesting, that human beings are of no matter or appreciable value in this nonchalant universe.' (*LY*, p. 179.) In fact the poems were widely noticed, though Hardy grumbled privately that reviewers did not appreciate either his comic intentions or his metrical experiments (see Bailey, p. 348 and *LY*, pp. 79 and 193).

As usual, Hardy began immediately to send corrections to Macmillan—a few in December, a few more in March 1918, a further list in December 1918. A revised text was issued in the Uniform Edition in 1919.

Other significant editions of *Moments of Vision* are:

The Pocket Edition (1919): set from the *Moments of Vision* plates, at an earlier stage than the Uniform Edition, but with a few unique variants.

The Wessex Edition (with *Satires of Circumstance*), Verse Volume IV (1919): with numerous textual revisions.

Collected Poems (1919): also much revised, but not identical with the Wessex Edition.

The Mellstock Edition, volume XXXVII (1920): a resetting of the Wessex Edition, but with some further revisions.

Collected Poems (1923).

The holograph of *Moments of Vision* is in the library of Magdalene College, Cambridge. It is the printer's copy, and shows both revision and rearrangement of the poems. The corrected table of contents shows, for example, that 'Signs and Tokens' was first placed where 'The Five Students' now stands; there is also a cancelled title, 'After the Battle', following 'I Met a Man' among the war poems (no such poem survives, but Hardy considered the title for 'Outside the Casement', which he later included in *Late Lyrics*). A tipped-in slip, bearing the title of the book in Hardy's hand, shows that he considered and then erased two other titles: *Moments from the Years*, and *Moments of Vision and other Poetry*. As Hardy's pencilled note to 'I thought, my heart' indicates, at least some of the pencilled annotations, and perhaps also the erased variants, were made after *Hol.* had been returned to Hardy by the printer.

Sir Sydney Cockerell's copy of the first edition of *Moments of Vision*, with corrections in Hardy's hand, is in the collection of Frederick B. Adams; those corrections that are unique in this text are reported in the notes below.

Explanatory Notes

'*We sat at the window*'. Hardy and his wife were in Bournemouth in July 1875, a year after their marriage (*EL*, p. 141).

A wet St. Swithin's day (15 July) is said to herald forty days of rain.

Afternoon Service at Mellstock. Hardy recalls his church-going as a child in *EL*, p. 23.

Apostrophe to an Old Psalm Tune. l. 12 William Henry Monk (1823–89) was musical editor of *Hymns Ancient and Modern* (first issued 1861), in which he was responsible for more than sixty arrangements.

At the Word 'Farewell'. Hardy described this poem as 'literally true' (*ORFW*, p. 179). His account of parting from Emma Gifford at the end of his first visit to Cornwall is in *EL*, p. 99. See also the scene in *A Pair of Blue Eyes*, Ch. VI, in which Stephen Smith leaves Elfride Swancourt.

First Sight of Her and After. In Cockerell's copy of *SP* (Adams), which contains corrections given to Cockerell by Hardy, the title is emended to 'The Return from First Meeting Her'.

The Rival. The *Westminster Gazette* review of *MV* (8 December 1917) called this poem 'a grim and characteristic fancy'. In his scrap-book of reviews, opposite this remark, Hardy wrote: 'The reviewer, having no sense of humour, misses the point.' (Bailey, p. 348.)

Heredity. *EL*, p. 284 quotes the following journal for 19 February 1889: 'The story of a face which goes through three generations or more, would make a fine novel or poem of the passage of Time. The differences in personality to be ignored.' The text then adds: '[This idea was to some extent carried out in the novel *The Well-Beloved*, the poem entitled "Heredity" etc.]'.

Near Lanivet, 1872. Hardy wrote to Gosse on 28 January 1918: 'By the way—have you noticed "Near Lanivet, 1872" in "Moments of Vision?" I mention it not for literary reasons, but private ones—because you knew my late wife, and the scene occurred between us before our marriage.' (Adams.) He made the same point of factuality in letters to Harold Child (Adams), to Mrs Henniker (*ORFW*, p. 179), and to Middleton Murry (Berg).

Copying Architecture in an Old Minster. Hardy and his wife lived in Wimborne, Dorset, from June 1881 to June 1883.

To Shakespeare. Professor Israel Gollancz, of King's College, London, wrote to Hardy on 7 February 1916, inviting him to contribute to the *Book of Homage* that Gollancz was preparing for the three-hundredth anniversary of Shakespeare's death. Hardy wrote the poem in less than two weeks: the manuscript is dated 14 February, and Gollancz acknowledged receipt on the 18th (DCM).

A letter from Florence Hardy to T. J. Wise, in the British Library (Ashley MS 5755) indicates that *MS1* is the 'original' manuscript.

The page of Cockerell's First Folio on which Hardy wrote a fair copy of the poem was reproduced in the Sotheby catalogue of the sale of Cockerell's books and MSS, 30 October 1956, p. 55.

l. 16 ***passing-bell***: 'If, after the early morning tolling, it is desired (and no doubt paid for) the tenor bell will toll the exact age of the deceased. . . . This was called the "minute bell."' John Symonds Udal, *Dorsetshire Folk-Lore* (Hertford: 1922), p. 182. A footnote refers to this line in Hardy's poem as an illustration of the custom. Udal was an acquaintance of Hardy's, and corresponded with him on folk-lore and dialect matters.

Quid hic agis?. The title is from the Vulgate text of 1 Kings 19:9; in the Authorized Version it reads: 'What doest thou here?' The verses that follow, ending 'and after the fire a still small voice', were one of Hardy's favourite Biblical texts. They are the reading for Evensong on the eleventh Sunday after Trinity; Hardy called that day 'Small Voice Sunday' (*SCC*, p. 306), and he liked to attend the evening service on that day to hear the passage read. His own Bible, now in DCM, has notes opposite these verses showing where Hardy attended church on this day from 1859 to 1870. See *EL*, pp. 50 and 203.

Before Knowledge. ll. 9–10 In *Hol.* these have been added in the right-hand margin.

The Blinded Bird. ll. 15–20 paraphrase 1 Corinthians 13:4–7.
l. 15 Above the line in *Hol.* Hardy wrote, and then erased:

Charity, who hath it?

The Faded Face. In a correction to the *WE* proofs, sent to R. & R. Clark on 26 July 1919, Hardy wrote concerning ll. 19 and 21: 'Stet. the original reading "over-wrung" instead of "rueness-wrung."' The reading 'rueness-wrung' does not appear in any printed text.

The Duel. The story of how the Duke of Buckingham killed the Earl of Cardigan in a duel in 1668, while the unfaithful Countess held Buckingham's horse, is told in the Countess of Cardigan's *My Recollections* (London: 1909), p. 124. Hardy read the brief account there, and copied it into his notebook (Purdy, p. 195).

At Mayfair Lodgings. The poem is based on an incident that occurred while Hardy was staying in London in December 1894 (*LY*, p. 35). Collins (p. 24) reports the following conversation with Hardy:

C.: Why, and how, 'need not the tragedy have come due'? Because she would have married him, and there would not now have been the tragedy of her dying apart from him?

H.: Yes.

The Background and the Figure. l. 12 Above *flower* in *Hol.* Hardy wrote and erased *figure*; below it he wrote and erased *shine out.*

Sitting on the Bridge. l. 26 Above the line in *Hol.* Hardy wrote and erased *On the West Front.*

Lines. 'To make the verses fit the music you would of course have to repeat the words of the last line but one in each verse.' Letter from Hardy to Dr C. W. Saleeby, 30 December 1917 (Adams).

'*In the seventies*'. The epigraph is from Job 12:4 (Vulgate).

The Occultation. In *Hol.*, the page has been cut off below line 8, and a new piece pasted on, suggesting that perhaps there had originally been further lines.

The Wound. Pinion (p. 132) notes a similar image in *Tess*, Ch. XXI: 'The evening sun was now ugly to her, like a great inflamed wound in the sky.' (*WE*, p. 173.)

A January Night. 'The poem "A January Night. 1879" in *Moments of Vision* relates to an incident of this new year (1879) which occurred here at Tooting, where they seemed to begin to feel that "there had past away a glory from the earth". And it was in this house that their troubles began.' (*EL*, p. 163.)

The Oxen. Hardy also used this folk-belief in *Tess*, Ch. XVII. When the poem was published in *The Times*, a note was added: 'No copyright reserved.'

MS 1 was reproduced in facsimile in the catalogue of the Ida O. Folsom sale, the American Art Association Anderson Galleries (New York, 6 and 7 December 1932), p. 39, where it is described as '"The Oxen", verses for Christmas Eve.' The present location of the manuscript is unknown.

On a Heath. Collins (pp. 24–5) records the following discussion:

C.: Who or what is it that is referred to in the last stanza?

H.: There is a third person.

C.: 'Another looming,' 'one still blooming,' 'a shade entombing'—are not there three different things?

H.: No, only one.

An Anniversary. l. 13 In a note to R. & R. Clark concerning proofs for *WE*, Hardy wrote on 19 June 1919: 'for "Knew nought of sogged wound" read "Knew of no sogged wound".' The former version does not appear in any printed text.

The Pink Frock. There is a description of 'the lady of the "Pretty pink frock" poem' in *LY*, p. 31.

In her Precincts. A copy of *MV* sold at the Sotheby sale of 22 and 23 June 1959 was inscribed by Hardy on the half-title: '"In her precincts", p. 90 (an experience) Thomas Hardy.' In the margin of the table of contents in *DCM3* opposite the title of this poem Hardy wrote '(Mrs. H - - bury).' Mr and Mrs Cecil Hanbury lived at Kingston-Maurward House in the early 1920s. Hardy was godfather to their daughter Caroline (see 'To C. F. H.' in *Human Shows*).

The Last Signal. William Barnes, the Dorset poet, was Hardy's teacher, friend, and neighbour. He died on 7 October 1886, and was buried on 11 October. As Hardy walked across the fields from Max Gate to the funeral the incident occurred that the poem describes (*EL*, p. 240). Hardy wrote an obituary of Barnes (*Athenaeum*, 16 October 1886; Orel, pp. 100–6), and a preface to *Select Poems of William Barnes* (London: 1908; Orel, pp. 76–82).

l. 7 Hardy's list of corrections to the *WE* proofs includes this note: 'for "Flashed out a reflex" read "Flashed back the fire".' The former phrase does not occur in any printed text.

The Chimes. The chimes are those of St. Peter's Church, Dorchester, which played the Sicilian Mariners' Hymn during Hardy's youth. Hardy notes the silencing of the chimes in a footnote to 'After the Fair' (in *Time's Laughingstocks*), and in a note to Ch. IV of *The Mayor of Casterbridge* (*WE*, p. 33).

The Figure in the Scene. EL, p. 104 describes this poem as a memory of one of Hardy's visits to Cornwall during his courtship of Emma Gifford. Two sketches by Hardy corresponding to the description in the poem are in DCM. On one, a pencil drawing, Hardy has written at the top 'Beeny Cliff, in the rain—Aug. 22, 1870', and at the bottom '"It never looks like summer." E. L. G. (on Beeny).' The other drawing is a pen-and-ink version of the same subject; on it Hardy has written '*Beeny Cliff* (Aug. 22. '70) / *The Figure in the Scene*', and has quoted ll. 3–5 of this poem.

l. 16 Beside *Immutable* in *Hol.* Hardy wrote and erased *Inseparable* and *?Inscribed?*, and below the line *There permanent.*

'*Why did I sketch*'. See preceding note. Below the title in *Hol.* Hardy wrote in pencil and erased (*The same story*).

Conjecture. l. 2 Emma Lavinia Hardy (Hardy's first wife), Florence Emily Hardy (his second wife), and Mary Hardy (his sister).

At Middle-field Gate in February. Hardy recalled the names of the 'bevy' in *EL*, p. 292.

Overlooking the River Stour. Hardy and his first wife, Emma, lived at Sturminster Newton, on the river Stour, from July 1876 to March 1878. He later called those years 'the Sturminster Newton idyll . . . Our happiest time.' (*EL*, p. 156.) He revisited the house in 1916, which may have been the occasion of the poem.

The Musical Box. From the Sturminster Newton period—1876–8 (*EL*, p. 156). In *Hol.*, to the left of the third line of each stanza, Hardy wrote in pencil and then erased the last two syllables of the preceding line—with the thought, perhaps, that this would reproduce the effect of a musical box's repetitions.

On Sturminster Foot-bridge. Another poem from the Sturminster Newton years (see preceding two notes, and *EL*, p. 156). Hardy was annoyed by a reviewer who remarked that 'one could make as good music as that out of a milk-cart' (*LY*, p. 79), and added the headnote to *CP23* to make his intentions clear. The lines, he wrote, were 'intended to convey by their rhythm the impression of a clucking of ripples into riverside holes when blown upon by an up-stream wind.' (*LY*, p. 193.)

Royal Sponsors. Hardy's book of reviews of his poetry, now in DCM, includes one of *MV*, written by J. C. Squire in *Land and Water* (13 December 1917). Squire quotes from the fourth stanza of this poem, remarking that 'the first two lines are thoroughly comic'. Beside this passage Hardy has written 'as intended to be'.

Old Furniture. ll. 26–30 are late additions to the *Hol.* text: see textual notes.

A Thought in Two Moods. l. 9 Below ⟨*prescience*⟩ in *Hol.* Hardy wrote and erased *forecast.*

l. 13 Above the line in *Hol.* Hardy wrote and erased:

When gaily she laughed.

The Last Performance. The pianist is Hardy's first wife, Emma. See *LY*, p. 153.

The Interloper. Collins asked Hardy what it was 'under which best lives corrode'. Hardy replied: 'Madness', but later emended that to 'Insanity', and wondered aloud how he could make the point clear. Collins suggested adding a motto, which Hardy did in *CP23*. (Collins, p. 25.)

l. 31 The Fourth Figure is from Daniel 3:25.

Logs on the Hearth. Hardy's sister Mary died on 24 November 1915. See *LY*, p. 170.

The Five Students. Hardy identified one of the students as his friend Horace Moule (who committed suicide in 1873).

Beside the last two stanzas in *Hol.* (ll. 30a–l in the textual note to the poem), Hardy wrote: [*Omitted from first edition.*] These stanzas were in fact never included in a printed text.

The Wind's Prophecy. l. 34 *Skrymer*: a sleeping giant in Norse mythology.

Molly gone. Molly is Hardy's sister Mary, who died in 1915. See note to 'Logs on the Hearth', above.

Looking Across. 'Out there' is the graveyard at Stinsford Church. It contained the graves of Hardy's parents, his first wife, Emma, and his sister Mary.

At a Seaside Town in 1869. Hardy identified the town as Weymouth, where he lived and worked in 1869 (*EL*, p. 84).

In *Hol.* the subtitle is an interlined addition.

The Glimpse. In *Hol.*, ll. 20–5 are inserted from the right-hand margin. The insertion seems first to have read:

In the empty rooms
Booming hollow as tombs!
But I never come near her,
Though nightly I hear her.

Hardy then cancelled the first line of the insertion and added above it the present ll. 20–2.

The Pedestrian. In *Hol.*, the subtitle is an interlinear addition.

l. 2 *Nox Venit*: John 9:4; in the Authorized Version 'the night cometh'.

At a Country Fair. A Hardy notebook in DCM contains this note: '*Blind Giant.*—His dimensions had attracted cupidity of an exhibitor, who had barely allowed him necessaries and kept him a sort of prisoner.' (Bailey, p. 399.)

'*It never looks like summer*'. The title is a remark of Emma Hardy's which Hardy wrote on a drawing that he had made of her on Beeny Cliff, Cornwall, in August 1870 (see note to 'The Figure in the Scene', above). Hardy revisited the scenes of his courtship in March 1913, a few months after his wife's death.

He fears his Good Fortune. *MS1* is marked, in Hardy's hand, [*First rough draft*].

He wonders about Himself. Hardy wrote in his journal for 28 November 1893: 'Poem. "He views himself as an automaton"'; the note is quoted in *LY*, p. 26 with the added note '(published)'.

ll. 10–11 In *Hol.*, beside these lines, Hardy wrote: '[Incorrectly printed in some Editions]'. The lines are in fact identical in all printed texts. Below the revised lines in *DCM3* Hardy wrote: 'the first draft read as above.'

Jubilate. Title: In *Hol.* Hardy wrote and erased *The merry underground dancing party*, and above the line: *The joyful.*

ll. 7–8 Exodus 28:15–30.

He revisits his First School. The village school that Hardy first attended is described in *EL*, p. 20.

'*I thought, my Heart*'. The third stanza, which is not in any of Hardy's books published during his lifetime, exists in four versions:

(1) on the verso of the *Hol.* text of the poem, where Hardy noted that 'a third verse, as overleaf, was not printed'; (2) the text quoted in Ruth Head's *Pages from the Works of Thomas Hardy* (London: 1922), p. 171, where it is described as 'unpublished third verse, specially communicated for this Selection'; (3) the text written by Cockerell into his copy of *MV*, with a note that it is 'from a copy I took at Max Gate Jan. 11, 1925'; (4) the text, in Hardy's hand, tipped in to his copy of Verse Volume IV of *WE*. Head's text clearly derives from *Hol.*, and Cockerell's from Head's, from which it differs only in accidentals. (I have not reported these differences in textual notes, since they almost certainly result from faulty copying on Cockerell's part.) The fourth version is based apparently on Head (whose italics it adopts); it is the latest text, and the most authoritative. Both the third and fourth examples are in the Adams collection.

At the bottom of *MS1* Hardy wrote and erased: *Another verse*, followed by what appears to read *I met her only etc.*

Midnight on the Great Western. A similar scene occurs in *Jude the Obscure*, Ch. V. iii (*WE*, pp. 331–2)—the arrival of Little Father Time.

'*I rose and went to Rou'tor Town*'. Purdy (p. 203) identifies 'Rou'tor' as Rough Tor (or Row Tor), a hill on Bodmin Moor in Cornwall, near where Hardy's first wife, Emma, lived before her marriage.

When Collins asked Hardy what 'the evil wrought at Rou'tor Town' was, Hardy replied: 'Slander, or something of the sort.' (Collins, p. 26.)

Old Excursions. In *MS1*, below the date, Hardy wrote: (*copied*).

In a Whispering Gallery. Hardy identified the gallery as the interior of the dome of St. Paul's Cathedral, London. (See Appendix B.)

The Clock of the Years. Epigraph: Job 4:15.

In the Garden. M. H. is Hardy's sister Mary (see *LY*, p. 170).
In *Hol.*, opposite l. 14, Hardy wrote in pencil and erased

strayed
Her where its finger played
?greyed?

The Tree and the Lady. In the *Hol.* table of contents, this title replaced 'The sound of her'. The latter title does not occur elsewhere in Hardy.
l. 7 Above *shiver* in *Hol.* Hardy wrote and erased *quiver.*

The Young Glass-stainer. Hardy noted the composition of the poem in his journal for 23 November 1893 (*LY*, p. 26). The subject resembles somewhat the situation of Sue Bridehead in the second part of *Jude the Obscure.*

Looking at a Picture. The date deleted from *Hol.*—March 1913—suggests that the occasion is the forty-third anniversary of Hardy's first meeting with his first wife.

The Choirmaster's Burial. Hardy's grandfather, also Thomas, was the leader of the Stinsford Church choir from 1801 or 1802 until his death in 1837. When he was buried 'there could be no such quiring over his grave as he had performed over the graves of so many, owing to the remaining players being chief mourners' (*EL*, pp. 10–16).

The Man who forgot. l. 25 Above *My* in *Hol.* Hardy wrote and erased *The man's.*

While drawing in a Churchyard. In *Hol.*, the fourth stanza is written below the fifth stanza, and below the zigzag mark that Hardy customarily used to indicate the end of a poem, indicating that the original poem consisted of only sixteen lines, not including the present ll. 13–16.

Poems of War and Patriotism. In 1899, at the beginning of the Boer War, Hardy wrote to Mrs Henniker: 'I constantly deplore the fact that "civilized" nations have not learnt some more excellent and apostolic way of settling disputes than the old and barbarous one, after all these centuries; but when I feel that it must be, few persons are more martial than I, or like better to write of war in prose and rhyme.' (*Letters* II, p. 232.) He was one of the first group of English men of letters to be summoned by the government in September 1914 'for the organization of public statements of the strength of the British case and principles in the war' (*LY*, p. 163).

Three of the war poems ('"Men Who March Away"', 'In Time of "The Breaking of Nations"', and 'A Call to National Service') were first published with notes stating that they were not in copyright, the evident intention being to increase circulation of the poems as a contribution to the war effort. Hardy had attached similar notes to two of his Boer War poems—'Embarcation' and 'A Christmas Ghost-Story'—though his motive then seems to have been not to support war but to stress its tragic human cost (see Volume One of this edition, pp. 116 and 121, and the notes on pp. 368–9).

'Men who March Away'. The poem was first printed in *The Times* on 9 September 1914, and in the *Times Literary Supplement* the following day. Hardy then added it to *SC*, which was already in production, and it appeared there as the last poem in the volume, labelled 'Postscript'. The copy-text for this last-minute addition was a cutting from the *TLS*, with corrections in Hardy's hand. Hardy also intended to include the poem in the first edition of *MV*: it is in the holograph, following 'His Country', and the title appears, cancelled, in the table of contents. It was omitted from the book, however, and was not included in 'Poems of War and Patriotism' until *CP* and the Wessex Edition of *MV* in 1919.

Hardy wrote to Arthur Symons on 13 September 1914: 'I am glad to hear that you liked the verses, though I fear they were not free from some banalities which it is difficult to keep out of lines which are meant to appeal to the man in the street, and not to "a few friends" only.' (Bailey, p. 417.) On 9 November he wrote in much the same vein to Cockerell, adding: 'You may possibly have suspected the "Friend with the musing eye" to be the author himself.' (Taylor.) In 1918, just after the end of the war, he sent a revised copy of the poem to Henry Newbolt, with a letter in which he wrote:

In an impulse . . . I send you the lines copied out, thinking you might like to have them as you have valued them, and as there were a few trifling errors in the newspaper copies. My mind goes back to the row of poor young fellows in straw hats who had fallen-in in front of our County Hall here—lit by the September sun, whom my rather despondent eye surveyed.

Well, it is all over now—at least I suppose so. I confess that I take a smaller interest in the human race since this outburst than I did before. (HRC.)

ll. 5 and 33 In Cockerell's copy of *SP* (Adams), which contains corrections given to Cockerell by Hardy on 25 May 1918, these lines are corrected to read:

To hazards whence no tears could win us;

The same revision appears in the list of corrections to *SP* that Hardy sent to Macmillan on 4 December 1918, but here, above the word *could*, Hardy has written *can*. (The list is inserted into *DCM2*.)

His Country. Written before the war (H): note to first edition only.

'A long study of the European wars of a century earlier had made it appear to him that common sense had taken the place of bluster in men's minds; and he felt this so strongly that in the very year before war burst on Europe he wrote some verses called "His Country", bearing on the decline of antagonism between peoples.' (*LY*, p. 162.)

England to Germany in 1914. *LY*, p. 164, dates the poem in October.

An Appeal to America on behalf of the Belgian Destitute. Hardy wrote the poem in response to a request from the Commission for Relief in Belgium, dated 9 December 1914 (Bailey, p. 419).

The Pity of It. Hardy had noted the presence in Dorset of such phrases as 'Ich woll' and 'er woll' in his journal in 1889 (*EL*, p. 290).

In March 1915 he wrote to Mrs Henniker: 'I, too, like you, think the

Germans happy and contented as a people: but the group of oligarchs and munition-makers whose interest is war, have stirred them up to their purposes—at least so it seems. I have expressed the thought in a sonnet that is coming out in the *Fortnightly*.' (*ORFW*, p. 166.) Two years later he wrote to her again: 'People are in strangely irritable moods I fancy. I said very harmlessly in a poem (sonnet) entitled "The Pity of It" that the Germans were a "kin folk, kin tongued" (which is indisputable) and letters attacking me appeared, denying it!' (*ORFW*, p. 177.)

In Time of 'the Breaking of Nations'. Jer. li. 20. (H)

The Jeremiah text in the Authorized Version reads: 'Thou art my battle axe and weapons of war: for with thee will I break in pieces the nations, and with thee will I destroy kingdoms.'

The long gestation of the poem is mentioned in both *EL* and *LY*. *EL*, p. 104, describes the summer of 1870, when Hardy was in Cornwall, courting his future wife, while in Europe the Franco-Prussian War was in progress. 'On the day that the bloody battle of Gravelotte was fought they were reading Tennyson in the grounds of the rectory. It was at this time and spot that Hardy was struck by the incident of the old horse harrowing the arable field in the valley below, which, when in far later years it was recalled to him by a still bloodier war, he made into the little poem of three verses entitled "In Time of 'the Breaking of Nations'".' *LY* (p. 178) quotes Hardy's account at the time of the publication of *MV* in 1917:

I believe it would be said by people who knew me well that I have a faculty (possibly not uncommon) for burying an emotion in my heart or brain for forty years, and exhuming it at the end of that time as fresh as when interred. For instance, the poem entitled 'The Breaking of Nations' contains a feeling that moved me in 1870, during the Franco-Prussian war, when I chanced to be looking at such an agricultural incident in Cornwall. But I did not write the verses till during the war with Germany of 1914, and onwards. Query: where was that sentiment hiding itself during more than forty years?

MS1 is identified in a letter from Florence Hardy to the collector Howard Bliss as the original manuscript (Bancroft). Hardy wrote *MS2* into Edward Marsh's book of manuscript poems in November 1918.

Cry of the Homeless. Hardy was solicited for a contribution to Edith Wharton's *Book of the Homeless* by Henry James, to whom Hardy wrote on 8 August 1915: 'I send the enclosed page, for what it may be worth, as not quite the right thing. I am sorry to think that being in verse it is awkward for one of the conditions—that of translation. However perhaps a prose rendering would be better than nothing. Anyhow I hope it may help, though infinitesimally, in the good cause . . .'. He added, in a postscript: 'Any more fit title may be given to the verses.' (Yale.)

Before Marching and After. Frank William George was a distant cousin of Hardy; he was killed in the Gallipoli campaign in August 1915. Hardy described him as 'almost the only, if not the only blood relative of the next generation in whom I have taken any interest.' (*ORFW*, p. 170.)

There are two manuscripts of the poem in HRC: one is marked in Hardy's hand (*Original MS*). The other is a fair copy. The typescript in the Fales Collection was probably made for inclusion in one of Florence Hardy's pamphlets: the contents were later changed, and 'Before Marching and After' was not included (see Purdy, p. 192).

Then and Now. ll. 5–7 At the Battle of Fontenoy in 1745, a British officer, Lord Charles Hay, is said to have invited the French guard to fire first. The French replied: 'We never fire first; *you* fire first.' The incident is reported in Voltaire's *Précis du siècle de Louis XV*, Ch. XV; see also the life of Lord Charles Hay in *DNB*.

Hardy wrote to Cockerell on 28 August 1914:

> As for myself, the recognition that we are living in a more brutal age than that, say, of Elizabeth, or of the chivalry which could cry: 'Gentlemen of the Guard, fire first'! (far more brutal indeed: no chivalry now!) does not inspire one to write hopeful poetry, or even conjectural prose, but simply makes one sit still in an apathy, and watch the clock spinning backwards, with a mild wonder if, when it gets back to the Dark Ages, and the sack of Rome, it will ever move forward again to a new Renascence, and a new literature. (*SCC*, p. 279.)

l. 19 Matthew 2:18. 'In Rama was there a voice heard, lamentation, and weeping, and great mourning . . .'. The context is Herod's slaughter of the innocents.

A Call to National Service. Purdy (p. 191) quotes a letter from Hardy to Cockerell, dated 31 March 1917, in which Hardy writes that the poem was 'written in a great hurry at the request of the N. S. [National Service] Department, and no proof was sent.'

The Dead and the Living One. *LY*, p. 171 calls this poem 'a war-ballad of some weirdness'.

ll. 34–6 in *Hol.* have been added at the foot of the page, below the date and tailnote.

A New Year's Eve in War Time. One of Hardy's 'literally true' poems: he described the incident in letters to Mrs Henniker (22 December 1916; *ORFW*, p. 175), and to Cockerell (15 January 1917, *SCC*, p. 284).

l. 18 See Revelation 6:8.

'*I met a man*'. Corrections on the proof of Mrs Hardy's pamphlet are in a hand other than Hardy's: perhaps Cockerell's.

l. 3 Exodus 34:29–35.

l. 25 1 Samuel 15.

The Coming of the End. There are two partial drafts of this poem on verso pages in *Hol.* On the verso of f. 9 ('Apostrophe to an Old Psalm Tune') Hardy wrote and cancelled the following:

The Coming of the End.

How it came to an end!
The meeting afar ⟨in the west⟩ from the crowd
And the love talk and laughters unpenned,
The parting when much was ⟨confessed⟩ avowed

(The second line may be incorrect: Hardy has uncharacteristically written a revision over a first draft, and then cancelled the whole line.)

On the verso of f. 139 ('He revisits his First School') he wrote and cancelled:

"Afterwards."
How it came to an end!
The meeting afar in the west,
And the lovedreams and laughters unpenned,
How it came to an end.

It came to an end,
Yes, the outgazing over the stream
With the sun on each serpentine bend

Late Lyrics and Earlier

History of Composition and Publication

The dated poems in *Late Lyrics* show that for this book Hardy had reached farther back into the past for poems than he had in his previous two volumes: there are two poems from the 1860s, one from the 1870s, two from the 1890s, and four from the 1900s. The fertile poetic period that had followed the death of his first wife in 1912 continued to be a rich source: seven poems are dated 1913 (in some cases tentatively), and all of these are in the elegiac mood of the 'Poems of 1912–13' in *Satires of Circumstance*; other poems from the following years revert to the same mood and themes. Ten of the *Late Lyrics* poems are from the war years, though only four could be called 'war poems'. Comparatively few of these poems had previously been published: twenty-one had appeared in newspapers and magazines, and six in pamphlets privately printed by Florence Hardy.

On 8 November 1921, Hardy wrote to Macmillan: 'since Moments of Vision was published in 1917 other poems have accumulated. . . . These poems with many others I have on hand would, I find, fill a volume quite as thick as Moments of Vision; and though I am by no means anxious to rush into print again—quite the reverse, indeed—the question arises whether it would not be advisable to bring them out—say early next year. . . .' (BL Add. MS 54924.) Clearly it *was* advisable: Hardy sent the manuscript in January 1922, revised proofs a month later, and received bound copies in May.

As usual, Hardy began at once to correct his text. He sent in his first revision a week after publication day, and it was made in the second impression in August; in September he sent a few more changes, which were made in the Uniform Edition (the third impression) in December 1922. In October he added still further corrections, in anticipation of the new edition of *Collected Poems*, which would include *Late Lyrics*. But even then he was not satisfied: 'I think I had better read the proofs of this additional part all the same,' he wrote to Macmillan, 'since in all human probability I shall never do so again.' (BL Add. MS 54925.) And he made yet another set of revisions when *Late Lyrics* was published in the Wessex Edition in 1926. These two—the second edition of *Collected Poems* (1923) and the Wessex Edition—are the only significant editions after the first.

The holograph of *Late Lyrics and Earlier* is in the Dorset County Museum. Like the holographs of Hardy's other books of verse it is the printer's copy, which was later bound; and like them it contains many authorial revisions and corrections. Other manuscripts exist of seven individual poems; two others, of 'The West-of-Wessex Girl' and 'The Marble-Streeted Town', which Hardy gave to the Plymouth Public Library, were destroyed by fire during the Second World War. There are also nine typescripts—presumably typed by Florence Hardy—and a number of proofs. These are reported in the textual notes.

Explanatory Notes

Apology. Hardy's longest critical defence of his poems caused him a good deal of doubt and anxiety. The essay was written, according to his Memorandum Book, during January 1922, when he was in bed with a chill, and it was sent to Macmillan with the holograph of *LL* on 23 January. By mid-February he was uneasy enough about the essay to send it to Cockerell for advice. 'I am sending it', he wrote in his covering letter,

> to ask your opinion whether I shall prefix it to the new volume or not. I don't *wish* to, and should not at all mind destroying it. It came into my mind mostly while lying in bed during the late weeks, and seemed then almost necessary.
>
> Is it uncalled for, or, if not altogether so, is it too cantankerous in respect of reviewers, etc., for a writer whose books are fairly well received nowadays . . . (*SCC*, p. 288).

Cockerell replied at once that it should be printed as it was, but three days later Hardy wrote again to say that he was 'abridging the whole somewhat, in spite of your saying you would not omit a word.' (*SCC*, p. 289.) Three days after that, he had apparently expanded it once more; on 21 February he wrote to Macmillan: 'As I had to modify and enlarge the Preface, I am sending a new MS. of it.' (DCM.)

In Hardy's first references to the essay it is called a preface, but in a postscript to his letter he explained that he had retitled it: 'I thought "Apology" more piquant than "Preface".' (*SCC*, p. 289.)

ll. 17–18 Hardy wrote to Gosse on 14 February 1922: 'By the way, your letter was most apt. I have now been able to put in among the short prefatory words that "some illustrious men of letters" have asked for the poems. How selfish of me to make use of you in this way!' (BL Ashley MS. B862.)

ll. 52–3 The quoted phrases are from Wordsworth's 'Ode: Intimations of Immortality', ll. 142 and 145.

l. 69 In *Hol.*, in place of *condemnatory*, Hardy has written *terminative*, with *condemnatory* written in pencil above it, and erased.

ll. 87–8 Job 37:16.

l. 92 Harrison, commenting on the *Collected Poems*, had written: 'My philosophy of life is more cheerful and hopeful than that of these Lyrics.' 'Novissima Verba.–II', *Fortnightly Review* (2 February 1920), 183.

ll. 99–101 The 'Romanist' is J. M. Hone, who had written an essay on Hardy for the *London Mercury*. Hardy lifted the two quoted phrases from the following:

> This Will [in *The Dynasts*] is the originating principle of all things, which works 'eternal artistries' in circumstance, an aimless activity of which individuals are the phenomena. The dark gravity of these ideas is scarcely reflected in Mr. Hardy's measures; and, indeed, the observations of the Superterrestrial Intelligences in the play often recall, by their rhythms, something from the book of the words in a light opera . . .
>
> Mr. Hardy refuses the consolation which the Frankfort sage [Schopenhauer] offered to the faithful. He is a bad Schopenhauerian—as one would say, a 'bad Catholic.' 'The Poetry of Mr. Hardy', *London Mercury* (February 1922), 399, 400.

ll. 113–14 Arnold, 'The Study of Poetry', in *Essays in Criticism*, Second Series.

ll. 122–3 See Acts 17:16–31.

ll. 187–8 Preface to *Lyrical Ballads*.

l. 202 Coleridge, *Biographia Literaria*, Ch. XIV.

l. 229 Hebrews 12:27. For other comments by Hardy on the 'readjustment' of the English Church, see *Letters* I, pp. 136–7; *LY*, pp. 121–2, 177.

l. 244 However, one must not be too sanguine in reading signs, and since the above was written evidence that the Church will go far in the removal of 'things that are shaken' has not been encouraging. (H): *WE*.

ll. 249–50 Preface to *Lyrical Ballads*. Wordsworth wrote: 'Poetry is the breath and finer spirit of all knowledge; it is the impassioned expression which is in the countenance of all Science.' Hardy has abridged and altered the sense of the latter clause.

l. 252 Auguste Comte, *Social Dynamics, or The General Theory of Human Progress*, vol. III of *System of Positive Polity*, trans. Edward Spencer Beesly (London: 1876), p. 60.

ll. 261–2 *In Memoriam*, LXXXVII: ll. 21–2.

The Maid of Keinton Mandeville. Hardy noted in his journal, 5 March 1878: 'Concert at Sturminster. A Miss Marsh of Sutton [Keinton?] Mandeville sang "Should he upbraid", to Bishop's old tune. She is the sweetest of singers—thrush-like in the descending scale, and lark-like in the ascending—drawing out the soul of listeners in a gradual thread of excruciating attenuation like silk from a cocoon.' (*EL*, p. 156.) *EL* adds: 'Many years after Hardy was accustomed to say that this was the most marvellous old song in English music in its power of touching an audience.'

Sir Henry Bishop (1786–1855), composer of the tune, was a popular writer of theatre music. The poem was published in the *Athenaeum* on his birthday, 30 April.

l. 14 In *TS*, *sleight* is written over an erasure, possibly *lure*.

Summer Schemes. l. 15 In *Hol.*, *growth* has been cancelled, *flags* written above, and the correction then erased.

Faintheart in a Railway Train. See note to 'Going and Staying' below.

Barthélémon at Vauxhall. The Morning Hymn ('Awake, my soul, and with the sun') was sung every Sunday in the Stinsford parish church that Hardy attended as a boy, and it remained one of his favourites (see *EL*, p. 14, *LY*, pp. 45 and 224). At one time he considered writing a story based on Barthélémon's life; he took biographical notes from *Grove's History of Music* (the notebook is in DCM), and drafted several possible plots. See Evelyn Hardy, 'Thomas Hardy: Plots for Five Unpublished Stories', *London Magazine* (November 1958), 37–9.

'*I sometimes think*'. F. E. H. is Florence Emily Hardy, Hardy's second wife. The dedication appears to be a late addition. The manuscript of the poem is reproduced in facsimile in *LY* opposite p. 225.

l. 13 In *DCM3* Hardy underlined *be full*, and wrote in the margin, in pencil, *? quite be.*

Jezreel. The advance of the British army under General Allenby across the Plain of Esdraelon in Palestine was announced in *The Times* on 23 September 1918. Hardy's poem is dated the following day. In a letter to Mrs Henniker he wrote: 'It was written very rapidly, and was published the day after, it being just a poem for the moment. I thought people did not seem to realize that Esdraelon and Jezreel were the same. Well, as to my having any affection for Jezebel, I don't think I can admit that: I have the same sort of admiration for her that I have for Lady Macbeth, Clytaemnestra, and such. Her courage was splendid.' (*ORFW*, p. 182.) For Hardy's biblical references, see I Kings 21:17–24 and II Kings 9:16–37.

Like some of Hardy's other war poems, 'Jezreel' was published in *The Times* with the note: (*No copyright*).

l. 9 In Cockerell's copy of *WE* Verse Volume V (Adams), Hardy also revised the line to that quoted in the established text.

'*The curtains now are drawn*'. In *Hol.*, below *I Major* Hardy wrote and erased: [*In her boudoir*]. and below *II Minor*: [*By her grave*].

'*According to the Mighty Working*'. The title is from the Order for the Burial of the Dead of the Church of England.

The West-of-Wessex Girl. The girl is Hardy's first wife, Emma, who was born in Plymouth and raised in Devon and Cornwall. The Hoe and St. Andrew's Church are in Plymouth.

Going and Staying. J. C. Squire, editor of the new *London Mercury*, wrote to Hardy in August 1919, asking for a contribution for the first number. Hardy replied: 'I am not up to date nowadays, and as a contributor should probably disappoint everybody. I daresay I could find some small poem of an inoffensive kind; but that would hardly be sufficiently striking, to my mind, and would have no connection with a new enterprise.' (Taylor.) Five days later he sent the first two stanzas of 'Going and Staying', offering as an alternative 'The Fiddler's Story' ('The Country Wedding'). When he returned the proof of the poem to Squire in October Hardy wrote: 'I am taking rather a liberty, but as the poem seems rather grey for a new and hopeful magazine I have annexed another, of quite a frivolous kind . . .' (Taylor), and he pasted to the proof the manuscript of 'Faintheart in a Railway Train'. 'Going and Staying' was published in the first number of the *London Mercury*; 'Faintheart', under the title 'A Glimpse from the Train', in November 1920.

At a House in Hampstead. Hardy was a member of the National Committee for acquiring Wentworth Place, the house where Keats lived in Hampstead; his poem was written for a memorial volume published by the Committee.

l. 5 Keats is buried in the Protestant Cemetery, Rome; Hardy visited the grave in 1887 (see 'Rome: at the Pyramid of Cestius', in *Poems of the Past and the Present*).

'A man was drawing near to me'. *EL* quotes Emma Hardy's recollections of the evening in March 1870 when Hardy first came to St. Juliot, Cornwall, remarking in a footnote: 'The verses entitled "A Man was drawing near to Me" obviously relate to this arrival.' (*EL*, p. 92.) The places named in the poem lie between St. Juliot and the nearest railway station at Launceston.

A Gentleman's Epitaph. l. 8 Quadrilles danced early in the nineteenth century. (H)

Several Weipperts wrote popular music in England at that time; John Weippert was director of the band at Almack's Rooms, where Hardy danced as a young man.

A Duettist to her Pianoforte. The duettists to whom the poem is dedicated are Hardy's wife, Emma Lavinia Hardy, and her sister, Helen Catherine Holder, wife of the vicar of St. Juliot, in whose house Hardy and Emma first met. Hardy recalls the two women singing duets during his first visit there (*EL*, p. 99).

'Where three roads joined'. Tresparrett Posts (in the cancelled subtitle) is an intersection north-west of St. Juliot, where three roads do join. For a map of the area see F. B. Pinion, *A Hardy Companion* (London: 1968), p. 352.

'And There was a Great Calm'. The poem was published in a special supplement to *The Times*, on the second anniversary of the Armistice. 'The request to write this poem', Mrs Hardy wrote (*LY*, pp. 214–15), 'had been brought to him from London by one of the editorial staff. At first Hardy was disinclined, and all but refused, being generally unable to write to order. In the middle of the night, however, an idea seized him, and he was heard moving about the house looking things up.'

On the day the poem was published, Hardy wrote to Harold Child: 'The Armistice Supplement makes a very good show. I am afraid I must have been rather obscure, for the writer of the leading article on the subject seems to think I ask, why did the Allies fight? But the meaning is, of course, why did the war originate: why did those who started it, whoever they were, do so. So far it looks as if they were the Germans, as we have all along supposed.' (Adams.)

The title appears twice in the New Testament: Matthew 8:26, and Mark 4:39.

Haunting Fingers. l. 23 In *P1* Hardy underlined *long*, and wrote in the margin *?loving*. He then cancelled the revision, and stetted *long*.

l. 35 Above *nebulous* in *MS1*, Hardy wrote and then erased: *musty rotting*.

l. 36 In the margin of *Hol*. Hardy tried and erased several alternative phrases, of which only *charnel earth* and *charnel mould* are legible.

The Woman I Met. The first idea for the poem may have come from an incident that Hardy recorded in his journal in 1891: 'Piccadilly at night. "A girl held a long-stemmed narcissus to my nose as we went by each other."' (*EL*, p. 308.)

l. 56 The Lock, or Lock-hospital, was a hospital for the treatment of venereal diseases in Southwark, London; the term became generic for such institutions.

'If it's ever spring again'. l. 3 In *DCM3* opposite this line Hardy wrote and erased:

I'll go where I { awaited / found one }

The same seems to have been erased opposite l. 9.

On Stinsford Hill at Midnight. The girl was learnt to be one of the Salvation Army. (H): *Hol.* It was said that she belonged to a body of religious enthusiasts. (H): *WE.* Hardy also wrote, and erased, the *Hol.* note in *DCM3*; in his own copy of Verse Volume V of *WE* he wrote: '[Omit this note in any new edition.]' (Adams.)

The occasion is described in *LY*, p. 28.

The Selfsame Song. In *Hol.* Hardy wrote and erased an alternative title: *The Changeless Song.*

The Wanderer. In *Hol.* Hardy wrote and erased an alternative title: *The Benighted Traveller.*

A Wife comes back. l. 23 In *DCM3* Hardy cancelled *clothed* and wrote in the margin *drest.*

l. 34 In *DCM3* he cancelled *age*, and then erased the cancellation.

At Lulworth Cove. In September 1820 Keats, on his way to Rome, landed one day on the Dorset coast, and composed the sonnet, 'Bright star! would I were steadfast as thou art.' The spot of his landing is judged to have been Lulworth Cove. (H)

Last sentence. For *judged Hol.* reads *supposed.*

Keats in fact did not write the sonnet there, but only made a fair copy of it. The date and note were apparently an afterthought: Hardy wrote them on a separate sheet, which is pasted to the end of the poem, over the zigzag mark which he characteristically used to indicate the end.

Two Serenades. In *Hol.*, ll. 9, 19, 31, and 42 are interlined additions to the original text.

End of the Year 1912. Emma Hardy had died on 27 November 1912.

'I worked no wile to meet you'. The *Hol.* page has been cut below l. 20, just above a zigzag mark indicating the end of the poem; this piece was turned over, and pasted on to the bottom of the page, and the last four lines were added.

An Autumn Rain-Scene. Hardy called this 'a very mild little poem', and a 'trifling' one (*ORFW*, p. 199).

The Beauty. 'The Regent Street beauty, Miss Verrey, the Swiss confectioner's daughter, whose personal attractions have been so mischievously exaggerated, died of fever on Monday evening, brought on by the annoyance she had been for some time subject to.'—London paper, October 1828. (H)

Hardy copied the sentence, from the *Dorset County Chronicle* for 16 October 1828, into his notebook in 1884, adding: 'Only 17. —Buried at St. George's burying-ground, Bayswater—body attempted by ressurectionists [*sic*].' The notebook is in DCM.

The Collector cleans his Picture. The collector is Hardy's friend, the Dorset clergyman-poet William Barnes. Barnes's daughter, Lucy Baxter (who wrote as 'Leader Scott'), describes his picture-cleaning hobby in her *Life of William Barnes* (London: 1887), pp. 151–2.

The *Hol.* text seems originally to have begun with l. 2, which is indented. Then l. 1 was added above it, and finally the epigraph was squeezed in between the new first line and the title. The page has been cut off below l. 39, and a separate sheet containing the last two lines pasted on.

The epigraph reads, in the Authorized Version: 'Son of man, behold, I take away from thee the desire of thine eyes with a stroke.'

On the Tune called the Old-hundred-and-fourth. The tune is from Thomas Ravenscroft's *Whole Book of Psalms*, published in 1621 and for many years the common hymnal of the English Church. Dr Gauntlett, in the cancelled title, is Henry John Gauntlett (1805–76), organist and composer of hymns, including the setting of John Keble's 'The voice that breathed o'er Eden'.

In *Hol.*, the third line of each stanza appears originally to have read: *On Sundays*, the lines being indented as Hardy's short lines customarily are; the lines were then lengthened and moved to the left margin.

The Opportunity. The poem is dedicated to Helen Paterson (1848–1926), the artist who illustrated the first edition of *Far From the Madding Crowd.* Hardy met her a few months before they both married. Purdy (p. 220) quotes a letter from Hardy to Gosse, dated 1906, in which Hardy recalls her:

> The illustrator of Far from the Madding Crowd began as a charming young lady, Miss Helen Paterson, and ended as a married woman,—charms unknown—wife of Allingham the poet. I have never set eyes on her since she was the former and I met her and corresponded with her about the pictures of the story. She was the best illustrator I ever had. She and I were married about the same time in the progress of our mutual work, but not to each other, which I fear rather spoils the information. Though I have never thought of her for the last 20 years your inquiry makes me feel 'quite romantical' about her (as they say here) . . .

Evelyn G. of Christminster. Evelyn Gifford was a cousin of Hardy's first wife, and daughter of Dr E. Hamilton Gifford, Canon of Worcester and later Archdeacon of London. Dr Gifford had married Hardy and Emma. The poem was written on the death of Miss Gifford, in September 1920.

Voices from Things growing in a Churchyard. l. 1 'Fanny Hurd's real name was Fanny Hurden, and Hardy remembered her as a delicate child who went to school with him. She died when she was about eighteen, and her grave and a head-stone with her name are to be seen in Stinsford Churchyard.' (*LY*, p. 223.)

l. 9 Benjamin Bowring, gent., is memorialized on a tablet in Stinsford Church. He died in 1857.

l. 19 Thomas Voss appears briefly in *Under the Greenwood Tree*, Part I, Chs. IV and V; Hardy said that he was the only character in the novel with a real local name (*EL*, p. 122; see also *EL*, p. 280).

l. 35 It was said her real name was Eve Trevillian or Trevelyan; and that she was the handsome mother of two or three illegitimate children, *circa* 1784–95. (H)

According to a cancelled passage in the typescript of *LY*, Hardy discovered her story in the Stinsford Register in 1921 (DCM). The passage is quoted in Richard H. Taylor, ed., *The Personal Notebooks of Thomas Hardy* (London: 1978), p. 277.

l. 41 Audley Grey, Esq., and his wife are commemorated by a monument in Stinsford Church. See John Hutchins, *History and Antiquities of Dorset*, 3rd edition (Westminster: 1861–73), vol. II, p. 567. The monument was erected in 1723.

The Children and Sir Nameless. Hardy wrote to Cockerell on 10 March 1922: 'The effigy of Sir Nameless I have dated back a hundred years further, to get rid of the doubt about the ruff. I *fancy* it was worn when real armour had ceased and dress-armour was in fashion; but I am not sure . . .' (*SCC*, p. 291). Cockerell had been helping Hardy with the proof-reading of *LL*.

At the Royal Academy. The poem is a versification of a note that Hardy made after visiting the Royal Academy's annual show in 1891: 'They were not pictures of *this* spring and summer, although they seem to be so. All this green grass and fresh leafage perished yesterday; after withering and falling, it is gone like a dream.' (*EL*, p. 308.)

Her Temple. l. 8 In *DCM3* Hardy underlined *None now*, and wrote in the margin in pencil: *? But none.*

A Two-years' Idyll. Hardy and his first wife lived in Sturminster Newton, Dorset, from 1876 to 1878; he later referred to the period as 'the Sturminster Newton idyll . . . our happiest time'. (*EL*, p. 156.) A cancelled draft of the title and first four lines of the poem is on the verso of 'Paradox', in the *Hol.* of *Human Shows.* It reads:

A Two-Years' Idyll
Never such joy was
Just those two seasons unsought
Sweeping like summertide wind on our ways;
Moving as straws

By Henstridge Cross at the Year's End. The typescript of the poem at Stourhead House was the property of Lady Hoare, and is inscribed by her: 'Sent me by Florence Hardy, from the great Poet, when first finished writing, Nov. 10th, 1919.'

The Chapel-Organist. Cockerell, reading proofs of *LL*, had apparently been confused by the poem. Hardy wrote to him:

I have altered a word or two in the first verse of 'The Chapel Organist', to make it clear that she is indulging in those reflections on the *last* night—immediately before her suicide—not, as it seemed to you, on a later occasion. Of course, it is all inferential since nobody could *know* the final thoughts of a woman who was dead when they found her: but this is a recognized licence in narrative art, though it should be veiled as much as possible. (*SCC*, pp. 290–1.)

ll. 45–6 Old-Hundredth, Saint Stephen's, etc., are names of traditional hymn-tunes.

ll. 65–6 The Evening Hymn that the congregation sings is 'Glory to thee, my God, this night'. The tune is Tallis, the words are by Thomas Ken. Ken was an Anglican Bishop, hence the liberal spirit of the Dissenters in singing his hymn.

After a Romantic Day. The cancelled epigraph in *Hol.* is from Joel 2:28.

The Two Wives. Hardy uses a similar plot in his story 'Fellow-Townsmen' in *Wessex Tales.*

A Procession of Dead Days. The second page of *Hol.* has been cut off below l. 40, and a new piece pasted on containing the last eight lines.

He follows Himself. In *Hol.* Hardy wrote in pencil and erased the following revisions:

l. 21 for *friend's*: *Love's*
l. 26 for *friend*: *Love*
l. 28 for *his*: *her*.

Hardy considered this change of gender again in *DCM3*; there the same changes are entered, but left tentative: each is marked *Qr* (for *query*).

'*O I won't lead a homely life*'. The Adams manuscript is a musical setting of the poem, in Hardy's hand, written on the back of a circular from an investment company, which is dated 23 August 1922. Hardy has provided alternative words to make the poem appropriate for a female singer. In the first stanza the alternative second line reads:

She cried, "As dad's and mother's Jill

The second stanza, in the alternative version, changes *she* to *I*, and alters the last line to read:

And sad was life for me!

Vagg Hollow. Hardy wrote in his journal for 20 April 1902: 'Vagg Hollow, on the way to Load Bridge (Somerset) is a place where "things" used to be seen—usually taking the form of a wool-pack in the middle of the road. Teams and other horses always stopped on the brow of the hollow, and could only be made to go on by whipping. A waggoner once cut at the pack with his whip: it opened in two, and smoke and a hoofed figure rose out of it.' (*LY*, p. 96.)

The Country Wedding. One of several narrative poems involving the 'Quire' of *Under the Greenwood Tree* (see also 'The Rash Bride' in *Time's Laughingstocks* and 'The Paphian Ball' in *Human Shows*). Bailey (p. 476) identifies the scene as Puddletown, near Dorchester.

Lonely Days. Purdy (p. 223) suggests that the diary from which the poem was versified may have been that of Emma Hardy. *Hol.* shows erased variations of the last four lines, now illegible.

The Marble Tablet. In March 1913, shortly after the death of his first wife, Hardy visited St. Juliot, Cornwall, where he had first met her, and arranged to have a memorial tablet placed in the church there. He returned with his second wife in September 1916 to see that the tablet had been properly designed and erected.

The Master and the Leaves. Hardy described the poem to Robert Graves, to whom it was sent for publication in the *Owl*, as 'a very trifling one'. (Bailey, p. 479.)

Last Words to a Dumb Friend. l. 40 In *Hol.* the line is a late addition, inserted from the margin.

On One who lived and died where He was born. Purdy (p. 223) sugests that the poem refers to Hardy's father.

The Sailor's Mother. The poem deals with the final scene of Hardy's story, 'To Please his Wife' (*Life's Little Ironies*).

Outside the Casement. *Hol.* shows that Hardy tried, and erased, an alternative title: *After the Battle*. The subtitle is an interlined late addition.

The Passer-by. Purdy identifies L. H. as Louisa Harding, a farmer's daughter whom Hardy knew in his youth. See 'Louie' in *Human Shows*, 'To Louisa in the Lane' in *Winter Words*, and *EL*, pp. 33–4.

On a Discovered Curl of Hair. The locket containing the curl and a miniature of Hardy's first wife, dated 1870, is in the Berg Collection. The portrait is reproduced in *EL* facing p. 96. See 'A Forgotten Miniature' in *Winter Words*.

An Old Likeness. In *Hol.*, the headnote and ll. 5–6 and 29–30 are late additions inserted from the margin.

Her Apotheosis. In *DCM3* Hardy considered restoring *LL*'s first-person reading in the second stanza, marking tentative pencilled revisions as follows:

l. 5 *them*: underlined, in the margin *? me*
l. 7 *them*: underlined, in the margin *? me*
l. 8 *their*: underlined, in the margin *? my*

The epigraph is an interlined addition to *Hol.*: it is from Isaiah 24:16 in the Vulgate, and may be translated: 'My secret, mine.'

'Sacred to the Memory'. Hardy's sister Mary died on 24 November 1915. The inscription on her tomb in Stinsford churchyard reads: 'Sacred to the Memory of Mary Elder Daughter of Thomas and Jemima Hardy . . .'.

A Military Appointment. In *Hol.*, (*Scherzo*) is an interlined addition.

The Lament of the Looking-Glass. l. 7 Above the line in *Hol.* Hardy has written and erased: *I've ? back images*.

l. 12 In *DCM3* Hardy underlined *within*, and wrote in the margin, in pencil, *?in/*.

The Chosen. The epigraph is from Galatians 4:24; the Authorized Version reads: 'Which things are an allegory'. It is a late addition to *Hol.*

The Inscription. The memorial brass in the poem closely resembles one in the church at Yetminster, Dorset, as described in John Hutchins's *The History and Antiquities of the County of Dorset*, 3rd edition (Westminster: 1861–73), vol. IV, p. 456.

l. 58 Hardy's revision in *DCM3* is confirmed by an identical revision which he made in Cockerell's copy of Verse Volume V of *WE*. (Adams.)

The Marble-Streeted Town. Hardy's first wife was born in Plymouth. Hardy visited the town in March 1913, shortly after her death. The date in *Hol.*, (*1913?*), suggests that he may have begun the poem then.

The Whitewashed Wall. The poem was written for *Reveille*, a quarterly for disabled soldiers and sailors, at the request of its editor, John Galsworthy (Bailey, p. 494).

The Seven Times. Purdy (p. 225) suggests that the poem may refer to seven journeys that Hardy made to St. Juliot, the last after his first wife's death.

The Sun's Last Look on the Country Girl. Mary Hardy died on 24 November 1915. The headnote appears to be a late addition to *Hol.*

The Colour. Bailey (pp. 496–7) quotes a Dorset children's rhyme, 'Jinny Jones', which resembles Hardy's poem in its question-and-answer form, and in the use of symbolic colours.

Murmurs in the Gloom. In *Hol.*, (*Nocturne*) is an interlined addition.

An Ancient to Ancients. Hardy cites examples of artists and works of art popular in England in his youth: 'The Bohemian Girl' (1843), an opera by Michael Balfe (1808–70), the painters William Etty (1787–1849), William Mulready (1786–1863), and Daniel Maclise (1806–70), and the novelists Edward Bulwer-Lytton (1803–73), Walter Scott (1771–1832), Alexandre Dumas (1802–70), and George Sand (1804–76).

The first page of *Hol.* has been cut off below the third stanza, and a new piece pasted on.

After Reading Psalms XXXIX, XL, Etc. The Latin phrases are all from the Book of Psalms in the Vulgate:

l. 4 38:10 ('Because thou didst it'.)
l. 8 60:3 ('Thou hast led me'.)
l. 12 40:13 ('Thou hast upheld me'.)
l. 16 38:6 ('Thou hast made my days'.)
l. 20 39:10 ('O Lord, thou knowest'.)
l. 24 64:5 ('Whom hast thou chosen?')

Surview. Epigraph, Psalm 119:59: 'I thought on my ways' (Authorized Version).

l. 18 I Corinthians 13:13.

APPENDIX A

General Preface to the Novels and Poems

[In a letter to Macmillan dated 25 October 1911, Hardy referred to a 'newly written *general* preface to all the books', which he was sending. (BL Add. MS 54923.) This preface had been written for the de luxe edition, which was then being planned (for an account of the history of this project see my introduction to Volume One of the present edition). When those plans failed, the essay was placed in the first volume of the Wessex Edition, *Tess of the d'Urbervilles*, published in 1912. The corrected proofs of the General Preface are in the Bancroft Library, University of California, Berkeley.]

In accepting a proposal for a definitive edition of these productions in prose and verse I have found an opportunity of classifying the novels under heads that show approximately the author's aim, if not his achievement, in each book of the series at the date of its composition. Sometimes the aim was lower than at other times; sometimes, where the intention was primarily high, force of circumstances (among which the chief were the necessities of magazine publication) compelled a modification, great or slight, of the original plan. Of a few, however, of the longer novels, and of many of the shorter tales, it may be assumed that they stand to-day much as they would have stood if no accidents had obstructed the channel between the writer and the public. That many of them, if any, stand as they would stand if written *now* is not to be supposed.

In the classification of these fictitious chronicles—for which the name of 'The Wessex Novels' was adopted, and is still retained—the first group is called 'Novels of Character and Environment', and contains those which approach most nearly to uninfluenced works; also one or two which, whatever their quality in some few of their episodes, may claim a verisimilitude in general treatment and detail.

The second group is distinguished as 'Romances and Fantasies', a sufficiently descriptive definition. The third class—'Novels of Ingenuity'—show a not infrequent disregard of the probable in the

Pt Bancroft
Title General Preface *P1*

12 many . . . any,] many, if any, *P1*   22 show a not infrequent] show a *P1*

chain of events, and depend for their interest mainly on the incidents themselves. They might also be characterized as 'Experiments', and were written for the nonce simply; though despite the artificiality of their fable some of their scenes are not without fidelity to life.

It will not be supposed that these differences are distinctly perceptible in every page of every volume. It was inevitable that blendings and alternations should occur in all. Moreover, as it was not thought desirable in every instance to change the arrangement of the shorter stories to which readers have grown accustomed, certain of these may be found under headings to which an acute judgment might deny appropriateness.

It has sometimes been conceived of novels that evolve their action on a circumscribed scene—as do many (though not all) of these—that they cannot be so inclusive in their exhibition of human nature as novels wherein the scenes cover large extents of country, in which events figure amid towns and cities, even wander over the four quarters of the globe. I am not concerned to argue this point further than to suggest that the conception is an untrue one in respect of the elementary passions. But I would state that the geographical limits of the stage here trodden were not absolutely forced upon the writer by circumstances; he forced them upon himself from judgment. I considered that our magnificent heritage from the Greeks in dramatic literature found sufficient room for a large proportion of its action in an extent of their country not much larger than the half-dozen counties here reunited under the old name of Wessex, that the domestic emotions have throbbed in Wessex nooks with as much intensity as in the palaces of Europe, and that, anyhow, there was quite enough human nature in Wessex for one man's literary purpose. So far was I possessed by this idea that I kept within the frontiers when it would have been easier to overleap them and give more cosmopolitan features to the narrative.

Thus, though the people in most of the novels (and in much of the shorter verse) are dwellers in a province bounded on the north by the Thames, on the south by the English Channel, on the east by a line running from Hayling Island to Windsor Forest, and on the west by the Cornish coast, they were meant to be typically and essentially those of any and every place where

> Thought's the slave of life, and life time's fool,

—beings in whose hearts and minds that which is apparently local should be really universal.

But whatever the success of this intention, and the value of these

23 events,] ~ *P1* 40 an untrue] not a true *P1*

novels as delineations of humanity, they have at least a humble supplementary quality of which I may be justified in reminding the reader, though it is one that was quite unintentional and unforeseen. At the dates represented in the various narrations things were like that in Wessex: the inhabitants lived in certain ways, engaged in certain occupations, kept alive certain customs, just as they are shown doing in these pages. And in particularizing such I have often been reminded of Boswell's remarks on the trouble to which he was put and the pilgrimages he was obliged to make to authenticate some detail, though the labour was one which would bring him no praise. Unlike his achievement, however, on which an error would as he says have brought discredit, if these country customs and vocations, obsolete and obsolescent, had been detailed wrongly, nobody would have discovered such errors to the end of Time. Yet I have instituted inquiries to correct tricks of memory, and striven against temptations to exaggerate, in order to preserve for my own satisfaction a fairly true record of a vanishing life.

It is advisable also to state here, in response to inquiries from readers interested in landscape, prehistoric antiquities, and especially old English architecture, that the description of these backgrounds has been done from the real—that is to say, has something real for its basis, however illusively treated. Many features of the first two kinds have been given under their existing names; for instance, the Vale of Blackmoor or Blakemore, Hambledon Hill, Bulbarrow, Nettlecombe Tout, Dogbury Hill, High-Stoy, Bubb-Down Hill, The Devil's Kitchen, Cross-in-Hand, Long-Ash Lane, Benvill Lane, Giant's Hill, Crimmercrock Lane, and Stonehenge. The rivers Froom, or Frome, and Stour, are, of course, well known as such. And the further idea was that large towns and points tending to mark the outline of Wessex—such as Bath, Plymouth, The Start, Portland Bill, Southampton, etc.,—should be named clearly. The scheme was not greatly elaborated, but, whatever its value, the names remain still.

In respect of places described under fictitious or ancient names in the novels—for reasons that seemed good at the time of writing them—and kept up in the poems—discerning people have affirmed in print that they clearly recognize the originals: such as Shaftesbury in 'Shaston', Sturminster Newton in 'Stourcastle', Dorchester in 'Casterbridge', Salisbury Plain in 'The Great Plain', Cranborne Chase in 'The Chase', Beaminster in 'Emminster', Bere Regis in 'Kingsbere', Woodbury Hill in 'Greenhill', Wool Bridge in

64 humanity,] human nature, *P1*   85 illusively] ⟨imaginatively⟩ *P1*
91 rivers] ⟨river⟩ *P1*

'Wellbridge', Hartfoot or Harput Lane in 'Stagfoot Lane', Hazlebury in 'Nuttlebury', Bridport in 'Port Bredy', Maiden Newton in 'Chalk Newton', a farm near Nettlecombe Tout in 'Flintcomb Ash', Sherborne in 'Sherton Abbas', Milton Abbey in 'Middleton Abbey', Cerne Abbas in 'Abbot's Cernel', Evershot in 'Evershed', Taunton in 'Toneborough', Bournemouth in 'Sandbourne', Winchester in 'Wintoncester', Oxford in 'Christminster', Reading in 'Aldbrickham', Newbury in 'Kennetbridge', Wantage in 'Alfredston', Basingstoke in 'Stoke Barehills', and so on. Subject to the qualifications above given, that no detail is guaranteed,—that the portraiture of fictitiously named towns and villages was only suggested by certain real places, and wantonly wanders from inventorial descriptions of them—I do not contradict these keen hunters for the real; I am satisfied with their statements as at least an indication of their interest in the scenes.

Thus much for the novels. Turning now to the verse—to myself the more individual part of my literary fruitage—I would say that, unlike some of the fiction, nothing interfered with the writer's freedom in respect of its form or content. Several of the poems—indeed many—were produced before novel-writing had been thought of as a pursuit; but few saw the light till all the novels had been published. The limited stage to which the majority of the latter confine their exhibitions has not been adhered to here in the same proportion, the dramatic part especially having a very broad theatre of action. It may thus relieve the circumscribed areas treated in the prose, if such relief be needed. To be sure, one might argue that by surveying Europe from a celestial point of vision—as in *The Dynasts*—that continent becomes virtually a province—a Wessex, an Attica, even a mere garden—and hence is made conform to the principle of the novels, however far it outmeasures their region. But that may be as it will.

The few volumes filled by the verse cover a producing period of some eighteen years first and last, while the seventeen or more volumes of novels represent correspondingly about four-and-twenty years. One is reminded by this disproportion in time and result how much more concise and quintessential expression becomes when given in rhythmic form than when shaped in the language of prose.

114–17 —that . . . them—] ⟨—that the features of spots which bear fictitious names were only suggested by certain real places, and are in no sense photographic descriptions of them—⟩ *P1* 131–2 vision—as in *The Dynasts*—that] vision that *P1* 133 is made conform to] ⟨does not depart from⟩ *P1* 137 seventeen or more] ⟨seventeen⟩ *P1* 140 becomes when] becomes—whatever its value—when *P1*

One word on what has been called the present writer's philosophy of life, as exhibited more particularly in this metrical section of his compositions. Positive views on the Whence and the Wherefore of things have never been advanced by this pen as a consistent philosophy. Nor is it likely, indeed, that imaginative writings extending over more than forty years would exhibit a coherent scientific theory of the universe even if it had been attempted—of that universe concerning which Spencer owns to the 'paralyzing thought' that possibly there exists no comprehension of it anywhere. But such objectless consistency never has been attempted, and the sentiments in the following pages have been stated truly to be mere impressions of the moment, and not convictions or arguments.

That these impressions have been condemned as 'pessimistic'—as if that were a very wicked adjective—shows a curious muddle-mindedness. It must be obvious that there is a higher characteristic of philosophy than pessimism, or than meliorism, or even than the optimism of these critics—which is truth. Existence is either ordered in a certain way, or it is not so ordered, and conjectures which harmonize best with experience are removed above all comparison with other conjectures which do not so harmonize. So that to say one view is worse than other views without proving it erroneous implies the possibility of a false view being better or more expedient than a true view; and no pragmatic proppings can make that *idolum specus* stand on its feet, for it postulates a prescience denied to humanity.

And there is another consideration. Differing natures find their tongue in the presence of differing spectacles. Some natures become vocal at tragedy, some are made vocal by comedy, and it seems to me that to whichever of these aspects of life a writer's instinct for expression the more readily responds, to that he should allow it to respond. That before a contrasting side of things he remains undemonstrative need not be assumed to mean that he remains unperceiving.

It was my hope to add to these volumes of verse as many more as would make a fairly comprehensive cycle of the whole. I had wished that those in dramatic, ballad, and narrative form should include most of the cardinal situations which occur in social and public life, and those in lyric form a round of emotional experiences of some completeness. But

The petty done, the undone vast!

180 petty] little *WE12*

The more written the more seems to remain to be written; and the night cometh. I realize that these hopes and plans, except possibly to the extent of a volume or two, must remain unfulfilled.

T. H.

October 1911.

l. 60. *1 Henry IV*, v. iv. 81.

ll. 149–50 Hardy wrote in his notebook in 1904: 'The paralyzing thought—what, of all that is thus incomprehensible to us, [the Universe] there exists no comprehension?' H. Spencer. *Autob.* See also Hardy's letter to Clodd, quoted in Volume One of this edition, pp. 385–6.

l. 164. *idolum specus*, 'the idols of the cave': Francis Bacon, *Novum Organum*, I, xxxix.

l. 180. Robert Browning, 'The Last Ride Together', l. 53.

APPENDIX B

Hardy's Notes for Hermann Lea

Hermann Lea was a local amateur photographer who knew Hardy from 1898 until 1921; for the last eight years of their friendship he lived in the cottage in which Hardy was born, in Higher Bockhampton. Lea was one of the early Dorset motorists, and took Hardy on many drives around the county; he estimated that he had driven Hardy 'many thousands of miles' during 1914–16 alone, but the touring began much earlier. Out of these excursions came two books: *A Handbook to the Wessex Country of Thomas Hardy's Novels and Poems* (Bournemouth: 1906), and *Thomas Hardy's Wessex* (London: 1913)—both illustrated with Lea's photographs of Hardy scenes.

According to Lea, Hardy took an active role in the preparation of *Thomas Hardy's Wessex*:

> Although I had visited most of these towns and villages and natural features, and had, moreover, a fairly wide selection of photographs covering the historical Wessex, there were still some places that demanded identification. Thus between 1910 and 1913, when the book was first published, my task necessitated many and frequent visits to Max Gate. As the work proceeded, Hardy grew increasingly interested and I found him ever ready to help me with suggestions, particularly in regard to which subjects should be used for illustration.
>
> Sometimes he wrote me notes regarding the places; sometimes he gave me information during my visits to Max Gate; and sometime he came with me to look at

certain somewhat obscure features to which he had referred in his writings, and which he himself was not too certain about.[1]

Certainly Hardy approved of Lea's work. In a letter to Macmillan dated 17 January 1911 (BL Add. MS 54923) Hardy describes *The Wessex Country* as 'fairly correct' on the relation between actual and imagined places, and four years later he wrote to Harold Child, who was writing a book on Hardy, that 'Lea's book, though not literary . . . is very accurate'. (Adams.)

Thomas Hardy's Wessex deals with only the first three volumes of Hardy's poems: *Wessex Poems*, *Poems of the Past and the Present*, and *Time's Laughingstocks*. In expectation of a later, expanded edition, Hardy prepared the two lists that follow. Both are in his own hand, and are in the collection of Richard Little Purdy.

I.

A Supplementary Chapter to Mr Lea's book may contain some of the following additional illustrations.

'Satires of Circumstance'

'Wessex Heights'—Ingpen Beacon: Wyll's Neck: Bulbarrow: Pilsdon: Yell'ham.
'When I set out for Lyonnesse'—Bockhampton from Heath Gate.
'Under the Waterfall'—Vallency Valley, Boscastle.
'Places'—Plymouth Hoe.
'The Coronation'—Westminster Abbey, interior.
'Aquae Sulis'—Bath.
'In the British Museum'—Elgin Marble Room.
'The Sacrilege'—Dunkery Beacon, Exmoor.
'The Abbey Mason'—Gloucester Cathedral, interior.

'Moments of Vision'

'Afternoon Service at Mellstock'—Stinsford Church, interior.
'Near Lanivet'—Handpost on the St. Austell Road.
'Copying Architecture'—Wimborne Minster, interior.
'To Shakespeare'—Stratford on Avon Church from the other side of the river.
'Sitting on the Bridge'—Grey's Bridge.
'The Last Signal'—The path to Winterborne Came.
'The House of Silence'—The Lawn, Max Gate.
'At Middle Field Gate'—Middle Hill Gate, Bockhampton Lane.

1. *Thomas Hardy Through the Camera's Eye*, ed. J. Stevens Cox, Monographs on the Life of Thomas Hardy, No. 20 (Beaminster: 1964), p. 28.

'On Sturminster Foot Bridge'—near Riverside, Sturminster.
'The Sunshade'—Swanage Cliffs.
'At a Seaside Town'—Weymouth Esplanade.
'The Pedestrian'—Coll-Hill, near Wimborne.
'He revisits his first school'—Bockhampton School.
'In a whispering Gallery'—Whispering Gallery, St. Paul's.
'Paths of Former Time'—The meadows behind Max Gate.
'A New Year's Eve in War Time'—Max Gate: inside the wall.
'I looked up from my writing'—Study window, Max Gate.

II.

Places (of Poem-scenes)

Dorchester. The Ballad Singer (Time's Laughingstocks)
The Chimes (Moments of Vision)
The Revisitation (Time's Laughingstocks)
Grey's Bridge. Sitting on the Bridge (Moments of Vision)
Stinsford Church. A Church Romance (Time's Laughingstocks)
Stinsford Churchyard. Friends Beyond (Wessex Poems)
Rain on a Grave (Satires of Circumstance)
Stinsford House. Noble Lady's Tale (Time's Laughingstocks)
Stinsford Church. Afternoon Service at Mellstock (Moments of Vision)
Stinsford Churchyard. Transformations (Moments of Vision)
Upper Bockhampton: House by the Well. The House of Hospitalities (Time's Laughingstocks)
Upper Bockhampton. The Rash Bride (Time's Laughingstocks)
Night in the Old Home (Time's Laughingstocks)
After the Last Breath (Time's Laughingstocks)
One We Knew (Time's Laughingstocks)
When I set out for Lyonnesse (Satires of Circumstance)
The Satin Shoes (Satires of Circumstance)
The Announcement (Moments of Vision)
The Oxen (Moments of Vision)
On the Heath. By the Barrows (Time's Laughingstocks)
A Roman Road (Time's Laughingstocks)
Bockhampton Lane. At Middle Field Gate (Moments of Vision)
Lower Bockhampton. He revisits first School (Moments of Vision)
The Dead Quire (Time's Laughingstocks)
Max Gate. Something tapped (Moments of Vision)
The House of Silence (Moments of Vision)
The Last Performance (Moments of Vision)
The Ageing House (Moments of Vision)
Who's in the next Room (Moments of Vision)

Everything Comes (Moments of Vision)
The Shadow on the Stone (Moments of Vision)
New Year's Eve in War Time (Moments of Vision)
The Photograph (Moments of Vision)
Road from Dorchester to Weymouth. Great Things (Moments of Vision)
Weymouth. At a Seaside Town in 1869 (Moments of Vision)
Max Gate. The Strange House (Late Lyrics)
The Garden Seat
End of 1912
Sturminster Newton. The Maid of Keinton.
Stinsford Hill. On Stinsford Hill
Came Rectory. The Collector
Old Neighbours and New
Stinsford Churchyard. Voices from things growing
[and others].

INDEX OF TITLES

INDEX OF FIRST LINES